# EMPLOYMENT, UNEMPLOYMENT
AND
# LABOR
UTILIZATION

# EMPLOYMENT, UNEMPLOYMENT

# AND

# LABOR UTILIZATION

edited by

**Robert A. Hart**
*University of Stirling*

Boston
UNWIN HYMAN
London   Sydney   Wellington

**Unwin Hyman, Inc.**
**8 Winchester Place, Winchester, Mass. 01890, USA**

the U.S. company of

**Unwin Hyman Ltd**
15/17 Broadwick Street, London W1V 1FP, UK

Allen & Unwin (Australia) Ltd,
8 Napier Street, North Sydney, NSW 2060, Australia

Allen & Unwin (New Zealand) Ltd in association with the Port
Nicholson Press, 60 Cambridge Terrace, Wellington, New Zealand

First published in 1988

**Library of Congress Cataloging-in-Publication Data**

Employment, unemployment, and labor utilization/ edited by Robert A.
Hart.
   p.   cm.
   ''Proceedings of a conference held at the Science Center Berlin in
September 1986'' – Introd.
   Bibliography: p.
   Includes index.
   ISBN 0-04-445120-2 (alk. paper)
   1. Unemployment – Congresses.  2. Hours of labor –Congresses.
I. Hart, Robert A.
HD5707.E46  1988
331.12'5 – dc19

88-10740
CIP

**British Library Cataloguing in Publication Data**

Employment, unemployment and labour
  utilization
  1. Employment, related to working hours.
  I. Hart, Robert A., *1946–*
  331.12'5

ISBN 0-04-445120-2

Typeset in 10 on 11 point Palatino by
Mathematical Composition Setters Ltd, Salisbury, Wiltshire
and printed in Great Britain by Biddles of Guildford.

# Contents

## SCIENCE CENTER BERLIN

The articles published in this volume are the proceedings of a conference financed by the Science Center Berlin. Immediate support was given by two research units in the Science Center, the Industrial Policy Unit and the Labour Market and Employment Unit.

# List of Contributors

| | |
|---|---|
| Katharine G. Abraham | *Brookings Institution and MIT* |
| John T. Addison | *University of South Carolina and University of Bamberg* |
| David N. F. Bell | *University of Glasgow* |
| Lutz Bellmann | *University of Hannover* |
| George Bittlingmayer | *Industrial Policy Unit, Science Center, Berlin* |
| Alison Booth | *The City University, London* |
| Christoph Büchtemann | *Research Unit Labour Market and Employment, Science Center Berlin* |
| John K. Dagsvik | *Central Bureau of Statistics, Norway* |
| Ronald G. Ehrenberg | *Cornell University and National Bureau of Economic Research* |
| Felix R. FitzRoy | *Industrial Policy Unit, Science Center Berlin* |
| Wolfgang Franz | *University of Stuttgart* |
| Daniel S. Hamermesh | *Michigan State University and National Bureau of Economic Research* |
| Robert A. Hart | *University of Stirling* |
| Mansanori Hashimoto | *Ohio State University* |
| Susan N. Houseman | *University of Maryland* |
| Olaf Hübler | *University of Hannover* |
| Seiichi Kawasaki | *Ritsumeikan University* |
| Heinz König | *University of Mannheim* |
| Edward P Lazear | *University of Chicago and Hoover Institution* |
| Olav Ljones | *Central Bureau of Statistics, Norway* |
| Jeanne Li | *Cornell University* |
| John P. Martin | *Economics and Statistics Department, OECD* |
| Georg Meran | *Free University of Berlin* |
| Axel Mittelstädt | *Economics and Statistics Department, OECD* |
| John D. Owen | *Wayne State University* |
| Winfried Pohlmeier | *University of Mannheim* |
| John Raisian | *Hoover Institution* |
| Erik R. de Regt | *University of Limburg* |
| Pamela Rosenberg | *Dickinson College* |
| Tuire Santamäki | *Labour Institute for Economic Research, Helsinki* |
| Fabio Schiantarelli | *University of Essex and Boston University* |
| George Sheldon | *Labor and Industrial Economics Research Unit, University of Basel* |

Steinar Strøm                University of Oslo
Toshiaki Tachibanaki        Kyoto University
Robert Topel                University of Chicago and National Bureau of
                            Economic Research
Laurence Weiss              University of California (San Diego) and
                            Goldman-Sachs
Tom Wennemo                 Central Bureau of Statistics, Norway
John D. Whitley             ESRC Macroeconomic Modelling Bureau,
                            University of Warwick
Nicholas Wilson             University of Bradford Management Centre
Robert A. Wilson            Institute for Employment Research, University of
                            Warwick
Klaus F. Zimmermann         University of Mannheim and University of
                            Pennsylvania

# Acknowledgements

This volume contains the proceedings of a conference held in Berlin in September 1986. The conference was fully funded by the Science Center Berlin and this is gratefully acknowledged. Immediate financial support came from two research units within the Science Center – the Industrial Policy Unit and the Labour Market and Employment Unit. Thanks are due to the Directors of these units – Professor Dr Meinolf Dierkes and Professor Dr Egon Matzner, respectively – for their backing and support.

Many thanks are due to Hanna Trautmann who gave excellent assistance with the organisation and running of the conference. First-class secretarial support was provided by two people: Ilona Köhler was involved at the conference organisational stage in Berlin while Ann Cowie dealt with the later editing work at Stirling. Further, Manfred Fleischer of the Industrial Policy Unit gave valuable adminstrative assistance in Berlin.

Finally, thanks are due to the Berlin Senate who recognised the international importance of this conference by providing participants with a splendid reception.

# CHAPTER 1

# *Introductory Overview*

## ROBERT A. HART

This volume contains the proceedings of a conference held at the Science Center Berlin in September 1986. It was designed to bring together economists from Europe, Japan and North America in order to present new research work of central importance to the OECD-wide debate on high and persistent unemployment rates and related employment problems. In a wide international context, the conference discussed relationships between employment and unemployment on the one hand and labor utilization and work intensity on the other. The latter two variables include standard working hours, overtime working, part-time working and flexible staffing arrangements. A recurring emphasis concerned the role of labor costs in employment/labor utilization decisions, and an important additional theme along these lines recognized the influence of job security policies.

To a large extent, European and North American research developments in this general area have followed quite distinct paths. This seems to have occurred primarily as a result of divergent policy emphases. A major example concerns the interest in the relationship between employment and hours of work on the two continents (for detailed comparative analyses, see Hart, 1987). Despite differing policy goals and institutional backgrounds, however, several of the key underlying economic problems are quite similar. Large mutual gains can be made from the exchange of ideas on theoretical and empirical methodology and this was one of the broad aims of the conference.

Ever since the first 1970s OPEC supply shock, an important policy debate has taken place in Europe, and also in Australasia, about the feasibility of tackling persistent unemployment by work sharing. This has generally involved analyzing the trade-off between employment (and/or unemployment) and average hours of work. Within this domain, the single most important issue has concerned the effects on employment and unemployment of reductions in the standard or normal workweek. (For early contributions see Brechling, 1965 and Ehrenberg, 1971a.) Several of the chapters in this volume give a state-of-the-art representation of theoretical and empirical approaches to modeling in this area. Ehrenberg also had a major early influence on dynamic modeling and some of the latest innovations along these lines are also presented.

1

Although there has been some limited interest, the topic of workweek reductions has not been so significant in North America. Nevertheless, North American economists have found the distinction between employment and labor utilization of great value in analyzing other labor market issues. The area particularly emphasized at this conference, has been the study of the effects of job security legislation on the labor market. Changes in job security provision involve differential costs of labor market adjustment at the extensive (employment) and intensive (labor utilization) margins. Correspondingly, a careful distinction between the stock and utilization components of the labor input is an essential precondition to much of the work in this field.

Hopefully, it will be clear from reading the chapters in this volume that a quite wide range of policy issues within the general domain of employment, unemployment and labor utilization have unifying threads of theoretical and empirical approaches running through them. For given issues, this book provides the added bonus in several of the papers of providing a wide range of international comparative empirical results, which, again, help labor market economists in establishing general methodology and common research ground.

As suggested by the foregoing comments, work on theoretical and empirical issues related to the demand for workers and hours forms a central, although by no means exclusive, theme running through the conference papers. In Chapter 2, Daniel Hamermesh provides a broad, internationally based, summary of work on the effects of job security legislation on the demand for workers and hours. While the emphasis is on job security, the paper nevertheless presents a very useful background resumé of many of the topics of concern in the remainder of the book. It also contains a wide review of recent research work. Much of the job security legislation constitutes fixed employment costs to the typical firm and Hamermesh discusses the links between employment adjustment on the one hand and the distinction between quasi-fixed and variable labor costs on the other. The reader is not only reminded of the main results from standard quasi-fixed cost theory but also is provided with a summary of a range of empirical problems that have involved measuring the influence of fixed costs on employment–hours demand decisions. Further, the author includes an analysis of job protection with only partial coverage and, in particular, the possibility of replacing permanent by part-time workers. Finally, in examining the effects of changes in job security policy on employment adjustment lags, Hamermesh underlines another important aspect of several later contributions by providing an internationally oriented empirical analysis based on several OECD countries. As Hamermesh himself freely admits, interpretation of theoretical and, particularly, empirical results in this field is not without difficulty and this view is underlined by the criticism provided by John Addison, who raises several important questions.

The volume continues on the specific issue of job security in the next two chapters. In a wholly theoretical contribution in Chapter 3, Edward Lazear contrasts the gains and benefits experienced through the North

American emphasis on employment-at-will in labor relations compared to a much greater prevalence of legislated job security provision in Europe. Lazear's coverage is comprehensive. He sets out to show that, in a very simple wage economy, mandatory job security rules are unambiguously inefficient. Even under broader labor market assumptions – to embrace such features as fixed employment costs and severance pay – Lazear maintains that market inefficiency would tend to result from the abolition of employment-at-will. He argues that it is preferable for governments to act as enforcers of private contracts explicitly undertaken between workers and firms rather than to impose their own job security rules. In a broad defense of these positions, Lazear examines critically a range of second-best arguments that have been advanced in support of job security. These include the seeming benefits of job security rules in markets experiencing wage rigidities and the apparent beneficial impact of job security on workers' investments in specific human capital. In further extensions the author considers job security rules in relation to part-time and short-time employment as well as temporary versus permanent employment. Lutz Bellmann attempts to establish a stronger relative case for job security over employment-at-will – both by extending the domain of the theoretical discussion and by introducing an empirical question mark.

By contrast, Susan Houseman in Chapter 4 is concerned with job security in an essentially empirical setting. Her prime concern is the European steel industry where practices of work sharing in order to preserve jobs have been quite marked. The work is undertaken within the context of a theoretical model that attempts to explain the reactions of employment and hours to changes in production. As with a later paper (see Booth and Schiantarelli, Chapter 8), the model pays particularly close attention to the role of union behavior and bargaining power. Highlighting an important aspect of labor market policy in Europe, a useful description is given of job protection and work-sharing policies in the steel sector in five European countries. The significance of such legislation for the differential adjustment of employment and hours is tested econometrically for the cases of the German and French steel industries as well as for the US economy. The attempted explanation of the different European/US experience is of considerable interest given the well-established contrast in the cyclical adjustment pattern of employment and hours between them (e.g. Gordon, 1982; Tachibanaki, 1987). Houseman provides an example of a relatively rare economic analysis (however, see also Whitley and Wilson, Chapter 12) that supports the device of work sharing as a means of preserving jobs. She argues on the basis of her empirical results that recourse to shorter working time has helped to preserve jobs that would have otherwise been lost during the restructuring of the European steel industry. Lest the European policymaker hurry to the drawing board, however, George Bittlingmayer provides a strong note of caution over the interpretation of Houseman's results.

The next group of papers, Chapters 4–7, are essentially theoretical in nature. They represent some of the most important new directions in modeling the relationships between workers and hours. All four papers give prominence, although by no means exclusive attention, to the effects of workweek reductions on employment, unemployment and hours. Until relatively recently, the dominant type of model in this field has focused on the comparative statics of a profit-maximizing/cost-minimizing firm (for recent examples see Raisian, 1978; Hart, 1984a; Calmfors and Hoel, 1987). This work differentiates between quasi-fixed and variable labor costs in the firm's cost function and between workers and average hours per worker in the production function. From this set-up, separate demand functions for workers and hours in terms of relative factor prices and scale influences are derived.

Labor costs associated with overtime working have been typically modeled as a piecewise linear schedule. Beyond standard daily or weekly hours, overtime is assumed to be paid at some fixed constant multiple of the standard wage rate. Recently Santamäki (1983, 1986) has investigated the effects on factor demand of a cut in standard workweek in the event of a modified overtime wage schedule that treats premium rates as a positive function of the length of working time and a negative function of the length of a standard workweek. In her contribution to this volume in Chapter 5, Tuire Santamäki considers another extension of the basic problem. Thus, she investigates the implications for conventional labor demand theory of non-homogeneity of standard and overtime hours within the production function. Santamäki then re-casts both the standard model and her production function modifications within a dynamic theory of the firm along the lines of Nickell (1984a) and others. The problem becomes one of optimal control with the firm, given a perfectly foreseen variation in output demand, seeking the optimal adjustment strategy over the business cycle. One seeming advantage of the control method is that it provides explanations as to why similar experiences of demand fluctuations may result in significantly different responses across firms. Optimal strategies to deal with business cycle fluctuations are now dependent not only on the structural parameters describing the firm but also on its operational environment with respect to the cycle. In a particularly valuable contribution, David Bell casts more light on the properties of the labor services specification chosen by Santamäki and suggests alternatives that (a) may fit better with certain stylized facts and (b) allow developments to take place in dynamic specifications that go beyond some of the modeling confines imposed by Santamäki.

The control theoretical approach is continued in Chapter 6 by Heinz König and Winfried Pohlmeier. This chapter provides a complete set of results to a control problem equivalent to a comparative static model of Ehrenberg (1971a), thereby also including the distinction between standard and overtime hours. Of considerable further interest, the model incorporates the effects of marginal employment subsidies and the taxation of overtime work. Both strategies are of significant policy interest in both Europe and the USA. This is the first time they have

4

been incorporated within a model dealing with dynamic aspects of the conventional problem. Also of interest is that the chapter considers the possibility of incomplete information of the timing of a standard hours reduction. While acknowledging the contribution of the dynamic approach to modeling, John Owen nevertheless sounds several notes of caution over the value of the current state-of-the-art technique to the policymaker.

In Chapter 7, Felix Fitzroy extends the conventional model in other directions. He replaces the typical partial equilibrium setting by a simple general equilibrium framework in order to study, primarily, the effect of technical progress on employment under a zero profit condition. In the simplest version of his model – which treats hours as exogenous – FitzRoy finds that employment is a decreasing function of both technical progress and average hours. A reduction of the workweek increases employment, a result at odds with most of the earlier work. Endogenizing overtime in a long-run equilibrium model, however, restores the more familiar standard hours result while technical progress increases employment. Aspects of disequilibrium and monopolistic equilibrium are also discussed. In interesting variations on FitzRoy's models, Georg Meran shows that the employment effects with respect to technical progress are sensitive to modeling assumptions.

Recent work by Hoel (1984) and Calmfors (1985) has examined the employment effects of cuts in the workweek in a situation where a large monopoly union sets the wage and leaves it to the employer to set the level of employment. Both static and dynamic versions of a model with this underlying theoretical structure are considered in Chapter 8 by Alison Booth and Fabio Schiantarelli. The authors extend previous union bargaining models by explicitly incorporating the distinction between endogenous overtime and exogenous standard hours. In a further extension they examine the problem by way of an efficient bargaining model in which firms and unions bargain over *both* wages and employment. George Sheldon provides a wide-ranging critique of Booth and Schiantarelli's contribution as well as of union bargaining models in general. His comments deal with the policy relevance of this type of model and, in particular, with the degree to which such models reflect the actual working time roles and objectives of European unions.

Three single-country empirical studies of the effects of hours reductions on employment and labor utilization are presented in Chapters 9–11. The first two emphasize the demand side of the labor market while the third is supply oriented.

In Chapter 9, Robert Hart and Nicholas Wilson derive and test demand equations for workers' average total hours and average overtime hours using detailed information on 52 establishments in the British metal working industry for five separate years, 1978–82. Of the 52 enterprises, 43 worked some overtime in one or more years of the study: these are classified as 'overtime establishments'. Hart and Wilson estimate cross-section and pooled cross-section/time-series labor demand equations based on all establishments as well as, separately, on the overtime and non-overtime establishments. Moreover, they estimate separate equations for workers, total hours and overtime hours. Results are compared with the underlying conventional theory. In his comments, Olaf Hübler suggests extensions and refinements to the estimation techniques and comments on some interesting related work on West German household panel data (see Hübler, 1987).

Erik de Regt is also concerned with the effects of standard working time reductions on the demand for workers and overtime hours in Chapter 10. In contrast to the UK work, however, this is a purely time-series study that concentrates on Dutch manufacturing industry from 1954 to 1982. In the spirit of Nickell (1984a), de Regt constructs a dynamic labor demand model developed from the underlying assumption of a cost-minimizing firm that seeks to minimize the present value of costs – with respect to the capital stock, number of workers and working time – given an expected future stream of output. As far as standard workers–hours demand theory is concerned, de Regt emphasizes the need for introducing two modifications. In the first place, he argues that it is necessary to include capital services rather than the capital stock in the production function in order to reflect the fact that, with a fixed capital stock, capital services are positively related to changes in working time. Secondly, he develops the underlying static theory in terms of 'efficiency hours' – with respect to both labor and capital services – thereby directly accommodating the possibility that returns to hours can vary with respect to the length of the workweek. At a micro level, Hübler (1987) also integrates the concept of efficiency hours in his West German study of overtime and standard working hours. Among a number of other issues, Seiichi Kawasaki raises problems over the matching of the static and dynamic theory in de Regt's work.

In sharp contrast to the foregoing analyses, John Dagsvik, Olav Ljones, Steinar Strøm and Tom Wennemo examine, in Chapter 11, the effects of a cut in the working day using a microeconometric discrete/continuous choice model based on Norwegian household data. The model concentrates on the labor supply of married couples and is notable for jointly estimating the labor supply of couples. Among other noteworthy points is that the model contains a detailed specification of the tax structure and, further, its stochastic arguments are based on the underlying theory. The structure of the model permits the authors to impose varying constraints on the length of the working day. They then examine the effects on the separate participation rates of males and females as well as on their separate supply of hours. Klaus Zimmermann discusses the strengths and limitations of the model in the context of existing related supply work that has focused on discrete/continuous choice models of the consumer.

With exceptional instances (especially Chapter 7), much of the work on the labor market implications of hours reductions in this volume is couched in terms of partial equilibrium analysis. In addition, the chapters have a decidedly microeconomic bias. By contrast, earlier studies by van Ginneken (1984) and Whitley and Wilson (1986) have reported on simulations of hours reductions in a range of European macroeconometric models. Unlike the micro work, such simulations generally point to somewhat favorable employment and unemployment responses. Whitley and Wilson provide a substantial extension to their earlier work in Chapter 12. They set themselves two main objectives. First, they explore what they believe to be a deficiency in the partial – largely demand-oriented – approaches, viz. the treatment of standard hours as an exogenously determined variable. In a medium or long-term perspective, they argue that normal hours are endogenously determined by largely supply-side factors and proceed to argue that assessing cuts in standard working time requires a complete demand/supply sub-model for hours that is itself integrated into a full macroeconomic system. Second, they explore the effects of hours reductions in sub-models within five UK macroeconometric models. Moreover, they attempt to standardize their simulations so as to facilitate model comparisons. As in the earlier macroeconomic studies cited above, the authors find employment impacts that are generally favorable in the short run and that then reduce somewhat in the longer term to a level above or below the starting value depending on the choice of model. Interestingly, this result is consistent with the dynamic (partial) theoretical analysis of König and Pohlmeier in Chapter 6. Axel Mittelstädt provides a healthy skepticism over these predictions as viewed against the background of recent OECD experience.

Demand-side relationships between part-time and full-time employment may be expected to mirror, to some degree, those between hours of work and employment. For example, relative changes in overtime rates or quasi-fixed costs of full-time workers should produce substitution responses in the number of part-time workers and/or worker utilization. Theoretically, such correspondence provides an interesting variation on the demand for workers and hours theme (FitzRoy and Hart, 1986). Surprisingly, little demand-side empirical work exists in this area (although, see Owen, 1979), so the work presented in Chapter 13 by Ronald Ehrenberg, Pamela Rosenberg and Jeanne Li is particularly welcome. The authors analyze aggregate time-series data for the US and, after controlling for cyclical influences, they detect an increase in involuntary part-time employment. This leads them to seek demand-side explanations of inter-industry variations in part-time employment/full-time employment in terms of relative cost differentials as well as health and private pension coverage and production technology. A supply-side equation is also modeled and estimated. To provide a truly international comparative flavor to this topic, Christoph Büchtemann incorporates in his comments a rich survey of related research activity in Europe, drawing attention to US/European differences and similarities in approach and interest.

A well-established literature has studied the demand for hours of work as part of a set of interactive choices that make up the firm's overall reaction to demand fluctuations. Typically, employment and inventories are also included within the choice set (e.g. Topel, 1982; Rossana, 1983). For certain firms, flexible staffing arrangements – such as agency temporaries, short-time hires and on-call workers – might also be included within the choice set. Flexible staffing may also be used to smooth labor supply fluctuations resulting from employee sickness, vacation, special leave and so on. In Chapter 14, Katherine Abraham carries out a theoretical and empirical study of these potential demand and supply influences on flexible staffing arrangements. Empirical work is based on a new survey of 400 US employers. Apart from testing demand and supply hypotheses, she also provides a thorough descriptive analysis of the survey data. Toshiaki Tachibanaki attempts to assess this relatively new area of research in the perspective of the conceptually related literature. He also suggests further avenues of investigation.

The study of significant differences in employment, hours and wage variability between Japan and the USA has provided a fertile area of labor market research in recent years. Mansanori Hashimoto and John Raisian are leaders in this field and, in Chapter 15, they extend their earlier empirical analyses. As far as major explanations are concerned, they concentrate on firm specific human capital arguments involving, in particular, the unique role of the Japanese bonus system. In his critical comments, John Martin argues that no dominant theory has yet emerged to explain the differences. In attempting to explain the trend growth in US unemployment during the 1970s and 1980s, Robert Topel and Laurence Weiss question, in the final chapter, the efficacy of demand-side policies and argue that higher unemployment is caused by supply responses to labor market structural uncertainty. They model formally a process whereby increases in future relative wage uncertainty reduce the expected return to specific human capital and increase the attractiveness of current period unemployment. One predicted outcome is that youth unemployment, involving relatively inexperienced workers, will rise more than proportionately to unemployment among older workers during uncertain periods. Wolfgang Franz in his comments concentrates particularly on this view of relatively high unemployment of young people in the context of West Germany and argues that the actual experience there does not fit comfortably with the Topel/Weiss explanations.

# CHAPTER 2

# The Demand for Workers and Hours and the Effects of Job Security Policies: Theory and Evidence

## DANIEL S. HAMERMESH

## 2.1 Introduction

Since the 1960s there has been a rapid spread of what can collectively be called job security policies. Some put restrictions on employers' behavior before workers are displaced, some provide income security to workers after displacement, and still others offer special treatment of specific groups of workers when permanent layoffs are contemplated. They are also diverse in orgin: some are negotiated between unions and management, while others are imposed by government.

My purpose here is to provide the background for examining how these policies affect labor demand. Reference is made to specific examples, but presenting the details of the array of specific policies is left to others (see, for example, Gennard, 1979, 1985). The nature of labor costs is discussed and linked to employers' optimizing behavior in the face of differing cost structures. Both the static demand for labor – the amount of employment and hours generated on average – and fluctuations in employment and hours – labour market dynamics – are discussed. The outcome is a guide to the qualitative effects of current and proposed policies on the demand for labor. An examination of empirical results on the effects of structures of labor costs on employment (most of which are unfortunately general rather than linked to specific policies) then suggests the potential quantitative impacts of the various policies.

## 2.2 The Nature of Labor Demand and Labor Costs

In this section I categorize labor costs facing employers and examine their impacts on the level of the changes in profit-maximizing labor inputs. I ignore the effects of differences in *average* labor costs among groups of workers, as I have analyzed and summarized evidence on them elsewhere (Hamermesh, 1986).

## 2.2(a)  Fixed Employment Costs

The simplest example of a labor cost structure is a fixed cost per worker, $V$, that the employer must pay each time period no matter how many hours a particular worker's services are utilized or how much the worker's hourly labor cost is. Examples of such costs include employer-provided health insurance (life insurance too in some cases); clerical costs of maintaining payroll and other records on the worker; and, in the United States, the (relatively low level of) taxes that finance unemployment insurance benefits.[1]

Following Rosen (1978), assume that the total cost of labor is $W(H)EH + VE$, where $W$ is the hourly wage rate, expressed as a function of hours per worker, and $H$ is the average hours worked per employee. Then the marginal cost of a worker is $WH + V$; the cost of an extra hour of labor is approximately $EW[1 + p]$, where $E$ is total employment, and $p$ is the elasticity of the wage rate with respect to hours. Under certain simplifying assumptions $p$ is the premium rate for overtime work. (I assume overtime is worked, but that it constitutes a small fraction of total hours.) Assume that production is characterized by:

$$Q = F[K, G(E, H)], \qquad (2.1)$$

where $K$ is the typical firm's capital input. I assume here that employment–hours substitution is separable from capital–labor substitution, which may or may not be correct.[2]

Consider the effect of an increase in $V$ if $W$ remains constant. Labor costs per worker rise, so that the cost of a given number of worker-hours rises. This increase has three separate effects. First, and most obviously, the scale effect reduces employers' labor demand by the product of the labor demand elasticity and the percentage increase in total labor costs for a given employment level. One impact of this increase is thus a decline in $EH$, total worker-hours demanded.

The second impact is a substitution effect on the firm's relative demand for employees and hours. The relative price of these two labor inputs, $[WH + V]/[EW(1 + p)]$, rises, inducing substitution away from employment and toward hours. As long as some substitution is possible, the imposed change will induce employers to lengthen workweeks by adding overtime hours and reducing employment to achieve a given rate of output. At a given wage rate and a constant premium for overtime work, increased fixed costs of employing a worker cause a decrease in the employment–hours ratio.

The third effect is more subtle and arises from the heterogeneity of labor inputs. Assume for analytical simplicity that there are only two types of labor, working $H_1$ and $H_2$ hours respectively, and that the firm uses $E_1$ and $E_2$ employees in each category. Total labor costs are then:

$$\Sigma[W_i(H_i)H_i + V_i]E_i, \tag{2.2}$$

where the subscript $i$ refers to the particular group of labor. Assume that production is characterized by:

$$Q = F[K, G(E_1, H_1, E_2, H_2)], \tag{2.1'}$$

so that labor inputs are still assumed to be separable from capital. If fixed costs of employment increase by the same nominal amount, the relative prices of employment and hours of the two types of worker change in proportion only if $V_1 = V_2$, $p_1 = p_2$, $W_1 = W_2$, and their employment and hours are the same, i.e. if the two groups of workers are functionally identical, so that the case is uninteresting.

In general, a constant nominal increase in the fixed cost of employment represents a greater percentage increase in the price of worker-hours of low- than of high-wage employees, and a greater increase in the price of employment relative to hours among low- than among high-skilled workers. If all six pairs of employment–hours combinations are $p$-substitutes, and labor is separable from capital, a constant nominal increase in $V_1$ and $V_2$ will induce substitution away from low-skilled worker-hours and toward high-skilled labor (in addition to the substitution away from labor generally and toward capital). Moreover, within each group of workers there will be substitution toward greater hours per worker, with greater substitution toward more hours per low-skilled employee.

Under different assumptions about the nature of production this conclusion does not necessarily stand up. For example, suppose hours of each type of worker must be the same ($H_1$ and $H_2$ are perfect $p$-complements), perhaps because a plant must operate for a shift of a given duration. We will still observe a relative decrease in total worker-hours of low-skilled employees, because there will be a relative decline in employment of low-skilled workers; but hours per worker will change identically for both groups.

When the assumption of separability of capital from labor in (2.1') is relaxed, it becomes difficult to draw general conclusions about the effects of changes in fixed costs. One might, for example, imagine that machine-tenders must work in shifts of fixed duration, while hours per worker of other employees are not complementary with the intensity of capital utilization. In that case a rise in the fixed costs of employing machine-tenders will reduce their employment, but it will also reduce the rate of utilization of capital and could increase the ratio of employment to hours among other workers, depending on the relevant substitution elasticities. Clearly, once one disaggregates labor and abandons capital–labor separability, very little can be concluded *a priori*.

A large array of policies can be viewed as mixing imposed changes in hourly labor costs and fixed employment costs.[3] Increases in payroll tax

11

rates to finance taxes on which there is a ceiling on earnings, and increases in the ceiling at a constant tax rate, raise the cost of employment if the ceiling is low, and have no effect on the cost of an additional hour. They are both equivalent to increases in fixed employment costs. If the ceiling is higher, the effect of these changes on the relative size of fixed and variable employment costs may differ.

Reductions in the standard workweek (which require penalty rates on hours beyond the normal week) raise the fixed cost of employment, since the cost of an additional worker is raised by the penalty times the reduction in the normal workweek; but the cost of an additional hour also increases for employees who had been working marginally less than the previous standard week. The net impact depends on the distribution of hours per worker before the change was imposed. Changes in the penalty rate for overtime pay, and restrictions on the amount of overtime that may be used, are other examples. In each case the impacts of the pure policy on labor–labor and employment–hours substitution will be attenuated because the marginal cost of an additional hour is raised; but, to the extent that the fixed-cost component of the change dominates, the ratio of employment to hours and the mix of workers employed will change in the directions indicated above. However, the potentially ambiguous effect of mixed policies underscores the importance of analyzing the specifics of each proposed change.

## 2.2(b)   Costs of Changing Employment

A variety of natural and imposed labor costs accompanies gross changes in a firm's employment. Costs of searching for and processing new employees, including advertising costs and part of the overhead costs of maintaining a personnel department; initial training costs (those that must be incurred to make the employee minimally productive in the firm), to the extent the employer shares in these costs; and payroll costs that accompany layoffs, including higher payroll taxes or direct payments, are some examples.[4]

Most of the analysis of the cost of adjusting employment has assumed that the average cost increases the larger is the change in employment. The assumption is embodied in Figure 2.1a in the positive slope of $CK$.[5] That average costs are increasing is usually rationalized by pointing to an ever-greater disruption of the firm's operations as the change in employment increases. Consider a standard downward-sloping labor demand schedule, $D_1$ (shown in Figure 2.1b), with the firm confronted by an imposed increase in the hourly cost of labor, from $W_0$ to $W_1$. We deal here with a decrease in equilibrium employment; a rise in employment can be handled *mutatis mutandis* with a similar analysis. In the absence of adjustment costs, employment would fall from $E_0$ to $E_1$. With these costs, though, an immediate drop in employment engenders costs equal to $OAFD$ in Figure 2.1a: making the entire adjustment at once leads to very large transactions costs. The profit-maximizing firm can do

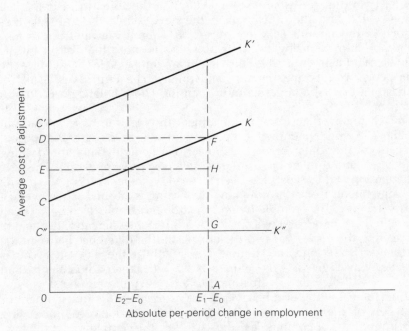

**Figure 2.1a**

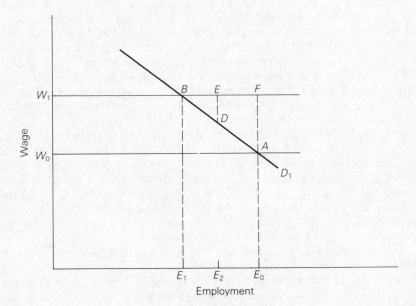

**Figure 2.1b**

better than this, for example by making half the adjustment in the first time period and the other half in the next. While the firm sacrifices profits in the amount *DBE* in Figure 2.1b when it is away from its new static profit-maximizing position, this loss is more than offset by the saving in adjustment costs. These latter are only O*AHE* – two times the per-period cost of making the adjustment. The firm saves *EHFD* of adjustment costs, a larger amount than the *DBE* of static profits that it forgoes.

Increasing average costs of adjustment thus lead firms to spread out changes in employment when a permanent change in wages is imposed. In general, the adjustment takes forever, with employment approaching the new static equilibrium asymptotically (see the Appendix). The bulk of attention to these costs has been focused on their effects on the timing of adjustment. Consider now how the timing is affected when average costs increase, for example by an upward shift from *CK* to *C'K'*. Even though the average cost of a particular adjustment is greater, the gain to spreading the costs over two periods is still the difference between the rectangle *EHFD* and the triangle *DBE*. Only if the line *CK* becomes steeper – average costs rise more rapidly with larger adjustments than before – will the rate of adjustment to a new equilibrium be slower.

Consider how the firm behaves if the average cost is independent of the size of the adjustment. Except for the possibility of increasing disruption to operations as the size of the employment change increases, independence appears to be a good characterization of the nature of adjustment costs, especially given the absence of any evidence on this issue. In this case the line *CK* in Figure 2.1a, becomes horizontal at *C"K"*. There is no saving of adjustment costs if the cut in employment is spread over two periods, and the firm loses profits in the amount *DBE* for one period. With the average cost independent of the size of the adjustment, the firm changes to its new profit-maximizing employment level in one jump *if it changes employment* (Rothschild, 1971).

The firm may not, though, vary employment at all. Assume that the rise in $W$ is permanent. If the total cost of the change, the area O*AC"G*, exceeds the present value of the gain in profits from making the change, the triangle *ABF* divided by the discount rate, the firm will hold employment at $E_0$. More generally, the greater are the total costs of adjustment, the stickier employment will be in response to shocks to product demand or wages. Adjustments may be spread out or concentrated in one period; but, as shown in the Appendix, regardless of the slope of the average costs as the size of the adjustment changes, an increase in the cost of making the adjustment reduces the variation in employment in response to a given demand shock.

The presence of adjustment costs changes the average level of employment in each time period (see Nickell, 1978). Consider a two-period case, in which period 1 is characterized by high product demand, shown in Figure 2.2a by the labor demand schedule $D_1$, while in period 2 labor demand is reduced to $D_2$, shown in Figure 2.2b. The wage rate is constant at $W_0$, and there are adjustment costs of O*R* per worker

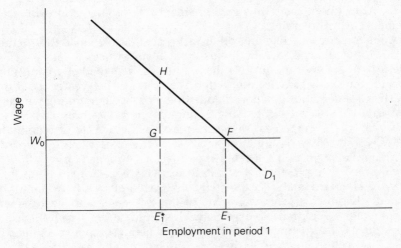

**Figure 2.2a**

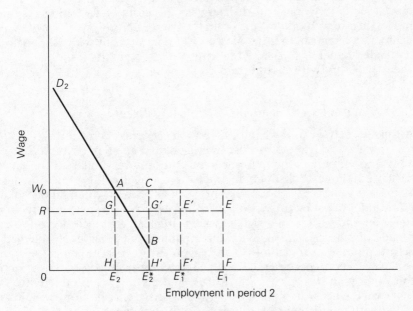

**Figure 2.2b**

discharged. If there were no such costs, the firm would set employment at $E_1$ and $E_2$ in periods 1 and 2 respectively. If it does so in the presence of these costs, it incurs additional costs of $EFHG$. The firm could make higher profits over the cycle if it reduced its first-period employment and raised its second-period employment. Indeed, it should set employment at levels $E_1^*$ and $E_2^*$ such that the sum of the triangles $FGH$ in Figure 2.2a and $ABC$ in Figure 2.2b is just equal to the rectangle $E'F'H'G'$ in Figure

15

2.2b. Adjustment costs thus lead to smoothing of fluctuations in factor demand over the cycle.

Adjustment costs, like any other factor cost, also reduce the average factor input. More generally, adjustment costs reduce average employment by a greater amount: (1) the greater the per-worker cost; (2) the greater the firm's rate of time preference; and (3) the greater the firm's elasticity of demand for labor. If adjustment costs differ among workers, the firm will also substitute labor of one type for that of another. If, for example, the average cost over an entire business cycle of employing older workers rises owing to an increase in the cost of laying them off, their employment will fall relative to that of younger workers (unless their supply is perfectly inelastic and relative wages are flexible).

In the standard analysis exposited above, asymmetries between hiring and discharge costs were ignored, so that increases and decreases in employment were treated identically.[6] It should be clear from the list of the sources of adjustment costs that there is no reason to expect the cost of a hire to be the same as that of a discharge. The total costs of the change, or the variation of average cost with the size of the change, need not be same for hires and discharges. The costs of searching for and processing new workers are entirely different from layoff costs. This distinction suggests that the elasticity of employment with respect to a particular demand shock and the length of the lag in the response to that shock will vary with its direction.

## 2.2(c)  Indirect and Potential Costs of Adjustment

A third variety of non-wage costs that affect firms' behavior differently from wages and fringes are costs imposed by regulation of the *process* of adjusting employment. In some senses these are similar to the costs discussed above. I distinguish them here because they relate to less aggregated problems of adjustment, such as who may be laid off, what information must be provided to employees, etc. Consider, first, regulations on the order in which workers are laid off. Included in such regulations are collectively bargained requirements that layoffs be made according to inverse seniority, and legal restrictions on layoffs of more senior workers. These regulations will not impose any cost on the firm *if* the wage paid to each worker exactly reflects his/her productivity. In that case the firm can abide by the regulations at no cost, for it would be indifferent about the order of layoffs in their absence.

The more likely case is that wages increase with tenure:

$$W = F(TN), \qquad F' > 0, \; F'' < 0, \qquad (2.3)$$

where $W$ is the wage rate and $TN$ is the worker's seniority. The positive relationship may be due to shared investment in firm-specific training (Becker, 1964) or be part of some long-term implicit contract between the worker and the firm (Lazear, 1981). Assume also that productivity rises

16

with tenure:

$$\pi = G(TN), \qquad G' > 0, \tag{2.4}$$

where $\pi$ is the worker's productivity per period, and that $F - G$ increases monotonically with $TN$. We assume more senior workers earn a wage above their current productivity as part of some optimal long-term implicit contract, perhaps because this wage–productivity relationship induces higher lifetime output by workers. Alternatively, the excess of wages over productivity among more senior workers might be 'explained' by custom.

Assuming now that there are no other costs of layoff or of hiring, how will the employer behave in the presence of fluctuations in product demand? The regulation of layoffs by inverse seniority obviously imposes an adjustment cost on the firm. However, the average cost is decreasing with the size of the adjustment: a small adjustment requires that the least senior worker, whose productivity exceeds the wage by the greatest amount, be laid off. That first layoff is quite costly. As more layoffs are made in a particular time period, the cost per layoff declines as more senior workers, for whom $W - \pi$ is greater, become subject to layoff. With a declining average cost of adjustment, it pays the firm to concentrate in one period all the layoffs it intends to make in response to expected changes in product demand. As in Section 2.2(b) above, though, the imposition of adjustment costs makes the employer less likely to change employment in response to a particular shift in product demand, and reduces the size of adjustments that do occur. These costs also represent an increase in total cost per worker, leading firms to reduce average employment over the cycle.

If wages do not equal productivity, the imposition of this regulation will lead to changes in relative employment by seniority. In the short run the workforce will clearly become more senior; but, with the regulation, the cost of employing more senior workers rises relative to that of more junior workers, especially in those firms whose product demand is more variable. This change in relative costs leads employers to undertake policies, such as a flattening of the wage–tenure profile, that eventually change the quit–tenure relationship and raise the ratio of junior to senior employees.[7] Even if no layoffs ever occur, the possibility of layoffs being conducted under inverse seniority, coupled with the systematic departure of wage rates from productivity, induces employers to seek a less senior workforce.

This point applies equally well to other restrictions on layoffs that differ by seniority. If restrictions are imposed on laying off more senior workers, employers will seek to substitute junior for senior workers by changing wage structures to alter the quit–tenure relationship. Conversely, if junior workers are protected, employers will try to steepen wage–tenure profiles and induce senior workers to remain on the job longer. Any restriction on severing members of a particular group of employees will lead employers to hire other groups of workers in preference to them.[8]

A second potential cost of adjustment is the requirement that information about planned changes in labor demand be made public. The extent of employers' opposition to such a requirement suggests it would reduce profits. One can view required prenotification as an increase in labor costs; alternatively, it might be viewed as a fixed cost of employing any labor. Under either view one can infer that it would reduce the aggregate amount of labor demanded over the business cycle. It would do this in existing plants and, perhaps more important, inhibit the formation of new capital that is $p$-complementary with the types of labor being protected.

Its potential effects are more complex than this, however. Workers' earlier awareness that their jobs are in jeopardy will lead them to change any decisions tht affect the extent to which they are tied to their current employers. Investment in firm-specific training will be reduced, so that the stock of firm-specific human capital will be smaller than otherwise at the time layoff occurs (Hamermesh, 1987). The reduced investment will increase workers' likelihood of quitting, for the discrepancy between their current wage and their alternative wages elsewhere will be reduced. To the extent that workers do not anticipate layoffs or plant closings well, requirements of openness about them will induce a more rapid reallocation of labor to expanding industries. However, those workers with the greatest past investment in training specific to the firm (and to the industry, if the entire industry is endangered) may act on the information by seeking governmental protection for their employers; with greater specific investment, public requirements of notification are more likely to lead to increased voice rather than more rapid exit.

The potential improvement in overall economic efficiency produced by publicity about impending layoffs comes at a cost to the declining firm and perhaps to those workers who remain with that firm. With employees bearing a reduced share of firm-specific investment, the firm's profits will decline still more rapidly than in the absence of the requirement, assuming the government does not try to protect the firm. Also if, as I assumed above, the difference between wages and productivity rises with tenure, the firm will be left with an increasingly older stock of workers as the date of layoff or plant closing approaches. Under the assumptions we have made this will lower profits still further and hasten the reduction in employers' demand for labor and the date at which the layoffs occur or the plant closes.

## 2.2(d)  Partial Coverage

The discussion has assumed that each particular job security policy applies uniformly to all workers and firms. (This assumption has been implicit in our use of a typical firm as the focus of analysis.) In reality, though, the policies do not apply equally to all employees in a firm, to all firms in an industry or to all industries in the economy. Most are characterized by partial coverage, which changes their impact on the economy and allows room for their net effects to be less than their gross effects on the firms to which they apply directly.

Consider, for example, a policy that increases adjustment costs in a particular sector of the economy. All the effects we discussed in Section 2.2(b) above apply in that sector. However, employees who are not working in this sector because of the increased labor cost will find work in the uncovered sector, if real wages in that sector can fall to absorb the increased supply. The policy of partial coverage thus leads to a reduction in the size of the covered sector and an expansion in the uncovered sector. This kind of two-tier policy gives employers a continuing incentive to substitute unprotected for protected workers and to contract services out to firms in the unprotected sector.

Partial coverage also affects the propensity of covered workers to quit their protected jobs. Since these jobs must be rationed (because of the supply of uncovered workers seeking them), incumbents are less likely to quit, for the alternative is a lower-paying, insecure job in the uncovered sector. Obversely, those in the uncovered sector have an increased probability of quitting, for the lower wage rates there combine with the attraction of protected jobs to induce more turnover. The economy-wide impact on turnover of job security policies involving partial coverage is unclear.

## 2.3  Analysis of Job Security Provisions

In this section I pigeonhole a variety of policies that have been undertaken to promote job security. While the set examined is by no means exhaustive, it is sufficiently representative to provide indications of how other policies might be categorized in light of the theoretical discussion. I discuss the policies in the order in which the various types of costs were considered in Section 2.2.

### 2.3(a)  Policies Affecting Fixed Costs

In the United Kingdom and the FRG a number of industries have collectively negotiated a **guaranteed periodic payment** (Gennard, 1979, pp. 43, 51). Such a policy converts an hourly, variable cost into a fixed cost exactly like those we discussed in Section 2.2(a). As such, it will reduce employers' demand for new workers even further below what it would have been, reduce the total number of employees, but raise hours worked by those remaining employed. In the long run, in so far as labor becomes more of a fixed cost, the policy will be a barrier to new firms entering the industry.

In 1975 British Steel negotiated an agreement to **limit overtime work**. This restriction is analogous to an increased penalty rate for overtime work, except that the penalty is infinite after some amount of overtime hours used. (If the ban were total, the overtime penalty would be infinite for even the first hour of overtime work.) Assuming the limit is effective (the firm would otherwise have used more overtime), this policy offsets fixed employment costs and induces firms to substitute workers for hours.

**Shorter workweeks** have been introduced in several countries recently. Thus France changed the standard workweek to 39 hours in 1982. The effect of such changes is unclear; it depends, as we saw in Section 2.2(a), on the distribution of current employees by the amount of hours worked per week. Many governments offer subsidies to short-time work, as in Japan, where only reductions of entire days are subsidized, or in the FRG, France and Italy, where reductions in hours generally are encouraged (Gennard, 1985). Such policies lower the price of workers relative to hours and provide an incentive to substitute additional workers for longer workweeks.

## 2.3(b)   Policies Affecting Adjustment Costs

The 1965 Redundancy Payments Act in the United Kingdom offered workers lump-sum payments if they were involuntarily severed through no fault of their own, payments that were in some cases 'topped up' by collectively negotiated plans (Gennard, 1979, pp. 41, 66). Such provisions represent adjustment costs in which the average cost is probably constant. If so, the policy will inhibit layoffs but will ensure that any layoffs that do occur are lumped together. In addition, the imposition of redundancy pay will inhibit employers from expanding employment when product demand rises, and will result in lower employment on average. Most redundancy payments, e.g. those created through collective negotiation in some German industries (Gennard, 1979, p. 64), increase with years of service. If the more senior workers are no more productive than junior workers, the ratio of their cost to their productivity relative to that of junior workers rises. This will induce employers to substitute toward more junior workers.

The United Kingdom's Temporary Employment Subsidy provided fixed payments to employers who agreed to forgo laying off employees who would otherwise have been discharged (Gennard, 1979, p. 31); Sweden offers training subsidies linked to workers' wage rates to employers who forgo layoffs (McKersie and Sengenberger, 1983). These policies **subsidize retention** of workers, and thus implicitly raise the relative cost of adjustment. As such, firms are less likely to vary employment over the cycle. However, because labor costs are subsidized, employment expands beyond what it otherwise would have been in those firms that qualify for the subsidy. In that sense, the policy can be viewed as a cost reduction in declining industries.

These policies are aimed particularly at collective layoffs. A host of specific policies designed to protect against unfair dismissals of individuals has arisen in Western Europe. Most (Gennard, 1985) define fair dismissal in terms only of a worker's conduct and provide for appeals to courts or labor tribunals. To some extent these policies do raise the cost of workers relative to hours, and thus tend to reduce employment–hours ratios. They are, though, explicitly related to adjustment, and as such they induce the effects that we noted in Section 2.2(b).

In the past several years there has been some loosening of the policies that have raised adjustment costs, both on collective layoffs and individual dismissals. For example, the FRG in 1985 increased the fraction of the workforce scheduled for layoff before the provisions of protective legislation become effective and exempted new firms from the legislation entirely. Spain in 1980 reduced the amount of redundancy payments required to be awarded to workers laid off because of economic factors (Gennard, 1985). There has also been a general loosening of the restrictions on individual dismissals to allow the invocation of economic necessity as a justification for such layoffs. All these changes reduce the impacts we noted above: they make adjustments more likely than under the more rigid legislation, and they increase average employment in the sectors covered by the legislation.

## 2.3(c)  Policies That Produce Indirect Costs

**Layoff by inverse seniority** characterizes most collective agreements in the United States and the United Kingdom. In the FRG, France and Italy, legislation requires that length of service and personal circumstances be included among the considerations governing the order of layoffs. The effect of these provisions on employment fluctuations is, as I showed in Section 2.2, unclear a priori. Assume, however, that they impose costs on the employer because they impose a different ordering from the (private) cost-minimizing ordering that the employer would choose. If so, they induce all the short- and long-run effects on employment, wage structures and mobility that were discussed in Section 2.2(c). Most important in terms of aggregate employment, they reduce cyclical fluctuations and also reduce average levels of employment.

**Limits or bans on hiring** have been introduced through collective negotiations in the German steel industry and elsewhere (Gennard, 1979, pp. 63, 72). Assuming that employers would hire workers into some jobs while discharging them from others, such a ban represents an additional adjustment cost. It will reduce employment fluctuations while raising labor costs, thus reducing the average amount of labor demanded.

**Prenotification** of impending plant closings or major layoffs must be provided to governments and/or employee representatives in a number of OECD countries. In the United Kingdom, Italy and the FRG, prenotification must be given to certain workers even in cases of impending individual dismissals. All such requirements operate as indicated in Section 2.2: they affect the speed with which adjustments take place, the willingness of firms to invest in new capital equipment and of workers and firms to invest in training, and the mobility patterns of workers in the affected firms.

## 2.3(d) The Partial Coverage of Job Security Legislation

A wide variety of **restrictions** in the various provisions of job security legislation make that legislation conform to the model of partial coverage that was outlined in Section 2.2(d). For example:

(1) Canada is considering requiring that part-time employees (those working no more than 20 hours per week) be covered by pensions (effectively decreasing problems that arise from partial coverage of protective legislation).[9]

(2) Exemptions from job security legislation exist for workers and firms that do not meet various criteria (Gennard, 1985). Thus in the United Kingdom claims of unfair dismissal are not allowed for employees with less than two years of seniority. The seniority requirement is even more stringent for part-time employees. In Italy, some of the legislation excludes employers of fewer than 35 workers, while in the FRG employers of fewer than 5 workers are excluded from employment protection leglislation generally.

(3) In Germany and Italy, prenotification requirements are much more stringent for white- than for blue-collar workers.

To the extent that employers can substitute part- for full-time workers, exemptions will result in an expansion of the part-time workforce. Similarly, they should favor the relative expansion of smaller enterprises, especially in those sectors in which economies of scale do not exist or are not very substantial. Indeed, to the extent that substitution by employers and consumers is possible, exemptions from the panoply of job security legislation may have created the beginning of two-tier societies, one with rigid job security requirements covering high-paid, senior, full-time workers in large firms, the other more flexible, with part-time, low-paid, insecure workers in small businesses. The high-paid tier will contract because of the imposed rigidity, while the low-paid tier will expand.

## 2.4 Evidence on the Effects of Labor Costs

### 2.4(a) Fixed Costs and Employment–Hours Substitution

The most important empirical issue to be addressed is whether employers' production functions allow for substitution *in the long run* between employment and hours per worker. To the extent such substitution is possible, policies that produce relative increases in fixed employment costs bias employers toward reducing employment and increasing hours. There are two strands of literature that bear on this issue. The first examines employment–hours trade-offs in the context of standard labor demand equations without actually attempting to measure relative fixed and variable costs. While it cannot, therefore, provide direct evidence on the effect of changes in labor cost structures on the mix of employment and hours, it can inform us whether an increase in the use of hours decreases or increases the demand for workers at a fixed level of output. The second strand tries to measure cost structures and, in most cases, to examine how they affect employers' demands for overtime.

Recent evidence from standard labor demand equations on this issue is quite mixed. For US manufacturing, 1963–1981: II, Rossana (1983) estimates a model of the demand for hours as a function of employment levels, measures of orders, and real wages.[10] This type of model is inspired, as are similar models discussed in this section, by Nadiri and Rosen (1969). The estimates suggest that for each 10 per cent long-run increase in employment there is a 1.5 per cent drop in hours per worker. Similar equations in Rossana (1985), estimated using monthly US data for 1959–1982: 6 over six two-digit SIC industries, find no significant effect of the stock of employees on the demand for hours. Somewhat perplexing, though, since they imply an asymmetry, equations describing employment demand for the same industries mostly show a small but significant *positive* effect of hours per worker on the demand for workers. However, since the hours and employment equations were not estimated jointly, this asymmetry may be a result of the estimation technique (or perhaps of a specification having insufficient grounding in microeconomic theory). Yamamoto (1982) finds negative effects of employment on hours, and vice versa, using quarterly data for Japanese manufacturing from 1970 to 1978. Faini and Schiantarelli (1985) observe the same relation between employment and hours for the Italian industrial sector, 1970–1980. In both cases, however, the short sample periods make it unclear whether or not these really represent long-run relationships.

One study of US data using similar models, but decomposing output changes into permanent and transitory components, estimates the size of an hours–employment trade-off using data on overtime hours (Crawford, 1979). For manufacturing 1958–1976 (monthly), it finds a small but significant positive relationship between employment levels and the demand for hours. Comparing this result to those cited above, it seems quite clear that this approach provides little evidence of a long-run trade-off between employment and normal hours, i.e. of whether hours and employment are substitutes or complements. This may be because such a trade-off truly does not exist: evidence for the very long run suggests hours per week are determined mainly by workers' preferences, not by production technology (see Hamermesh and Rees, 1984). However, in so far as these studies do not even attempt to measure the relative costs of hours and workers, their lack of evidence is not too critical.

Several studies of the demand for overtime hours have attempted to divide employment costs into fixed and variable components. Their choice of data allows for much greater variability in the underlying marginal costs of employment and hours, and thus at least makes it possible to measure the extent of substitution of employment for hours.

23

The three analyses for the US summarized in Ehrenberg and Schumann (1982) and that study itself all suggest that higher fixed costs of employment do reduce the long-run employment–hours ratio. In all these studies, though, the trade-offs are quite small: a one-third increase in the relative cost of an hour of overtime would produce no more than a 4 per cent decline in the ratio of overtime to other hours. A somewhat larger effect is produced for West Germany using time-series data, 1964–1983, by König and Pohlmeier (1986).

Using annual data, 1951–1981, for West Germany, Hart and Kawasaki (1987) decompose payments to labor, particularly payroll taxes, into fixed and variable measures and examine their effects on employment and hours. Their model treats hours, employment and the capital stock as jointly determined by their lagged values, fixed and variable payroll taxes, output, non-wage fixed and variable labor costs, and capital costs. The authors find surprisingly that a cut in the payroll tax ceiling in a tax structure with a high ceiling relative to the average wage level increases employment and reduces hours per worker. They attribute this perverse result to their use of a model that includes both capital and labor. Hart and Kawasaki also produce the expected finding that decreased variable payroll taxes reduce the employment–hours ratio.

While the evidence seems fairly clear that an increase in the fixed costs of employment induces only slight substitution away from workers and toward hours, holding total worker-hours constant, this does not mean the negative employment effects of job security policies that impose fixed employment costs are small. Elsewhere (Hamermesh, 1986) I have summarized an immense body of evidence on the elasticity of labor demand with respect to labor costs. The overwhelming bulk of studies that use modern estimation techniques finds that the net (including all adjustments among firms) long-run constant-output labor demand elasticity characterizing broad aggregates of industries is between .1 and .5. The total elasticity, which allows for scale effects, is larger still. That being the case, policies that increase the fixed costs of employment may reduce the employment–hours *ratio* only slightly, but can effect substantial reductions in the *total* amount of worker-hours employed.

## 2.4(b)  Adjustment Costs and Lagged Labor Demand

There is a huge mass of empirical evidence demonstrating that the demand for workers and hours lags behind output. Moreover, the lags in the adjustment of employment are greater than those in the adjustment of hours per worker. Hamermesh (1976) summarizes a large number of early studies demonstrating this fact. More recent evidence corroborates this conclusion in more carefully specified models. Using a model like that of Nadiri and Rosen (1969), but decomposing changes in product demand into expected and unexpected components, Topel (1982) suggests a similar conclusion based on data for 1958–1975 for six US manufacturing industries. For the automobile industry Chang (1983) demonstrates this both for the United States and for the state of Michigan.

The average length of the lags of employment and hours behind output changes is not so closely determined as are their relative lengths. However, the evidence summarized in Hamermesh (1976) suggests that nearly all the adjustment is completed within one year. Recent studies of the FRG and France (Bucher, 1984) using similar techniques produce similar results. Early studies on aggregate US data (Sargent, 1978a; Meese, 1980) that paid close attention to the structure of expectations and its implications for error terms in the estimating equations found very long lags of employment behind output (average length over one year). These may well be artifacts of the estimating procedure rather than reversals of previous evidence. More recently, Shapiro (1986) has employed a dynamic expectational model of the adjustment of production labor, non-production labor and capital that suggests that adjustment lags for workers exceed those for hours per worker, and that the lags are not very long. It seems safe to conclude that the lags in adjusting labor inputs are fairly short.

Theoretical work underlying the estimation of lagged factor adjustment rests on the theory of adjustment costs, in most cases on an increasing average cost. Whether empirical results stem from these costs has not been demonstrated. However, Morrison and Berndt (1981) use annual US data for 1952–1971 to show that the adjustment of non-production worker employment to changes in output demand is much slower than that of production workers. Assuming that adjustment costs are quadratic, Shapiro (1986) infers that they are substantial for adjustments of non-production worker labor, but quite small for adjustments of production workers. Similar findings are reported for the British engineering sector for 1963–1978 by Nissim (1984).[11] De Pelsmacker (1984) finds the same qualitative results for Belgian auto plants from 1976 through 1982.

Assuming that the lags arise from adjustment costs, there is some evidence that these costs are asymmetric. Hamermesh (1969) demonstrates for a group of three- and four-digit SIC US manufacturing industries that the lag of layoffs behind output changes is shorter than that of new hires behind output changes. Inferentially, the average cost of increasing employment rises more rapidly than that of employment declines. What this finding implies about potential asymmetries in the effects of job security policies is unclear without a specification of how those policies affect adjustment costs.

The short-run effects of specific policies have received very little serious empirical attention. Nickell (1979) examines British manufacturing data, 1955–1976, and finds that the lag in employment rose during this period, while the lag in hours declined. He attributes these changes to the increased requirements of job security policies. More recently Nickell (1982) has shown that between 1967 and 1977 an increase in the use of unfair dismissal legislation caused a reduction in both hiring and flows from employment, with the latter dominating (so that the net effect was a reduction in unemployment). For the United States, Hamermesh (1978) shows that expansion of the unemployment insurance program, which is financed by what is essentially a fixed tax, produced at least some short-run substitution away from employment and toward increased hours per worker. Implicitly the UI system increased the speed of adjustment of employment to changes in product demand.

As a further test of some of these ideas, I examine dynamic employment–output and hours–output relations in 12 OECD countries. This exercise extends Nickell's (1979) examination of these relationships for the UK. I concentrate on determining whether and how the rate of adjustment to changes in product demand changed in the 1970s from what it had been earlier. We have seen that many countries adopted policies during the 1970s that were designed to slow the adjustment of employment to output shocks. At the same time, though, we know that large increases occurred in the price of energy, which is a $p$-substitute for labor. These changes may also have altered the lag structure in employment–output and hours–output relations (though there is no *a priori* reason to believe this happened). All we can test, therefore, is whether changes in lag structures occurred.

For each country with available data, an integrated vector-autoregression model was estimated for the manufacturing sector:

$$Y_t = a Y_{t-1} + \Sigma\, b_i Q_{t-1} + ct + \varepsilon, \qquad (2.5)$$

where $a$, $b_1$ and $c$ are parameters; $Y$ is the dependent variable (in logarithms); $Q$ is the logarithm of output; $t$ is a time trend, and $\varepsilon$ is a disturbance term. The dependent variable $Y$ is either employment or total hours worked. For all countries the 'early' time period ended in 1973: III and the 'late' time period began with 1973: IV. This break point is chosen to coincide with the first oil shock. Obviously the timing of the impacts of job security policies differs in different countries, and it would be more appropriate to search for structural changes in each country separately. Failing that, we follow standard practice and use the oil shock to demarcate the point at which the structure may have changed. For most countries the initial observation in the early period is 1961: I, and the final observation in the late time period is 1985: II.[12]

The detailed results of estimating equation (2.5) are available from the author. For the six large countries – Canada, France, the FRG, Japan, the United Kingdom and the United States – the estimates are fairly satisfactory, though there is some tendency for Durbin's $h$-statistic to reject the null hypothesis of no serial correlation in the employment equations. The average lag of employment adjustment in the six large countries exceeds that of hours adjustment in 11 out of the 12 pairs of equations estimated. Among the smaller countries – Austria, Finland, Greece, Ireland, the Netherlands and Norway – the estimates are less precise (Greece and Finland) or imply lags of ridiculous length (Ireland).

Recognizing that the application of a common specification to data

26

**Table 2.1**
Comparison of average duration of adjustment lag (number of countries)[a]

| | Employment | | |
| --- | --- | --- | --- |
| Hours | Early > late | Early < late | Total |
| Early > late | 2 | 2 | 4 |
| Early < late | | 2(3) | 2(3) |
| No hours equation | (1) | (3) | |
| TOTAL | 2(3) | 4(8) | |

[a]Excludes Ireland

from a large number of economies will produce some anomalies, it is still worth while examining common trends in the results. The numbers without parentheses in Table 2.1 are totals including only the six large countries, while those in parentheses include all 11 countries except Ireland. Considering only the employment–output equations (the last line of the table), there is a tendency for the average lag of employment adjustment to have lengthened in the 1970s. (The probability of observing an increased lag in at least 8 of 11 countries is only .11 if the population probability is .5.) However, considering the $2 \times 2$ contingency table for the seven countries for which both employment and hours equations are estimated, Nickell's result that employment lags have lengthened, but hours lags have shortened, does not hold up. This diversity of changes in the average length of adjustment lags is observed in only two of the seven countries – Japan and the United Kingdom.

The results of this exercise are consistent with the hypothesis that changes in job security policy have induced slower adjustment of employment changes to shocks to output demand. They are not consistent with the additional claim that the same policy changes have encouraged employers to adjust more rapidly along the margin of hours per worker. Whether or not we have demonstrated anything more than a correlation of the growth of job security policies with increases in employment lags remains for other studies that examine the effects of specific job security policies on particular economies and industries (for example, Houseman in this volume, Chapter 4).

## 2.4(c)  Indirect Costs

Whether or not policies that alter employers' behavior in retaining workers increase labor costs depends on whether or not the wage–seniority relationship arises out of a seniority–productivity relationship.[13] Evidence on this issue is still sparse and deserves a more thorough review than is possible here, but the best conclusion at this point is that there is a positive relation between seniority and productivity, though one that is weaker than the wage–seniority relation.

There is remarkably little evidence on the employment effects of specific policies that attempt to prevent layoffs by changing indirect costs. Metcalf (1984) uses cross-section British data on industries to show that the Temporary Employment Subsidy succeeded in reducing permanent layoffs. (His results also show that short-time compensation increased layoffs, which is hard to credit.) As we saw in Section 2.4(b), Nickell (1982) demonstrates a similar effect of unfair dismissal legislation in the UK. The difficulties with broad-brush empirical work that uses gross measures in aggregate time-series equations to estimate the effects of complex policies are by now well known. It seems clear that serious evaluation of policies that affect indirect costs will require both more detailed specification of the programs' parameters and use of more disaggregated data. At this point we simply have very little information on the employment effects of anti-layoff programs that operate by affecting costs indirectly.

If markets worked well, in the sense that information was good, there would be little need for many programs restricting employers' rights to lay off workers. For example, if workers know that a permanent layoff is impending, they will reduce investment in firm-specific capital to the point where its value will be zero when the layoff occurs. The evidence (Hamermesh, 1987) indicates that substantial firm-specific investment takes place immediately before the layoff, implying that workers' information about impending layoffs is not very good. This suggests that requiring prenotification can prevent useless investment in firm-specific capital, and can aid adjustment by encouraging workers to substitute general training that will make subsequent job search easier. Indeed, evidence for a particular labor market (Folbre *et al.*, 1984) and for a nationwide sample of workers (Addison and Portugal, 1987b) indicates that prenotification does reduce the costs of dislocation.

### 2.4(d)  Partial Coverage – Substitution of Unprotected for Protected Workers

There have been no studies of whether or not protective legislation covering only part of an economy has induced a relative expansion of the uncovered sector. However, all the direct evidence suggests that partial coverage produces substantial substitution away from employment in the covered sector. Gennard (1985) argues that protective legislation and, more important, increased non-wage costs have resulted in an expansion of the sectors of the British economy and the kinds of employment that are not covered by the legislation and not so heavily subject to non-wage costs. Similarly, in the FRG he notes that firms have been spurred by employment regulation to use more subcontracting and more part-time labor.

Owen (1979) uses cross-section data for the United States in 1973 to estimate the degree of substitution between full- and part-time workers. He finds that changes in their relative wages had large effects on relative demand. This suggests that policies that increase the relative costs of employing full-time workers can produce large reductions in their employment, and large increases in the demand for part-timers. Disney and Szyszczak (1984) show that part-time employment in the UK was sharply affected when legislation expanded employment protection for part-time workers.[14]

## 2.5 Conclusions

Simple regressions that include the existence or magnitude of expenditures under a particular job security program cannot yield any useful information about its effects: those depend in a complex way on how the program affects costs; and, as we have seen, the paths through which costs may be changed are quite diverse. They include possible effects on the employment–hours ratio, on employment adjustment, and on the level of total labor input through their effects on average labor costs. The evidence suggests there is a short-run trade-off between employment and hours per worker, but that in the long run policies that affect the structure of labor costs have only a slight impact on employment. They do, however, affect the magnitude of adjustments in employment in response to changes in product demand. Also, when average labor costs are changed by job security policies, levels of employment demand will change through the standard routes of capital–labor substitution and scale effects.

The discussion in Section 2.4 makes it apparent how little we know about how job security programs in general affect labor costs, and what the impacts of particular policies have been. The few studies of job security policies that were enacted in the industrialized countries during the 1970s and early 1980s do suggest that they achieved their aims, but at the expense of reducing total worker-hours in protected employment. Better evidence is provided by studies of the impact of labor costs more generally: these suggest that the policies could have produced some short-run increase in employment. Given the lengths of lags in adjustment, though, the evidence indicates that it is unlikely that they induced a substitution of employment for hours that lasted beyond several years. Moreover, to the extent that they raised labor costs, as most did, they contributed to a decline in total worker-hours through the elasticity of demand for labor services.

The discussion of the theory of labor costs and the evidence on it imply that job security policies can induce a temporary substitution of employment for hours, and can permanently mitigate short-run employment fluctuations – both decreases and increases in employment. They accomplish this at the cost of reducing the equilibrium level of labor input and of output. They thus offer an industrialized economy a choice between greater employment stability (with fewer total hours worked on average) and greater employment fluctuations (with more total hours worked on average). Moreover, to the extent they cover only part of the labor market, they help create a two-tier labor market consisting of secure jobs in a declining sector and insecure jobs in an expanding sector.

## Appendix

Let the firm maximize:

$$\int_0^\infty [F(L) - wL - C(\dot{L})]e^{-rt}\, dt, \tag{2A.1}$$

where $L$ = labor input, $w$ = cost per unit of labor services, $r$ is the firm's discount rate, $C(\dot{L})$ is the adjustment cost, and I have assumed labor is the only input in a production function $F$, with $F' > 0$, $F'' < 0$. Assume that the marginal cost of adjustment can be increasing and in particular that $C$ is quadratic:

$$C(\dot{L}) = a\dot{L} + b\dot{L}^2, \qquad a > 0, b \geqslant 0. \tag{2A.2}$$

(The marginal cost of adjustment is then $2b\dot{L} + a$.) The Euler equation describing the firm's profit-maximizing path is:

$$2b\ddot{L} - 2br\dot{L} + F'(L) - w - ra = 0, \tag{2A.3}$$

where $\ddot{L}$ denotes $d^2L/dt^2$.
   If $b > 0$, the steady state is described by $\dot{L} = \ddot{L} = 0$ and $L^*$ such that:

$$F'(L^*) = w + ra. \tag{2A.4}$$

(This is the standard marginal productivity condition for labor demand, with the user-cost of adjustment added.) Assume that the firm has $L = L_0^*$ at $t = 0$, and that $w$ increases. The new equilibrium is shown as $L^*$ in Figure 2A.1. The line along which $\ddot{L} = 0$ is negatively sloped, for as $L$ increases in (2A.3), $F'(L)$ decreases, as must $\dot{L}$. The adjustment path from $L_0^*$ to $L^*$ is indicated by the arrow. A similar analysis applies if the firm begins at $L_1^*$, and is then shocked at $t = 0$ by a wage decrease.
   If $b = 0$, the marginal cost of adjustment is constant in $\dot{L}$, and (2A.4) holds for all $t$. Thus any change in $w$ causes the firm to adjust instantaneously to the new $L^*$ that satisfies (2A.4). That this is true when $b = 0$, but adjustment is slow when $b > 0$, shows that a more rapid increase in the marginal cost as $\dot{L}$ increases reduces the rate of adjustment. A higher marginal cost of adjustment – $a$ – reduces $L^*$, as does a higher discount rate. Employment on average is lower where adjustment costs are greater.
   That greater adjustment costs reduce employment fluctuations when shocks occur can be seen by assuming the firm is in equilibrium at $t = 0$,

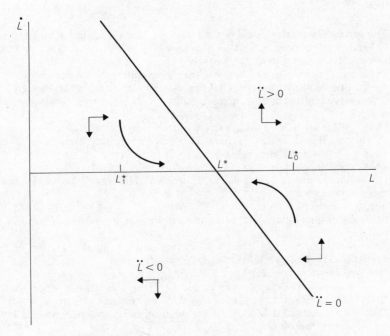

**Figure 2A.1** Phase diagram of employment adjustment

given $w_0$, and that $w$ changes temporarily to $w_1$ for some known period of time, $T$. The maximand (2A.1) becomes:

$$\int_0^T [F(L) - w_1 - a\dot{L} - b\ddot{L}]e^{-rt}\,dt + \int_T^\infty [F(L) - w_0 - a\dot{L} - b\ddot{L}]e^{-rt}. \quad (2A.1')$$

Since the firm's adjustment is slower when $b$ is greater, the shock to $w$ will result in a smaller movement away from $L_0^*$ by $t = T$ than if $b$ were smaller. If $b = 0$ the firm will choose either to maintain $L = L_0^*$ for all $t$, or to jump to $L_1^*$ at $t = 0$, then jump back to $L_0^*$ at $t = T$. With constant marginal adjustment costs the fluctuation will be the same size *if it occurs*; but the employer's willingness to vary $L$ at all decreases as $a$ is larger.

## Acknowledgements

A previous draft of this study was prepared under contract to the Organization for Economic Cooperation and Development. Helpful comments were received from John Martin, John Addison and participants in the Experts' meeting in Paris in April 1985.

# Notes

1 Though this last statement is not quite correct, the low ceiling on the taxable base under this program makes this component of payroll costs function essentially as a fixed cost per worker.

2 Evidence (Hamermesh, 1986) on the separability of capital from labor subgroups suggests, though, that this assumption is not right, though it is unknown whether the evidence generalizes to employment–hours substitution.

3 Hart (1984b) analyzes a wide variety of these combinations.

4 In this section I usually ignore general equilibrium impacts of these payments that work through labor supply to the firm.

5 This exposition is based on Hamermesh and Rees (1988).

6 However, the original analysis of this problem (Holt et al. 1960) did examine these asymmetries.

7 See, for example, Mincer and Jovanovic (1981) or Mitchell (1982) for evidence of a negative effect of tenure on the quit probability, other things equal.

8 As I discuss in Section 2.2(d) below, this is a general implication of the partial coverage of protective legislation.

9 See Wall Street Journal, 22 April 1986, p. 1.

10 This equation has little basis in economic theory, because it ignores fixed labor costs (or assumes implicitly that they are constant over time, which is clearly incorrect) and because it includes as independent variables both employment and output.

11 However, Nissim also has the strange result that the lag of skilled worker employment behind changes in skilled workers' wages is shorter than the adjustment lag of unskilled employment behind changes in unskilled wages. This result is inconsistent with the findings of lags behind output in the same study.

12 The exceptions are: France, with the late time period ending in 1984: IV; Greece and the United Kingdom, with the early period beginning in 1963: I; the Netherlands, with the late period ending in 1985: I; and Norway, for which observations for 1971: I–1972: III are excluded because of missing data.

13 Despite one recent argument to the contrary (Altonji and Shakotko, 1987), I assume that the wage–seniority relationship is not merely an artifact resulting from incorrectly analyzed data.

14. Because the study lacks a satisfactory relative price variable and uses interaction terms without the matching main-effect variables, the results in Disney and Szyszczak (1984) are less reliable than those in many of the other studies discussed in this survey.

# COMMENT

## JOHN T. ADDISON

In this interesting theme paper, Professor Hamermesh has set himself the unenviable task of analyzing the consequences of a plethora of job security provisions and regulations. Such arrangements are distinguished in terms of their impact on fixed employment costs and the costs of adjusting employment, and their coverage. Having anchored his discussion in this manner, he then engages the extant empirical literature, and in the process offers some new material of his own on the relative speeds of adjustment of hours and employment behind changes in output.

Increases in the fixed costs of employment are said to have relatively straightforward effects if labor is separable from capital in the three-factor production function. Thus, for example, *given low wage ceilings* for payroll taxes, increases in either the ceiling or tax rates reduce the employment–hours ratio, lower the overall demand for labor, and lead to a substitution away from low-skilled worker-hours toward high-skilled labor, *inter al.* Similarly, a reduced workweek raises fixed employment costs, although the magnitude of the negative effect on employment vis-à-vis hours depends on the distribution of actual hours worked prior to the change and in particular on the relative number of hours worked between the old and the new workweeks.

Turning to the direct costs of adjusting employment, much of Hamermesh's discussion is predicated on the argument that average costs rise with the scale of the adjustment because of disruption effects. Such transaction costs produce phased rather than instantaneous adjustment to exogenous changes in wages or demand. Indeed, other than producing a slimmed down labor force to begin with, their magnitude may rule out any change in employment even if average costs are independent of the size of the adjustment. At the end of his discussion, Hamermesh introduces the caveat that the response of employment to changes in demand will vary with the direction of the demand shock because of asymmetries between hiring and discharge costs. This is an interesting point but one that is imprecisely articulated. The problem with the discussion is that it seemingly fails to recognize that transaction costs – associated with hiring and training costs, search costs, and moving costs – are one factor motivating long-term worker–firm attachments. Viewed in this light, the more interesting question devolves on stock adjustment and factor utilization decisions, where the former comprise permanent layoffs and new hires and the latter temporary layoffs. In the absence of such considerations, one has to question why no attention is paid to downward wage adjustments.

As I began Hamermesh's subsequent discussion of indirect and potential costs of adjustment, I thought the issue of long-term attachments was about to be tackled since the focus now shifts to seniority

33

practices. In the event, such practices are seen as being exogenously determined. It is first noted that if the worker's wage exactly reflects his productivity, there will be no adjustment cost associated with an inverse seniority (last-in-first-out) rule. If, as is typically the case, productivity rises with seniority but by less than does the wage, it is argued that the employer will concentrate all his (temporary) layoffs in one period because the marginal costs of adjustment will fall with the scale of adjustment. I do not disagree with this argument, although I would prefer to couch it in terms of other cost advantages attaching to the layoff of more senior workers on the lines suggested by Haltiwanger (1984). However, I find myself in sharp disagreement with the second part of the argument that sees an increasing gap between the wage and marginal revenue product as somehow economically arbitrary, but yet prompting employers when confronted with the introduction of a seniority rule to alter wage–tenure profiles and thereby secure greater quits among the protected category. There are any number of theoretical reasons associated with profit-maximizing behavior that produce a growing gap between the wage and marginal revenue product as the worker's seniority with the firm grows. A sample of such arguments would include deferred compensaton as a device to defer worker shirking; an insurance function to protect workers against low productivity outcomes later in their careers; an adverse selection or screening argument; and, of course, even a standard firm-specific human capital model would point to the same outcome over certain ranges of the tenure profile once allowance is made for opportunistic behavior. In short, there is a natural or endogenously derived seniority system in many employments that has first to be analyzed before making predictions as to the impact of legislated job security provisions on adjustments costs.

Also in this section of the paper, Hamermesh tackles the interesting question of advance notification. Here I have to say that, although he correctly identifies the costs to firms and the gain to society from an advance notification rule, I do not agree with the argument that, because the coefficient on tenure fails to fall in the run-up to job loss, this is (a) evidence of labor market ignorance and (b) illustrative of the gains to workers. I amplify both arguments below.

Finally, Hamermesh's thoroughly appropriate discussion of partial coverage might have benefited from further elaboration. One fundamental issue that needs to be addressed here is whether partial coverage is an example of a market escape route or indicative of policymakers serving several constituencies. Coverage may well be the most important factor conditioning the impact of legislated changes in job security and justifies further analysis.

In the middle section of the paper, Hamermesh pigeonholes various types of job security practices/policies according to whether they impact on fixed employment costs or the costs of adjusting employment. Here, I propose to delve a little more deeply into one of his cases but preface these comments with two more general observations. First, one unresolved issue in his discussion is the distinction between collectively negotiated and externally imposed job security arrangements. Both here and elsewhere I would like to have seen some comment on the role of negotiated job regulations as devices to cope with the problems raised by information asymmetries. Second, I detect signs in this discussion of the difficulty of rigidly dichotomizing job security practices into the fixed costs/adjustment cost framework.

But my main observation has to do with the late and unlamented Temporary Employment Subsidy (TES) introduced by the British in August 1975. This measure, as Hamermesh correctly argues, implicitly raised the relative cost of adjustment by subsidizing the retention of workers. But did TES stabilize employment over the cycle as he suggests? It is not in doubt that TES reduced the marginal costs of labor to the firm (over the range of the prospective redundancy program and for the duration of the subsidy). However, the policy was associated with displacement to the extent that there was a substitution in consumption away from the output of non-subsidized firms. Also, one has to look to the longer-term effects of job subsidization and the changes that it produces in economic behavior. The market has an inbuilt mechanism leading firms to guarantee wages and employment status to some degree independent of the vagaries of the cycle. It might thus be predicted that implicit contracts would be less likely to specify job security, the greater the stabilization in the variance of the employee's income stream achieved via governmentally financed measures. In other words, one effect is to produce a substitution of public for private provision. Indeed, over the longer term, might not the use of job subsidies as a feature of countercyclical policy even reshape implicit contracts in such a way as to raise the equilibrium rate of unemployment?

Some other brief observations on TES follow. First, the flat-rate nature of the subsidy was discriminatory in outcome since it preserved jobs with relatively low hiring and training costs (and layoff costs). Second, by reducing the cost of labor along the employment dimension, TES presumably led to a rise in the employment–hours ratio. Third, and more generally, TES posed a political problem identical to that referred to earlier by Hamermesh in his discussion of advance notification: it provided a natural incentive for subsidized groups to engage the polity. Thus, laggards in the recovery phase may be expected to lobby governments to extend the life of the program. Finally, it should not go unsaid that job subsidization of this nature is implicitly a beggar-thy-neighbor policy, destined to invite retaliation from those countries to whom one is exporting one's unemployment.

I now turn to the empirical material assembled by Hamermesh. One is struck in equal measure by the masterful review of the literature and the general imprecision of that literature for the purpose at hand. Thus, the evidence on employment–hours trade-offs is difficult to interpret. The safest conclusion is that it is dangerous to infer anything from models that fail to distinguish between stocks and labor utilization. The over-

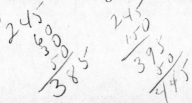

35

time studies do demonstrate that increases in the penalty rate raise the employment–hours ratio, albeit fairly modestly, but the impact of higher fixed employment costs on that ratio is opaque. In this latter context, I learned much from Hart and Kawasaki's (HK) (1987) paper on the effect of changes in payroll taxes in a system where the ceiling is high. In such circumstances one might predict that reductions in the ceiling would, by increasing the ratio of fixed to variable costs, reduce the employment–hours ratio. HK's simulations suggest exactly the opposite. This outcome is in part explained by lower *total* payroll taxes and hence positive scale effects. Although the HK model has its own idiosyncracies – one being a negative association between the direct wage and the capital stock in the factor demand equation – the overwhelming strength of this analysis lies in its attempt to parameterize the effects of a specific regime, and in its recognition of the simultaneous determination of the mix of payroll tax contributions with employment–hours allocation given exogenous changes in the wage ceiling. Clearly, not only the height of the ceiling is relevant in predicting the effects of such changes.

I also find it difficult to draw any firm conclusions from the material on the lagged adjustment of employment and hours behind changes in output, particularly when international comparisons are being made. That the lags in employment behind output are greater than those reported for hours comes as no great surprise. The greater lags in the adjustment of new hires than observed for layoffs is more interesting, but no distinction is drawn between temporary layoffs (stock utilization) and permanent layoffs (stock adjustment) and no mention is made of wage flexibility.

It is very tempting to conclude that the greater lags in the adjustment of employment to output observed in a number of European countries than in the US are attributable to the greater restrictions on the employer's use of labor in the former group. But one must exercise extraordinary caution in drawing inferences from cross-country comparisons. To take a rather different example: it is often argued that the greater reliance upon layoffs in the US reflects that country's imperfectly experience-rated UI system. The problem here is that in many European countries the UI system is not experience rated at all! Clearly, cross-country differences in relative speeds of adjustment of employment and hours to changes in output have causes other than job security regulations. I find Robert Gordon's (1982) analysis instructive in this regard. Gordon finds that a much larger fraction of the variability in the (manufacturing) wage bill takes the form of nominal wage changes relative to changes in hours and employment in Britain and Japan than in the US.

Hamermesh's own calculations of mean lag lengths are perhaps rather more interesting for what they fail to reveal; namely, the absence of any evidence to suggest that employers have adjusted more rapidly along the hours dimension in more recent years. Hamermesh's break point in the various countries' time-series data coincides with the first oil price shock. It is not derived endogenously, which could be a problem in that countries responded very differently in their macro policies to the shock and presumably introduced job security policies that differed in nature, scope and timing. Neither of these issues is addressed. In any event, Hamermesh finds some evidence of increasing employment lags over the more recent interval, which is at least consistent with, though by no means confirmation of, the effects of policies geared to slowing the adjustment of employment to output shocks. I note in parenthesis that some of Hamermesh's findings are not replicated in other data sets (cf. Mairesse and Dormont, 1985).

Turning finally to the evidence on indirect or potential costs of adjustment, my interpretation again diverges from that offered by Hamermesh. I would suggest that the Medoff and Abraham (1980) result appears less iconoclastic *if* one is not wedded to the argument that the coefficient on tenure in the conventional earnings function test exclusively picks up the return to job-specific training investments. (Note that the general training component of tenure is supposed to be captured in the age or 'other experience' variable.) There is now an emerging body of evidence to suggest that much purportedly firm-specific capital is in fact general capital. An extreme view is presented by Altonji and Shakotko (1987), who report that, having controlled for heterogeneity bias using an IV methodology, the effect of tenure on wages is small and that general labor market experience (and purposive mobility) account for the bulk of wage growth over a career. A less extreme finding is available from Addison and Portugal's (1987a) analysis of displaced worker earnings, which suggests that tenure on the lost job is productive of income in the post-displacement job. Both sets of results might seem to imply that Hamermesh need not be unduly exercised by an apparent divorce between wage structure and productivity. That said, acceptance of the Altonji and Shakotko findings, in particular, does raise important questions for the supervision, sorting and risk aversion models, on the basis of which I have strongly criticized Hamermesh's original interpretation of the wage–productivity–tenure nexus.

A related problem is that Hamermesh views investments in firm-specific training as continuing to the very point of (permanent) layoff, from which he infers substantial information deficits on the part of workers (and firms?). This provides one important reason why he comes down in favor of an advance notification requirement. Abstracting from the measurement issue, I agree that there are benefits to society from advance notification for the reasons given by Hamermesh, but I see little to suggest that the worker will gain any breathing space during which interval he will substitute search for worthless training investments. In short, for all the reasons discussed by Hamermesh, the notional lead time of the notified worker will be eroded. There is of course no inconsistency between this statement and empirical results showing that workers gain from advance notification in terms of a reduced spell length of unemployment following displacement (Addison and Portugal, 1987b).

I will keep my concluding comments brief. Legislated job security rules have to be purchased by those who are unable to find employment and by those who value job security less. It would appear to be incumbent on those who favor the erection of a panoply of job security legislation to identify the sources of market failure that prevent efficient matches being made in the labor market *and* to make explicit the trade-offs involved. Hamermesh has made an heroic effort to identify the latter but, as he himself concludes, our knowledge of the precise impact of specific programs is rudimentary. What does seem to be clear is that legislated job security does not in practice help those who encounter the greatest difficulty in locating good jobs, for reasons that have to do with the skill endowments they bring to the market. Indeed, if Hamermesh's 'new labor market segmentation' scenario is substantially correct, and I am sympathetic to this view, then such workers are precisely those most at risk from job protective legislation.

Hamermesh's study patently cannot provide any comfort to those who regard state intervention as a solution to the job security problem. Unfortunately, however, Hamermesh ultimately fails to define the nature of the problem because he glosses over the very considerable degree of job security enjoyed *de facto* by workers in both union and non-union regimes (Addison and Castro, 1987) *and* the theoretical factors that underpin bonding. My major criticism is that the role of the market has been downplayed in this otherwise wide-ranging discussion and that at times the distinction between voluntary and mandated practices is unnecessarily blurred. But there is much that I agree with in this interesting analysis. As is conventional, I have focused here on areas of disagreement.

# CHAPTER 3

# Employment-at-Will, Job Security, and Work Incentives

## EDWARD P. LAZEAR

There are major differences between American and European rules of labor relations. One frequently cited apparent difference relates to the rules governing job security. The doctrine that governed the American labor scene at least until quite recently is employment-at-will. Under this doctrine, the worker serves at the employer's pleasure, and dismissal is held to be the unilateral privilege of the employer. No reasons need be given for termination and workers have no right to protest the dismissal. Most European countries differ. There, labor law often provides for job security in a number of ways. Workers who believe that they have been dismissed for unjust reasons often have access to friendly courts. Frequently, explicit severance pay formulas are dictated by the state so that workers who are laid off are entitled to some lump-sum compensation. As the required payment rises, employers find that termination becomes increasingly costly and, at the extreme, employers are denied any right to fire a worker.

These seemingly different environments would be expected to give rise to different employment and layoff patterns. Proponents of job security have argued that there are benefits that accrue to the firm as well as to the worker from a denial of employment-at-will. Opponents argue that job security rules generate unemployment. But even articulate opponents of state-mandated job security point out potential benefits from voluntary elimination of employment-at-will (see Fischel, 1984, pp. 1074–5).

It is argued that despite the apparent benefits from job security rules, the government's role should be limited to enforcement of explicit employment contracts between workers and firms. Any benefit that can be achieved by a government-dictated job security rule can be duplicated by a privately contracted one. Neither contract costs nor enforceability problems present a compelling argument against this view.

Although employment-at-will was the rule in the United States for most of its history, that picture is changing. The National Labor Relations Act, which requires unionized firms to bargain in good faith, was perhaps the first significant deviation from employment-at-will. Since job security and grievance procedures are legitimate topics for negotiation, employers who are required to bargain over these issues do not enjoy complete employment-at-will.

More recently, the Civil Rights Act of 1964 created a major and direct deviation from employment-at-will. Employers are no longer free to dismiss workers if the dismissal violates anti-discrimination provisions of Title VII. This gives workers job security rights that were not enjoyed previously. Even the unprotected class of white males under 40 years old can look forward to some coverage through age discrimination provisions that bind the employer after the worker turns 40.

A third and more subtle deviation from employment-at-will takes the form of unemployment compensation that has at least some experience rating incorporated into the formulas. If a firm is charged, even in part, for a laid-off worker's unemployment compensation, the layoff becomes more costly.[1] These payments are not dissimilar from severance pay, which amounts to a deviation from employment-at-will.

Finally, courts have looked at employment terminations 'without cause' as breaches of unwritten labor contracts in a number of circumstances. The ability of workers to impose costs on an employer through legal expenses creates a deviation from the strictest interpretation of employment-at-will. The movement by courts in the direction of job rights makes more important an investigation into the soundness of the employment-at-will doctrine.

Proponents of retaining the doctrine argue first that job security rules in general, and large severance pay requirements in particular, cause employers to be more cautious about hiring new labor. An employer knows that, once he hires an employee, the worker can be dismissed only at significant cost. As a result, employers hire fewer workers than they would in the absence of restrictions on dismissal.

An additional problem is that most severance pay requirements can be circumvented by dismissing the worker before he becomes a permanent employee, that is, before he becomes vested in the right to receive severance pay. This is actually a function of the typical severance pay formula, but an exemption from severance pay requirements for temporary employees is quite common. The result is a substitution of temporary labor for permanent labor with dismissals occurring just before the vesting date. Thus, it is argued that the attempt to improve job security actually undermines it.

Proponents also point out that countries compete for business, and that plants are most likely to be located in countries that are the least restrictive.[2] To the extent that a country benefits from increases in the demand for its labor, restrictions on firms drive them elsewhere, causing workers to suffer.

Eventually, proponents argue, the outcome is an increase in the price of the final product. Consumer surplus is lost and generally inefficient conditions result.

On the other side of the discussion are proponents of job security rules

40

who argue that there are significant economic benefits to the provisions, and especially those mandated by the state. This is contrary to most economists' presumption that contracts entered into voluntarily by both parties must benefit both sides. The efficiency argument for state-mandated job security must rest on some comparative advantage in enforcement that the government enjoys. Perhaps it is the introduction of a third party who can somehow lower the social costs of engaging in some transactions. The alternative is that job security provisions are an easy way to transfer resources from capital to labor. These points are explored below and the following issues are examined: First, pro-ponents of job security suggest that more employment may result because employers are not free to dismiss their workers. Second, it is argued that job security provisions 'insure' workers by preventing employers from laying them off during bad times. Third, workers are more likely to make commitments to their firms when they feel that their jobs are secure. Job security can thereby raise productivity. Fourth, even if all agents in the economy are not made better off, workers may be made better off. Thus, supporters claim that the transfers brought about by job security laws may be desirable. These issues are explored with more rigor below.

The major conclusions of the analysis are:

1  There is no case where a state-dictated job security is warranted. Although it may be beneficial, under rare circumstances, to deviate from employment-at-will, the government need only enforce explicit job security contracts between workers and firms.
2  The best argument for job security rules – that workers will not undertake investment in firm-specific capital without them – is incorrect. It is true that such investment may not occur, but job security rules do nothing to remedy the situation.
3  It is possible, but not certain, that abolition of employment-at-will makes workers better off. If it occurs, it is at the expense of other scarce factors. Further, it is generally dominated by direct transfers, say through the tax system, from one group to the other.
4  A perfectly flexible competitive labor market can offset the effects of state-mandated job security or severance pay. Whether that occurs in practice remains an empirical question.

## 3.1  The Efficiency Effects of Job Security Rules

### 3.1(a)  *General Issues of Efficiency*

In the simplest of all worlds, mandatory job security rules are unam-biguously inefficient. Those rules cause distortions in an otherwise efficient factor market. The first section proves that rigorously.

Suppose there are two periods, 1 and 2. Define job security as a rule that says that an individual who works in period 1 is guaranteed employment in period 2 at a wage equal to or greater than the period 1 wage. Let $L_i = s_i(w_1, w_2)$ be the labor supply of each of $M$ workers where $L_i$ is the amount of labor supplied and $w_i$ is the wage in period $i$. Further, let $D_i(w_i)$ be the demand for labor by each of $N$ firms. The market equilibrium determines $w_1$ and $w_2$ such that equations (3.1a) and (3.1b) hold:

$$ND_1(w_1) = Ms_1(w_1, w_2) \tag{3.1a}$$

$$ND_2(w_2) = Ms_2(w_1, w_2). \tag{3.1b}$$

For simplicity of notation in what follows, it is assumed that $M = N$. The surplus generated in period 1 and period 2 by an economy with employment-at-will is given by

$$H = M \int_0^{L_1^*} [D_1^{-1}(x) - s_1^{-1}(x; w_2)] \, dx + M \int_0^{L_2^*} [D_2^{-1}(x) - s_2^{-1}(w_1; x)] \, dx \tag{3.2}$$

where $L_i^*$ is the equilibrium amount of labor hired in period $i$ when $w_1$ and $w_2$ are determined as the solutions to (3.1a) and (3.1b). $s_1^{-1}$ is the inverse with respect to $w_1$ and $s_2^{-1}$ is the inverse with respect to $w_2$.

Strict job security can be defined as a situation where the amount of labor hired in period 2 is equal to the amount of labor hired in period 1. That is, employers are forced to pay a wage in period 2 equal to the one in period 1 and to retain all workers in period 2 who worked in period 1. The constraint is binding only if at $(\bar{w}, \bar{w})$, $s_2(\bar{w}, \bar{w}) \geqslant s_1(\bar{w}, \bar{w})$.[3] Define $\bar{L}$ as the amount of labor used in each period. Then total consumer surplus is given by:

$$\bar{H} = M \int_0^{\bar{L}} [D_1^{-1}(\bar{L}) + D_2^{-1}(\bar{L}) - s_1^{-1}(\bar{L}; \bar{w}) - s_2^{-1}(\bar{w}; \bar{L})] \, dx. \tag{3.3}$$

To prove that job security reduces surplus, it is sufficient to show that

$$H > \bar{H}.$$

It follows trivially that employment-at-will dominates because equation (3.2) could always replace $L_1^*$ and $L_2^*$ with the $\bar{L}$ used in (3.3). Under these circumstances, the surplus is the same. Given that the constraint to hire as many in period 2 as in period 1 is binding, employment-at-will must strictly dominate as well. Thus, in this simplest economy, job security rules are necessarily inefficient.

### 3.1(b) Work Sharing and Job Security Rules

It is sometimes alleged that job security rules provide insurance to workers, because workers can be certain that they will continue to be employed. Work sharing occurs as a general practice in European countries where job security rules are in force. Work sharing appears to be less prevalent in the United States. This section investigates the efficiency effects of work sharing.

A decrease in labor can be accomplished by a reduction in the number of workers or by a reduction in the number of hours worked per worker. Whenever there are fixed costs of hiring a worker or of coming to work, a decline in demand for labor should always be accomplished, at least in part, by a reduction in the size of the workforce. Job security, defined as the inability to dismiss workers, prevents the appropriate reduction and results in inefficiency. It is important to point out that this occurs because most countries allow firms to adjust the number of hours worked per day, but do not permit (or place large penalties on) an actual layoff. If the law treated reduction in hours in the same way it treats an actual layoff, no inefficiency need result. It is the asymmetry that induces firms to use too many workers and to work them for too few hours per day during downturns. This is now shown rigorously.

Suppose that $Z_1$ is the amount of labor hired in period 1. $Z_1$ is the product of $M_1$, which is the number of workers employed in period 1, and $L_1$, which is the number of hours worked per worker. For any given $Z$, the choice of $M$ and $L$ that minimizes social cost is the solution to

$$\min_{M,L} \left[ \int_0^L s_1^{-1}(x; w_2) \, dx + (M)(F) \right] \tag{3.4}$$

where $F$ is the fixed cost per worker (e.g. a hiring cost, setup cost, or transportation cost). This is minimized subject to the constraint

$$(M)(L) = Z. \tag{3.5}$$

Substituting (3.5) into (3.4) yields

$$\operatorname*{Min}_{L} \left[ \int_0^L s_1^{-1}(x; w_2) \, dx + \frac{FZ}{L} \right].$$

The first-order condition is

$$\frac{d}{dL} = s_1^{-1}(L; w_2) - \frac{FZ}{L^2} = 0, \tag{3.6}$$

which the second-order condition reveals to be a local minimum. Substitute (3.5) back into (3.6) to write the first-order condition as

$$s_1^{-1}\left(\frac{Z}{M}; w_2\right) - \frac{FM^2}{Z} = 0. \tag{3.7}$$

43

Using the implicit function theorem,

$$\frac{dM}{dZ}\bigg|_{(3.7)} = \frac{-\left[\dfrac{1}{M}(s_1^{-1})' + FM^2/Z^2\right]}{-\dfrac{Z(s_1^{-1})'}{M^2} - \dfrac{2FM}{Z}} > 0. \tag{3.8}$$

Equation (3.8) implies that when $Z$ falls, say during a cyclical downturn, the optimal number of workers falls. The inability to reduce heads, and the necessity to substitute a reduction of hours, violates (3.6) and results in inefficiency.

Although a rule that constrains employers' ability to reduce hours is necessarily inefficient, it is possible that workers can be made better off by the rule. This occurs when workers have concave utility functions and cannot share output through any alternative system of side payments. It is important that no side payments be made, however. For example, a two-part wage always dominates in the case where all workers are identical. It is necessary to lay some workers off during the downturn, but the firm can compensate workers in the form of voluntary severance pay for the layoff. This amounts to an insurance payment to workers who lose their jobs. Since this eliminates an inefficiency, the total surplus is higher and compensation that makes at least one side better off without harming the other can be established. The argument breaks down when information about workers' alternatives and productivity at the firm is imperfect or when voluntary severance pay arrangements are not credible. These points are explored in later sections.

### 3.1(c)   Can Workers Be Made Better off by Job Security Rules?

It is possible, although not certain, that a job security rule can bring about a transfer of rents from one specific factor, say land, to labor. This generally implies an inefficiency, however, so it must be assumed that no direct transfer can be effected as an alternative. Consider the situation in Figure 3.1.

Suppose the demand for labor is $D_1$ in period 1 and $D_2$ in period 2. Suppose further that the supply of labor is $s(w)$ and, for simplicity, depends only on the wage in the current period. With employment-at-will, $L_1$ are employed in period 1 and $L_2$ are employed in period 2. The surplus to the worker is area $ACG$ + area $ABE$. If job security prevails, the two-period demand curve is $D_1$, because of the perfectly inelastic function for period 1. Thus, $L_1$ are employed in both periods. Under these circumstances, surplus to the worker is area $ACG$ + area $ABE$ + area $BCGE$. The difference is area $BCGE$, so the workers' surplus is greater with job security.

Of course, job security implies an inefficiency: there is overemployment of $L_1 - L_2$ labor in period 2, which means that total surplus is lower than it would be with employment-at-will. Area $EGF$ is the social cost of job security. With job security, the workers' surplus in period 2 is $ACG$,

44

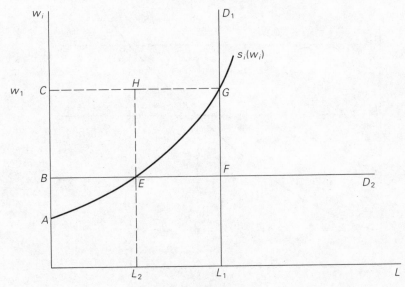

**Figure 3.1**

but the firm's surplus is negative $BCGF$. The firm would prefer to be permitted to employ only $L_2$ in period 2 at a price of $w_1$ and to make a direct payment $HGE$ for that right. Then lost surplus to the firm is only $BCHE + HGE$, which is less than $BCGF$. But workers are no worse off. Their surplus in period 2 is still $ACHE + HGE = ACG$ as it was with job security. Thus, direct transfers dominate.

It need not be the case that job security makes workers better off, even ignoring the possibility of direct transfers. Consider Figure 3.2. Here, demand is perfectly inelastic in each period, but demand in period 2 lies below that in period 1. The two-period constrained demand curve is $\bar{D}$, which lies halfway between $D_1$ and $D_2$. ($\bar{D}$ gives the per-period marginal product when workers must be hired for the two periods.) With employment-at-will, $L_1$ are employed in period 1 and $L_2$ in period 2, yielding a surplus of $AHE + ABG$. If job security is instituted, then $L$ are employed. Surplus is $ACF + ACF$. The difference in surplus between employment-at-will and job security is area $HEFC - BCFG$. Since $HEFC > BCFG$, employment-at-will yields more surplus. In this case, all surplus goes to the workers so workers are better off with employment-at-will.[4]

The case described by Figure 3.1 shows how forcing the employer to retain workers makes workers better off, given that there is no alternative method of bringing about transfers. The case in Figure 3.2 shows that even if society is concerned only with its workers, and even if there is no other way to accomplish transfers to labor from, say, land, workers may well be better off without job security.

There is a difference between already employed individuals and those who are not yet employed. In the situation illustrated by Figure 3.2, an

45

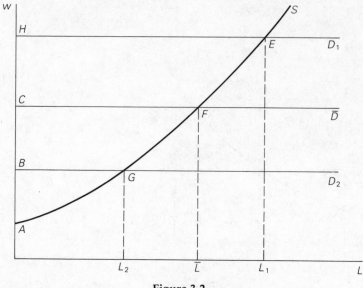

**Figure 3.2**

unanticipated announcement of job security makes all $L_1$ employed workers better off, especially if they must be retained at their period 1 wage. But this further depresses demand for other labor in period 2 (in this case it would be zero). Thus, the individuals who are new workers in period 2, as the period 1 workers become old, suffer relative to those who are already employed. When they are hired in period 3, fewer are employed and they are employed at wage $\bar{w}$.

### 3.1(d)   Severance Pay vs. Strict Job Security

It might seem that the purest job security rule, which bans dimissal in period 2 for workers who were employed in period 1, is equivalent to an extremely large level of severance pay. After all, the requirement that an employer pay a worker an extremely high severance pay payment is tantamount to preventing the firm from dismissing the worker. State-mandated severance pay can always be offset by corresponding changes in the wage payment. To undo a job security rule, it is necessary to offer severance pay. Doing so renders the job security rule indistinguishable in effect from state-mandated severance pay. Both can be undone by a competitive labor market with no constraints on borrowing and lending. For arbitrary levels of severance pay or job security rules, the allocation of labor is unaltered in this purest economy.

To see this, first consider a labor market without any government-mandated or voluntary severance pay. The supply and demand conditions of equations (3.1a) and (3.1b) yield competitive wages $w_1^*$ and $w_2^*$.

46

work, where $A_i$ is the worker's alternative use of time in period $i$. Similarly, firms continue to hire labor so long as

$$M_i > w_i^*$$

where $M_i$ is the worker's marginal product in period $i$. The worker who is just indifferent between working and not working is the one for whom

$$A_i^* \equiv w_i^*, \quad i = 1, 2. \tag{3.9}$$

Similarly, the firm that is just indifferent between hiring and not hiring the worker is the one such that

$$M_i^* \equiv w_i^*, \quad i = 1, 2. \tag{3.10}$$

Now, suppose that the government imposes a requirement that all workers who worked in period 1 be paid $Q$ as severance pay if they are not employed in period 2. The market offsets severance pay completely if the equilibrium is such that the marginal worker and marginal firm remain $A_i^*$ and $M_i^*$ as defined by (3.9) and (3.10). Then the same workers work and the same firms employ labor as without state-mandated severance pay.

With severance pay, workers work in period 2 iff

$$A_2 + Q < w_2'$$

and firms employ labor iff

$$M_2 + Q > w_2'$$

where $w_2'$ is the resulting market wage in period 2, given the existence of severance pay. Thus, to ensure that the same workers work, it is necessary that

$$w_2' = A_2^* + Q \tag{3.11a}$$

and

$$w_2' = M_2^* + Q \tag{3.11b}$$

or

$$w_2' = w_2^* + Q \tag{3.12}$$

since $A_i^* = M_i^* = w_i^*$. Equation (3.12) can be solved for arbitrary $Q$. Thus, in period 2, wages are increased simply by the amount of severance pay and all is restored.

A similar argument applies to period 1, but there is a slight difference. Risk-neutral workers now view the value of working in period 1 as

$$w_1' + (Q) \text{ (probability receive } Q \text{ in period 2)}$$

because working in period 1 entitles them to severance pay in period 2 if a layoff occurs. This can be rewritten

$$w_1' + Q\left(\frac{L_1^* - L_2^*}{L_1^*}\right). \tag{3.13}$$

Similarly, firms view the wage paid in period 1 as given by equation (3.13) because each worker hired in period 1 has the right to receive severance pay if not employed in period 2. Thus, to bring about the same allocation of resources as achieved in the absence of severance pay, it is necessary that

$$A_1^* = w_1' + (Q)\left(\frac{L_1^* - L_2^*}{L_1^*}\right) \tag{3.14a}$$

$$M_1^* = w_1' + (Q)\left(\frac{L_1^* - L_2^*}{L_1^*}\right) \tag{3.14b}$$

or

$$w_1' = w_1^* - (Q)\left(\frac{L_1^* - L_2^*}{L_1^*}\right). \tag{3.15}$$

since $w_1^* = A_1^* = M_1^*$. Thus, the wage in period 1 is lower by the value of the severance pay. That too is easily achieved for arbitrary $Q$.

Thus, the government-mandated severance pay will be offset by higher market wages in period 2 and lower market wages in period 1 so that the allocation of resources is unchanged.

There is an additional requirement for the offset to work. The requirement is that the worker can make an up-front payment for the job. Otherwise, profits are lower with severance pay, which distorts investment in capital. To see this, note that the same amount of labor is employed in each period so output and therefore revenue is unchanged. But costs are different. Without severence pay, costs are

$$C^* = w_1^* L_1^* + w_2^* L_2^*. \tag{3.16}$$

With severance pay, costs are

$$C' = w_1' L_1^* + w_2' L_2^* + (Q)(L_1^* - L_2^*). \tag{3.17}$$

48

Substitution of (3.12) and (3.15) into (3.17) yields

$$C' = w_1^* L_1^* + w_2^* L_2^* + QL_2^*. \tag{3.18}$$

So $C' > C^*$ by $QL_2^*$. Thus, each of the $L_1^*$ workers must make a payment of $QL_2^*/L_1^*$ in period 1 to keep profit the same. So long as there are no constraints on borrowing and lending, all is well. But any inability or apprehension by workers on this score causes some serious problems.

This is not a technical detail. Without the ability to extract a payment from workers before the job even begins, it is impossible to maintain profit at its previous level and also achieve efficiency in both periods. But for a number of reasons elaborated below, workers may have cause to resist making up-front payments to the firm. If a payment of $QL_2^*$ is not made, then firms cannot offer a sufficiently high wage in period 2 to achieve efficiency. To do so implies that the wage in period 1 must be too low to achieve efficiency in period 1. Thus, the effects of severance pay are offset completely only if there are no limitations on buying the job.

It is also true that severance pay effects are neutral only when the payment made by the firm is received by the worker. There can be no third-party intermediary that receives any of the payment. If this occurs, then incentives are necessarily distorted. Thus, an unemployment insurance system that does not have perfect experience rating will induce inefficiencies. This is shown rigorously:

Define $Q$ as the amount of severance pay received by the worker and $Q'$ as the amount paid by the firm. An imperfect experience-rated system has $Q' < Q$. (It may be true that the system as a whole is solvent by charging firms a fixed fee, independent of layoff experience or size of the workforce. But this independence guarantees that those components of cost do not affect the firm's marginal calculation.) First consider period 2. The proof that there is underemployment in period 2, given efficient employment in period 1, follows.

For efficiency in period 2, the same firm and same worker must view the work/no work decision as a marginal one. Thus, necessary is that

$$w_2' = A_2^* + Q \tag{3.19a}$$

$$w_2' = M_2^* + Q' \tag{3.19b}$$

or, substituting (3.19b), (3.9), and (3.10) into (3.19a),

$$w_2^* + Q' = w_2^* + Q$$

or

$$Q = Q'.$$

Unless $Q = Q'$, inefficiency must result. The inefficiency takes the form of underemployment. For $Q > 0$, the supply price for any given worker rises by $Q$. For $Q' > 0$, the demand price for any given worker rises by $Q'$. Since $Q > Q'$, the supply price rises by more than the demand price so the equilibrium wage is too high to induce efficiency in period 2.

A similar argument reveals that there is overemployment in period 1. Firms are reluctant to hire workers because they know that employment carries with it a commitment to pay severance pay in period 2. But workers are sufficiently more anxious to work in period 1 because the right to severance pay that they receive exceeds the cost to the firm of paying.[5]

The results of this section are somewhat surprising when put in the context of international comparisons. Consider a European country that has strict severance pay laws, but no state unemployment compensation system. Payments are made directly from firms to workers at dismissal. Under this system, so long as up-front payments can be made, there are no inefficiencies introduced by this European deviation from employment-at-will. Neither underemployment in good times nor overemployment in bad times results because wages adjust to offset any detrimental effects. Contrast this situation with the one in the United States. Even though many believe employment-at-will to be the law of the land, state-run unemployment compensation is pervasive. As Topel (1983) has shown, the experience rating is far from perfect for many firms in many states. As a result, $Q > Q'$ so that overemployment in good times and underemployment in bad times is the result. If these are the facts, and if impediments to perfect offsets are ignored, then the conclusion is not that Europe has too few layoffs during downturns, but that the United States has too many. The rhetoric that surrounds contrast between employment-at-will and job security may be just that. The issue may be one that depends more on implicit prices induced by the unemployment compensation system than on court doctrine.

An example is instructive. France, which is generally thought to be a country that has significant job security, mandates a severance pay scheme in which the minimum separation indemnity cannot be less than a sum equal to either 20 hours of pay for hourly employees or one-tenth of a month's salary for monthly employees, multiplied by the number of years of employment; workers with over 10 years' seniority receive an additional 1/15 of a month's salary times the number of years of employment. Table 3.1 calculates the severance pay for a worker with an annual salary of $25,000 and years of service ranging from 0 to 30. State unemployment compensation in most US states far exceeds these French minimums, even for reasonably senior workers. Depending on the state, the firm's marginal cost of unemployment benefits may exceed the French amounts, too. In practice, French firms may have severance pay allowances that are far more generous than the minimum mandated amount. Additionally, some European countries do have state unemployment insurance that is funded by employers (see Bundett and Wright, 1986, pp. 13–14). But Topel's data suggest that many firms operate in the range where the *marginal* cost of an unemployed worker is

**Table 3.1**
Severance pay under French law for worker earning $25,000/year

| Years of service | Payment | Percentage of annual salary | Years of service | Payment | Percentage of annual salary |
|---|---|---|---|---|---|
| 0 | 0 | 0.0 | 16 | 4167 | 16.7 |
| 1 | 208 | 0.8 | 17 | 4514 | 18.1 |
| 2 | 417 | 1.7 | 18 | 4861 | 19.4 |
| 3 | 625 | 2.5 | 19 | 5208 | 20.8 |
| 4 | 833 | 3.3 | 20 | 5556 | 22.2 |
| 5 | 1042 | 4.2 | 21 | 5903 | 23.6 |
| 6 | 1250 | 5.0 | 22 | 6250 | 25.0 |
| 7 | 1458 | 5.8 | 23 | 6597 | 26.4 |
| 8 | 1667 | 6.7 | 24 | 6944 | 27.8 |
| 9 | 1875 | 7.5 | 25 | 7292 | 29.2 |
| 10 | 2083 | 8.3 | 26 | 7639 | 30.6 |
| 11 | 2431 | 9.7 | 27 | 7986 | 31.9 |
| 12 | 2778 | 11.1 | 28 | 8333 | 33.3 |
| 13 | 3125 | 12.5 | 29 | 8681 | 34.7 |
| 14 | 3472 | 13.9 | 30 | 9028 | 36.1 |
| 15 | 3819 | 15.3 | | | |

zero. Under these circumstances, the American system encourages too many layoffs.

An argument similar to the one on severance pay can be made for a strict job security rule. Formally, that rule says that a worker has the right to receive some $w_2$ in period 2. But the employer has the ability to 'buy out' of that position by offering some severance pay $S$. The employer offers up to

$$S = w_2 - M_2$$

to buy out of the job security requirement. The worker accepts iff

$$A_2 + S > w_2$$

or iff

$$A_2 + w_2 - M_2 > w_2$$

or iff

$$A_2 > M_2.$$

This is the standard efficiency condition. As above, period 1 wages and 'signing bonuses and penalties' can be levied to bring about efficiency in period 1, as well as zero profit. Thus, job security rules can be undone by the market.

It seems that neither state-mandated severance pay nor strict job security rules have any effect because they can be undone by the market. Undoing requires that a number of conditions are met. First, borrowing and lending must be costless so that the worker can divorce consumption timing from earnings timing. Second, strategic bargaining in period 2 over wages on severance pay cannot be a problem. These requirements may be too severe to permit a complete offset of the government-imposed rule.

## 3.2  Second-Best Cases for Job Security

In this section, some arguments for job security are presented. All of these cases depend on the existence of some imperfection that prevents the economy from adjusting in the ways described above.

### 3.2(a)  Minimum Wages and Job Security

It is possible to make a case for job security rules if one believes that there are significant wage rigidities in the economy. Even in this situation, the case is not an unambiguous one. Perhaps the best case for restrictions on employment-at-will rules can be made when it is assumed that wages are rigid downward. Indeed, there is evidence to support the reasonableness of the hypothesis for the American labor market (see Gordon, 1982). If wages are not sufficiently flexible, then it might be beneficial to institute job security provisions. Proponents of job security rules can argue correctly that employers react too dramatically to changes in demand for product or technology and that their desires to dismiss the worker must be tempered by job guarantees.[6] To see this, consider the following example.

Suppose that demand were perfectly inelastic in period 1, but quite elastic in period 2. Figure 3.3 illustrates the situation. Suppose that the supply of labor in each period were given by $s_i(w_i)$ so that labor supply is independent of wages in other periods. If wages were free to adjust, labor employed in period 1 would be $L_1$ and in period 2 would be $L_2$. Now assume that wages are rigid downward and that firms adjust optimally to that fact. Since the demand for labor is perfectly inelastic in period 1, it is still perfectly inelastic; the demand for labor will be unchanged in period 1. Thus $L_1$ are employed at wage $w_1$. But in period 2, the downward rigidity of wages implies that the wage remains at $w_1$ and no labor is hired. Alternatively, suppose that job security is guaranteed so that anyone employed in period 1 may continue to be employed in period 2. Then the firm's demand is the solution to the two-period problem, where labor is constrained to be the same in both periods. In this case, since demand is perfectly inelastic in period 1, the demand, conditional on no layoff in period 2, is also perfectly inelastic.

52

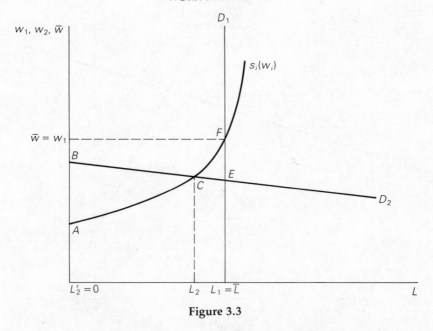

**Figure 3.3**

This implies that employment equals $L_1$ in both periods. Is the surplus generated by the constrained situation greater than that when firms may lay workers off? In this case, yes. Since surplus in period 1 is the same, and since surplus in period 2 is zero with employment-at-will (no workers are employed), the question boils down to determining whether the surplus associated with work in period 2 at level $L_1$ is positive. The surplus is equal to area $ABC$ minus area $CFE$. As drawn, it is clearly positive, so the job security rule undoes some of the damage caused by wage rigidity and is beneficial.

But it need not be so. Figure 3.4 provides a counter-example. If wages were free to adjust, employment in period 1 would be $L_1$ and in period 2 would be $L_2$. With rigid wages, employment in period 2 is $L_2'$. A job security rule that prohibited employers from laying off workers in period 2 would alter the demand in period 1. However, since demand is perfectly inelastic in period 1, the two-period demand curve is also perfectly inelastic. Thus, employment in periods 1 and 2 equals $\bar{L}$. Under employment-at-will, given wage rigidity, surplus equals area $ABF$ + area $ABCH$. With job security, surplus equals area $ABF$ + area $ABCH$ + area $HCG$ − area $CFG$. The difference between the two equals area $CFG$ − area $HCG$. Since $CFG > HCG$, employment-at-will dominates. Thus, even when an argument can be made for job security as an offset to other inefficiencies, the validity of the argument becomes an empirical question. Under some demand/supply scenarios, the economy is better off living with the wage rigidity than countering it with job security rules.

It can be argued that a state-mandated job security rule is unnecessary, and even harmful. Consider the case described by Figure 3.3.

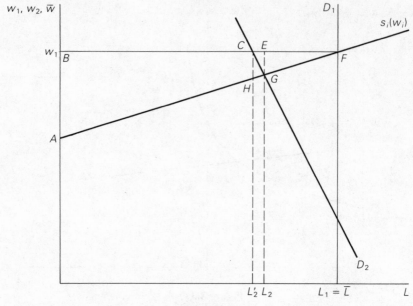

**Figure 3.4**

Since surplus is available from a job security rule, worker and firm should agree *ex ante* to such a rule, and the worker should be willing to pay for the job security right. The advantage to contracts that are merely enforced by the state is that no job security contract would be written when the case of Figure 3.4 prevails. Thus, there would be no worry about the state actually making things worse.

The problem is that this begs the question. The Coase Theorem argument of the previous paragraph may well be inconsistent with the assumption of wage rigidity, unless that too is government imposed. Worker and firm contracting to institute job security in return for lower wages is tantamount to denying that wages are rigid.

A better argument against state-mandated job security rules is that they are a fix for some other malady. If the problem is caused by a government-dictated minimum wage, a more appropriate remedy is removal of that minimum. Only if the wage rigidity is endogenous (as in Hall and Lazear, 1984), might a job security rule make sense in the second-best context. Even then, the case is far from clear.

### 3.2(b)  *Specific Capital as a Rationale for Job Security Rules*

Even those who have argued in favor of employment-at-will and against job security[7] recognize that the efficiency of some actions must rely on reputation of the firm. To the extent that reputation is not a perfect enforcement device, there may be a role for job security rules. As

Kennan (1979) has pointed out, agents do not have correct incentives to invest in specific capital because the separation decision is distorted.

The view that specific human capital provides a role for job security rules is, so far as I can ascertain, simply incorrect. That view holds that the worker may have insufficient incentive to undertake an investment that is specific to a particular firm if he is uncertain that he will retain employment. It is surely correct that workers may not have sufficient incentives to engage in specific human capital investment, but job security rules do nothing to solve the problem. A rule that makes the worker sufficiently confident to undertake the investment also robs the firm of the ability to punish the worker financially if he does not undertake the investment. Thus, the worker feels no financial impact of the investment and, as a result, does not undertake it.

Let us be somewhat more rigorous. There are two conditions that must be met: first, the worker underinvests in specific human capital; second, a job security rule remedies the situation.

The worker's decision to invest in specific human capital depends on returns relative to costs. The following conditions create a situation that meets the first criterion, namely, that the worker underinvests in specific human capital. Suppose that the worker can take an action in the first period that is unverifiable by the firm until the second period. Suppose that the action consists of investing $1.00 in period 1 in specific human capital that raises his productivity by $1.50 so that taking the action is socially efficient. If the worker receives $X$ in period 2 for having taken that action, and if $X > 1$, then the worker invests. The problem as the worker sees it is that he is in a compromised position *ex post*. A Nash bargaining approach among risk-neutral players suggests that the worker might expect to receive $0.75 for the investment because threat points are moved in a way that yields a split-the-difference solution. This means that the worker underinvests in specific capital.[8] Note further that there is no sharing of costs that will help. Irrespective of what the firm does in period 1, the situation in period 2 is unchanged. Sunk costs are sunk so the worker can expect to receive only $0.75 (or some other bargaining solution amount).

It might appear that if the firm covered $0.25 of the cost by paying a higher wage in period 1, the problem would be solved. But this is not the case. Since the firm cannot observe until period 2 whether or not the investment has been made, failure by the worker to make the investment merely changes the threat points. In this example, the worker's wage offer falls back by $0.75: if the worker makes the investment, he nets

$$w_1 + \$0.25 \text{ in period } 1 + (w_2 + \$0.75) \text{ in period } 2 - \$1.00 \text{ investment.}$$

If he does not, he nets

$$w_1 + \$0.25 \text{ in period } 1 + w_2 \text{ in period } 2.$$

The second amount is larger so he does not make the investment. Sharing the costs does not solve the problem. This example meets the first criterion: the worker underinvests in specific human capital.

The issue then turns to criterion 2: does a job security rule help? To make the case as strong as possible, permit a job security rule not only to guarantee employment, but also to allow the wage dictated for period 2 to deviate from $w_1$. Thus, let the job security rule guarantee the worker employment at wage $W_2^*$. This guarantee cannot affect investment. If the worker does not invest, he receives

$$w_1 \text{ in period } 1 + w_2^* \text{ in period 2.}$$

If he does invest, he receives

$$w_1 \text{ in period } 1 + w_2^* \text{ in period 2} - \$1.00 \text{ investment.}$$

The former dominates; the worker does not invest. In fact, he is less likely to invest with the job security rule than without it.

The reason that a job security rule is not a remedy is that it does not distinguish between employees who have acted appropriately and those who have not. Of course, in theory it could. But that requires that society devote resources to case-by-case examination. There is no reason to presume that the government has a particular advantage in this activity. If it does, then no job security rule is warranted. The government, with its superior information-gathering technology, should merely enforce contracts made between workers and firms. Those contracts need not specify employment guarantees. In the specific capital case discussed above, it is sufficient to specify that the firm pay at least $1.00 when the worker undertakes the investment. The government, as a cheap third-party enforcer, ensures that the terms are carried out.


## 3.2(c)   Job Security with a Wage Guarantee as an Impediment to Rent Seeking

One argument that can be made for employment and wage guarantees by a third party is that such guarantees eliminate the incentive to invest in outside offers. Some wasteful investment can be avoided by such a rule.

Return to the situation described in the last section. A worker invests in specific capital in period 1 and receives wages in period 2. Let us modify that example slightly so the failure to undertake the investment is not the problem. To do that, suppose that the value of the $1.00 investment is $3.00, so that a Nash bargaining solution would yield an increase in the period 2 wage of $1.50. (Again, there is nothing special about the Nash solution. It is merely an example.) The worker is willing to undertake the investment. But he can raise his share of the rent in period 2 by changing the threat point. Suppose that, by searching, he can increase his best outside offer. The wage that he receives in period 2 rises by the Nash bargaining fraction, in this example by 0.5 of the change in the outside offer. Of course, this activity is socially wasteful. It can be eliminated, however, by a job security rule with a specified wage. If the worker received the full $3.00 increase associated with the $1.00 investment, there would be no gain to search. It would be impossible to drive his wage up beyond that level, so search that changes the threat point, but still leaves the outside offer below the worker's value in the current firm, is useless. A job security rule that required that the firm employ the worker in period 2 at the $3.00 higher wage does the job. It is necessary that the government do it because a promise by the firm to pay the high wage in period 2 is not credible. When period 2 arrives, worker and firm are back in the same bargaining situation, irrespective of what the firm promised in period 1. Thus, without the government rule, the worker would have the incentive to engage in wasteful search.

Although a government-imposed job security rule improves the situation in this simple case, there are two points that are relevant. First, the government must possess a great deal of information about each firm/worker relationship. What is necessary is that the government guarantee the correct wage in period 2, not merely the wage that was paid in period 1. Simply stating that the worker is entitled to employment in period 2 at $w_1$ is no help. Since $w_1$ is necessarily below the worker's value after having made the investment, the same incentives for wasteful search remain.

Second, and related, the government need not impose a job security rule. Even if the government had all the relevant information, it would be sufficient merely to enforce any voluntary contract made between worker and firm in period 1. Doing this would provide the worker/firm pair with incentives to agree on a low period 1 wage in return for the $3.00 higher period 2 wage to eliminate wasteful search. The government's promise to enforce the contract makes the firm's promise to pay credible. Additionally, since the government enforces only an explicit contract, it does not need any information about the worker's productivity that may be costly to obtain. Thus, enforcement of contracts dominates because it is always as good as job security, and is superior when the government is at a disadvantage in gathering the costly information. (It seems unreasonable that the government would have knowledge about the value of the worker's specific human capital that is actually superior to that of the worker and firm.)

### 3.2(d)  Job Security and Insurance

There is a large literature that views the employment contract as an insurance arrangement.[9] Insurance has the same *ex post* enforceability problems as specific human capital. In the second period, the firm, if not constrained, would like to force the worker to receive no more than the value of his alternative. A job security rule of the sort described above can solve the problem. If the firm is constrained to employ the worker at the optimal insurance wage, the government solves the credibility problem.

The same criticisms that were made in the last section apply here. First, not all firm/worker pairs will have the same optimal insurance wage. Thus, the job security rule must be tailored to each situation. This requires a great deal of information on the government's part. Second, the government-imposed job security rule is unnecessary. It is better to use the government to enforce explicit contracts made between workers and firms. Then, no information or rule uniformity is required.

### 3.2(e)   Contract and Enforcement Cost Arguments

It is sometimes argued that a state rule dominates a private explicit contract because the former is cheaper to enforce. The argument is incorrect. Consider a worker who is wrongfully dismissed. If an explicit contract is present, the worker may take action, but must resort to the courts (or some other adjudicating body). That action may be too costly. But a job security rule does not help. The wronged worker must still take the firm to court to redress the wrong. The presumption that the court will find in the worker's favor need not differ. The court can be stern or lenient on firms whether the contract is a private explicit one or a state-dictated job security rule. Thus, enforcement costs are not conserved by a state-mandated job security rule.

Contract costs are somewhat less straightforward. Suppose that it is too costly to write explicit contracts between worker and firm so that the rule that applies is the one mandated by the state. If the rule is job security, the worker rather than the firm wins when the case comes to trial. But, in a competitive market, the workers must pay the expected cost to the employer in reduced wages. The job security rule transfers income from those who would not have been fired to those who would have been. For reasons discussed above, it is far from clear that this transfer is desirable.

### 3.3   Extensions

### 3.3(a)   Part-time and Short-term Employment

One alleged effect of job security rules is the substitution of part-time labor for full-time labor. This is because part-time workers are often exempted from job security coverage. A rule that causes labor substitution that would not occur in a competitive economy is inefficient. But the inefficiency is a direct result of the specifics of the job security rule. A rule that treated part-time work as a continuous extension of full-time work would not have adverse substitution effects. The substitution is induced because of a non-linearity in the formulas.

## 3.3(b)  *Temporary vs. Permanent Employees*

A similar argument pertains to temporary vs. permanent employees. It is correct that job security rules as they are generally implemented induce substitution of temporary for permanent help. This results because the formula for severance pay usually specifies no payment for employees who have worked for less than, perhaps, six months. The discontinuity in the formula places value on dismissing the worker before he completes the six-month probationary period.

That problem is easily remedied by an appropriate severance pay formula. If the marginal product of workers with experience level $t$ is given by $M(t)$, if workers are paid wage $w(t)$, and if the severance pay formula is given by $Q(t)$, then the true cost of a worker at time $t$ is

$$w(t) + Q'(t). \tag{3.20}$$

To avoid any distortion in relative demand for labor types, it is necessary that

$$\frac{w(t_0) + Q'(t_0)}{w(t_1) + Q'(t_1)} = \frac{M(t_0)}{M(t_1)} \text{ for all } t_0, t_1. \tag{3.21}$$

There are enough degrees of freedom in (3.21) so that, for any given wage structure, severance pay formulas can be set in a non-distortionary fashion. For example, if wages were set correctly in the absence of severance pay so that

$$\frac{w(t_0)}{w(t_1)} = \frac{M(t_0)}{M(t_1)},$$

it is now necessary that

$$\frac{w(t_0) + Q'(t_0)}{w(t_1) + Q'(t_1)} = \frac{w(t_0)}{w(t_1)}.$$

If

$$\frac{Q'(t_0)}{Q'(t_1)} = \frac{w(t_0)}{w(t_1)},$$

equality is guaranteed and no distortion occurs. It seems that it is the particular form of the formula, and not the existence of severance pay or job security rules, that induces a substitution from permanent to temporary work.

The argument is correct only if wages are given exogenously. In fact, even the severance pay formula with six-month cliff vesting should not induce a substitution of temporary for permanent workers. If wages are determined endogenously by the market, the fact that $Q'$ is infinite at six months is irrelevant. It could easily be offset by a corresponding change in wages at that point. For example, lowering wages at the six-month anniversary by an amount just sufficient to offset the value of the accrued severance pay would induce firms to behave efficiently. Of course, we do not see firms engaging in these kinds of offsets. There is at least one obvious reason. If offsets took this form, the firm has effectively undone the severance pay. Since, on the six-month anniversary, the firm 'charges' the worker in lower wages for the value of the vested severance pay, the firm takes back with one hand what it gives with the other. Worker welfare is unaffected and the government is likely to take a negative view of firms that offset in this particular fashion. Put alternatively, to the extent that the government wants the severance pay or job security rules to be effective, it must also ensure that firms are not permitted to take corresponding actions that offset the provisions. This is analogous to undoing a limitation on mandatory retirement by changing pension formulas so that workers 'choose' to retire at the previous age of mandatory retirement.

## 3.4 Conclusion

It has been argued that job security rules may, under pathological circumstances, be welfare improving. However, those rules never need be imposed by the government. Instead, the government's willingness to enforce private explicit contracts between workers and firms is a superior alternative. This conclusion is only reinforced by the recognition that abolition of employment-at-will in most circumstances produces market inefficiencies and, in the long run, lower income for workers.

## Acknowledgements

Comments by Lutz Bellmann, John Cogan, Robert Hall, Bengt Holmström, Kevin M. Murphy, Rita Ricardo-Campbell, Sherwin Rosen, Myron Scholes and Mark Wolfson are gratefully acknowledged. Support was provided by the National Science Foundation.

## Notes

1 The point is less obvious than it appears. Since equilibrium wages adjust to take account of unemployment benefits, it is possible that the situation without unemployment compensation has a lower layoff cost than the one with unemployment compensation. This point is discussed in more detail below.
2 Fischel (1984) is an exception. There it is argued that firms choose the environment that is most efficient. If workers are willing to pay more through

lower wages than the restrictions cost firms, the firms will voluntarily locate in the more restrictive environments.

3  Since the contract is one-sided so that workers have the option to leave if they desire, the labor supply for each period is unaltered.

4  A two-good economy, with only output, $Q$, and labor, $L$, generates this demand curve if

$$Q = Q^* \text{ for } L = L^*$$
$$= 0 \quad \text{otherwise}$$

and 'tastes' shift between period 1 and 2 so as to raise the value of leisure relative to that of output.

5  Feldstein (1976) and Topel (1983) examine the effects of an imperfectly experience-rated unemployment system on unemployment rates.

6  See Hall and Lazear (1984) for the theoretical treatment of this excessive responsiveness argument.

7  See Epstein (1984) for a coherent defense of employment-at-will. Rosen (1984) makes the point that reputations as a bonding equivalent is a 'slippery notion'. Fischel (1984) points out that 'Employment contracts that are not terminable at will and informal grievance-resolution machinery are two measures that firms might employ to reduce the risk of opportunistic behavior.'

8  This is true for any bargaining solution with expected wage less than $1.00.

9  The literature finds its roots in Baily (1974) and Azariadis (1975). An example that is more closely related to the current case is Harris and Holmström (1982).

# COMMENT

## LUTZ BELLMANN

Lazear's contribution focuses on welfare effects of legal restrictions on the employer's right to lay off workers. First of all, Lazear argues against state-mandated job security rules because they do not improve welfare or even imply welfare losses: 'There is no case where a state-dictated job security is warranted' (p. 41). The most important single results are the following. The market can undo state-mandated severance pay in principle, but in practice the necessary requirements for this undoing (i.e. wealth and credit constraints for the workers, incentive compatibility problems on the firm's side) may not be fulfilled. Therefore, the workers are not able or are unwilling to make up-front payments to the firms. It follows that those severance pay rules usually distort capital investment. Lazear shows that, in a second-best context, rigid wages and specific human capital may lead to an efficient continuation of labor contracts when demand declines. But he argues that the government should merely concentrate on enforcing explicit contracts signed by employers and employees which prespecify the remuneration of the employees.

My first point concerns Lazear's argument that workers do not invest in their specific human capital in the case where reputation is not a perfect enforcement device. In this case no job security rule – state-mandated or not – would solve the problem (pp. 54ff.). I believe that the assumption made by Lazear that the firm does not observe the worker's productivity resulting from human capital formation before the end of the first period is too restrictive. Extending his model, the possibility that firms can devote resources to monitor workers to detect malfeasance should be considered, too. The probability of detecting the worker shirking can be regarded as an endogenous variable, which is determined by the ratio of supervisors to workers. The wages paid to the supervisors have to be compared with the resource losses owing to workers' shirking. Furthermore, there are incentives for workers to increase their effort, because senior positions in the hierarchy are better remunerated than junior positions. Two properties of this rank-order-tournament are worth mentioning. First, long-term labor contracts are a precondition for the functioning of these promotion incentives. Second, recruitment of supervisors from outside the firm causes disincentives. Therefore, junior workers of the firm can be viewed as a third party: if the firm lays off a senior worker, the supervisor position must be filled with a worker one rung down on the seniority ladder. 'The "third-party", which gains from any separation is therefore made up of all the less senior workers whose seniority is increased as a result' (Carmichael, 1983, p. 252). Thus the contract is self-enforcing, whereas job security results from self-commitment of the firm and is not dictated by the state.

My second point is also connected with specific human capital.

Looking at this topic in the context of the rank-order-tournament introduced above provides an example of a contract with rigid wages, because wages are attached to jobs. Lazear has pointed out that a job security rule may be defended by endogenous wage rigidity (p. 54). But perhaps it is even better to monitor workers and make their wages partially dependent on their performance. Hashimoto and Yu (1980, p. 543) have noted that these systems are prevalent among executives and workers with long years of tenure. So, again, employment-at-will is not the preferred adjustment mechanism. Instead, resources are devoted to overcome informational imperfections.

My third point relates to enforcement costs of contracts. Employment-at-will contracts avoid enforcement costs because the threat of dissolution can lead to a self-enforcing agreement, as is shown in the theory of repeated games (Telser, 1981). But, as Rosen (1984, p. 985) has noted, most terms of labor contracts are left unspecified. This leads him to ask. '... why is it that the implicit terms should not be actionable, as they are, for example, in commercial law?' (Rosen, 1984, p. 986). Therefore, he argues that in union contracts, and less formally in non-union firms, grievance procedures exist that involve costs that are lower than those caused by an inefficient large number of layoffs.

My last point concerns reasons why it might be useful for both the employer and the employees to adopt severance pay systems. One reason might be to induce the worker to quit during a recession. Such a strategy avoids expensive case-by-case appraisal of the employees in order to find out who should be laid off. Schellhaaß (1984, p. 288) has collected severance pay data from 93 firms in the Federal Republic of Germany for the year 1983. He finds that for workers with 30 years of tenure the severance payments range between 25 and 290 per cent of annual earnings. These great differences indicate that it might be beneficial for a firm to use severance pay systems as an active strategy for employment adjustment. The potential importance of this topic is illustrated far more by the findings of Schellhaaß than by the payments under French law mentioned by Lazear in Table 3.1.

# CHAPTER 4

# Shorter Working Time and Job Security: Labor Adjustment in the Steel Industry

## SUSAN N. HOUSEMAN

---

Historically, reduction of working time has been a quality of worklife issue. More recently, a number of European unions and governments have promoted working time reduction as a solution to high unemployment. A somewhat different and important motivation underlying the surge of interest in these measures is employment security. Since the mid-1970s severe macroeconomic recessions and restructuring of large segments of their economies have placed strains on traditional European employment relationships characterized by strong job security. Working time reduction measures serve to protect job security in the short run.

The paper draws upon the steel industry case, contrasting European and American experiences. Although the European and American steel industries have undergone similar restructuring in recent years, they have effected large-scale employment reductions in markedly different ways. Differences in methods of workforce reduction measures are consistent with and, it is argued, rise in part from past employment practices and associated levels of job security. The paper documents cross-country differences in employment adjustment and considers some of the economic consequences of more extensive use of shorter working time measures in Europe during cyclical fluctuation and structural decline in demand.[1]

The paper is organized in four sections. Section 4.1 develops a simple theoretical framework for explaining firms' adjustment of employment and hours to changes in production. The model highlights the potential role of various institutional and behavioral factors in explaining cross-country differences. It stresses that worker rights in jobs, or other factors affecting labor's bargaining power, may influence optimal adjustment strategies in efficient contracts, and that job security provisions, provisions constraining firms' employment decisions, may be mechanisms to ensure efficient resource allocation.

Section 4.2 provides background on past and current labor adjustment practices and government policy in Continental European and US steel industries. While layoff in the United States has been the norm, in Continental Europe steel companies have implemented large workforce reductions with minimal resort to dismissal, instead relying on shorter working time measures. The discussion emphasizes the continuity between workforce reduction programs implemented during restructuring and past employment practices, and the supporting role of government policy.

Section 4.3 presents the results of estimated employment and hours equations for the US, West German and French steel industries. Fundamental differences in the short-run adjustment of employment versus hours are found between the United States and European countries both prior to and during restructuring. While the economic impacts of these differences during adjustment to cyclical fluctuation are argued to be small, they are more important during restructuring, affecting short-run labor allocation as well as capital investment and long-run industry structure.

Section 4.4 concludes with a summary of results, and relates shorter working time measures to other developments in European industrial relations.

## 4.1  A Model of Short-Run Labor Adjustment

The radically different methods of workforce adjustment and associated levels of job security documented below in the European and US steel industries are evident, more generally, in the differential employment and hours adjustment patterns in their economies. This section develops a simple theoretical model designed to elucidate a number of potential factors affecting these adjustment patterns.

Theoretical models underlying many empirical investigations of labor adjustment assume non-linear adjustment costs to explain less than instantaneous employment and hours adjustment to changes in production. Often the motivation for analyzing labor adjustment patterns has been the so-called short-run increasing returns to labor puzzle. The list of adjustment costs typically includes various hiring and firing costs and adverse morale effects. Following Nadiri and Rosen (1969), a number of authors extend the basic partial adjustment model to incorporate the dynamic interdependence of factors of production in the adjustment process. Input prices, in general, are taken as exogenous.

The more recent implicit contract literature, adopting a quite different approach, models the joint determination of wage and employment variables. A primary motivation of this literature is to explain the phenomenon of short-run wage rigidity and to determine the circumstances under which labor adjustment is efficient. The literature stresses long-run attachments between firms and workers, uncertainty over future demand, and costs incurred by workers in the event of layoff. By jointly determining wage and employment variables across all states of nature, firms are able to offer more risk-averse workers a form of insurance.

The model developed below is similar in key respects to standard implicit contract models, although demand is known with certainty.[2] The principal motivation of the model is to address the issue of cross-country differences in labor adjustment and to highlight the impact of certain behavioral and institutional factors on adjustment patterns.[3] As in implicit contract models emphasis is placed on adjustment costs to workers from layoff, and it is assumed contracts are efficient with employment and compensation variables jointly determined. Unlike most of the literature, however, the model incorporates non-monetary in addition to monetary adjustment costs, and studies the effects of the division of income between labor and capital on resource allocation. Legal or implicit job rights, or other factors affecting labor bargaining power, are shown to influence employment and hours adjustment.

To focus on the short-run labor adjustment problem, capital is assumed fixed and production is expressed as a function of a variable labor input. Labor input can be adjusted through the number of employees and the hours worked per employee. Thus, average hours may be written

$$h = h(L, Q)$$

$$\frac{\partial h}{\partial L} < 0 \quad \frac{\partial^2 h}{\partial L^2} > 0$$

where $L$ is the number of workers and $Q$ is the level of production.

The optimal adjustment of employment and hours depends on the size and nature of the underlying labor adjustment costs. I distinguish between two types. The first is essentially a monetary loss. Examples include search costs, moving or commuting costs, and a lower alternative wage, such as may result from the loss of a return on firm-specific human capital. The second type of cost, non-monetary losses, relates to job-specific locational and work attributes valued by workers. Workers may develop strong attachments to workplace and community, which typically grow over time[4] and which are broken at high personal cost. Such social factors are treated extensively in empirical studies of displaced workers, and were stressed by all steel employer and employee representatives interviewed for this study. This category of costs in the model is intended to crudely capture a wide range of negative effects resulting from unemployment, job switch and moving.

Monetary losses are modeled simply as the difference between total compensation in the declining industry, $w$, and the alternative compensation or unemployment insurance, $A$. Non-monetary costs are modeled as an absolute decrease in utility, $-B$. Utility is assumed to be a negative function of hours worked and additively separable in income and hours. Workers are identical in preferences and alternative opportunities. Using indirect utility functions and normalizing prices to one, the utility of a worker on the job is

$$V = V_1(w) + V_2(h),$$

whereas the utility in the event of uncompensated dismissal is[5]

$$V = V_1(A) - B.$$

The firm selects wages, employment levels, hours, and severance payments so as to minimize costs subject to a production constraint and a constraint that it guarantee workers or a union some minimum expected utility. This utility level defines the division of rents between labor and capital, and proxies for labor's bargaining power or workers' rights to their jobs and income.[6] Because of asymmetries in hiring and layoff, labor adjustment in an upturn and a downturn are treated separately.

## 4.1(a)  Labor Adjustment in a Downturn

First suppose the firm experiences a drop in demand representing either a one-time permanent decline or a cyclical decline with the expectation of a rise in the next period. Employment in the preceding period is taken as given. The essential points about labor adjustment can be captured in a one-period model of employment and hours determination following a decline.[7] Given optimal output, the cost-minimization problem for the firm is

$$\text{min. } wL_t + s(L_{t-1} - L_t) \tag{4.1}$$

$$\text{s.t. } L_t[V_1(w) + V_2(h)] + (L_{t-1} - L_t)[V_1(s+A) - B] = \bar{V}L_{t-1}$$

$$Q_t = Q(L_t, h_t)$$

where $s$ is the severance payment, $L_{t-1}$ is employment in the preceding period, and $L_t < L_{t-1}$. With equal probability of layoff, $\bar{V}$ is each worker's expected level of utility. An alternative interpretation of this formulation is one in which a union with utilitarian preferences represents workers.[8] In this case, $\bar{V}$ is the average level of worker utility.

Expressing $h$ as a function of $L$ and denoting the Lagrangian on the utility constraint as $\lambda$, first-order conditions for cost minimization include

$$w - s + \lambda[V_1(w) + V_2(h) + \frac{\delta V_2}{\delta h}\frac{\delta h}{\delta L}L_t - V_1(s+A) + B] = 0 \tag{4.2}$$

67

$$\frac{\delta V_1}{\delta w} = -\frac{1}{\lambda} \tag{4.3}$$

$$\frac{\delta V_1}{\delta s} = -\frac{1}{\lambda} \tag{4.4}$$

From (4.3) and (4.4) the marginal utility of income is equated between retained and dismissed workers; with utility that is additively separable, incomes also are equalized. However, with non-monetary losses, and possible differences in hours worked, in general, utilities of retained and dismissed workers will differ. Below, it is assumed that $B$, the disutility of being laid off, is large relative to $V_2$, the disutility associated with time spent on the job, over the relevant range, and that dismissed workers are worse off. Thus, even with severance payments, unemployment is involuntary.

Making substitutions from equations (4.3) and (4.4), (4.2) may be simplified to

$$\frac{\delta h}{\delta L} = \frac{w - s - \dfrac{\delta w}{\delta V_1}\,(V_2 + B)}{\dfrac{\delta w}{\delta V_1}\dfrac{\delta V_2}{\delta h}\,L_t} \tag{4.5}$$

which has the familiar interpretation that the firm hires labor such that the marginal rate of substitution of hours and the number of workers equals the inverse ratio of their marginal costs. The numerator of the right-hand expression, the marginal cost of keeping an additional worker in a downturn, is the wage less the severance payment less the difference in utility between a worker who keeps his job and one who is laid off. The denominator, the marginal cost of hours, represents the greater disutility of longer hours to the workforce. An increase in non-monetary adjustment costs, $B$, lowers the marginal cost of retaining workers. If the second-order conditions for cost minimization are met, an increase in $B$ will lead to more employment and fewer hours worked in a downturn.[9]

Labor adjustment costs alter the opportunity cost of labor and lower optimal employment adjustment. Efficient contracts must specify employment as well as total compensation, since at the optimal wage firms would otherwise hire too few workers. In this context, income and job security provisions specifying severance payments, employment and hours are not inefficient constraints on restructuring, but rather mechanisms to ensure efficient resource allocation.

An increase in $\bar{V}$, which captures labor's bargaining power, in general, will lead to an increase in both employment and compensation and a reduction in hours.[10] Intuitively, firms will meet the higher $\bar{V}$ constraint partly through higher wages and severance payments and partly through lower labor productivity associated with higher employment

68

levels and shorter hours. Conversely, workers take the higher utility partly in the form of higher compensation and partly in the form of greater job security. Because of non-monetary adjustment costs and the value of leisure, employment adjustment is sensitive to income distribution, even in a partial equilibrium model.[11]

### 4.1(b)  Labor Adjustment in an Upturn

During an upturn, similar pressure to adjust through hours rather than employment exists only to the extent that firms expect a decline in the future and newly hired workers' jobs or incomes are protected by contract or by law. Consider, then, a firm experiencing a cyclical upturn with the implication that $L_{t-1} < L_t$ but that $L_t > L_{t+1}$. In a two-period model the firm faces the following cost-minimization problem:

$$\text{min. } w_t L_t + \rho[w_{t+1} L_{t+1} + s_{t+1}(L_t - L_{t+1})]$$

$$\text{s.t. } L_t[V_1(w_t) + V_2(h_t)] + \phi L_{t+1}[V_1(w_{t+1}) + V_2(h_{t+1})]$$

$$+ \phi(L_t - L_{t+1})[V_1(s_{t+1} + A) - B] = \bar{V} L_t \qquad (4.6)$$

where $\rho$ and $\phi$ are the firm's and the workers' discount factors, respectively. $\bar{V}$ is the minimum expected utility, defined across two periods, that the firm must guarantee workers.

With some rearranging and substitution of terms, the first-order condition for optimal hours and employment may be written

$$\frac{\delta h_t}{\delta L_t} = \frac{w_t + \rho s_{t+1} + \dfrac{\delta w}{\delta V_1}[\bar{V} - w_t - V_2(h_t) - \phi(V_1(s_{t+1} + A) - B)]}{\dfrac{\delta w}{\delta V_1}\dfrac{\delta V_2}{\delta h_t} L_t} \qquad (4.7)$$

The firm sets the marginal rate of substitution of hours and employment equal to the marginal cost of employment divided by the marginal cost of hours. As above, the marginal cost of hours is the disutility to workers associated with working longer hours. The marginal cost of employment in the current period includes not only the current wage but also future obligations to the newly hired worker. The second term in the numerator of the right-hand expression is the dicounted value of the future severance payment, while the third term captures the difference between average worker utility and the lower utility of a worker who is laid off in the next period. Thus, future obligations to workers raise the marginal cost of hiring labor and result in greater adjustment through hours in a cyclical upturn.

### 4.1(c)  Model Assumptions

In the model, bargaining power, individual preferences and union objectives affect wage and employment outcomes. In addition, government policy may alter the marginal costs of adjusting hours versus employment levels or relieve bankruptcy constraints. These behavioral and institutional factors are discussed below to review explanations of slow employment adjustment in Europe in general, and in the steel industry in particular, compared to the United States.

Clearly, employment adjustment outcomes depend on underlying individual preferences and on how these preferences are weighted in a group decision. With respect to the former, the model assumes that non-monetary adjustment costs are important, and therefore have a significant impact on optimal employment and hours adjustment.

With respect to the latter, the model effectively asumes a union representing workers has a utilitarian objective function, which involves an equal weighting of members' preferences. An alternative and common modeling of union behavior assumes seniority-based layoffs and a majority voting rule that aggregates these preferences. Consequently, the union reflects the median worker's preferences, a situation which is likely to result in higher wages and more layoffs in a downturn.[12] Similarly, in an upturn, expansion of employment will not be inhibited by the expectation of future severance payments. The bread and butter issue orientation of American unions often is contrasted with the supposedly broader working-class orientation of European unions. Such differences would warrant different modeling of the union objective function, and may account for some of the cross-country variation in labor adjustment patterns.

Labor law and government policy represent potentially important institutional factors that account for cross-country differences in adjustment. The strong job security and slow employment adjustment in Europe often is attributed to legal restrictions on employer discretion in dismissing workers for economic reasons. European legislation typically requires a minimum period of notification and consultation with worker representatives and a minimum severance payment or the development of a social plan for redundant workers. In game theoretical terms, such legislation effectively raises labor's threat point, enhances its bargaining power and thus improves the wage–employment outcomes for labor in a cooperative solution.[13]

Expectations concerning worker rights and employer obligations exist outside of those specified in the law or legal contracts. Such expectations may have a powerful impact on employment adjustment practices even in the absence of explicit contracts or through their effects on bargaining power in the negotiation of contracts. The implicit contract literature deals precisely with the former situation. According to theory, various reputation mechanisms operate to enforce implicit agreements on employment and wage outcomes across contingent states. For example, employers will have difficulty recruiting during an upturn if they have laid off too many workers in preceding downturns. In addition to reputation mechanisms, problems of worker morale and productivity or industrial action may prevent employers from breaking implicit agreements or increase labor's bargaining power in negotiations. Moral considerations further inhibit employers from deviating from practices deemed socially fair. If expectations are a function of the past, then traditional employment relations of job security may have a strong inertia and employment adjustment practices may be slow to respond to changes in economic variables.

Government policy frequently alters the marginal costs of adjusting employment levels versus average hours, and could be easily incorporated in the above model. In Europe, unemployment insurance compensation for short-time work and special government labor subsidies have been instrumental in financing various shorter working time arrangements, and thus in saving employment for workers in selected industries or companies. One interpretation of such intervention is that the government has an efficiency-improving role in providing social insurance, particularly in the event of a firms' bankruptcy. An alternative interpretation is that it reflects labor's power in the political sphere.

## 4.2 Shorter Working Time and Workforce Reductions in Steel

The European steel industry, like the American, has undergone extensive restructuring since the mid-1970s. The decline in production, the shedding of excess capacity and the modernization of antiquated plant and equipment have been accompanied by large workforce reductions. Table 4.1 provides annual production and employment data for West Germany, France and the United States from 1962 to 1984. During 1962–74 production was characterized by fairly steady growth in each country while employment gradually fell, reflecting productivity gains. Between 1974 and 1975 production fell by over 20 per cent in all three countries and, although subsequently fluctuating with the business cycles, it has never approached the peak levels of 1973–74. During 1974–84 employment fell by 57 per cent in the United States, 39 per cent in Germany, and 56 per cent in France.

Unlike the US industry, however, the steel industry in Continental Europe has achieved massive reductions in labor with minimal resort to layoff.[14] Instead, companies have made extensive use of various forms of shorter working time: early retirement, reduction of the workweek, increased holiday, and worksharing. This section describes historical and current workforce adjustment measures in the steel industries of selected European countries. Explanations of the strong job security are discussed, and labor adjustment patterns are contrasted with those in the United States both before and during the crisis. Much of the information presented in this section is based upon extensive interviews with labor, steel company and government representatives in six European countries in 1984 and 1986, and with their counterparts in the United States in 1986.

71

**Table 4.1**
Production of crude steel and employment of manual workers, 1962–84

| | USA | | West Germany | | France | |
|---|---|---|---|---|---|---|
| | Production '000 tons | Employment[a] | Production '000 tons | Employment[b] | Production '000 tons | Employment[b] |
| 1962 | 98,328 | 402,662 | 32,563 | 208,926 | 17,234 | 129,081 |
| 1963 | 109,261 | 405,536 | 31,597 | 200,306 | 17,554 | 129,413 |
| 1964 | 127,076 | 434,654 | 37,339 | 206,174 | 19,781 | 130,080 |
| 1965 | 131,462 | 458,539 | 36,821 | 200,017 | 19,599 | 124,433 |
| 1966 | 134,101 | 446,712 | 35,316 | 186,581 | 19,594 | 117,069 |
| 1967 | 127,213 | 424,153 | 36,744 | 177,822 | 19,658 | 111,036 |
| 1968 | 131,462 | 420,684 | 41,159 | 178,801 | 20,403 | 107,115 |
| 1969 | 141,262 | 415,301 | 45,316 | 181,209 | 22,510 | 109,962 |
| 1970 | 131,514 | 403,115 | 45,041 | 180,628 | 23,774 | 109,891 |
| 1971 | 120,443 | 366,982 | 40,313 | 169,378 | 22,843 | 107,368 |
| 1972 | 133,241 | 364,074 | 43,705 | 165,502 | 24,054 | 106,381 |
| 1973 | 150,799 | 392,851 | 49,521 | 171,688 | 25,270 | 107,872 |
| 1974 | 145,720 | 398,212 | 53,232 | 174,020 | 27,020 | 110,490 |
| 1975 | 116,642 | 339,945 | 40,415 | 164,094 | 21,530 | 107,017 |
| 1976 | 128,000 | 339,021 | 42,415 | 161,682 | 23,221 | 103,305 |
| 1977 | 125,333 | 337,396 | 38,985 | 153,969 | 22,089 | 93,844 |
| 1978 | 137,031 | 339,155 | 41,253 | 148,603 | 22,837 | 84,885 |
| 1979 | 136,341 | 341,931 | 46,040 | 150,665 | 23,360 | 76,776 |
| 1980 | 111,835 | 291,483 | 43,838 | 144,176 | 23,172 | 65,729 |
| 1981 | 120,828 | 286,219 | 41,610 | 135,061 | 21,245 | 59,987 |
| 1982 | 74,577 | 198,477 | 35,880 | 126,371 | 18,403 | 57,498 |
| 1983 | 84,615 | 168,852 | 35,729 | 116,360 | 17,582 | 53,335 |
| 1984 | 92,528 | 170,694 | 39,389 | 106,934 | 18,827 | 48,531 |
| Growth rates | | | | | | |
| 1962–74 | 3.3 | −0.1 | 4.1 | −1.5 | 3.7 | −1.3 |
| 1974–84 | −4.5 | −8.5 | −3.0 | −4.9 | −3.6 | −8.2 |

[a] annual average figure
[b] year-end figure
Sources: EUROSTAT, *Iron and Steel Yearbook;*
American Iron and Steel Institute, *Annual Statistical Report.*

## 4.2(a)  The Tradition of Job Security

European workers, in general, enjoy relatively strong employment security. Whether or not it is a principal or independent cause of differential adjustment, European labor law restricting employer discretion in dismissing workers reflects different rights and obligations in Europe than in the United States, and different underlying conceptions of the nature of the employment relation. Legal restrictions on employment practices, such as the requirement that dismissal be for just cause, advance notification and consultation requirements, rights to severance pay, and restrictions on temporary employment establish worker rights in jobs and mirror and reinforce worker expectations of employment security. Owing to legal recourse and effects on employee expectations about job security, these laws are likely to increase labor bargaining power in downturns. European dismissal law contrasts with the employment-at-will doctrine operating for the most part in the United States.

In the context of generally strong employment security, European steelworkers have received special treatment. In the early development of the iron and steel industry, companies often monopolized local labor markets, blocking the entry of other industry into, and hence the economic diversification of, steel regions. With the strengthening of unions and development of collective bargaining in the twentieth century, agreements often provided strong job guarantees. However, job security in an industry facing cyclical not structural downturns served the mutual interests of employers and employees.

Within Germany, steelworkers enjoy a privileged legal status, and its implications for bargaining power warrant special mention. The German system of codetermination was first established following World War II in the steel industry. Although codetermination has been extended to large companies in all sectors, parity codetermination, or equal representation of workers and management on the Supervisory Board, exists only in steel. Because the Supervisory Board must approve major management decisions, labor has been in a position to block plant closures and layoffs.

The employment practices that evolved in Europe differed from those in the United States, where layoff was common. Athough US employers had similar interests in maintaining a stable workforce and the union was powerful, collective agreements focused on providing income security. Steelworkers negotiated supplementary unemployment benefits, which in addition to protecting income no doubt discouraged job search when recall was anticipated. With a seniority-based layoff system, older workers effectively received strong income and job guarantees.

## 4.2(b)  Shorter Working Time and Employment Adjustment during Restructuring

The workforce reduction measures adopted by the European and US steel industries during restructuring are consistent with previous employment practices and job security. Steel companies on the Continent have effected large workforce reductions largely without recourse to layoff. The basic formula for workforce reduction has been natural attrition, accelerated by early retirement and accompanied by a reduction of hours through the shortening of the workweek, an increase in holidays, or work sharing.

Prior to the crisis, normal retirement on the Continent was 65 and early retirement 62. All countries have lowered the age of early retirement. In France and Belgium workers are retiring at 50, in West Germany at 55, in Luxembourg at 57 and in the Netherlands at 57½.[15] Early retirement schemes typically are open to most of the eligible workers on a voluntary or required basis.[16] Therefore, accompanying early retirement have been extensive retraining and internal transfer programs whereby younger workers fill positions vacated by retirees. During restructuring, the steel industries in all Continental countries also substantially reduced average working time. In Luxembourg, steelworkers gained an additional 12 holidays, representing a 4.6 per cent reduction in annual working time. In France, the average working week has been lowered to 33½ hours in certain plants, in Belgium to 35 hours for most steelworkers, in the Netherlands to 36 hours, and in West Germany to 38 hours.[17]

At the same time, companies in West Germany, France, Belgium and the Netherlands have put large portions of their workforce on short-time. Workers on short-time receive unemployment insurance from the state for hours not worked, which companies typically supplement. Table 4.2 provides statistics on the utilization of short-time work since 1974 in West Germany and since 1980 for other countries.

In addition to shorter working time measures, France recently introduced an elaborate retraining program. Also, rather than using work sharing, the Luxembourg steel company ARBED created a separate profit-making division, the so-called 'anti-crisis division', which subcontracted out extra workers to the state or to other companies. Finally, France and West Germany have experimented with job buy-out schemes.

European governments have played an important role in underwriting job security. Unemployment insurance for short-time work is an

**Table 4.2**

Percentage of the workforce affected by short-time work (annual average)

|      | West Germany | France | Belgium | Netherlands |
|------|--------------|--------|---------|-------------|
| 1975 | 20.0         |        |         |             |
| 1976 | 13.5         |        |         |             |
| 1977 | 18.6         |        |         |             |
| 1978 | 7.2          |        |         |             |
| 1979 | 1.1          |        |         |             |
| 1980 | 3.0          | 2.5    | 13.2    | 11.5        |
| 1981 | 8.5          | 8.3    | 19.2    | 20.2        |
| 1982 | 20.2         | 8.3    | 21.5    | 28.0        |
| 1983 | 29.2         | 14.4   | 26.4    | 17.7        |
| 1984 | 5.8          | 1.3    | 12.8    | 0.4         |
| 1985 | 0.2          | 0.8    | 5.9     | 0           |

*Sources:* West Germany – Arbeitgeberverbandes Eisen und Stahlindustrie; other countries – EUROSTAT.

automatic mechanism by which steel companies can shift the costs of hours adjustment onto the state. Further, all governments have subsidized the costs of early retirement. In France, the government is covering 30 per cent of the salary and 50 per cent of the administrative costs of workers in retraining. In Luxembourg, the government absorbed most of the company losses on workers in the anti-crisis division.

The principal method of workforce reduction in the US steel industry has been layoff. Steel companies made little use of short-time work, in part because of union opposition.[18] In further contrast to trends in Europe, paid leave time has been cut. In the late 1960s, senior workers received an additional nine weeks of vacation every five years. The scheme, designed to avoid displacement from technological improvements, was abolished as part of a 1983 package of concessions.

The industry did establish an extensive income security program in 1977 for senior workers affected by permanent layoff. Eligibility depends on age and service; many of the pensioners are in their late 40s or early 50s. According to Davis and Montgomery (1986), the pension provides an average replacement rate in terms of after-tax income of about 50 per cent and, subject to limitations, may be supplemented by income from another job. The program has constituted a major labor cost to companies. The American early retirement program, however, differs fundamentally from the European in that it is not used, for the most part, to preserve jobs for younger workers.[19]

Differences in European and US government labor policy toward steel mirror cross-country differences in firms' employment practices. While European policy such as support for early retirement and short-time work has been oriented toward promoting job security and avoiding dislocation, US policy has been designed to assist the worker following layoff. US steelworkers have been major recipients of government funds for income support and retraining.

Early retirement programs, as the principal mechanism of workforce reduction in Continental Europe and of income security for senior workers in the United States, represent a large part of total labor adjustment costs and illustrate the different orientation of European and US labor policy. Based on unpublished data from the Statistical Office of the European Communities (EUROSTAT), European industry representatives and USX Corp., cost comparisons of early retirement programs were made for West Germany, France and the United States over the 1980–83 period.[20] The French government covered about 90 per cent of these costs and the West German an estimated half to three-quarters. The US government has assisted in a relatively minor and indirect way through unemployment insurance (UI) payments, whose duration of 26 weeks is far shorter than in Europe. While retirees accounted for a much larger percentage of leavers in Europe that in the United States, and while the terms of early retirement in Europe were more generous, the average per worker cost to companies was lower and early retirement costs as a percentage of total labor costs were about the same or lower in

Europe than in the United States.[21] Thus, European governments have played a major role in underwriting the costs of job security.

The job security of European steelworkers goes well beyond any legislated protection. In explaining their extensive reliance on working time reduction measures, union, employee and government representatives in each of five countries also stressed the importance of the tradition of job security. This factor may help explain differences with the United States, where the workforce also is well organized. The worker morale problems a firm encounters in laying off workers and a union's ability to mobilize workers to strike depend, in part, on worker expectations of their own job security and their notion of socially fair employment practices. Layoff in the European steel industry, unlike in the United States, would have constituted a major departure from the past.

## 4.3  Employment Adjustment and its Impacts on Restructuring

The preceding sections provide a framework for understanding cross-country differences in job security and labor adjustment. The objective of this section is first to document employment and hours adjustment patterns that are consistent with the theoretical predictions of Section 4.1 and the institutional discussion of Section 4.2 for the West German, French and US steel industries. In addition, it explores some of the economic consequences for an industry experiencing both cyclical fluctuations in demand and structural decline.

### 4.3(a)  The Data

Monthly data on production, hours and employment are used to estimate employment and hours output elasticities. The production variable measures crude steel output and is expressed in tons. Employment refers to production workers only. Employment is sampled at the end of the month in Europe and in the middle of the month in the United States. Hours are total hours worked by manual labor during the month. An average hour figure was derived by dividing total hours by employment in the United States, and by a two-month employment average in Europe. The data sources for France and West Germany are EUROSTAT steel publications. For the United States, production and hours data were obtained from the American Iron and Steel Institute. US employment figures are from the Bureau of Labor Statistics.[22]

### 4.3(b)  The Model

Separate employment and hours equations were estimated for each country over two time periods: 1969–73[23] and 1974–84. The former essentially represents adjustment to cyclical fluctuations in employment; the latter to structural decline. The equations estimate a basic partial adjustment model. Dependent variables are the natural log-arithm of employment, average hours and total hours. In each equation the right-hand-side variables are the logarithm of production, month dummy and time trend variables.[24]

The purpose of the exercise is to quantify cross-country differences in the magnitude and timing of labor adjustment and differences between pre- and post-1974 adjustment patterns. Because labor adjustment patterns may differ significantly across countries and time periods, the minimum of restrictions was imposed on the lag structure. Estimated equations included 6–12 month leads and 12–24 months lags in addition to current production.[25] Estimated coefficients were not sensitive to the specification of the lag structure. Tables 4.3–4.5 summarize the results of a representative set of employment, average hours and total hours equations, respectively. Hours equations include the natural logarithm of current production and 12 lags; employment equations also include one lead, owing to the measurement of employment in Europe. Because employment in West Germany and France is measured at the end of the month, interpretation of the lag structure for the employment equations differs slightly from that in the United States, as estimated adjustment is shifted forward by about a half a month. Serial correlation was a problem, particularly for the employment equations. Equations were corrected assuming the error term follows a first-order autoregressive process.[26]

## 4.3(c)   Adjustment to Cyclical Fluctuation

Tables 4.3–4.5 reveal the strikingly different patterns of employment and hours adjustment between West Germany and France, on the one hand, and the United States, on the other, both before and after 1974. Turning first to the 1969–73 period, the coefficients on the production variables suggest that employment adjustment in West Germany and France is small in any given period, and is spread over a long time. The United States differs both in the timing and in the magnitude of the employment adjustment. Adjustment of employment in the concurrent period is relatively large, with an elasticity of .314, declines sharply over subsequent periods, and is virtually complete after six months.

Most of the short-run adjustment of labor input in West Germany and France occurs through adjustment in average hours worked. From Tables 4.4 and 4.5, the coefficients on the average hours equations closely track those on total hours and, as in the United States, the bulk of the hours adjustment occurs in the same month as the change in production. Although the timing of the adjustment of total hours is similar across countries, the magnitude is considerably less in West Germany and France than in the United States. The six-month hours–output elasticity is .451 in Germany, .148 in France, and .943 in the United States. A possible explanation for the lower elasticity in Europe is that during slack periods workers are engaged in activities like maintenance or construction, which are not captured in production

**Table 4.3**
Employment adjustment

*Dependent variable: in (production workers)*

| | 1969–73 | | | 1974–84 | | |
|---|---|---|---|---|---|---|
| | *West Germany* | *France* | *USA* | *West Germany* | *France* | *USA* |
| In production, lag month | | | | | | |
| −1 | .014 | .010 | 0 | .001 | .003 | .029 |
| | (.016) | (.018) | (.011) | (.005) | (.007) | (.026) |
| 0 | .007 | −.001 | .314 | .008 | .005 | .230 |
| | (.016) | (.019) | (.011) | (.005) | (.008) | (.033) |
| 1 | .010 | .012 | .131 | .010 | .007 | .044 |
| | (.016) | (.019) | (.011) | (.005) | (.008) | (.033) |
| 2 | .025 | −.004 | .055 | .010 | .003 | .072 |
| | (.016) | (.017) | (.011) | (.005) | (.008) | (.033) |
| 3 | .037 | −.010 | .029 | .007 | −.002 | .043 |
| | (.015) | (.019) | (.011) | (.005) | (.008) | (.032) |
| 4 | .029 | −.009 | .015 | .013 | −.005 | .008 |
| | (.014) | (.019) | (.011) | (.005) | (.008) | (.032) |
| 5 | .025 | .042 | −.011 | .013 | −.005 | .045 |
| | (.014) | (.018) | (.011) | (.005) | (.008) | (.033) |
| $\sum_{6}^{12}$ | .231 | .107 | .103 | .053 | −.034 | .131 |
| | (.028) | (.046) | (.016) | (.015) | (.031) | (.034) |
| time | −.004 | −.013 | −.080 | .003 | −.076 | .045 |
| | (.023) | (.010) | (.013) | (.005) | (.008) | (.007) |
| time$^2$ | −.003 | 0 | .005 | −.004 | −.001 | −.007 |
| | (.003) | (.001) | (.002) | (.0004) | (.0007) | (.0007) |
| $R^2$ | .99 | .97 | .99 | .96 | .99 | .99 |

*Notes:* Standard errors are in parentheses. An intercept and month dummy variables were included in regressions, but are not reported.

measures. Unfortunately, data such as those on the use of subcontractors for such tasks, which would help shed light on this issue, are unavailable.

Despite the radically different patterns of employment and hours adjustment between the US and European steel industries, their impacts on labor allocation during periods of cyclical fluctuation may be relatively unimportant. At issue is the extent to which laid-off workers are productively employed in other sectors of the economy and the extent to which they remain unemployed until recalled to their previous job. Historically, the US steel industry has been one of the heaviest users of the unemployment insurance system. Lilien (1980) has estimated that, over the 1960–74 period, on average 88 per cent of the workers laid off in the Primary Metals industry, of which steel is the major component, were rehired. Arguably, during this period the steel industry effectively used the UI system to retain a large permanent workforce over the business cycle. Under these circumstances layoff is like another form of hours adjustment.[27]

**Table 4.4**
Average hours adjustment

*Dependent variable: in (average monthly hours worked)*

| | 1969–73 | | | 1974–84 | | |
|---|---|---|---|---|---|---|
| | West Germany | France | USA | West Germany | France | USA |
| In production, lag month | | | | | | |
| 0 | .390 | .254 | .467 | .489 | .212 | .309 |
| | (.078) | (.097) | (.043) | (.033) | (.035) | (.057) |
| 1 | −.078 | −.149 | −.037 | −.103 | −.036 | .132 |
| | (.089) | (.105) | (.051) | (.036) | (.036) | (.094) |
| 2 | −.001 | −.042 | −.008 | .018 | .022 | −.137 |
| | (.087) | (.098) | (.051) | (.036) | (.037) | (.094) |
| 3 | .153 | .127 | −.076 | .012 | −.021 | .104 |
| | (.086) | (.098) | (.051) | (.036) | (.037) | (.092) |
| 4 | −.184 | −.133 | −.049 | −.008 | −.004 | −.132 |
| | (.086) | (.109) | (.051) | (.036) | (.037) | (.093) |
| 5 | .050 | .103 | .109 | −.037 | .030 | .066 |
| | (.086) | (.112) | (.051) | (.035) | (.039) | (.094) |
| 12 $\sum_{6}$ | .003 | .015 | −.027 | −.067 | .053 | −.053 |
| | (.073) | (.112) | (.051) | (.037) | (.051) | (.060) |
| time | −.014 | −.058 | .056 | −.012 | .001 | −.012 |
| | (.042) | (.022) | (.034) | (.004) | (.006) | (.006) |
| time$^2$ | −.001 | .004 | −.007 | .001 | 0 | .001 |
| | (.005) | (.003) | (.004) | (.0003) | (.001) | (.001) |
| $R^2$ | .92 | .98 | .96 | .90 | .94 | .94 |

*Notes:* Standard errors are in parentheses. An intercept and month dummy variables were included in regressions, but are not reported.

In West Germany and France temporary layoff is virtually unknown. One explanation is that advance notice requirements preclude companies from using layoffs for short-run adjustment. Instead, short-time has been used extensively in West German and French steel, and is covered by the UI system. The system of short-time whereby workers may not work for one or more weeks is, in fact, quite similar to the practice of temporary layoff. Thus, the adjustment processes in Europe and the United States are more similar than employment and hours output elasticities would indicate.

## 4.3(d) Adjustment to Structural Decline

In the post-1974 period the differences in employment and hours adjustment patterns between Europe and the United States persist, although countries generally adjust labor more slowly. After 1974 in

**Table 4.5**
Total hours adjustment

*Dependent variable: ln (total monthly hours worked)*

| | 1969–73 | | | 1974–84 | | |
| | West Germany | France | USA | West Germany | France | USA |
|---|---|---|---|---|---|---|
| ln production, lag month | | | | | | |
| 0 | .379 | .264 | .789 | .496 | .221 | .583 |
| | (.062) | (.100) | (.044) | (.036) | (.032) | (.056) |
| 1 | −.058 | −.156 | .090 | −.104 | −.030 | .167 |
| | (.077) | (.106) | (.050) | (.037) | (.034) | (.096) |
| 2 | .022 | −.047 | .047 | .023 | .018 | −.100 |
| | (.076) | (.099) | (.050) | (.037) | (.035) | (.099) |
| 3 | .186 | .110 | −.051 | .021 | −.025 | .184 |
| | (.076) | (.099) | (.050) | (.038) | (.035) | (.097) |
| 4 | −.150 | −.122 | −.026 | .009 | −.013 | −.122 |
| | (.076) | (.111) | (.050) | (.037) | (.035) | (.098) |
| 5 | .071 | .099 | .094 | −.023 | .024 | .092 |
| | (.076) | (.112) | (.051) | (.037) | (.037) | (.099) |
| $\sum_{6}^{12}$ | .259 | .140 | .074 | .045 | −.111 | .120 |
| | (.057) | (.116) | (.055) | (.044) | (.042) | (.060) |
| time | −.018 | −.075 | .028 | −.007 | −.079 | .030 |
| | (.029) | (.023) | (.038) | (.006) | (.005) | (.005) |
| time$^2$ | −.004 | .004 | −.001 | −.003 | −.002 | −.006 |
| | (.004) | (.003) | (.005) | (.0005) | (.0004) | (.0004) |
| $R^2$ | .98 | .98 | .99 | .98 | .99 | .99 |

*Notes:* Standard errors are in parentheses. An intercept and month dummy variables were included in regressions, but are not reported.

West Germany and France employment appears almost completely unresponsive to short-run changes in production. Instead, changes in average hours account for virtually all of short-run labor adjustment. West Germany continues to show a large, immediate response in average hours, which probably captures the extensive use of short-time work, as is shown in the statistics of Table 4.2.

In the United States, labor adjustment patterns after 1974 are similar to those before 1974, with a relatively large employment response in the concurrent month. Much of the decline in total hours adjustment is accounted for by less proportionate adjustment of average hours. These findings are consistent with restrictions on short-time work, supported by the union.

The economic implications of short-run adjustment through hours versus employment levels are more complex and important in the case of structural decline than in the case of cyclical fluctuation. First, however, it should be noted that the low estimated European employ-ment–output elasticities in the post-1974 period do not imply that these steel industries failed to achieve substantial employment reduction. With employment reduction accomplished primarily through attrition, accelerated by early retirement and job buy-outs, the rate of reduction may depend more on the demographic characteristics of the workforce, like age, than on short-run production changes. In the decade following 1974 the steel workforce declined by 35 per cent in West Germany and 51 per cent in France. From Table 4.1 the rate of workforce reduction increases dramatically after 1974 in West Germany and France. Further, both countries achieve substantial gains in labor productivity, particu-larly France beginning in the late 1970s. In the regression equations this reduction is captured by the time trend variables. Job security in Europe applies to individuals, and arguably saved few if any jobs permanently. The medium-run effect of greater reliance on hours rather than employ-ment adjustment in the short run was more to smooth the rate of employment reduction than to lower it.

Short-run labor adjustment practices, however, may have profound effects on the restructuring process and long-run configurations of the industry. The adjustment of labor input primarily through hours rather than layoff renders closures difficult. Thus, particularly in a multi-plant operation, strong job security may affect optimal production allocation, investment and closure decisions.

In another study, I used plant level data for the steel industry in seven European Community countries, to examine the effects of job security on production and capacity allocation. Using technological and loca-tional variables as the determinants of production and capacity allo-cation across plants, cross-country differences in allocation criteria and changes within countries over time were linked to job security and employment adjustment practices. Strong job security implied greater allocation to less efficient plants. Furthermore, the study found little evidence that the least efficient capacity Community-wide was being closed. In general, strong job security favored equal proportionate cutbacks in capacity across plants and companies. By affecting invest-ment and closure decisions, the methods of labor adjustment have longer-run impacts on the patterns of production and hence employ-ment in a restructured industry (Houseman, 1985).

The method of workforce reduction also has quite important impli-cations for income distribution. Most obviously, short-run adjustment through hours results in more equitable treatment of the existing workforce.

Finally, the choice between employment versus hours adjustment in the short run has effects on the reallocation of labor to other sectors, which are likely to be important in the case of a structural decline in demand. First, the use of hours adjustment delays the availability of workers to other sectors of the economy. The efficiency of a policy that smoothes employment reduction through shorter working time measures depends upon the dynamics of the local labor market: its economic dependence on the declining industry and ability to absorb large numbers of workers with that industry's skills. The limited evidence on dislocated steelworkers in the United States suggests that they experience unusually long spells of unemployment (see Flaim and Seghal, 1985). While beyond the scope of the current study, this issue deserves careful empirical analysis.

Second, implicit in different speeds of workforce reduction are differences in the characteristics of those released from steel. Early retirees and quits accounted for a greater proportion of leavers in Europe than in the United States. Older workers are more likely to exit the workforce, while those leaving voluntarily are presumably more geographically and occupationally mobile.

## 4.4  Conclusion

Underlying differences in labor adjustment patterns in Europe and the United States are differences in the job security of the workforce and in the utilization of shorter working time measures. Restructuring industries have been important users of shorter working time measures, and this paper contrasts experiences in European and US steel industries to document cross-country differences in labor adjustment and to explore possible causes and their economic consequences.

Explicit and implicit worker rights in jobs, attitudes toward mobility, union objectives and government policy are interrelated, reinforcing factors, which help explain the widely divergent patterns of employment and hours adjustment in Europe and the United States. In steel, differences in European and US labor adjustment practices existed long before restructuring of the industry. Placed in its historical and institutional context, the extensive reduction of working time in Europe has been a natural outgrowth of past job security and supporting government policy. In the United States, layoff and government policy oriented toward assisting dislocated workers had been the norm.

Use of shorter working time measures, however, has quite different economic consequences during cyclical and structural decline in demand. During cyclical fluctuations, the implications of the different employment and hours adjustment practices in European and US steel on labor allocation are likely to be minimal, since most American steelworkers were on temporary layoff. During restructuring, their implications for labor allocation are more complex and important. While the European steel industry did effect large workforce reductions, shorter working time measures saved thousands of jobs for younger workers in the short run. The effects on labor allocation depend upon the mobility of dislocated steelworkers, and the ability of the regional economy to absorb large numbers with their skills. In addition, strong job security and the use of shorter working time measures in Europe rendered plant closure difficult, and thus may have had long-term impacts on industry structure and regional employment by affecting capital investment decisions.

In conclusion, shorter working time measures in Europe have been an important mechanism to preserve job security for the workforce. In this capacity, the growth in shorter working time is closely linked with other developments in European industrial relations, notably workforce flexibility. For example, reductions in average working time increasingly are tied to greater flexibility when hours are worked. The effect is to lower expected labor costs, in part by lowering the marginal costs of adjusting labor through hours rather than workers. Thus, shorter working time and workforce flexibility together help preserve job security of the workforce in the short run and ensure the economic viability of the system for the future.

## Notes

1  Although steel is a special case, it is representative of an important set of industries. Many of the political pressures for working time reduction and examples of their application in Europe have come from sectors like steel, which face economic pressures to restructure and implement large work-force reductions.

2  Houseman (1985) incorporates uncertainty into a similar model. Uncertainty does not alter the basic results of the model.

3  Few models directly address the problem of cross-country differences,
.  although frequent reference is made to institutional factors such as employ-ment security legislation and unemployment compensation for short-time work (see, for example, Moy and Sorrentine 1981). An exception in the literature is FitzRoy and Hart (1985), which focuses on differences in the structure of social security taxes.

4  To the extent that these factors are important and grow over time, labor is theoretically similar to putty-clay models of captial in which, once invest-ment takes place and the form of capital determined, capital becomes less mobile.

5  If the worker is employed, the constant term $B$ also captures the disutility of hours worked at an alternative job.

6  This modeling is appropriate for both European and US steel where wage and employment and/or severance payment variables (i.e. the total wage bill) are negotiated. More generally, in Europe job security legislation, which often requires consultation with worker representatives and the development of a social plan, restricts employers' prerogative to lay off workers and arguably gives workers some power in determining employ-ment levels. Moreover, as is assumed in the implicit contract literature, employers may have understandings with workers concerning employment adjustment policies.

7  With no hiring costs, labor demand in this period would be unaffected by an increase in the next period.

8  With a utilitarian objective function the union maximizes the sum of worker utilities.

9  This and other comparative static results are treated in an appendix available from the author.

10 In examining the impact of labor's bargaining power on adjustment patterns, it would be more desirable to have a dynamic model that takes into account both the hiring and dismissal process, rather than one that takes the labor force attached to the firm as fixed. Higher labor costs may induce substitution of capital for labor. However, the impact of higher capital–labor ratios on measured employment and hours–output elasticities is ambiguous.

11 In more common formulations where utility is a function only of income and prices, utility maximization is equivalent to income maximization and resource allocation would be insensitive to income distribution in this partial equilibrium model.

12 Grossman (1982) contrasts the outcomes of this model with those of the standard implicit contract model, in which workers face equal probability of layoff. As noted above, the latter formulation is equivalent to one in which a union representing the workers has a utilitarian objective function.

13 Legislation, of course, may set conditions above any optimal outcome and thus operate as a constraint on efficient wage–employment bargains.

14 Workforce reduction measures and job security in British steel differed significantly from those used in other European countries. Plant closures and productivity agreements negotiated at the British Steel Corporation, primarily after the election of Prime Minister Thatcher, resulted in large-scale redundancies.

15 For the Netherlands, this involved a special measure implemented three times. Otherwise, the age of early retirement is 60.

16 Because workers receive a large percentage of their previous pay until the age of normal retirement and a normal pension thereafter, the schemes have been popular.

17 In practice, the distinction between a reduction in average weekly hours and an increase in holiday is less clear cut. Often average hours are calculated over a time period longer than a week. Thus, workers may work longer hours during the course of the week and receive compensation in the form of extra days off rather than overtime pay.

18 With a seniority-based layoff system, many senior workers opposed pay cuts accompanying large reductions in hours; unlike in Europe, in the United States short-time work generally is not covered by the unemployment insurance system.

19 A 1983 provision allowed workers age 60 to retire early on a voluntary basis. This component of the early retirement system is relatively small.

20 Owing to space constraints I do not discuss in detail methodology or results, which are more fully treated in Houseman (1986). The USX data come from the Davis and Montgomery study.

21 The company costs in 1983 of those retiring between 1980 and 1983 were estimated to be 2.3–3.7 per cent of total labor costs in West Germany, 2.4 per cent in France, and 4.1–4.9 per cent in the United States.

22 The EC and US definitions of the steel industry differ slightly in terms of product coverage, which would affect measurement of employment and hours variables. These differences, however, should not significantly affect estimated elasticities.

23 Employment and hours equations for West Germany and France and employment equations for the United States also were estimated over a longer period: 1962–73. (Hours data for the US are available only since 1969.) The estimated coefficients in the 1962–73 equations were quite similar

to those in the 1969–73 equations, except for France where estimated hours adjustment is greater in the longer time period. The qualitative comparison between France and the United States made below is not sensitive to time period, however.

24  The time trend variables are assumed to capture movements in capital stock and input and output prices.

25  The approach adopted in this paper follows that in Sims (1974). Lead variables were included as a test of the exogeneity of the right-hand variables. Except for the average hours equations, F-tests showed that the lead variables were not significant.

26  Assumptions of higher-order serial correlation were tested, but had little effect on the estimated coefficients and their significance.

27  Of course, workers on layoff may accept temporary employment elsewhere. However, the same argument applies to European workers on short-time. Further, with company SUB payments the percentage make-up was quite high and thus there was little financial pressure on steelworkers to seek alternative employment. In fact, layoff became so popular that inverse seniority rules were applied in certain parts of the industry.

# COMMENT

## GEORGE BITTLINGMAYER

Cyclical industries and industries in long-term decline can adjust the number of workers or average hours per worker. Which of these two is the better social policy? Susan Houseman offers the reader three essays on this question, one theoretical, one institutional and one empirical – thereby displaying a command of the three skills that Joseph Schumpeter considered essential for good economic research.

The first section presents a model of how a firm adjusts the number of workers in the face of union power and declining or increasing demand. Because it is intrinsic to the topic at hand, I will focus on the first case of declining demand. The firm attempts to minimize its labor plus severance costs subject to the constraint that the value of the union's utilitarian objective function, which takes into account the utility of those working and those laid off, cannot fall below an exogenously given level. Although I have no objections to the way the technical details are carried out, it seems to me that posing the outcome of union–employer haggling over working hours and employment as a Lagrangian minimization problem will not be the last word on this issue. I would note, for example, that if there is no effective opposition by labor, that is, if the value of the constraint is low enough, the minimization problem (4.1) implies zero workers, provided that the severance pay $s$ is less than the wage $w$, as it should be if working reduces utility. The assumption of a utilitarian objective function also supresses conflict of interest within the union, yet a policy that favors one margin – fewer hours worked on average – over the other – fewer workers – will have different implications for different workers. At a more general level, it seems to me that not enough effort was made to distinguish between what is optimal from the union's point of view, what is optimal from the point of view of the firm facing a union with certain notions about how total working time should be reduced, and what is optimal from society's view. Another way to make this point is to note that the solution to the firm's constrained cost-minimization problem depends on the exogenously given value of the union's constraint, but that this value can be too high or too low from society's point of view. The deliberate short-term focus also sidesteps the important observation that, in a competitive labor market, workers in a cyclical industry will get wage premiums to compensate them for unemployment risk.

Section 4.2 is a review of developments in the European steel industry. Its strengths and weaknesses seem to be a consequence of the way the information was collected, namely interviews with steel executives, union leaders and government officials. On the plus side, economists should do more first-hand learning about the industries they study. The attitude of many economists in the past has been that of a biologist who refuses to observe plants and animals in the field. The weakness of this section is that it takes the differences between the European and US approach to workforce reduction as largely the product of a different 'tradition'. I do not doubt that this is what people say, but I question whether economists are well advised to adopt this view. Any culture contains contradictory 'traditions', and if instead European firms had a laissez-faire hire and fire policy, but not US firms, there would undoubtedly be strains in the European and US traditions that one could offer as rationalizations. This explanation even fails on its own terms. Why have workers in the steel industry in France or West Germany been better able to protect their interests than the other workers in their respective countries? Is the steel industry 'tradition' different? I would look to the specific political and economic circumstances that enable labor to achieve its goals through the political process in some cases but not in others. For example, the more homogeneous local labor forces or the greater obstacles to mobility – some linguistic, others government induced – may play a role in explaining the different approach of European firms and unions. Culture and tradition certainly have their influence, and they have to be taken as given for the problem at hand, but the calculus of cost and benefit for what is essentially an economic problem should not be so readily dismissed.

The third part of Houseman's paper is an econometric study. Three variables – the number of workers, average hours worked and total hours worked – are in turn regressed on production of crude steel plus a time trend. These are interesting results that are fairly persuasive in showing that the US steel industry adjusts the number of workers much more readily than the West German or French steel industries to short-term swings in production. Of particular interest is the tendency for the European adjustments to spread themselves out over a longer period.

A technical issue does merit discussion. These regressions are very much like cost function estimates in which costs are regressed on output. There is, however, a long literature that concerns itself with problems that arise in estimates of cost and production functions. If current production is a function of the number of workers and an error term reflecting luck, production problems, changes in the mix of steel products, and so on, then the coefficient on current production will be biased downward.[1] This is in essence an 'errors-in-variables' problem, and, as is well known, the extent of the bias depends on the variance of the measurement error and the variance of the 'true' values of the independent variable. If the random fluctuations and the changes in output mix are large compared to the planned fluctuations (conditioned on a constant output mix), the bias in the estimated coefficients will be large.

The potential problems this implies for the coefficients in Tables 4.3, 4.4 and 4.5 can be illustrated by looking at French steel output over the years 1969–74, that is, the years over which the adjustment to cyclical fluctuation is estimated. (See Table 4.1 for the data.) French steel output increases gradually, the difference between the highest and lowest value being 12.3 per cent. On the other hand, the difference between the highest and lowest US value over the same period is 25.2 per cent, twice as large, and that for West Germany 22.8. With comparatively little variation in the French data, it is hardly surprising that the significant French adjustment coefficients in Tables 4.3, 4.4 and 4.5 are lower.[2]

In a sense, of course, this statistical discussion simply confirms Houseman's point that the Europeans have placed short- and medium-term stability of employment first and profitability of the steel firms second. The extent of the bias is simply a measure of the extent to which production is smoothed for the sake of social policy. However, this point could be made more directly by simply comparing month-to-month, quarter-to-quarter or year-to-year percentage changes in employment, where I suspect the Americans would have lost hands down, and by showing that the French and West Germans were more willing to reduce the output of crude steel per employee below long-term trend during the mid-1970s, that is, less willing to cut employment when output dropped. The reader can verify this with Table 4.1 as well. West German output per worker increased at an annual rate of 5.7 per cent from 1962 to 1974, fell by one-fifth in a single year, 1975, and did not substantially increase above the 1973–74 level until 1984. Yearly increases in output per worker in the US, in contrast, were 3.4 per cent in the years 1962–74 and 4.0 per cent, slightly greater, in the years 1974–84.

These comments in no way detract from the substance of the results of course, namely that labor is more of a fixed factor in Europe than in the US. But this, it seems to me, is different from showing that shorter working hours are a good idea. Whether we should adjust hours per worker rather than the number of workers in the face of a long-term decline in output or in the face of cyclical fluctuations cannot be answered with these data. In order to come to the conclusion that Houseman does reach, namely that shorter working time will 'ensure the economic viability of the system in the future', it seems to me that the cost per job saved per year that arises because of shorter working time has to be compared to the cost of other alternatives. How does shorter working time compare to building sidewalks to nowhere, to retraining programs that take effect as soon as it is clear that restructuring has to take place, or to the social costs of relocation and unemployment? Hours worked per year in West Germany, for example, are already lower than for any major industrialized country. An arguable alternative to shorter working hours for an industry confronted with long-term, inevitable decline (which also takes cognizance of the consequences for aggregate productivity and the aggregate standard of living) is to find structural policies that are more responsive to new economic realities than those practiced in the Continental European steel industries over the last decade and a half.

# Notes

1 The downward bias in cost function estimates is lucidly discussed in Friedman (1955). Also see Johnston (1960) and Walters (1963) for treatments cast in terms of the econometric issues.
2 In private correspondence Houseman gives the coefficients of variation of seasonally adjusted production data for the US, France and West Germany as 11.2, 7.9 and 6.9, respectively, for the years 1962–73. This includes the years 1962–68, which were not included in the regressions in Tables 4.3, 4.4 and 4.5, but during which French and West German production levels were substantially below the levels for 1969–73. Thus, these values overestimate the variability of production during this later period.

# CHAPTER 5

# *Implications of the Non-Homogeneity of Standard and Overtime Hours on the Structure and Cyclical Adjustment of Labor Input*

## TUIRE SANTAMÄKI

### 5.1  Introduction

Several studies have established that studying labor market phenomena associated with changes in the labor input without differentiating between workers and hours per worker as well as between variable and quasi-fixed labor costs may produce seriously misleading inferences. The subject of the relative marginal productivities of the two components of labor input continues to be a debatable issue with mixed empirical evidence.

The significance of the productivity of hours has been further evoked by the general working time debate, where the separate implications of changes is standard and overtime hours have been emphasized. It is noteworthy, however, that the numerous econometrical studies on returns to total hours are unable to yield information on the returns to each dimension of the hours input that is of concern to those engaged in the debate. Although the arguments have been founded on the different role of standard and overtime hours, this distinction has been neglected[1] in modeling the production activity.

In this paper, we distinguish between standard and overtime hours in the production function, too, and it is our purpose to examine the implications of this distinction for the optimal choice of workers and hours. The production function is specified in Section 5.2. Section 5.3 focuses on the problem of how a cut in standard hours affects the optimal structure of labor input if the marginal product of total hours depends on their distribution between standard and overtime hours. In Section 5.4, a dynamic decision-making model is developed for a demand-constrained firm to analyze the optimal adjustment of hours

90

and employment during a business cycle, while Section 5.5 characterizes the impacts of the productivity differences on the adjustment pattern of the firm.

## 5.2 Specification of the Production Function

First of all, we allow for the fact that the marginal contribution to output of an additional manhour differs as between the employment of a new worker or extending the average workweek of an existing worker. There is, however, no established way to model even the short-run production function differentiating between the stock of wokers $N$ and the average productive hours $H$.

Following Ehrenberg (1971b), the function form is generally chosen from the class of multiplicatively separable functions. For instance, Ehrenberg (1971b), de Regt (1984) and Calmfors and Hoel (1985) assume that the flow of labor services is given by $h(H)N$, where $h$ is strictly concave, while Nickell (1978), Ström (1983) and Hoel (1986) assume a unit elasticity w.r.t. $H$. Several additional alternatives emerge in other studies; e.g. Rossana (1984) specifies a production function $F(HN, N)$, concave in the arguments $HN$ and $N$.

For our purposes, we need a parametrically specified production function to obtain unambiguous results on the effects of cutting standard hours and/or to arrange the various elementary policies into sequences during a business cycle. We follow the majority of previous studies by assuming that the underlying production technology can be adequately approximated by the constant elasticity specification and, allowing for the marginal product of hours to depend on the number of standard hours,[2] we postulate

$$Q = N^\alpha H_s^{\beta_1} \left(\frac{H}{H_s}\right)^{\beta_2} = f(N, H, H_s) \quad \tfrac{1}{2} < \beta_2 < \alpha < 1 \qquad (5.1)$$

where $Q$ is the level of output
$N$ is the number of workers
$H$ is the average number of productive hours per worker
$H_s$ is the standard number of hours per worker

First, some properties of the function are briefly discussed.

(i)   If $\beta_1 = \beta_2 = \beta$, then the marginal productivity of total hours is independent of the length of standard workweek, and then equation (5.1) reduces to $Q = N^\alpha H^\beta$.

(ii)  As to the parameter restrictions, their mutual order of size is required by the sufficiency conditions of our model.[3] The empirical evidence on output elasticities is not conclusive. A common empirical finding is that the labor input exhibits increasing returns and, for models that separate $N$ and $H$, this is usually found to be the result of increasing returns to average hours ($0 < \alpha < 1 < \beta$).

This has provoked attempts either to rationalize the finding or to show that is is due to some kind of specification error. The main examples on the rationalization of empirical findings are provided by Feldstein (1967), Craine (1973) and more recently by Anxo (1986). Alternative explanations offered, for example, by Nadiri and Rosen (1969), Tatom (1980), Leslie and Wise (1980), Hart and Robb (1980) and Hart and McGregor (1988) suggest that increasing returns are observed owing either to the omission of variables that are positively correlated with the length of average hours or to the misspecification of dynamic factor demand equations (Latham and Peel, 1979). Even then, higher returns to hours per worker than to workers have often been observed,[4] the findings being in contradiction with the sufficient conditions underlying the derivation of the factor demand functions.

(iii) The order of size for parameters $\beta_1$ and $\beta_2$ is determined by the mutual productivity of normal and overtime hours, which continues to be an important issue. Many authors – labeled institutionalists by Leslie and Wise (1980), with probably an unrivalled knowledge of the labor market in practice – consider the productivity of overtime to be fairly low, while others – in fact basing their statements inaccurately on observations of increasing returns to total hours – argue that overtime hours are extremely productive and efficient.

The production function specification (5.1) permits both of the cases, but in discussing the results we *a priori* assume that overtime hours are marginally less efficient than standard hours, or $\beta_1 > \beta_2$.[5] Then,

$$f_{HH,} = (\beta_1 - \beta_2) F_H / H_s > 0. \tag{5.2}$$

i.e., *ceteris paribus* the marginal product of total hours is negatively related to the number of overtime hours. Moreover, our specification is symmetric w.r.t. overtime and 'undertime' hours, which is of significance in our dynamic model context with a possible labor-hoarding outcome. Then, for $\beta_1 > \beta_2$, the undertime hours are more efficient and overtime hours less efficient than standard hours, while the opposite holds for $\beta_1 < \beta_2$.

(iv) Although the marginal product of total hours is influenced by the length of the standard workweek, $H_s$, the same is not true for the ratio of the marginal products of total hours and employment, or

$$\frac{d(f_H/f_N)}{dH_s} = \frac{f_N f_{HH,} - f_{NH,} f_H}{(f_N)^2} = 0. \tag{5.3}$$

## 5.3 Effects of a Cut in Standard Working Hours: Implications of the Non-Homogeneity

In the conventional model of the demand for labor input (Rosen, 1968; Ehrenberg, 1971b; Bell, 1982; and Hart, 1984a), employment and hours decisions are considered in an optimization framework of a firm, whose behavior is assumed to be one of minimizing the total labor costs subject to the constraint of the production or labor services function. The costs are comprised of the quasi-fixed labor costs, and standard and overtime wages with a constant overtime pay premium. Then the firm confronts the problem

$$\min C = \begin{cases} nN + wH_sN + \rho w(H - H_s)N & H > H_s \\ nN + wH_sN & H \leqslant H_s \end{cases} \tag{5.4}$$

subject to the production constraint

$$F(N, H) - Q = 0 \tag{5.5}$$

$$F_N, F_H > 0; \ F_{NN} \leqslant 0; \ F_{HH} \leqslant 0; \ F_{NH}, F_{HN} > 0,$$

where $C$ is total labor costs,
   $n$ is the quasi-fixed labor cost,
   $w$ is the standard wage rate, and
   $\rho$ is the overtime pay premium, $\rho > 1$.

   From this model follows the well-known result concerning the structure of the labor input: *ceteris paribus*, a change in standard hours has an opposite effect on equilibrium hours. For instance, a reduction in standard hours increases the marginal cost of an additional employee relative to additional utilization, because more hours need to be paid at premium rates. The (substitution) effect of reducing the standard workweek is to increase equilibrium hours and to decrease employment,[6] as long as the institutional overtime restrictions are not binding.
   As to our alternative production function (5.1) with $H_s$ as an explicit argument, we note that changes in factor proportions stem again from an ensuing rise in the marginal cost of an additional employee $MC_N$, or

$$MC_N = n + wH_s + \rho w(H - H_s) \quad H > H_s \text{ and} \tag{5.6}$$

$$\partial MC_N / \partial H_s = (1 - \rho)w < 0. \tag{5.7}$$

This emerges since both the marginal cost of overtime hours ($MC_H$) and the ratio of marginal products ($F_H/F_N$) remain unchanged (cf. equation (5.3)), and hence it may be shown that

$$\frac{\partial H}{\partial H_s} = -\frac{\beta_2(\rho - 1)}{\rho(\alpha - \beta_2)} < 0, \tag{5.8}$$

i.e. we obtain the familiar result of opposite changes in standard and optimal hours.
   Since a higher proportion of total hours is now made up of overtime hours, the employment effect is not necessarily negative as in the

traditional case. It may easily be shown that

$$\text{sgn}\,\frac{\partial N}{\partial H_s} = \text{sgn}\left(\frac{\beta_2 - \beta_1}{\beta_2} - \varepsilon_{HH_s}\right), \tag{5.9}$$

where $\varepsilon_{HH_s}$ is the elasticity of optimal hours w.r.t. standard hours, or

$$|\varepsilon_{HH_s}| = \frac{(\rho - 1)wH_s}{n - (\rho - 1)wH_s}. \tag{5.10}$$

Hence, the favorable employment effect presupposes that

$$|\varepsilon_{HH_s}| < (\beta_1 - \beta_2)/\beta_2. \tag{5.11}$$

Then, although labor utilization rises as a result of a cut in standard hours, employment may also improve, but only if the additional usage of less efficient overtime hours is insufficient to compensate for the production loss due to shorter standard hours.

The established theory of the demand for hours then yields a negative relationship between standard and optimal hours for firms operating in the overtime regime. However, the result appears to be crucially dependent on the form of the overtime pay premium, the constant premium excluding any changes in the marginal cost of hours as a result of shorter standard hours. To give further insight into the importance of the wage cost function even for qualitative inferences, we will finally examine the implications of perhaps a more realistic wage cost function with a variable overtime pay premium.

We take the view that an overtime pay premium that is proportional to the ratio of total to standard hours is a reasonable approximation to the institutional, stepwise rising premium system, aggregated over time and over employees. Hence, we postulate a premium function[7]

$$z = \rho\,\frac{H}{H_s} \qquad \rho > 1, \tag{5.12}$$

which combined with a Cobb–Douglas production function (either homogeneous or non-homogeneous normal and overtime hours) yields a positive relation between standard and optimal hours, or

$$\frac{\partial H}{\partial H_s} > 0. \tag{5.13}$$

The outcome is now due to the fact that shortening standard hours implies a rise in the marginal cost of labor utilization too, and, furthermore, the rise is higher than that of the marginal cost of an additional employee.[8]

For a demand-constrained firm with homogeneous hours, the employment effect of shortening standard hours is then necessarily positive, while in the case of non-homogeneous hours the corresponding condition is given by

$$\varepsilon_{HH_s} > -\frac{(\beta_1 - \beta_2)}{\beta_2}. \tag{5.14}$$

Since the elasticity $\varepsilon_{HH_s}$ is now positive from equation(5.13), in our case of less productive overtime hours ($\beta_1 > \beta_2$) the cut in standard hours unambiguously favors employment at the expense of labor utilization.

Obviously, these kinds of conclusions are based on *ceteris paribus* responses of a simple partial model and hence they are not directly applicable to policy debate. The final outcome also depends on scale and capital substitution effects as well as any repercussions induced. Since average hours are output invariant, however, these additional aspects tend to be more relevant in the determination of employment than in that of optimal utilization.

## 5.4 Development of the Dynamic Model of the Firm

The remaining sections are devoted to aspects of the cyclical adjustment of hours and employment. In particular, the effects of the non-homogeneity of standard and overtime hours are to be uncovered. For this purpose, the basic model of the firm with a usual Cobb–Douglas technology is developed in this section, while the next section centers upon the differences that are caused by the alternative specification of the production function.

To focus on the economic and technical substitutionability of the two dimensions of the labor input, we will examine the case of a demand-constrained firm that meets the perfectly foreseen output demand totally and chooses the optimal composition of labor services to produce the goods to be sold.

The following notation is adopted in the model:

| | |
|---|---|
| $p$ | is the unit price of output |
| $X(t)$ | is the output demand at time $t$ |
| $A(t)$ | is the rate of recruitment at time $t$ |
| $D(t)$ | is the rate of firing at time $t$ |
| $n$ | is the quasi-fixed non-wage cost per employee |
| $N(t)$ | is the number of employees at time $t$ |
| $H(t)$ | is the average productive hours of work per employee at time $t$ |
| $a$ | is the unit recruitment cost |
| $d$ | is the unit firing cost |
| $\delta$ | is the natural rate of decrease of employment due to voluntary departures and |
| $r$ | is the rate of discount. |

To simplify the analysis, $p$, $n$, $a$, $d$, $\delta$ and $r$ will be assumed positive and constant over time. To study how the various policies are linked during a business cycle, we need some tractable assumptions regarding the expected demand and the production and cost functions.[9]

As discussed previously, in the basic model we specify a Cobb–Douglas production function

$$Q = H^\beta N^\alpha \quad \tfrac{1}{2} < \beta < \alpha < 1. \tag{5.15}$$

The variable labor costs $V(H)$ include three elements: standard wages, overtime wages and variable non-wages. We will describe the variable labor costs per employee with a piecewise smooth function $V(H)$,

$$V(H) = \begin{cases} wH_s & H \leqslant H_s \\ wH & H > H_s \end{cases} \tag{5.16}$$

where $H_s$ denotes the standard number of hours.

It should be particularly noted that we have assumed that, below standard hours, even the variable labor cost per employee is fixed. This formulation is of critical importance for the labor-hoarding outcome (defined as the discrepancy between paid and productive working hours) to arise.[10] In this basic model, we neglect the overtime pay premium system, too, although its implications for policy characteristics could be easily shown.

Finally, as in most of the related studies (see Nickell, 1974; Leban and Lesourne, 1980, 1983; and Leban, 1982), we also assume that a recession at rate $\mu - \gamma$ between time points $t_0$ and $t_1$ perturbs the upward trend of an exponential growth at rate $\gamma$, or

$$X(t) = \begin{cases} X_0\, e^{\gamma t} & t \in (0, t_0) \\ X_0\, e^{\gamma t_0}\, e^{-(\mu - \gamma)(t - t_0)} & t \in (t_0, t_1) \\ X_0\, e^{\gamma t - \mu(t_1 - t_0)} & t \in (t_1, \infty) \\ \gamma > 0, \mu - \gamma > 0 \text{ and } \gamma < r\alpha.[11] \end{cases} \tag{5.17}$$

A simple demand cycle with constant rates of change in demand both in expansion and in recession, separately, is illustrated in Figure 5.1.

Our analysis is then explicitly concerned with the optimal adjustment to a single recession. Later on, however, we will deal with the validity of our results in a strictly cyclical set-up, i.e. if recession phases repeatedly perturb the upward trend of output demand.

Assuming the firm wants to maximize the net present value discounted at rate $r$ over an infinite time horizon, the optimal control problem of the firm may be set as follows:

$$\max \int_0^\infty \{pX(t) - aA - dD - nN - V(H)N\}\, e^{-rt}\, dt \tag{5.18}$$

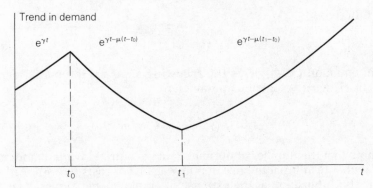

**Figure 5.1** Illustration of a demand cycle

subject to

$$\dot{N} = A - D - \delta N \tag{5.19}$$

$$N^\alpha H^\beta - X(t) = 0 \quad \tfrac{1}{2} < \beta < \alpha < 1 \tag{5.20}$$

$$A \geqslant 0 \tag{5.21}$$

$$D \geqslant 0 \tag{5.22}$$

$$H \geqslant 0 \tag{5.23}$$

with $N(0)$ given and $V(H)$ and $X(t)$ defined in equations (5.16) and (5.17) respectively.

Next, we shall directly characterize the strategies that may be optimal over the business cycle thus skipping over the details of the mathematical analysis.[12] We shall first describe the elementary policies and then indicate the feasible ways in which the policies may be linked with each other.

## 5.4(a) Elementary Policies

For this model, we are left with three feasible policies: the recruitment policy, the firing policy and the hours adjustment policy (numbered V, VI and VII, respectively, in Santamäki, 1986).

RECRUITMENT POLICY (V):

In this mode, the number of productive hours is constant, or

$$H_V = H_a = \frac{\beta[(r + \delta)a + n]}{(\alpha - \beta)w} > H_s \quad \text{if} \tag{5.24}$$

$$\frac{(r + \delta)a + n + wH_s}{wH_s} > \frac{\alpha}{\beta} \tag{5.25}$$

and otherwise

$$H_V = H_s. \tag{5.26}$$

Then, equation (5.24) yields the following signs for the partial derivatives of $H_a$ w.r.t. exogenous parameters:

$$H_a = H_a(\overset{+}{r}, \overset{+}{\delta}, \overset{+}{a}, \overset{+}{n}, \overset{-}{\alpha}, \overset{+}{\beta}, \overset{-}{w}). \tag{5.27}$$

We note that the number of optimal hours is output invariant and, also, the familiar result that the rise in non-wage labor costs $[(r+\delta)a + n]$ will favor labor utilization at the expense of employment. In particular, the higher the rate of voluntary quits ($\delta$), the higher the level of hours at which hiring occurs. This is owing to the fact that the average employment tenure of a worker decreases and hence the proportion of hiring cost to be recovered at each moment of time rises.

We also note the indirect way in which standard hours now affect optimal decisions; e.g. a reduction in standard hours only extends the range of parameter values in which $H_a$ is optimal. This conclusion is due to our simple specification of the labor cost function $V(H)$, adopted for convenience only. The number of employees is then demand determined and, therefore, the stock of workers increases in expansion and decreases in recession. Since, by definition, the rate of recruitment is positive in this mode, the feasibility of this policy in recession requires that $\delta > (\mu - \gamma)/\alpha$, or the decrease in employment owing to voluntary departures to be stronger than that required by the fall in production activity.

FIRING POLICY (VI):

The firm may resort to dismissals only if the interest and amortization of the firing cost are not higher than the sum of standard wages and the quasi-fixed non-wage labor cost, or if

$$(r+\delta)d \leqslant n + wH_s. \tag{5.28}$$

Then the number of average hours is again constant, or

$$H_{VI} = H_d = \frac{\beta[-(r+\delta)d + n]}{(\alpha - \beta)w} > H_s \quad \text{if} \tag{5.29}$$

$$\frac{-(r+\delta)d + n + wH_s}{wH_s} > \frac{\alpha}{\beta} \quad \text{and} \tag{5.30}$$

$$H_{VI} = H_s \text{ otherwise.}[13] \tag{5.31}$$

From equation (5.29) we get the following signs for the partial derivatives of $H_d$ w.r.t. exogenous parameters:

$$H_d = H_d(\bar{r}, \bar{\delta}, \bar{d}, \overset{+}{n}, \alpha, \bar{\beta}, \bar{w}). \tag{5.32}$$

We note, in particular, that the rise in the rate of voluntary quits ($\delta$) or in the firing cost ($d$) now lowers the level of productive hours at which firing occurs.

For the policy to be feasible, the rate of firing must be positive, which presupposes that $(\mu - \gamma)/\alpha > \delta$. Then the recession rate $\mu - \gamma$ must be great enough for the natural turnover to be insufficient in reducing the stock of workers, while in expansion the firing policy cannot be feasible.

HOURS ADJUSTMENT POLICY (VII):

The stock of employees decreases at rate of natural turnover, $\dot{N} = -\delta N$, and the adjustment in labor input is accomplished through changes in labor utilization. Equating the rates of change in production and output demand, we obtain an explicit solution for the rate of change in productive hours:

$$\frac{\dot{H}}{H} = \frac{\gamma - \mu + \alpha \delta}{\beta} \quad t \in (t_0, t_1). \tag{5.33}$$

Obviously, productive hours always increase in expansion ($\mu = 0$), while in recession the course of hours depends on the rate of decrease in output demand. In particular, for slight recession rates or if $u = \mu - \gamma < \alpha \delta$, working hours increase even in a cyclical downturn.

We also note that the number of optimal hours may be fewer than standard hours, i.e. the labour-hoarding outcome is possible in this mode.

### 5.4(b) Feasible policy sequences or strategies

The admissibility of policy sequences depends on the values of structural parameters. In this paper, we shall restrict to the case of interior solutions in both the recruitment and firing modes, or $H_v = H_a > H_s$ and $H_{vi} = H_d > H_s$.

The alternative strategies or policy sequences are then as follows:

(a) $(\mu - \gamma)/\alpha < \delta$      a.1   V

(b) $(\mu - \gamma)/\alpha > \delta$      $\begin{cases} \text{b.1} & \text{V–VII–V} \\ \text{b.2} & \text{V–VII–VI–VII–V} \end{cases}$

(c) $(\mu - \gamma)/\alpha = \delta$      c.1   V–VII–V

In Case b we have two main strategies, which may be further divided into subcases depending on whether or not average hours fall below standard hours in the hours adjustment mode VII. The strategies b.1

and b.2 may be divided into the following subcases:

b.11  V–VII–V, $H_V = H_a$ and min $H_{VII} > H_s$
b.12  V–VII–V, $H_V = H_a$ and min $H_{VII} \leqslant H_s$
b.21  V–VII–VI–VII–V, $H_V = H_a$, $H_{VI} = H_d$, min $H_{VII} > H_s$
b.22  V–VII–VI–VII–V, $H_V = H_a$, $H_{VI} = H_d$, min $H_{VII} \leqslant H_s$.

Hence, even in this simple model we are left with six qualitatively different strategies that are optimal for different subsets of structural parameters.

To analyze the model completely, we should characterize the alternative strategies, compute the policy switch times for each case and determine the optimality criteria in terms of parameters describing the firm and its operational environment. Keeping in mind the purpose for which we make use of our model, we choose to proceed in a more limited way. We shall illustrate two strategies: the hours adjustment strategy (b.11) and the mixed firing–hoarding strategy (b.22).

CHARACTERIZATION OF THE HOURS ADJUSTMENT STRATEGY b.11: V–VII–V

We denote by $e_1'$ and $e_1$ the dates at which recruitment ends and resumes, respectively. In this strategy, recruitment stops before the top of the demand cycle and does not resume until the next upswing; the total time during which recruitment is blocked is given by

$$E_1 = e_1 - e_1' = \frac{\mu}{\gamma + \alpha\delta}\,(t_1 - t_0). \tag{5.34}$$

In addition, the hours adjustment phase (VII) is approximately symmetrically distributed around the recession.

It is a striking aspect of the result that the length or the timing of the period during which recruitment is blocked is independent of any cost variables. This also implies that in this model there is no relationship between the degree of labor fixity and the lead time at the turning points of hours per worker as compared to corresponding employment. It is the turning point of employment that leads the turning point of hours per worker in expansion when the firm faces an expected demand decline, while the opposite order holds in face of the next cyclical upturn. The significance of the hours–workers distinction is also apparent in the different timing of the changes in these two dimensions of the labor input.

Obviously, our model yields the common predictions regarding both the average levels as well as the amplitudes of absolute variations in hours and employment: first, the greater the degree of labor fixity, the lower is the average level of employment and the more intense is the labor utilization; second, employment variations accompanying demand changes will be smaller and hours variations higher the greater the degree of labor fixity.

CHARACTERIZATION OF THE MIXED FIRING–HOARDING STRATEGY b.22:
V–VII–VI–VII–V

This strategy represents the most diversified, and perhaps the most interesting, policy sequence. The firm resorts to firing in recession with $H_{VI} = H_d > H_s$, while around the trough of the cycle productive hours are below standard hours or the firm hoards labor.

The rates of change in output demand, employment and working hours during the various policies in strategy b.22 are briefly illustrated in Figure 5.2.

For this sequence, there are six dates during a demand cycle at which policies change:

- $e_1$ and $e'_1$, the dates at which recruitment begins and ends
- $e_2$ and $e'_2$, the dates at which firing begins and ends, and finally
- $s_0$ and $s_1$, the dates at which labor hoarding begins and ends.

In this strategy,

- the recruitment always stops before the top of the cycle and does not resume until the next upswing,
- the dismissal of workers takes place in recession, and
- the labor-hoarding phase is unsymmetrically placed around the trough of the cycle, the proportion $(\gamma + \alpha\delta)/\mu$ of the total length appearing in the downswing.

Figure 5.3 gives an alternative way to characterize the strategy by sketching the time paths of the control and state variables. The vertical axis shows log(base $e$)-values of the variables so that piecewise linear curves describe the time paths with constant, but discretely varying, rates of change.

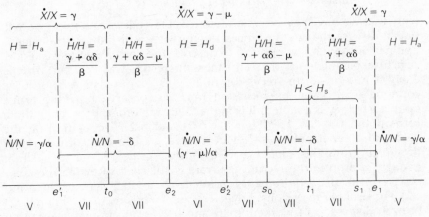

**Figure 5.2** Illustration of strategy b.22

101

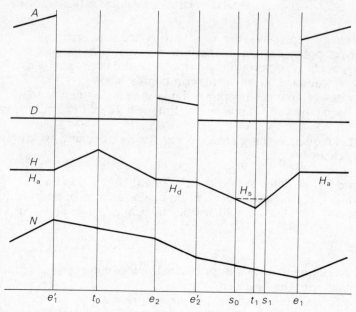

**Figure 5.3** Time paths of the control and state variables in strategy b.22

Figure 5.3 clearly shows the different time patterns in the adjustment of hours and employment. It is employment that always starts to decline in late expansion and only begins to improve in the next upswing, whereas the turning points in hours per worker exactly coincide with those of the autonomous demand cycle.

## 5.4(c) Optimality of the various strategies

Now that we have characterized two feasible policy sequences, we will briefly discuss the circumstances in which each of the six strategies is optimal. Although it is possible to describe the outcome in terms of any structural parameter, perhaps the most interesting way is to perform the analysis in terms of the recession rate $\mu - \gamma$. Then, *ceteris paribus*, if we continually increase the recession rate and observe how the firm's optimal strategy is adapted, it is in the following order that each of them turns optimal: a.1, c.1, b.11, b.12, b.21 and b.22. Depending on the values of other parameters, however, b.12, b.21 or both of them may disappear from the sequence. Obviously, if the recession is slight enough, a drop in the recruitment rate is sufficient to match the labor services with the requirements dictated by product demand (a.1 and c.1). For stronger recessions, however, hours adjustment (b.11 and b.12) or even dismissals of workers (b.21 and b.22) turn optimal in bringing about the requisite decreases in labor input.

102

## 5.4(d)  *Validity of the results in a strictly cyclical set-up*

So far, we have assumed that, after the slump, the original upward trend in output demand is expected to continue forever. Now we ask how far in the future the next turning point of the cycle must be for our conclusions to hold even in the strictly cyclical set-up.

We have found that it is $t_0 - e_1'$ units of time in advance that the firm must be able to forecast the upper turning point of the cycle in order to be able to behave optimally. Furthermore, it takes $e_1 - t_1$ units of time in the next upswing to complete the adjustment. For example, if recession periods with identical characteristics repeatedly perturb the upward trend in output demand at rate $\gamma$, the duration of each expansion phase must be longer than

$$(e_1 - t_1) + (t_0 - e_1') = E_1 - (t_1 - t_0) \tag{3.35}$$

for the cures not to overlap. It turns out that this requirement is not too restrictive.[14]

## 5.5  Implications of the Non-Homogeneity on the Cyclical Adjustment of Labor Input

In this section, we seek to analyze the implications of the alternative production function $f(N, H, H_s)$ as specified in equation (5.1) for the cyclical adjustment of hours and employment.

In what follows, we indicate by bar the solutions for the endogenous variables in this model variant. It turns out that the solutions are obtained by simply replacing $\beta$ with $\beta_2$, where $\beta$ is the elasticity of output w.r.t. total hours in the usual production function, which does not allow the two basic components of total hours to be unravelled. Hence the effects may be traced by differentiating the solutions w.r.t. $\beta$ and noting that $\beta_2 < \beta$, if overtime hours are inherently less productive than standard hours, or if $\beta_1 > \beta_2$.[15]

For $\beta_2 < \beta$, we get the following conclusions concerning the different policy options:

*Recruitment policy:*
(1)  $\bar{H}_a < H_a$, or recruitment takes place at a lower level of hours.
(2)  The range of parameter values in which $\bar{H}_a$ (instead of $H_s$) is optimal becomes more limited.
(3)  The ratio of recruitment to employment, $\bar{A}/\bar{N}$, remains unchanged, but for any given level of output the number of workers is greater, and hence the number of newly hired workers rises, or $\bar{A} > A$.

*Firing Policy:*
(1)  $\bar{H}_d < H_d$, or firing takes place at a lower level of hours.
(2)  The range of parameter values in which $\bar{H}_d$ (instead of $H_s$) is optimal becomes more limited.

(3) The ratio of firing to employment, $\bar{D}/\bar{N}$, remains unchanged, but for any given level of output the number of workers is greater, and hence the number of dismissals rises, or $\bar{D} > D$.

*Hours adjustment policy:*
(1) The speed at which optimal hours increase in expansion and decrease in recession accelerates.

In general, the model results in a less steady pattern of employment, although the average level of employment appears to be higher.

Next, we go on to characterize the changes in the policy switching times in the cases of the two strategies previously described.

STRATEGY b.11: V–VII–V (NO LABOR HOARDING)

The length of time during which recruitment is blocked, $E_1 = e_1 - e'_1$ remains constant. The same is approximately true for the timing, too, although the more accurate result implies that the start of the hours adjustment policy is consequently slightly deferred.

STRATEGY b.22: V–VII–VI–VII–V (LABOR HOARDING INCLUDED)

The total time during which recruitment is blocked becomes shorter and hence recruitment ends later and begins earlier in the next upswing. The labor-hoarding phase commences sooner after the prolonged firing phase, although the duration of the labor-hoarding period turns out to be ambiguously affected by the change in parameter $\beta$.

The last results concern the optimality of the six optional strategies (see p. 99). We first note that the optimality criteria of strategies a.1 and c.1 remain unchanged: if the requisite decrease in labor input is less than or exactly equal to the reduction that is attributable to voluntary departures, then the cyclical adjustment is accomplished by varying the rate of recruitment only. Accordingly, strategy b.11 becomes optimal when the recession rate crosses the critical value of $\alpha\delta$, or $\mu - \gamma > \alpha\delta$. Furthermore, given that $H_{VI} = \bar{H}_d < H_d$, it is a slighter recession, *ceteris paribus*, that results in the optimal adoption of each of the strategies b.12, b.21 and b.22 in turn.

## 5.6 Conclusions

The point of departure for this paper is the notion that the marginal productivity of hours may differ as between standard and overtime hours. Therefore, we specify a short-run production function allowing the marginal product of total hours to depend on their distribution between the two components. The implications for the optimal choice of hours and employment are then analyzed in two different contexts.

First we ask how the optimal response to a reduction in standard hours is affected by the non-homogeneity of hours. In the traditional model with a constant overtime pay premium, a reduction in standard hours increases the marginal cost of an additional employee relative to additional utilization, more hours needing to be paid at premium rates. Thus, the effect of reducing the standard workweek is to increase equilibrium hours and to decrease employment. We have shown how this conventional result should be modified if an overtime pay premium proportional to the ratio of total to standard hours is introduced, or, alternatively, if standard and overtime hours are not homogeneous. The introduction of a variable overtime premium yields a positive relation between standard and average hours, which is in accordance with empirical evidence. The non-homogeneity of hours combined with a constant overtime pay premium, in turn, yields the conventional result of opposite changes in standard and average hours. Even in the latter case, however, employment may improve as a result of shorter standard hours, but only if the additional usage of less efficient overtime hours is not sufficient to compensate for the production loss incurred.

The other problem concerns cyclical aspects. We develop a dynamic model of a cost minimizing firm that faces a perfectly foreseen variation in output demand. The solutions obtained from the control theoretical model establish how the optimal strategy over the business cycle depends on the values of structural parameters characterizing the firm and its operational environment. Then the analysis makes it understandable why, e.g., a similar autonomous fluctuation of output demand may give rise to quite different responses among various firms. As to the hours productivity, in particular, we have considered the case in which a rise in the relative proportion of overtime hours diminishes the marginal product of total hours. In comparison with the case of homogeneous hours, this model produces more, although cyclically less stable employment. This outcome arises since the use of overtime working instead of additional employees becomes less advantageous. In the downturn, however, it becomes more plausible that the firm resorts to laying off workers.

## Notes

1  See, however, Hart & McGregor (1988) and Santamäki (1984).
2  Hart & McGregor (1987) transform overtime hours to standard hour equivalents by writing $\bar{H} = H_s + k(H - H_s)$, $\bar{H}$ being the argument in the Cobb–Douglas function, and $k$ being the coefficient which reflects the productivity of an overtime hour relative to a standard hour.
3  The same restriction also ensues from the traditional model of labor demand with a constant overtime pay premium. Also in Hart and McGregor (1987), the second-order condition requires that returns to workers exceed the returns to standard hour equivalents.
4  For findings of higher output elasticity of workers ($\varepsilon_H < \varepsilon_N$), however, see e.g. Åberg (1985).
5  See Hart and McGregor (1988) for indication that returns to overtime working are significantly lower than those for normal hours.

6  We assume that equilibrium occurs in the overtime region, which presupposes that

$$-\frac{F_H}{F_N}(n + wH_s) + \rho wN < 0.$$

7  The second-order parameter restriction is now $2\alpha > \beta$, which permits the possibility of $\beta > \alpha$, too.

8  Since the change in the marginal cost of labor utilization depends on the precise form of the premium function, it is obvious that without an appropriate specification the effects of changes in $H_s$ cannot be unambiguously signed. For realistic values of structural parameters, our conclusion (5.13) holds in the case of a linear premium function too; i.e. for $z = 1 + \rho(H - H_s), \rho > 0$.

9  For a more detailed presentation of the model, see Santamäki (1986).

10 In our model, labor hoarding represents planned excess capacity that arises from the cyclical fluctuation in output demand combined with the specified cost structure, and hence it is not due to any kind of uncertainty or any expected supply shortages in the labor market.

11 The sufficiency of the optimality conditions requires that the growth in employment is less than the rate of discount, which poses the parameter restriction $\gamma/\alpha < r$, or $\gamma < r\alpha$

12 For details, see Santamäki (1986), Chs 2 and 3.

13 More precisely, in the particular case of $(r + \delta)d = wH_s + n, H_{V1} \in (0, H_s)$

14 For instance, let us consider the case in which strategy b.11 is optimal and assume the following values for the structural parameters needed in applying equation (5.34): the output elasticity w.r.t. workers $\alpha = 0.72$, the rate of voluntary departures $\delta = 0.05$, the expansion rate $\gamma = 5\%$ p.a., the recession rate $\mu - \gamma = 6\%$ p.a. and the length of the recession phase $t_1 - t_0 = 2$ years. Then each expansion phase must last about 0.8 years or 10 months for our analysis to remain valid.

15 The comparison is then made between two cases with equal production contribution of total hours $H$. For $H^\beta$ to be equal to $H_s^{\beta_1} \cdot H^{\beta_1}$, where $\beta_1 > \beta_2$, we must have $\beta_2 < \beta$.

# COMMENT

## DAVID N. F. BELL

I would like to focus on three issues raised by Tuire Santamäki's paper. The first concerns the specification of the production function and the overtime premium. The second relates to the modeling of labor services in a dynamic context. The final section suggests an alternative to the Santamäki dynamic formulation that is more consonant with the main stylized facts relating to UK overtime working.

### The Labor Services Function

Equation (5.1) in her paper gives the labor services function favored by Santamäki to model the effects of a cut in standard hours. Ignoring employment, this function can be written

$$L = H_s^{\beta_1} \left( \frac{H_s + H_0}{H_s} \right)^{\beta_2} \tag{1}$$

where $H_0 = H - H_s$ is overtime hours. The level sets of this function satisfy the relation

$$\frac{dH_0}{dH_s} = - \frac{[\beta_1(H_0 + H_s) - \beta_2 H_0]}{\beta_2 H_s}.$$

From this result it is clear that the specification is consistent with zero overtime hours. The marginal rate of substitution (MRS) between standard and overtime hours approaches $\beta_1/\beta_2$ as overtime hours fall toward zero. Thus overtime hours will be used only if

$$\rho \leqslant \frac{\beta_2}{\beta_1},$$

where $\rho$ is the overtime premium. It is a stylized fact that the premium is greater than unity, implying that this labor services specification is consistent with the use of overtime only if $\beta_2 > \beta_1$. This contrasts with Santamäki's argument concerning relative returns to total and overtime hours in that she maintains that there is no restriction on the relative size of $\beta_1$ and $\beta_2$ in her labor services function. Part of the confusion may arise because $\beta_1$ and $\beta_2$ cannot be directly interpreted as 'returns' to total and overtime hours respectively because total hours are a mixture of both standard and overtime hours. It is clear when the function is rewritten as in (1) above that returns to both categories of hours are dependent on both $\beta_1$ and $\beta_2$.

In contrast, the MRS approaches infinity as standard hours approach zero. Thus the labor services function has the desirable property that

107

standard hours will not be reduced to zero. It also collapses to a simple formulation when $\beta_1 = \beta_2$ and, following the argument above, employers would make use of overtime hours only if the overtime premium was unity.

Note further that the homotheticity of this functon (it is homogeneous of degree $\beta_1$) implies that the decision to make use of any overtime hours depends only on the ratio of $\beta_1$ to $\beta_2$ and not on the amount of standard hours already being worked. If a non-homothetic function is utilized, this property will no longer hold. Take, for example, a simple alternative formulation to (1)

$$L = H_s^{\beta_1}(1 + H_0)^{\beta_2} \tag{2}$$

where along any labor services contour

$$\frac{dH_0}{dH_s} = -\frac{\beta_1 H_0}{\beta_2 H_s}.$$

This implies that, the greater the number of standard hours already being used, the lower is the overtime premium necessary to induce overtime working. This point should be apparent from Figure 1, which plots labor services contours for this function and for that suggested by Santamäki along with the 'expansion path' for both functions for a given fixed overtime premium. With the Santamäki formulation, a rise in the demand for labor services will elicit increased demand for standard and overtime hours of similar proportions, while under the alternative suggested here expansion will be accommodated mostly through additional overtime working. These conclusions are, of course, conditional on a simpler cost function of the form $c = wH_s + w\rho H_0$ than the piecewise linear formulation used by Santamäki where, of course, fixed employment costs are also included. Nevertheless, the argument presented here illustrates some of the particular properties of the Santamäki function and shows that alternatives with similar, but not identical, properties exist.

The variable overtime premium where overtime working becomes increasingly expensive as more of it is used adds further complication to the analysis. Under this scheme the costs of hours can be written

$$C = wH_s + wzH_0 = wH_s + w\rho\left(1 + \frac{H_0}{H_s}\right)H_s,$$

which implies that the isocost lines are quadratic and convex to the origin as would be the case with a piecewise linear cost function that took account of rising overtime premia and may account for the change in sign that Santamäki observes in the predicted relationship between standard and total hours.

While the ability of these theoretical models to generate predictions of relationships between standard and overtime hours is of some interest,

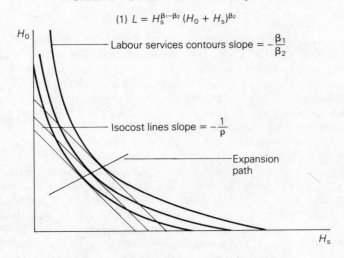

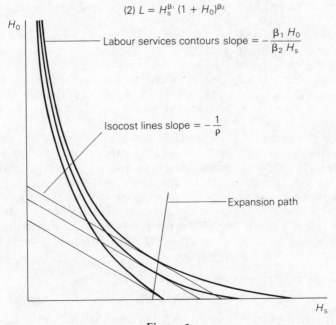

**Figure 1**

it is clear from the preceding discussion that there may be a number of alternative formulations with properties that correspond to the stylized facts concerning hours of work. The next investigative stage should be to try to discriminate between such alternative formulations by attempting to fit them in an econometric framework.

## Dynamic Models

The dynamic model presented in Section 5.4 of the paper is a development of Nickell's work on dynamic labor demand. The firm, rather than optimizing over points in workers, standard hours and overtime hours space, instead develops policies that control recruitment, firing and labor utilization. The Nickell model uses fixed coefficients and an earnings function that is horizontal and then upward sloping to prevent firms cutting hours dramatically to induce quits. It then seeks to maximize the net present value of the firm subject to the constraints that demand must always be met and that the stock of employees depends on recruitment, firing and quit rates. Leban and Lesourne extend the Nickell model to allow for flexible technology and prices. Santamäki has flexible technology and also an earnings function that distinguishes between standard and overtime hours. Her results concur with the conventional wisdom derived from the simpler static model. Greater voluntary quits induce higher levels of hours since hiring costs have to be written down more quickly. With no recruitment or firing policy, hours are adjusted to fluctuations in demand and labor hoarding may occur, etc.

Santamäki has varied the standard model through her introduction of non-wage employment costs more explicitly. Barron, Lowenstein and Black (1984) explore a variation of the same type of model by having a 'sink' into which layoffs can be deposited and subsequently recalled. This is used to explain the high incidence of layoffs in the US, though no attempt is made to show how the model can explain the much lower use of layoffs in Europe.

The emphasis in all these models is on the dynamics of the labor market. The results are not generally at variance with those from similar static models. A common feature is the perfect foresight with which employers are credited. There are no 'surprises'. This is perhaps an area that might be explored more extensively as an alternative to dynamic models. Once factor supplies and product demand become uncertain, firms' strategies seem likely to turn more towards utilization of the workers they know as being unlikely to shirk and away from policies based on the external labor market.

## A Variation on the Santamäki Model

One of the stylized facts concerning overtime working in the UK is that the major source in the variation of aggregate hours worked is not changes in the number of overtime hours worked by individuals but rather changes in the proportion of employees working overtime. The decision to offer additional overtime working appears then to be essentially binary rather than being continuous over the range of overtime hours. This is consonant with firms responding to higher demand by using an additional shift. In the aggregate, if many firms introduce additional shifts, there will be an increase in the number of

110

workers reported as working overtime, without necessarily any increase in the average number of overtime hours per worker doing overtime.

One might think of firms facing a static cost function of the form

$$C = nN + wH_sN + \rho wH_0k(\rho)N$$

as an alternative formulation to Santamäki's equation (5.4) (using the same notation) where $H_0$ and $H_s$ are exogenously given (by the technical requirements of shift working, say) and the employers' choice variables are $N$ and $k$ where $k$ is the proportion of workers working overtime. One might also bring in supply considerations by allowing $\rho$ to be itself a positive function of $k$ in order to incorporate the notion that higher premiums may have to be offered to induce supply of overtime hours from the marginal worker.

In a dynamic context this will reduce to a problem very similar to that outlined by Barron *et al.* if the overall size of the workforce remains fixed. The trick would be to treat workers not assigned to overtime working in a similar fashion to layoffs and find the optimizing strategy for assigning overtime instead of the optimal layoff strategy.

Santamäki's paper shows how one can specify static and dynamic models that give a greater wealth of realism in their treatment of working time. As a first step in checking whether the theory corresponds with the stylized facts, this is very useful. Clearly there are alternative specifications that could also generate some of these broad generalizations. It is always worth bearing in mind that stylized facts are not necessarily consistent across countries and that more powerful specifications are likely to be able to accommodate such differences. Finally, it is only when subjected to empirical testing that any definitive discrimination between alternative specifications is possible.

111

# CHAPTER 6

# A Dynamic Model
# of Labor Utilization

## HEINZ KÖNIG AND WINFRIED POHLMEIER

## 6.1 Introduction

Constraints on demand management policies owing to already high
government budget deficits or because of doubts about their effectiveness have led economists and policymakers to focus attention on
specific labor market policies for stimulating employment. Besides early
retirement schemes, reductions in weekly working hours and legal
restrictions on overtime work, taxation of overtime premiums and
general or marginal wage costs subsidies have been proposed for job
creation. In West Germany, for instance, labor unions argue that a
reduction of standard working hours and of overtime work would result
in a substantial improvement in employment. In fact, simulation studies
by the Ifo-Institute (1983) suggest that a reduction of two hours per
working week without corresponding wage compensation could induce
an increase in employment of about 370,000–510,000 jobs. In the political
discussion, similar arguments are debated concerning overtime work,
which amounted to 70 hours per year on average for every employee in
1985.

There are various approaches to model variations in labor utilization
and employment. Adjustment costs (for instance, Oi, 1962; Baily, 1977),
uncertain demand (Baily, 1974) as well as the existence of implicit
contracts (Azariadis, 1975, 1981) are used to demonstrate that, in
response to price falls of increasing severity, firms will first reduce hours
of work and only later start on layoffs. Analogously it may be argued
that non-inventory-carrying firms will react to positive shifts in demand
by a higher degree of utilization of labor, i.e. with overtime work, and, if
the demand shift is considered to be permanent, will increase the labor
stock.

In this paper we disregard such sophisticated approaches like the
existence of implicit contracts and assume a (neo-classical) cost-
minimizing firm facing four types of labor costs: (i) the standard wage
rate, i.e. the negotiated wage rate including a firm-specific premium for
normal working hours; (ii) the overtime working hours wage rate; (iii)
adjustment costs for hiring and firing; and (iv) non-wage labor costs

independent of the rate of labor utilization. In a control-theoretic approach we will discuss the comparative statics with respect to these variables as well as the effects of different wage costs subsidies schemes including taxation of overtime work. We will also present the dynamic features of the model. Finally, we will turn to the problem of the employment-hours decision when firms are uncertain with respect to the time of occurrence of a reduction in standard working hours per week.

## 6.2  A Dynamic Model of Employment–Hours Decisions

Since the seminal work of Feldstein (1967) and Rosen (1968) the importance of treating hours worked and persons employed separately as factor inputs has in general been recognized, although macro-econometric studies on the employment function still regard both dimensions of labor utilization to be equivalent. In a neoclassical framework, Hart (1984a,b) has extended this approach to model the effects of non-wage labor costs for the static case.

In the following we proceed in the spirit of Ehrenberg's work (1971a) by using a labor services function to analyze the influences of changes in various categories of labor costs and wage costs subsidies, including taxation of overtime premiums, on the level of employment and the rate of labor utilization. We consider a model in which wage and non-wage parameters are taken as exogenously determined by the firm, which chooses an optimal cost-minimizing path for the mix of overtime hours per worker and the number of employees to achieve the level of labor services over the whole planning period. Some deficiencies of this approach may be stressed:

(i)   The assumption of homogeneity of labor as well as independence of marginal contributions to labor services of an hour of one employee to the hours of another may be questioned.
(ii)  The neglect of other input factors, especially capital, and substitution effects induced by factor-price changes seriously restrict the policy implications of the model. However, apart from comparative static results, we have been unable to deal in a control-theoretic approach with more than two control variables in a way that offers an explicit analytic solution.
(iii) Although labor services functions are easily interpreted in a static (timeless) sense, they might lead to difficulties in a dynamic context owing to the stock-flow characteristics of persons employed and hours worked.

We therefore consider this function as a package of contracts offered to workers in the unit production period. This means that the firm optimizes labor input over the whole planning period, determining employment and effective working hours at each instant of time.

We assume a representative firm requiring a constant flow of labor

113

services over time according to a neoclassical production function:

$$L = L(N, h) \text{ with } L_N, L_h > 0 \quad L_{NN}, L_{hh} < 0 \quad L_{Nh} > 0, \tag{6.1}$$

where $L$ represents the amount of labor services, $h$ the average hours per worker and $N$ the number of workers. The factor 'employment' is assumed to be quasi-fixed, i.e. changes in the employment of workers are associated with positive costs of adjustment. These are purely hiring costs with no additional effect on production activities. For simplicity, the adjustment costs function is of the conventional quadratic form:

$$C(A) = \frac{a}{2} A^2 \quad a > 0, \tag{6.2}$$

where $A$ denotes the number of newly hired employees. Wage costs, $W$, consist of standard or negotiated wage payments and overtime wage costs:

$$W(h, N) = [\bar{w}\bar{h} + w(h - \bar{h})]N \quad h > \bar{h}, \tag{6.3}$$

where $\bar{h}$ is the fixed standard hours, $\bar{w}$ the standard wage rate, and $w$ the overtime wage rate, which is assumed to be independent of the size of overtime employment per worker. We neglect, therefore, the fact that overtime premiums may depend on the amount of overtime work, on specific firm or industry group arrangements and so forth.[1] Non-wage labor costs are assumed to be proportional to the employment level and, thus, independent of the rate of labor utilization. We ignore the complex structure of non-wage cost schemes caused by complicated non-linear social security schemes in various countries.[2]

The firm's decision problem is to minimize the present value of labor costs over an infinite horizon:

$$\min \int_0^\infty C(t)e^{-rt} \, dt, \tag{6.4}$$

where $r$ (the interest rate) is a discount factor, and where

$$C(t) = [\bar{w}\bar{h} + w(h - \bar{h})]N + bN + C(A) - S(N, A) \tag{6.5}$$

subject to

$$\dot{N} = A - qN \tag{6.6}$$

$$h = \phi(N, L) \quad \phi_N = -\frac{L_N}{L_h} < 0 \quad \phi_{NN} > 0, \tag{6.7}$$

where $q$ denotes the quit rate, $b$ the non-wage labor costs per worker, $\phi(\bullet)$ is the inverted labor services function and $S(\bullet)$ are the marginal

114

employment subsidies. Two types of marginal employment subsidy schemes are frequently discussed in the literature. Both are based on the general form $S = s \cdot B$, where $S$ indicates the amount of the subsidy, $B$ the subsidy base and $s$ the subsidy rate, which can be made time dependent with a decreasing rate over time. The type I subsidy scheme, proposed by Homlund (1981), takes changes in employment as a subsidy base:

$$S = s_I(A - kN) = s_I[\dot{N} + (q - k)N], \tag{6.8a}$$

where $k$ is the the threshold parameter. Equation (6.8a) includes two important special cases of subsidization. For $k = 0$ any newly employed worker is subsidized. Net increases in employment are subsidized if $k = q$. Since the subsidy scheme is symmetric, meaning that employment reductions are taxed, the latter subcase is nothing but a tax on increases in the average hours of work, $S = s_I \phi_{\bar{h}}^{-1} \dot{h}$. The type II subsidy scheme uses the difference between actual employment and some reference employment level $N_0$ (e.g. initial employment level) as the subsidy base:

$$S = s_{II}(N - N_0). \tag{6.8b}$$

Taking $\bar{N} = \phi^{-1}(\bar{h})$ instead of $N_0$, the type II subsidy scheme can be regarded as a tax on overtime hours with vanishing taxes if effective hours equal standard work hours. As Chiarella and Steinherr (1982) have shown, both schemes are technically equivalent for $k = 0$ so that we disregard an explicit derivation of the comparative static results with respect to the type II subsidy scheme.

By the elimination of $h$ through (6.7), the optimization problem reduces to a simple control problem with the level of employment as state variable and hirings as control variable, while the optimal path of average hours is determined by the optimal path of $N$ via (6.7). For the following analysis we assume only the region with positive overtime to be relevant. Furthermore, we posit for the elasticity of the marginal rate of substitution between hours and employment:

$$\eta(\phi_N, N) = \frac{\phi_{NN}N}{\phi_N} < -2. \tag{6.9a}$$

Condition (6.9a) is nothing but the second-order necessary condition for cost minimization in the static case. For a labor services function of the Cobb–Douglas form $L = \alpha_0 N^\alpha h^\beta$, the inequality reduces to $\alpha > \beta$. If the labor services function is linear homogeneous in $N$ and $h$, the inequality becomes:

$$\frac{1}{1 - \omega} > 2\sigma, \tag{6.9b}$$

where $\omega$ is the elasticity of labor services with respect to the number of

115

workers and $\sigma$ is the elasticity of substitution between hours and workers.

Although formulation (6.9b) is not so meaningful if one adopts the interpretation of the instantaneous labor services function as a relationship between labor services and contract conditions and employment level, it yields more insight into the shape of the isoquant required for a cost minimal path. For linear homogeneous labor services functions, inequality (6.9b) requires either high productivity of workers in terms of the elasticity of labor services with respect to the number of workers or a low substitutability between workers and hours.

With the inequality (6.9a) holding, $-C(\bullet)$ is jointly concave in the state and in the control variable. Since the state equation is linear in $A$ and $N$, the necessary conditions for optimality are also sufficient for $\lambda(t) \geqslant 0$.

Application of the maximum principle yields the following necessary conditions for the type I subsidy scheme:

$$\lambda = C_A - s_I = aA - s_I, \tag{6.10}$$

where $\lambda$ is the present value of the shadow price of employment. Equation (6.10) reveals that, along the optimal path, the type I subsidy scheme reduces the marginal adjustment costs and lowers the shadow price of employment. The time path of the shadow price is given by:

$$\dot{\lambda} = (r+q)\lambda + \bar{w}h + w(h - \bar{h}) + b + w\phi_N \cdot N + s_I k. \tag{6.11}$$

Solving the differential equation above leads to:

$$C_A - s_I = \int_t^\infty [\bar{w}h + w(h - \bar{h}) + b + w\phi_N N + s_I k] e^{-(r+q)(t'-t)} \, dt'. \tag{6.12}$$

At any instant of time the firm hires new workers until the net marginal hiring costs balance the discounted value of all costs arising from the employment of an additional worker. These employment costs consist of four parts: the wage costs per worker including the overtime wage payments per worker, the non-wage costs per worker, and the costs of reduction of the subsidy owing to a higher subsidy threshold. Employment costs are reduced by the term $w\phi_N \cdot N$, which gives the cost reduction owing to the reduction of overtime working.

The equilibrium solution is given by (6.11) for $\lambda = 0$:

$$(r+q)qaN + \bar{w}h + w(\phi - \bar{h}) + b + w\phi_N \cdot N + (k - r - q)s_I = 0, \tag{6.13}$$

where we used $C_A = aA = aqN$. Defining the LHS of (6.13) as $G(N, \nu)$, with $\nu$ as the vector of the parameters of the model, we get by the application of the implicit function rule:

$$\frac{\partial N}{\partial \nu_i} = -\frac{G\nu_i}{G_N} \quad \text{and} \quad \frac{\partial h}{\partial \nu_i} = \phi_N \frac{\partial N}{\partial \nu_i}, \tag{6.14}$$

where

$$G_N = (r + q)qa + w\phi_N(2 + \eta) > 0. \tag{6.15}$$

Instead of a detailed mathematical exposition, we present the effects of parameter changes on equilibrium employment and utilization in Figure 6.1. Most of the results reported in Figure 6.1 are intuitively appealing and have been derived by several other authors within a static framework (e.g. Hart, 1984a,b; Ehrenberg, 1971a). The reduction in standard hours leads to an increase in the marginal costs of employment relative to those of an additional hour and, therefore, not to an increase in employment but to an increase in overtime work. A higher quit rate induces an increase in working hours and a decrease in the number of employees. If we interpret the discount factor $r$ as an indicator of uncertainty (i.e. the higher $r$, the higher uncertainty), the results exhibit similar properties to investment models with uncertain demand expectations: a higher degree of uncertainty leads to a reduction of capacity (here: $N$) and higher utilization rates (here: $h$). The effect of the subsidy rate $s_I$ on equilibrium employment is undetermined. If $r + q > k$, the employment effect of an increase in the subsidy rate is positive, meaning that subsidization of gross employment increases as well as subsidization of net employment increases yields positive employment effects when the subsidy rate is raised. A higher subsidy threshold, as one would expect, discourages employment.

The functioning of the type II subsidy is somewhat different. Since it basically subsidizes the level of employment, the type II scheme does not lower adjustment costs but reduces employment costs. Introducing type II subsidization yields instead of equations (6.10)–(6.12):

$$\lambda = C_A = a \cdot A \tag{6.16}$$

$$\dot{\lambda} = (r + q)\lambda + \bar{w}\bar{h} + w(h - \bar{h}) + w\phi_N N + b - s_{II} \tag{6.17}$$

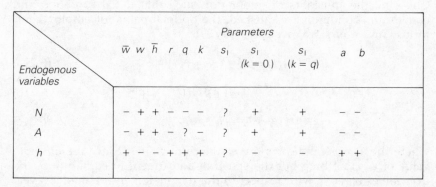

| Endogenous variables | $\bar{w}$ | $w$ | $\bar{h}$ | $r$ | $q$ | $k$ | $s_I$ $(k=0)$ | $s_I$ $(k=q)$ | $s_I$ | $a$ | $b$ |
|---|---|---|---|---|---|---|---|---|---|---|---|
| $N$ | − | + | + | − | − | − | ? | + | + | − | − |
| $A$ | − | + | + | − | ? | − | ? | + | + | − | − |
| $h$ | + | − | − | + | + | + | ? | − | − | + | + |

**Figure 6.1** Effects of parameter changes on equilibrium employment, hiring and utilization

$$C_A = \int_t^\infty [\bar{w}\bar{h} + w(h - \bar{h}) + b + w\phi_N N - s_{II}]e^{-(r+q)(t'-t)} \, dt'. \quad (6.18)$$

Equation (6.18) nicely shows that, in constrast to the type I scheme, type II subsidization lowers all future costs due to the employment of an additional worker. Since the reference employment level enters the cost function as a fixed component, it neither has an effect on the equilibrium values of $N$, $A$ and $h$ nor influences the adjustment path. Comparative statics at equilibrium under the type II scheme leads unambiguously to an increase in employment and a decrease of effective hours when $s_{II}$ is raised.

## 6.3  Dynamic Features of the Employment–Hours Decision

The optimal path of employment and hiring is given by equations (6.6) and (6.11) where we use $\lambda = a\dot{A}$:

$$\dot{N} = A - qN \quad (6.19a)$$

$$\dot{A} = (r+q)A + \frac{1}{a}[\bar{w}\bar{h} + w(\phi - \bar{h}) + b + w\phi_N N + (k - r - s)s_I]. \quad (6.19b)$$

Approximating the differential equation system above linearly around the equilibrium values of $A$ and $N$ and evaluating the roots of the characteristic equation associated with the linearized system yields:

$$\psi_{1/2} = \frac{r}{2} \pm \frac{1}{2}\sqrt{r^2 + 4\left[q(r+q) + \frac{w\phi_N}{a}(2+\eta)\right]}, \quad (6.20)$$

where all quantities are evaluated at equilibrium. Since the roots of the system are real and of opposite sign, equilibrium will be a saddlepoint. Choosing the constants of integration such that initial condition and equilibrium condition are satisfied, the optimal paths for employment, hirings and hours are given by:

$$N(t) = N^* + (N_0 - N^*)e^{\psi_2 t} \quad (6.21a)$$

$$A(t) = A^* + (\psi_2 + q)[N(t) - N^*]e^{\psi_2 t} \quad (6.21b)$$

$$h(t) = \phi[N^* + (N_0 - N^*)e^{\psi_2 t}], \quad (6.21c)$$

where the asterisk indicates the equilibrium values. Since the absolute value of $\psi_2$ is nothing but the speed of adjustment to equilibrium, the derivatives of $|\psi_2|$ with respect to the parameters of the model reveal information about the influence of parametric changes on the speed of the firm's optimal adjustment policy. For the parameters of major

118

interest we find:[3]

$$\frac{\partial |\psi_2|}{\partial \bar{w}} > 0 \quad \frac{\partial |\psi_2|}{\partial \bar{h}} < 0 \quad \frac{\partial |\psi_2|}{\partial w} \lessgtr 0 \quad \frac{\partial |\psi_2|}{\partial s_1}\bigg|_{k < r+q} < 0 \quad \frac{\partial |\psi_2|}{\partial k} > 0.$$

(6.22)

These results are somewhat surprising, at least in terms of labor union arrangements. Reduction of the standard workweek displays two negative effects: it reduces equilibrium and it increases the speed of adjustment to equilibrium because of the higher cost pressure faced by the firm. The same argument holds for an increase of the standard wage rate, which raises the firm's cost of disequilibrium and, thus, forces the firm to faster adjustment. The adjustment paths of two firms with the same initial level of underemployment and different arrangements of the standard workweek are depicted in Figure 6.2.

The effects of an increase in the overtime wage rate are ambiguous. Thus, an increase in the overtime premium may induce a higher employment level not necessarily combined with a slowdown in the speed of adjustment. The policy effects of an increase in the subsidy rate of the type I scheme are also ambiguous. If $k < r+q$ we find that an increase in the subsidy rate results in a slowing down of the adjustment process, whereas an increase in the threshold parameter $k$ increases adjustment forces. The same trade-off exists for the type II subsidy scheme. Taxation of overtime work will induce firms to adjust more slowly to the long-run equilibrium level of employment. The dynamic optimal path is shown in Figure 6.3, where the slopes of the $\dot{N} = 0$ line and the $\dot{A} = 0$ line are given by:

$$\frac{\partial A}{\partial N}\bigg|_{\dot{N}=0} = q \qquad \frac{\partial A}{\partial N}\bigg|_{\dot{A}=0} = -\frac{w\phi_N(2+\eta)}{a(r+q)} < 0.$$

(6.23)

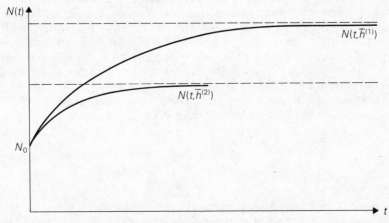

**Figure 6.2** Adjustment path of two firms with different standard working hours $(\bar{h}^{(1)} > \bar{h}^{(2)})$

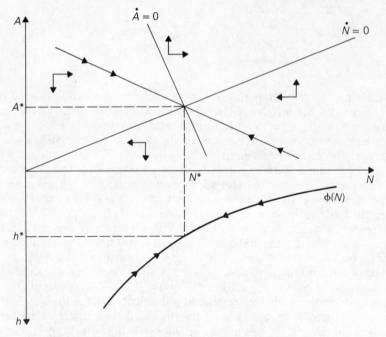

**Figure 6.3**  Optimal path of the firm

The model indicates that the optimal employment policy implies smoothing of demand for workers. If a firm's actual employment level is below its equilibrium value, the optimal adjustment policy suggests starting with a high number of acquisitions and reducing the number as the level of underemployment becomes smaller. If actual employment is above equilibrium, it is optimal for the firm to acquire only a few workers and to increase the number of acquisitions when the level of overemployment decreases. Condition (6.9) implies an additional smoothing effect at least for the Cobb–Douglas case, since the isoquant must show a strong curvature for the cost-minimal path to exist. If the convexity condition holds for the Cobb–Douglas case ($\alpha > \beta$), the hours adjustment path is always characterized by higher growth rates in absolute values than the employment path:

$$\frac{\dot{h}}{h} = \left(\frac{\phi_N \cdot N}{\phi}\right) \frac{\dot{N}}{N} = -\frac{\alpha}{\beta} \frac{\dot{N}}{N}. \tag{6.24}$$

The result is intuitively appealing. Since employment changes cause adjustment costs to rise, it is optimal for the firm to change hours more quickly than the employment level if it has to adjust factor inputs to a new equilibrium.

120

## 6.4 Optimal Employment–Hours Decision under Uncertainty

This section deals with a special type of uncertainty. Firms are assumed to have perfect knowledge about the size of the cut in standard working hours that unions are demanding (e.g. 35-hour workweek). But there exists uncertainty with respect to the timing of the cut, meaning that the firms do not know in which of the forthcoming bargaining rounds the cut will be introduced. In our model we posit that the representative firm can reduce the probability of the introduction of a cut in standard working hours through active employment policy.[4] We disregard the phenomenon of free-rider behavior of firms that profit from the employment policy of other firms without contributing to it. For the Federal Republic of Germany this is not such an unrealistic assumption, since German firms are well organized in employers' associations that are fairly subdivided by regional and industrial group criteria; this implies that free-rider behavior by a single firm is unlikely. For simplicity we ignore adjustment costs. The firm can instantaneously adjust its employment level to a parameter change.

The following approach corresponds to the line of limit pricing models where a seller is aware that his pricing policy affects the probability of entry of competing suppliers. Let $F(t)$ denote the probability that the cut in standard working hours has occurred at time $t$, with $F(0) = 0$. Then $f(t) = \dot{F}(t)$ is the density function of the random variable $t$. The probability of a cut in standard working hours at time $t$ under the condition that the cut has not yet taken place is given by:

$$\frac{f(t)}{1 - F(t)}. \tag{6.25}$$

We assume that the conditional probability of a cut in standard working hours is an increasing convex function of average working hours:

$$R(h) = \frac{f(t)}{1 - F(t)} \quad R' > 0, R'' > 0. \tag{6.26}$$

In addition, if

$$-C^{(2)} < \max_{N} - C^{(1)}(N) = \max_{N} - \{\bar{w}\bar{h}^{(1)} + w(\phi(N) - \bar{h}^{(1)}) + b\}N \tag{6.27}$$

holds, where $-C^{(1)}$ is assumed to be strictly concave in the employment level $N$, as in the preceding sections, and $\bar{h}^{(1)}$ are the standard working hours before the reduction, $\bar{h}^{(2)}$ is the new level of standard working hours after the reduction, and the constant $C^{(2)}$ denotes the expected minimum cost the firm can achieve at time $t$ after the reduction:

$$-C^{(2)} = \max_{N} - \{\bar{w}\bar{h}^{(2)} + w[\phi(N) - \bar{h}^{(2)}]\}N. \tag{6.28}$$

121

For a risk-neutral firm that minimizes the present value of costs from labor services over an infinite horizon, the optimal employment–hours decision may be described by:

$$\max_{N} \int_0^\infty -e^{-rt}\{C^{(1)}(N)[1 - F(t)] + C^{(2)} F(t)\}\, dt \tag{6.29}$$

subject to

$$\dot{F} = R(h)[1 - F(t)] \tag{6.30}$$

$$F(0) = 0 \tag{6.31}$$

$$h = \phi(N). \tag{6.32}$$

This is a straightforward control problem, with employment level $N$ as control variable and $F$ as state variable. The corresponding Hamiltonian to (6.29) is given by:

$$H = e^{-rt}\{- C^{(1)}(N)[1 - F(t)] - C^{(2)} F(t) + \lambda(t)[R(\phi(N))(1 - F(t))]\}. \tag{6.33}$$

Necessary conditions for optimality are:

$$\lambda = \frac{C_N^{(1)}}{R'\phi_N} \tag{6.34}$$

$$\dot{\lambda} = (r + R)\lambda + C^{(2)} - C^{(1)} \tag{6.35}$$

with the transversality condition

$$\lim_{t \to \infty} \lambda(t)e^{-rt} F(t) = 0. \tag{6.36}$$

Given the convexity assumption on $C^{(1)}(N)$ and inequality assumption (6.27), Kamien and Schwartz (1971) have shown for a problem of similar type that the optimal path of the control variable is time independent. Thus, a firm's optimal path for employment and hours in the pre-reduction period is:

$$N(t) = N^*, \quad h(t) = \phi(N^*) = h^*. \tag{6.37}$$

For a constant employment path, the solution of the flow equation (6.30) yields the probability path of working time reduction

$$F^*(t) = 1 - e^{-R(h^*)}. \tag{6.38}$$

Since a time-independent employment level implies $\dot{\lambda} = 0$, solving

122

(6.35) for $\lambda$ and equating it with (6.34) yields:

$$\frac{C^{(1)} - C^{(2)}}{r + R(h^*)} \, R'\phi_N = C_N^{(1)}. \qquad (6.39)$$

The RHS of (6.39) are the marginal employment costs at some time $t$ in the pre-reduction period, which are positive for $R' > 0$. This means that the threat of a reduction in standard working hours leads to an increase in employment in the pre-reduction period. In the pre-reduction period, firms create additional jobs and take into account higher costs for labor services in order to lengthen the pre-reduction period. The expected length of the pre-reduction period is given by

$$E^*(t) = \frac{1}{R(h^*)}. \qquad (6.40)$$

The firm that ignores its influence on the probability of the introduction of cuts in working hours (i.e. $R' = 0$) employs fewer workers and faces a shorter expected pre-reduction period than a firm that does not. It can be shown that $\lambda^*(t)$ reflects the marginal contribution of the state variable $F$ at time $t$ to the objective function. The higher the probability of cuts in standard working hours, at any time $t_0$, the higher the expected discounted value of costs from labor services will be.

Defining from (6.39) the implicit function:

$$F(N^*, \nu) = C_N^{(1)}(r + R) - (C^{(1)} - C^{(2)})R'\phi_N = 0, \qquad (6.41)$$

with $\nu$ the vector of parameters of the model and $N^*$ the optimal employment level in the pre-reduction period, we get, by the application of the implicit function rule:

$$\frac{\partial N^*}{\partial \nu} = -\frac{F\nu_i}{F_N}, \; \frac{\partial h^*}{\partial \nu_i} = \phi_N \frac{\partial N^*}{\partial \nu_i}, \; \frac{\partial E^*(t)}{\partial \nu_i} = -\frac{R'}{R^2} \phi_N \frac{\partial N^*}{\partial \nu_i}, \qquad (6.42)$$

where

$$F_N = C_{NN}^{(1)}(r + R) + C_N^{(1)}R'(1 - \phi_N) - (C^{(1)} - C^{(2)})(R'\phi_{NN} + R''\phi_N^2) > 0. \qquad (6.43)$$

The effects of parameter changes on employment and hours in the pre-reduction period as well as the effect on the expected length of this period are presented in Figure 6.4. In contrast to the deterministic model, a reduction of standard working hours has a positive temporary effect on employment, while the expected length of the pre-reduction period increases. The explanation of this phenomenon is simple. A factor that leads to an increase in labor costs causes a policy that tries to delay the occurrence of this factor. Since in our model the reduction of

| | Parameters | | | | |
|---|---|---|---|---|---|
| | $\overline{w}$ | $w$ | $\overline{h}^1$ | $\overline{h}^2$ | $b$ |
| $N^*$ | − | ? | + | − | − |
| $h^*$ | + | ? | − | + | + |
| $E^*(t)$ | − | ? | + | − | − |

Figure 6.4 Effects of parameter changes on employment and effective hours in the pre-reduction period and the expected length of the pre-reduction period

standard working hours causes higher costs of labor services, firms reduce their average hours and increase employment to lower the probability of the introduction of a cut in standard working hours.

## 6.5 Summary and Perspectives for Further Research

We shall dispense with the usual caveats about the limitations of this model. Some of them have been mentioned at the beginning and some more may be introduced by the discussant. Instead we shall summarize the main results and indicate some avenues for future research.

1  As far as reductions of weekly working hours as an instrument of active employment policy are concerned, we may state two ambiguous results. First, in a deterministic model with perfect foresight, such a policy may induce employment in the short run via a higher speed of adjustment but reduce − given wage costs − the equilibrium employment level in the long run. Second, where the firm is uncertain about the timing of the cut of weekly working hours, this policy might even raise the equilibrium level of employment in the pre-cut period.
2  Taxation of overtime work will induce firms to adjust more slowly to the long-run equilibrium level, but also induce firms to employ more workers at any point of time.
3  Marginal employment subsidies improve employment. An increase in the threshold stimulates the speed of adjustment, whereas an increase in the subsidy rate induces a reduction.
4  The existence of adjustment costs − as has been shown in other studies − results in an increase in effective working hours and a decrease in the level of employment.

It is unnecessary to stress the deficiencies of this approach. Further research should be directed to incorporating capital or other input factors relevant in the case of supply-side shocks, uncertainty of expectations with respect to future demand conditions, heterogeneous labor, and, last but not least, a more detailed story about firms' price-setting behavior and bargaining power with respect to wage contracts, especially overtime premiums and non-wage labor costs.

## Acknowledgements

We gratefully acknowledge financial support of this study by the Sonderforschungsbereich 5.

## Notes

1  For an endogenization of the overtime premium see, for example, König (1986).
2  See, for instance, Hart and Kawasaki (1987) for an empirical approach and Bell (1982) for an analysis of the employment–hours decision problem when there is a non-linear non-wage cost scheme.
3  For the derivation of (6.22) we assumed $3\phi_{NN} + \phi_{NNN} \cdot N < 0$, which holds e.g. for a labor services function of the Cobb–Douglas form and a labor services function of CES form, if the elasticity of substitution is less than or equal to unity.
4  In this way we try to model the behavior of German labor unions demanding weekly working hours reductions in case unemployment rates stay at a high level even in boom phases.

# COMMENT

## JOHN D. OWEN

The paper by König and Pohlmeier considers the effect on employment of labor market parameters. The latter include those contained in labor market subsidies designed to increase employment. Employment-determining parameters also include the wage rate paid for standard hours; the overtime premium; the 'adjustment cost' of hiring a new employee; non-wage labor costs that depend on employment but not on hours worked per employee; the quit rate; and the rate of discounting future costs. The authors are interested in the sign and magnitude of the effect on employment of a change in one of these parameters. They are also interested in the speed with which the new employment equilibrium is reached. In a later section of the paper they consider whether a cost-minimizing firm will introduce 'work sharing' if it anticipates that a reduction in worktime through union pressure is likely and if it believes that it can reduce the probability of a near-term, negotiated reduction in hours by voluntarily cutting hours and increasing employment.

The authors seek answers to these questions with the aid of a model that makes strong assumptions. For example, the various parameters change once in an initial period, then remain constant in all subsequent periods. Parameters do not change in an interactive way. For example, a reduction in the standard hours schedule does not produce any change in the hourly wage rate. Perhaps the strongest assumption, however, is that the demand of a firm for labor services is not only constant after the initial period but also constant within that period; i.e. it is not affected by any of the parametric changes considered. Further, the labor services obtained by the firm are assumed to be a function of the number of employees and the hours worked per employee. This labor services function is also assumed to be constant over time and to be invariant to any changes in the labor market parameters.

By these assumptions, once the level of employment in a period is known, the hours per employee are also given, by means of this simple labor services function.

In their model, the employer is assumed to have just one variable under his control: the number of new hires in each period. New hires, together with the stock of employees (given from the previous period) and the constant quit rate, determine the level of employment in that period, and hence the level of hours per worker.

These variables, together with the parameters of the model, determine the level of the employer's labor costs in each period. The firm has an infinite time horizon, which it discounts at a constant rate. Its task is to choose the number of new hires in each period so as to minimize the present value of these labor costs.

In this model, a change in the value of a parameter does not cause the employer to move immediately to the level of employment that will, in the long run, be appropriate. The cost of a new hire is assumed to increase with the square of new hires in a given period. This non-linearity provides an incentive for the employer to move gradually to a new equilibrium. The authors use optimal control theory to predict the path of employment to its new equilibrium level.

In their dynamic analysis, they confirm a number of results that have been found in static analyses. A more generous policy of stimulating employment will generally yield a larger increase in employment. A reduction in standard hours will reduce employment and increase hours per worker. A reduction in the quit rate will have the opposite effect.

They can also obtain other types of results from their model: they point out that changes in the value of parameters will influence the speed with which the employer moves to a new equilibrium as well as its level. For example, a lower level of the standard workweek increases the speed of adjustment. At the lower level of standard hours, wage costs are increased. This factor helps to offset the cost of rapid adjust-ment to a new equilibrium and so speeds that process. In their discussion of the effects of a likely union campaign to reduce hours, they demonstrate that this may make voluntary work sharing by the employer a minimum cost solution.

Overall, I found this paper to be an interesting and useful contribution to the discussion of labor market policy. In their closing remarks, however, the authors invite their discussant to critique their assump-tions. I now turn to that task.

In my view, the models presented here rest upon a restrictive set of assumptions. For this reason, while the results are of interest to economists, they may be of limited use to the policymaker.

Perhaps the most restrictive assumption is that labor services are constant over time and are invariant to changes in the model's param-eters. This means that trends in wages and other variables are not considered. It also eliminates uncertainty about future demand, and hence a major reason for the use of overtime hours rather than new hires. And, most important, it rules out negative changes in the demand for labor services that might result from lower standard hours, higher standard wages, or a higher overtime premium. This would appear to be in conflict with experience as well as with economic theory. For example, recent experience with reductions in standard working hours as an employment-generating device has been described as disappoint-ing – i.e. as not consistent with the assumption that a decline in hours is offset by a compensatory increase in employment, with total labor services demand remaining constant.

Finally, I also have some questions about the measurement of the cost of hiring a new employee in this model. It appears to be treated simply as a dollar cost and is not allowed to influence the labor services function, the relation between effective labor input and employment and hours. But surely much of the cost of hiring a new worker is his low productivity while he is learning his job, and the lower productivity of other, more experienced workers, who divert some of their own effort to his training. In this training period, more employees are required (at a given level of hours per worker) per unit of labor services provided. Hence, a constant labor services function assumption may underestimate employment growth in this transitional period.

# CHAPTER 7

# Employment and Hours in Equilibrium and Disequilibrium

## FELIX R. FITZROY

## 7.1 Introduction

More than a decade after pioneering studies by Feldstein (1967), Rosen (1968), Lucas (1970), Ehrenberg (1971a) and others had emphasized the distinction between hours and workers in production functions, the possibility of increasing employment by reducing working hours has beome a major political issue in several European countries. While union spokesmen see obvious employment benefits from 'redistributing work' and of course maintaining purchasing power through increased hourly wages, economists who have addressed the issue, such as Neumann (1984), Hoel (1986) or Hart (1987), emphasize cost or relative price effects that could reduce employment.

Most of the arguments, pro or contra, have been made in a static, partial equilibrium framework. However, actual changes in working time have usually been accompanied by growing productivity as a result of 'technical progress', which itself affects employment. Furthermore, increasing real wages have led to greater demand for leisure and repeated bitter conflicts between employers and their associations and organized labor, often on a nationwide scale, over reductions in the standard working week (Bienefeld, 1972). The historical changes in working time have generally been substantial and irregular, in marked contrast to the steady growth in real wages over most periods.

One problem with incorporating working time and unemployment into models of general equilibrium is that unemployment itself implies some deviation from the conditions of a perfectly competitive, Arrow–Debreu economy. In this paper we assume a given set of firms, and consider variation of employment by these firms under various conditions. Thus we are considering 'short-run' unemployment, without relying on entry of new firms, though we do also discuss some determinants of entry. In this framework we shall emphasize the contrasting results obtained by imposing some very elementary general equilibrium requirements.

In Section 7.2(a) we start with the simplest case where hours of work are exogenous for the firm, which chooses employment at a given wage. Employment is then a declining function of hours under a concavity assumption. If the wage is chosen so that maximum profit is zero, this result also holds but then technical progress *reduces* employment unless hours are reduced. Convexity, however, reverses these results! In Section 7.2(b) we consider the more realistic case of exogenous standard hours and endogenous overtime, and again obtain similar results.

As usual in partial models, the unrestricted demand for overtime or total (overtime plus standard) hours is a decreasing function of standard hours, and of the wage. Imposing the firm-equilibrium or zero-profit wage does not change this counterfactual result, but generates hours that decrease with the technical progress parameter.

In Section 7.2(c) we turn to the intensive margin and add a supply function for hours per worker. The general equilibrium specification closes the model and determines all variables as functions of technical progress and the premium wage ratio. Essentially the twin requirements of zero profits and intensive margin equilibrium use up the degrees of freedom, and standard hours are no longer an exogenous variable or policy instrument, but are rather determined as a declining function of technical progress.

The assumption of zero profits and homogeneous firms does not seem to be a good representation of at least the medium-run reality, which is relevant for current policy discussions of working time. Thus in Section 7.2(d) we turn to the equilibrium–disequilibrium combination of heterogeneous firms making positive profits with equilibrium at the intensive margin. Standard hours are now undetermined, total hours are, realistically, proportional to standard hours, and both employment and profits are strongly increasing functions of standard hours. Most significantly, the wage rate is a *decreasing* function of standard hours. This model thus reveals the distributional conflict involved in the working time decision, a conflict that is manifest in the historical record. The conflict also cuts across traditional boundaries however, because employment by existing firms is so sensitive to standard hours. Reducing unemployment *requires* a distribution of welfare from employed workers to the owners, and thus poses a fateful dilemma for organized labor.

In Section 7.2(e) related results are derived in a simple model of monopolistic equilibrium. Conclusions are drawn and the policy relevance of the various results is discussed in a final Section 7.3.

## 7.2  Models of Employment and Hours

### 7.2(a)  *Exogenous Hours*

The simplest approach to start with is to assume that hours, $h$, are essentially determined by centralized collective bargaining or legislation, as is at least approximately true in Europe, and that employers choose employment, $N$, to maximize profit. If $w$ is 'the' wage rate, then profit in real terms is

$$\pi = Q - whN - Z, \tag{7.1}$$

where $Q$ is output and $Z$ is a fixed cost. The production function is given by

$$Q = Q(h, N, t), \tag{7.2}$$

where $t$ represents a productivity or technical progress parameter, so $Q_t > 0$, where subscripts denote partials. Also we have $Q$ concave and increasing in $N$, increasing in $h$, and $Q = 0$ for $h$ or $N = 0$. The first-order condition gives

$$Q_N = wh, \tag{7.3}$$

and differentiating with respect to $h$ we have

$$\hat{N}_h = (w - Q_{Nh})/Q_{NN} < 0 \text{ if } Q_N \text{ is concave in } h, \tag{7.4}$$

where $\hat{N}(h, t, w)$ is demand for employment. By concavity and (7.3) we have $Q_{Nh} < Q_N/h = w$ so that (7.4) follows, and one has the partial equilibrium result that lowering hours with a given wage should increase employment by existing firms.[1] However, (maximum) profit may then decline because, if

$$\hat{\pi} = Q(h, \hat{N}, t) - wh\hat{N} - Z, \tag{7.5}$$

it follows by the envelope theorem that

$$\hat{\pi}_h = Q_h - w\hat{N}, \tag{7.6}$$

which *may*[2] be positive if $Q$ is concave in $h$. *Marginal* firms then cannot survive if $h$ is reduced, so this loss of employment must be balanced against the increase in employment by surviving firms (with positive profit).

Consider next the effect of increased productivity (technical progress) on employment in this model. Differentiating (7.3) with respect to $t$ we obtain

$$\hat{N}_t = - Q_{Nt}/Q_{NN} > 0, \tag{7.7}$$

as economists often claim. However, if we now define the zero-profit wage, say $w^0 = w^0(h, t)$, by $\hat{\pi}(h, t, w^0) = 0$, and differentiate this condition together with the corresponding first-order condition, $Q_N = w^0 h$, we obtain

$$\hat{N}_t^0 = (Q_t - NQ_{Nt})/NQ_{NN} < 0 \text{ when } Q_t \text{ is concave in } N \qquad (7.8)$$

as the response of employment demand at the zero-profit wage. Similarly, $w_t^0 = Q_t/hN$ but $w_h^0 = \hat{\pi}_h/hN$ is ambiguous[3], and when $Q_h$ is concave in $N$ we have

$$\hat{N}_h^0 = (Q_h - NQ_{Nh})/NQ_{NN} < 0, \qquad (7.9)$$

where $\hat{N}^0 = \hat{N}(h, t, w^0)$. Thus the simple requirement of zero profits as a condition for (long-run) equilibrium with free entry actually reverses the partial equilibrium or constant-wage demand response in a manner that appears to support the folk-wisdom that 'work can be redistributed' and that technical progress destroys jobs. Of course, when $w_h^0 > 0$, the equilibrium wage must decline with a fall in hours (if $t$ is held fixed) in order to obtain more employment, and this component of the bargain has always been strongly resisted by organized labor. We now turn to various generalizations.

## 7.2(b)  Endogenous Overtime

Allowing employers to choose some positive level of overtime hours, or pehaps shorter-than-standard hours as well, greatly complicates matters. If we write $C(H, S, t)$ for the cost of $H$ hours when $S$ are standard hours, then the use of overtime premium wages implies that $C_S < 0$ when $H > S$. We now require that $\pi = Q - CN$ be concave in $(H, N)$, and the condition for optimal $\hat{H}$ is

$$Q_H = C_H N. \qquad (7.10)$$

Total differentiation of the two necessary conditions (7.10) and (7.3) with respect to standard hours, $S$, yields ambiguous conclusions. Only in the usual piecewise linear case does it follow that $\hat{N}_S > 0$, so that reducing standard hours should reduce the demand for labor. Our confidence in this result is not enhanced by the result, which goes back to Ehrenberg (1971), that total hours are a decreasing function of standard hours. This is clearly contradicted by the historical experience of total hours declining secularly as standard hours were intermittently reduced (Bienefeld, 1972). Adding equilibrium conditions to the general case is not illuminating, so we proceed to solve a specific example.

Suppose the production function is Cobb–Douglas, or

$$Q = tH^{\alpha}N^{\beta} \qquad (7.11)$$

and cost is given by

$$C = W(H - S) + wS + T_c$$

$$= WH - S(W - w) + T_c$$

$$= W(H - Sx) + T_c, \tag{7.12}$$

where $T_c$ represents total non-wage labor – or complementary – cost, $W$ is the overtime rate, $w$ is the standard wage, and $x = (W - w)/W$ is the premium ratio, which is unchanged when both wage rates are changed proportionately. First-order conditions (7.3, 7.10) with this specification yield

$$\hat{H} = \alpha(T_c - Sx)/(\beta - \alpha)W, \tag{7.13}$$

with $\alpha < \beta < 1$ by the second-order condition, and

$$\hat{N}^{1-\beta} = \alpha t \hat{H}^{\alpha-1}/W. \tag{7.14}$$

As usual in partial analysis, lowering $S$ raises $\hat{H}$ and reduces $\hat{N}$. To close the model, impose zero (maximum) profit, so that

$$(1 - \beta)t\hat{H}^{\alpha}\hat{N}^{\beta} = Z. \tag{7.15}$$

Using (7.14) we can write this condition as

$$\hat{H}^{\beta - \alpha} = \alpha^{\beta}(1 - \beta)^{1 - \beta}t/Z^{1 - \beta}W^{\beta} \tag{7.16}$$

and then from (7.13) we get

$$W_0^{\alpha}(T_c - Sx)^{\beta - \alpha} = \gamma t, \tag{7.17}$$

where $\gamma$ is a constant, and $W_0$ is the equilibrium (overtime) wage for zero profit in terms of the other parameters. From (7.16) it is then clear that reducing standard hours requires a reduction in wages to maintain zero profits (holding the ratio $x$ constant).

Next we can obtain zero-profit demand for hours and employment, say $\hat{H}_0$, $\hat{N}_0$, from (7.13), (7.14) and (7.17) as

$$\hat{H}_0^{\alpha} = \alpha^{\alpha}(T_c - Sx)^{\beta}/(\beta - \alpha)^{\alpha}(\gamma t)^{\beta} \tag{7.18}$$

$$\hat{N}_0^{1-\beta} = \alpha^{\alpha}(\beta - \alpha)^{1-\alpha}/\gamma(T_c - Sx)^{1-\beta}. \tag{7.19}$$

Total hours still increase when standard hours are reduced unless there is an offsetting increase in productivity, $t$. In this case, employment demand will decline. After these somewhat unsatisfactory results we now turn to the supply of hours.

133

## 7.2(c)  Intensive Margin Equilibrium

To obtain a convincing model of hours in the long run it seems essential to incorporate worker preferences for consumption and leisure as a normal good. For a simple example, let utility be

$$U = \ln(Y - k) + \lambda \ln(L - H) \text{ with } \lambda, \, L - H > 0, \tag{7.20}$$

where $Y = W(H - Sx)$ is worker income, $L - H$ is leisure, and $\lambda, k$ are constants. The optimal supply of hours, $\tilde{H}$, follows easily from (7.20) with $L = 1$ by choice of units as

$$\tilde{H} = \lambda(WSx + k)/(1 + \lambda)W. \tag{7.21}$$

For equilibrium at the intensive margin,[4] equate supply with demand ($\hat{H}$) from (7.13) and find the equilibrium wage $W^* = W^*(Sx)$ given by

$$W^* = (T_c - Sx - k)/ASx, \tag{7.22}$$

where $A$ is a constant. We can then impose the zero-profit condition (7.16) and set $W^* = W_0$, which yields

$$\gamma t(ASx)^\alpha = (T_c - Sx)^\beta \tag{7.23}$$

in the special case $k = 0$.[5] Equation (7.23) can be interpreted as the definition of equilibrium standard hours, say $S = S^*(t, x)$ in terms of technical progress and the premium ratio. Clearly $S_t^* < 0$, so we have at last obtained a plausible result, namely that standard hours must *decrease* with technical progress to maintain equilibrium at the intensive margin as well as the zero-profit condition.

The intensive-margin equilibrium, zero-profit wage from (7.16) and (7.22) can be written $W_0^*$, and we have easily

$$W_0^* = (T_c - S^*x)/AS^*x. \tag{7.24}$$

Thus technical progress requires shorter standard hours from (7.22), which in turn generate higher zero-profit wages for intensive equilibrium by (7.24).

Finally, we derive corresponding equilibrium hours and employment, say $H_0^*$ and $N_0^*$, by substituting (7.24) into (7.13) and (7.14), so that after some algebra we have

$$H_0^* = \alpha AS^*x/(\beta - \alpha) \tag{7.25}$$

$$N_0^* = B_0/(T_c - S^*x), \tag{7.26}$$

where $B_0 = \alpha^\alpha(\beta - \alpha)^{1-\alpha}/\gamma$ is a constant. These results are quite sensible. In accord with long-run trends, actual, endogenous equilibrium hours are proportional to standard hours (7.25), and employment *increases* with technical progress and declining standard hours by (7.26). The model now leaves no scope for policy measures such as changing standard hours, since these are determined through the zero-profit and intensive-margin equilibrium conditions.

## 7.2(d)  Disequilibrium

The most plausible equilibrium–disequilibrium constellation that remains to be investigated is the combination of equilibrium at the intensive margin with unrestricted profits. This allows the more realistic case of heterogeneous firms, some of which attain positive profits. In spite of conceptual and measurement problems, there is ample evidence for the existence of persistent, firm-specific rents (Mueller, 1986), and this assumption, coupled with efficient allocation of employed workers' time entailed by intensive equilibrium, would appear to be a better basis for policy considerations than the various models we have considered hitherto.

To obtain hours and employment in this case we substitute the intensive-equilibrium wage ($W^*$) from (7.22) into the demand functions (7.13) and (7.14) and get

$$H^* = \alpha A S x / (\beta - \alpha) \tag{7.27}$$

$$N^{*1-\beta} = \alpha^\alpha (\beta - \alpha)^{1-\alpha} t (A S x)^\alpha / (T_c - S x). \tag{7.28}$$

Again, $H^*$ is proportional to $S$, and $N^*$ clearly increases with $Sx$ as well as $t$. A firm's maximum profit now becomes

$$\pi^* = (1 - \beta) t H^{*\alpha} N^{*\beta} - Z, \tag{7.29}$$

and using (7.27) and (7.28) we find that

$$\pi^* = [B^* t (Sx)^\alpha (T_c - Sx)^{-\beta}]^{1/1-\beta} - Z, \tag{7.30}$$

where $B^*$ is another constant. Clearly, maximum profit increases rapidly with standard hours, so it is understandable that employers have always been so vehemently opposed to hours reductions. The income and leisure of employed workers increase when standard hours are cut, so this parameter bears the crucial distributional burden in the present model that is so strongly suggested by the historical evidence (Bienefeld, 1972).

However, the distributional conflict is not only between employers and employees, but also between the employed and the unemployed. The positive response of $N^*$ to $S$ (7.28) means that firms will cut employment unless technical progress *more* than offsets the effect of reduced standard hours. At the extensive margin of employment it is of course also true that any profit-reducing changes will force marginal firms to close down

135

in the long run, thus providing an additional source of conflict and unemployment.

## 7.2(e)  Monopolistic Equilibrium

In this final model we revert to the simplest case where hours, $h$, are an exogenous parameter for firms and households. Great simplification can be obtained by assuming general symmetry in the following sense. There are $n$ firms each producing a different good, $i = 1, ..., n$ but with identical cost functions. Each worker-consumer has the same concave utility function

$$U = U(D_1, ..., D_n), \tag{7.31}$$

where $D_i$ is consumption of $i$, which is symmetric so that if $U_i = \partial U / \partial D_i$, then

$$U_i(D, ..., D) = m(D), \text{ say, for all } i, \tag{7.32}$$

or the marginal utility of each commodity is the same when the quantities consumed are all equal. Next we suppose that each employed worker has nominal assets, $a$, so the budget constraint is

$$A = a + hw = \Sigma P_i D_i, \tag{7.33}$$

where $A$ is nominal wealth and $P_i$ is the price of $i$. Since all wealth is spent on consumption and labor is the only factor of production, it follows by Walras' Law that in equilibrium

$$anN = h\pi, \quad \text{or } aN = \pi, \tag{7.34}$$

where $nN$ is total employment and $\pi$ is the profit of any firm. The Lagrangian for the worker is

$$L = U + \mu(A - \Sigma P_i D_i) \tag{7.35}$$

and the first-order conditions define demand functions $\hat{D}_i(\mathbf{P})$ satisfying

$$U_i(\hat{D}_1, ..., \hat{D}_n) = \mu P_i, \tag{7.36}$$

where $\mathbf{P} = (P_1, ..., P_n)$.

Then in symmetric equilibrium with $\hat{D}_i = \hat{D}(P)$, say, $P_i = P$ we have from the budget

$$A = nP\hat{D} \tag{7.37}$$

and $\mu = mn\hat{D}/W$ from (7.32).

136

Next we define total demand faced by firm $i$ as

$$\hat{Q}_i = E\hat{D}_i(h, \mathbf{P}), \tag{7.38}$$

where $E$ is total employment. The production function is $Q(h, N)$ so by (7.38) we have an induced demand for employment by firm $i$,

$$\hat{N}_i = \hat{N}(h, \hat{Q}_i) \tag{7.39}$$

satisfying

$$Q(h, \hat{N}_i) = \hat{Q}_i = E\hat{D}_i \tag{7.40}$$

and total employment is

$$\begin{aligned} E &= \Sigma\hat{N}_i \\ &= n\hat{N}(h, \hat{Q}) \end{aligned} \tag{7.41}$$

in symmetric equilibrium.

Profit attained by firm $i$ at price $P_i$ is now

$$\pi_i = P_i\hat{Q}_i - wh\hat{N}_i. \tag{7.42}$$

Write $\hat{Q}_i' = \partial\hat{Q}_i/\partial\hat{P}_i$; then the condition for an optimal price $P_i^*$ is

$$\hat{Q}_i + P_i^*\hat{Q}_i' = wh\hat{N}_Q\hat{Q}_i'. \tag{7.43}$$

In terms of the absolute value of demand elasticity, $e$, we obtain from (7.43)

$$P_i^* = w\hat{N}_Q e/(e-1). \tag{7.44}$$

Next we return to the conditions (7.37) and (7.41) for symmetric equilibrium in order to write the first-order condition (7.44), which then holds simultaneously for all firms, in the form

$$(a + hw)\hat{N} = \eta nw\hat{Q}\hat{N}_Q, \tag{7.45}$$

where $\eta = e(e - 1)$. But this immediately gives

$$h + a/w = \varepsilon\eta n, \tag{7.46}$$

where

$$\varepsilon = \hat{Q}\hat{N}_Q/\hat{N} \tag{7.47}$$

is the elasticity of demand for employment. Now in the case that

137

elasticities $\varepsilon, \eta$ are constant (independent of hours) we can compare equlibria with different hours as follows.

When $a$ and $n$ are fixed, $h$ must be an increasing function of $w$ from (7.46). Individual demand, $\hat{D}_i$, then certainly increases with $h$. But since production $Q(h, N)$ also rises with hours, the effect on employment from (7.40) is essentially ambiguous. There are two opposing effects, a productivity and a wealth effect, and the net result can be obtained only from specific functional forms. By (7.44) the response of the equilibrium price is also ambiguous. The foregoing suggests that the *real* wage is likely to decline with a reduction of hours if equilibrium is to be maintained, and of course the employment effect remains open. Notice from (7.46) that, if profits are zero, then reducing $h$ will also reduce the number of firms, again suggesting employment reduction. With heterogeneous firms, the usual partial equilibrium argument that cost increases will drive out marginal firms retains its force. In all, it is difficult to draw any very firm conclusions from this model of general interdependence.

The model is of course very special and artificial in many ways. However, it is unlikely that natural (but complicated) generalizations such as endogenous (total) hours would yield more clear-cut conclusions, so we now turn to some general considerations and lessons from the various models.


## 7.3  Policy Conclusions

As is usual in economic models incorporating equilibrium interdependencies, even qualitative results are often very sensitive to the precise nature of technical assumptions. As is intuitively very plausible, many of the results obtained above depend on output-response elasticities to changing hours. Many important considerations such as capital and its utilization, and the problems of division of labor and work organization caused by substitution from hours to workers, particularly for small firms, have been omitted. These issues are likely to tilt the scales further against employment benefits from hours reductions.

We have mentioned the heterogeneity of firms and dangers to marginal firms. Most employment creation in the US in recent years has occurred in new or small firms, which are handicapped in Europe in various ways. A surprising neglect in most of the literature is the heterogeneity of workers. Uniform working time seems basically as anomalous as uniform consumption, when it is not dictated by externalities or interdependencies. Unions in Europe are adamantly opposed to greater individual flexibility of working time, which seems to be becoming increasingly feasible with modern technology and organizational possibilities. From a welfare point of view, flexibility would seem to be much more important than mandatory changes in standard *and* uniform working hours.

Reducing high and persistent unemployment is a professed goal of organized labor in Europe. Yet there is little public recognition that this goal is almost certainly incompatible with what union spokesmen claim as a major achievement and cornerstone of their philosophy – uniform pay scales under centralized bargaining with little or no regard for local variations in cost of living and the financial health of the employer. Uniformly high wages based on the ability to pay of industry leaders are probably one of the major barriers to entry by new firms (next to limited venture capital) and a cause of unemployment in the majority of firms with lower productivity. At the macro level, wages above equilibrium that responded insufficiently to supply shocks in post-OPEC Europe have been well documented (Bruno and Sachs, 1985).

The most relevant of our theoretical models is probably the model of Section 7.2(d), together with the intensive equilibrium considerations in 7.2(c). The problem is that reduced standard hours and higher wages are compatible with equilibrium at the intensive margin (7.22), but that reduced hours also reduce profit and employment *unless* technical progress is sufficient to compensate for this effect. Heterogeneity is again the key practical modification for policy interpretations, as emphasized above. More research is clearly needed on the true costs of hours reductions in the short and the long run, so that realistic trade-offs can be debated.

## Notes

1 Of course, if $Q_N$ were a convex function of $h$, this result would be reversed. The evidence on this point is mixed, and the true relationship no doubt depends on the value of $h$ and workers' effort. In a range where effort is declining, (local) concavity seems plausible, but on the other hand hours may represent a utilization factor for capital with single-shift working, suggesting a linear relationship.
2 See note 3 below for conditions.
3 It is easy to verify that the sign of $w_h^0$ is positive or negative according as the elasticity of hours is greater or less than the (output) elasticity of workers in the Cobb–Douglas case.
4 Now we require parameters such that $\bar{H}$ and $\hat{H}$ are both $< 1$.
5 We assume $k = 0$ in the following to simplify the results without altering qualitative response.

# COMMENT

## GEORG MERAN

The main purpose of FitzRoy's paper is to show that the usual discussion of how the choice of labor hours in a world with technical progress affects employment is inappropriately conducted in a short-run, partial equilibrium context. This can be verified by means of simple long-run models characterized by the explicit introduction of a labor market and zero-profit conditions representing competitiveness. These models lead to different results from those obtained in the former framework, mainly owing to the introduction of the zero-profit condition. It is interesting to note that, if work hours are not taken to be exogenously given but are dependent on labor market conditions, then the qualitative results of the partial equilibrium context may re-emerge. FitzRoy shows, for example, that in a long-run equilibrium model a reduction in work hours leads to a reduction of employment as well. On the other hand, technical progress causes a reduced demand for labor. However, these results no longer apply if work hours are endogenous. Here technical progress increases, and a rise in standard hours decreases, employment.

My comment addresses the question of how these results vary with some modifications and elaborations of the underlying models. I confine myself to two examples.

(1)  FitzRoy's results obtained in his first model with exogenous work hours are dependent on how firms' profit vanishes in a competitive economy. He chooses (real) wages such that profits disappear. However, if firms maximize nominal profits with respect to $N$ (FitzRoy's symbols),

$$\max \pi = pQ(h, N, t) - whN - Z,$$

where $p$ is the product price, then the zero-profit condition implicitly defines the price function $p^0(h, t)$ from

$$\hat{\pi} = p^0(h, t)Q(h, \hat{N}, t) - wh\hat{N} - Z = 0.$$

Now, the usual comparative static analysis leads to conditions determining the employment effects of work hours and technical progress different from those obtained by FitzRoy (his equations (7.8) and (7.9)). Instead we obtain the partial derivatives:

$$\hat{N}_h^0 = \frac{1}{pQ_{NN}Q} \left[ Q(w - Q_{Nh}) + Q_N(pQ_h - wN) \right]$$

and

$$\hat{N}_t^0 = \frac{1}{Q_{NN}} (Q_t Q_N/Q - Q_{Nt}),$$

where the last equation collapses to zero, i.e. technical progress has no employment effect, if a Cobb–Douglas function with multiplicative (neutral) technical progress is inserted.

(2) The variety of contractual agreements observed in the mainly unionized labor market suggests that FitzRoy's remuneration schemes adopted in equation (7.12) may be too restrictive. The construction of optimal contracts yields income–work-hours–employment schemes that are far more general and, from a welfare-theoretical point of view, better. Utilizing common models of labor contracts it is instructive then to ask how technical progress affects the choice of work hours and employment. For this purpose I assume a slightly modified model of FitzRoy's (1981). Assume unions maximize the (known) expected utility of a representative member of a union with $N_u$ members by stipulating an optimal contract $C = (y, h, N, s)$

$$\max_{C} \frac{N}{N_u} U(y, L - h) + \frac{N_u - N}{N_u} U(s, L)$$

s.t.

$$\pi = ptQ(h, N) - yN - s(N_u - N) - Z = 0,$$

where $U$ is specified according to FitzRoy's equation (7.20), $y$ is income of employed workers and $s$ is severance pay to unemployed union members.

If technical progress affects output multiplicatively and if production is given by a Cobb–Douglas function, one can easily derive[1] with the help of the first-order conditions that work hours are *independent* of technical progress. This contradicts FitzRoy's outcome, where standard work hours decrease with technical progress. Thus, more flexibility in terms of a generalized labor contract raises questions about the role of work hours as a remedy against unemployment. This is in the spirit of FitzRoy's warning not to overrate the positive employment effects of work hours reduction. Of course, more empirical work is required to determine the technological structure under which these results are derived.

## Note

1. The derivation follows the usual procedure. For details, see FitzRoy (1981).

141

# CHAPTER 8

# Reductions in Hours and Employment: What Do Union Models Tell Us?

ALISON BOOTH AND FABIO SCHIANTARELLI

## 8.1 Introduction

A long-term aim of the labor movement in Europe is to reduce the standard working week in order to improve the quality of life for workers. Faced with the high unemployment levels of the 1980s, labor organizations are also arguing that the shorter working week will alleviate unemployment through the provision of new jobs. 'There is no viable solution to unemployment today other than sharing out the amount of work to be done among more people, thanks to a cut in working hours' (European Trade Union Institute, 1983). Thus the European Trades Union Congress (ETUC) and the International Labour Office (ILO) are currently pressing for a shorter working week. However, it is clear that few unions believe that this reduction in hours should be accompanied by a drop in real income for those in employment. The UK Trades Union Congress (TUC, 1984) for example suggests that claims should be made 'for reduced working time with no loss of pay in all negotiations'.

Labor organizations argue that a reduction in the standard working week will cause employment to increase, first, because more workers will be needed to produce a level of output that is assumed to remain the same or even to increase because of increased demand for leisure-related activities (ETUI, 1983). Secondly, it is argued that hours can be reduced while real income remains constant because workers will be healthier and less tired, hence absenteeism and accidents will decline and productivity will increase. Thirdly, with long-run trend productivity growth, workers may forgo part of the increase in real wages in order to have more leisure, with favorable employment consequences.[1]

Employers, on the other hand, argue that a reduction in hours will not be accompanied by increased employment, largely because the reduction in hours (keeping real income per worker constant) will increase labor costs. Firms will therefore reduce their production levels and their demand for workers, and unemployment will rise. Thus the Confederation of British Industry (CBI, 1979) estimated that British unemployment would increase by 100,000 if there were a standard 35-hour working week.

The employment effects of a cut in hours represent an important and controversial issue, which has received little attention in the literature. Notable exceptions fall into two categories. First, there are the fixed-price models of Hoel (1986) and Brunstad and Holm (1984). When firms are constrained in the output market, it is possible to specify simple models in which a reduction in hours has favorable employment effects. However, when firms are on their labor demand functions, the results are ambiguous and depend upon both the precise nature of the production function, and whether real hourly wages or daily wages are kept constant. Secondly, there are the contributions based on the monopoly union model of wage determination, as in Calmfors (1985) and Hoel (1984). Here the employment result is also indeterminate.

In this paper we discuss the employment consequences of a cut in hours on the basis of two models of wages and employment determination – the monopoly union model and the efficient bilateral bargaining model. In Section 8.2, we use, as in Calmfors (1985), the static monopoly union model in which actual hours are exogenously fixed. By adopting a specific formulation for the utility and production functions, we can summarize in a convenient and precise way the factors determining the employment outcomes of a change in hours and assess their empirical likelihood. In Section 8.3 we make the model dynamic, by assuming the existence of convex adjustment cost for the firm, associated with changes in employment, and by adopting an intertemporal formulation for the union's utility function. The optimal open-loop policy is derived for this simple differential game and the problem of time inconsistency in the absence of binding contracts is discussed. The time-consistent feedback solution is also obtained and the effect of a cut in hours is analyzed for both cases. In Section 8.4 we return to the static monopoly union model, assume that standard hours are exogenously fixed, but allow firms to choose actual hours worked in a model with overtime and fixed employment cost. Finally, in Section 8.5 we discuss the problem in the context of an efficient model in which firms and unions bargain about wages and employment. The analysis is carried out for the cases of hours fixed exogenously throughout and for the case of an initial optimal level of hours.

## 8.2  The Monopoly Union: The Basic Model

In many sectors of the economy, there are two levels of hours worked – the standard or normal level of hours, and the actual or total number of hours. The standard level of hours is determined by either legislation or collective bargaining, and the actual level of hours comprises standard hours plus some overtime as the employer may require. Initially, we suppose that there is no overtime, and that hours are exogenously determined by some central authority at $H$.[2]

Suppose there is a single trade union in one particular sector of the economy, representing workers who are employed in a number of perfectly competitive firms. The union sets the level of wages unilaterally, given the firm's demand for labor. Suppose that the economy is fully unionized, so we can generalize from the sector under examination to the economy. Assume also that the capital stock and the number of shifts are kept fixed and that workers, $N$, and hours, $H$, enter as separate factors in the production function, i.e. $F = F(N, H)$, where $F_H$, $F_N > 0$, with the subscripts denoting partial derivatives. The demand for labor can be written as $N = N(Y, H)$, where $Y = WH$ and $W$ and $Y$ denote respectively the real cost of an hour of work and of a worker per period; $N_Y$ is negative, whilst $N_H$ is positive (negative) if $F_{HN}$ is positive (negative), i.e. if the factors are cooperant (non-cooperant). Therefore, an exogenous reduction in hours will have two employment effects: first, a direct effect keeping $Y$ (or $W$) constant and, secondly, an indirect effect transmitted through the induced variation in the wage. The direct effect depends upon the precise nature of the production function.[3] The indirect effect depends also upon the wage determination model adopted.

What does the monopoly union model predict will be the effect of a reduction in $H$ on the wage level? Suppose that workers are identical and that their utility function, when employed, is $U = U(Y, L)$, where $Y$ is income and $L$ is leisure. The utility of workers not employed by the firm is $\bar{U}$, which depends upon unemployment income and the time endowment of leisure. Workers are assumed to be identical and are all members of a single union; the union maximizes the sum of utilities of its fixed membership, $M$, where total trade union utility, $V^U$, is defined as $N[U(Y, L)] + (M - N)\bar{U}$, subject to the firm being on its demand function for workers. As is well known, optimal wage and employment will be in this case independent of $M$. For models with endogenous membership see Booth and Ulph (1985) and Kidd and Oswald (1987).

Even in the context of the simple monopoly union model, the effects of a change in $H$ on $Y$ (and therefore $N$) are in general ambiguous (see Calmfors, 1985). In order to make some progress and to identify the basic factors at work, it is instructive to choose a particular parameterization of the production function and of the utility function. Suppose that each worker's utility function is Stone–Geary so that only the excess of leisure and income above a vital minimum ($L_0$ and $Y_0$) generates utility. In this case

$$U = (Y - Y_0)^\varepsilon (L - L_0)^{1 - \varepsilon},$$

where $\varepsilon$ is the elasticity of utility with respect to income. Suppose that the production function is Cobb–Douglas, such that $F = bH^\gamma N^\alpha$, with $0 < \alpha < 1$ and $\gamma > 0$,[4] where $b$ is an efficiency parameter, $\gamma$ is the elasticity of output with respect to hours, and $\alpha$ is the elasticity of output with respect to the number of workers. The value of the elasticity of output with respect to hours depends upon two opposite effects. It is possible that work intensity decreases with the length of the working day because of a fatigue effect ($\gamma < 1$). Alternatively, longer working days imply that down-times (owing to set-up and closing-down operations, etc.) represent a smaller proportion of total hours paid for ($\gamma > 1$). It is difficult *a priori* to say which of the two effects dominates.

It is easy to show that the elasticity ($\eta$) of employment with respect to hours can be decomposed in the following way:

$$\eta_H^N = \eta_H^N \bigg|_{Y=\bar{Y}} + \eta_H^N \bigg|_{H=\bar{H}} \eta_H^Y$$

$$= \frac{1}{1-\alpha}\left[\gamma - \frac{1-\varepsilon}{\varepsilon}\frac{H}{L-L_0}\frac{Y-Y_0}{Y}\frac{\varepsilon\dfrac{Y}{Y-Y_0}-\dfrac{1}{1-\alpha}}{\varepsilon\dfrac{Y}{Y-Y_0}-\dfrac{1}{1-\alpha}-\dfrac{Y_0}{Y-Y_0}}\right]. \quad (8.1)$$

Equation (8.1) shows that $\eta_H^N$ has an ambiguous sign. The term in brackets simplifies to $\gamma - [(1-\varepsilon)/\varepsilon](H/L)$ if we assume that the utility function has a Cobb–Douglas form and therefore both $L_0$ and $H_0$ equal zero. In the more general Stone–Geary case, under the plausible assumption that $\varepsilon[Y/(Y-Y_0)] - 1/(1-\alpha)$ is negative, a reduction in hours is more likely to have a positive effect on employment if: (i) $\gamma$ is small, so that there is a big efficiency loss when labor is employed for long hours; (ii) $\varepsilon$ is small, reflecting a lower elasticity of utility with respect to income as opposed to leisure; (iii) workers already have only a small amount of leisure available; (iv) the vital level of leisure time, $L_0$, is high and the vital level of consumption, $Y_0$, is low.[5] Notice that the condition guaranteeing an increase in utility following a cut in hours $\gamma - [(1-\varepsilon)/\varepsilon][H/(L-L_0)][(Y-Y_0)/Y] < 0$ is not as strict as the one guaranteeing an increase in employment. It is, therefore, possible to envisage situations in which unions ask for a cut in hours even if this does not increase the number of workers hired by firms.

A further insight into the problem can be obtained by analyzing the empirical evidence available concerning the parameters of interest. The econometric estimates of $\gamma$ have a large range of variation. Feldstein (1967), Craine (1973) and Leslie (1984) obtain estimates of $\gamma$ that are greater than 1; whereas the work by Leslie and Wise (1980) suggests that $\gamma$ is less than 1. De Regt (1984) finds that $\gamma$ is not well determined, and could be on either side of unity. Given the simple form of the utility function we are using for illustrative purposes, it is not easy to find direct empirical evidence on the value of $\varepsilon$. Nevertheless, estimates obtained by Bean (1986), using an intertemporally additively separable utility function in which each component has a Stone–Geary form and contains consumption, leisure and public expenditure, suggest a value of $\varepsilon/(1-\varepsilon)$ close to unity. $L_0$ is likely to lie in the interval between 0 and 8 hours. Finally, one could use the level of supplementary benefits, housing benefits, etc. as a proxy for $Y_0$. This latter assumption yields a value of the replacement ratio $Y_0/Y$ that has fluctuated between 0.45 and

0.55 in the last two decades. (See DHSS, 1983.) Even if we take the lowest estimate for $\gamma$ (0.64 in Leslie and Wise, 1980), the available empirical evidence therefore suggests that the employment effect of a cut in hours is more likely to be negative.[6] Notice that, for a plausible range of parameters, union utility may also decrease; which is a puzzle. If union utility declines, unions would not be acting rationally in seeking a reduction in hours in the first place.

## 8.3 A Dynamic Analysis of the Monopoly Union Model

Up to this point it has been assumed that there are no specific costs associated with variations in the level of employment. In this section we analyze the consequences of changes in hours in the context of a dynamic model of firms' behavior with convex adjustment costs. The assumption of a monopoly union will be maintained: the only modification is that the union now maximizes an intertemporal utility function.

Let $X$ be the level of gross hiring and $\delta$ be the quit rate. The firm will choose $X$, taking the wage rate as given, in order to solve the following problem:

$$\max V^F = \int_0^\infty e^{-rt}[F(N, H) - WHN - g(X)] \, dt$$

$$: \operatorname{sgn}(g') = \operatorname{sgn}(X), \quad g(0) = 0, \quad g'' > 0 \tag{8.2}$$

subject to:

$$\dot{N} = X - \delta N, \quad N(0) = N_0, \tag{8.3}$$

where $r$ is the firm's discount factor. Using Pontryagin Maximum principle and denoting with $\psi$ the costate variable evaluated at $t$, the open-loop optimal policy is described by the following equations:

$$X = f(\psi) \quad f' > 0 \tag{8.4}$$

$$\dot{N} = f(\psi) - \delta N \tag{8.5}$$

$$\dot{\psi} = (r + \delta)\psi - F_N(N, H) + WH. \tag{8.6}$$

The union, as the Stackelberg leader in this dynamic game, will choose a path for the wage rate, $W$, in order to solve the following problem:

$$\max_W V^U = \int_0^\infty e^{-\rho t}[NU(WH, H) + (M - N)\bar{U}] \, dt \tag{8.7}$$

subject to equations (8.5) and (8.6) describing the optimal path of $N$ and $\psi$ for the firm, where $\rho$ is the union's subjective rate of time preference.

Denote with $\mu$ and $\phi$ the costate variables associated with equations (8.5) and (8.6), respectively. Application of the Maximum Principle yields the following necessary conditions for an interior solution:

$$\dot{\mu} = (\rho + \delta)\mu + \phi F_{NN}(N, H) - U(WH, H) + \bar{U} \tag{8.8}$$

$$\dot{\phi} = (\rho - \delta - r)\phi - \mu f'(\psi), \tag{8.9}$$

where, under the assumption that $U_{YY}$ is negative for concavity of the Hamiltonian:

$$W = W(N, \phi, H); \quad W_N = -\frac{U_Y}{NHU_{YY}} > 0 \quad W_\phi = -\frac{1}{NHU_{YY}} > 0 \tag{8.10}$$

$$W_H = -\frac{U_{YY}W + U_{YH}}{HU_{YY}} \gtrless 0.$$

$\phi$ in this problem is the marginal contribution to the union objective function of the shadow price of an additional worker for the firm, $\psi$. Since the latter variable is free to jump, it is optimal for the union to set $\phi(0) = 0$ at the beginning of the planning period. If the union is allowed to reoptimize at time $s$ where $s > 0$, it will always have the incentive to reset $\phi(s)$ equal to zero, altering the policy announced at time zero, which will generally generate a value of $\phi(s)$ different from zero. This is the well-known time-inconsistency problem (see for instance, Calvo, 1978, and Miller and Salmon, 1985). In the presence of binding contracts the differential equation system described by equations (8.5), (8.6), (8.8) and (8.9) characterizes with equation (8.10) the evolution over time of $N$, $\psi$, $\mu$ and $\phi$. It is possible to show (see, for instance, Levhari and Liviatan, 1972) that if $\lambda_i$ is a root of the system then so is $\rho - \lambda_1$. This means that (local) stability can be ruled out. We will assume that $\rho$ is small enough so that two of the roots are positive and two are negative. In this case the system has a saddle path structure. Moreover, under the assumption of quadratic adjustment costs so that $g(x) = (b/2)X^2$, after simple but tedious algebra, it can be shown that in the steady state $dN/dH \gtrless 0$ as:

$$-\frac{\eta_H^{U-\bar{U}}}{\eta_Y^{U-\bar{U}}\eta_Y^{U_1}} - \frac{\eta_H^{F_N}\eta_N^F F_N}{\eta_Y^{U_1}Y} + \frac{\eta_H^{F_N} F_N}{\eta_Y^{U-\bar{U}}Y} - \frac{\eta_H^{F_N} F_N}{\eta_Y^{U_1}Y} + \frac{\eta_H^{U_1}}{\eta_Y^{U_1}\eta_Y^{U-\bar{U}}} \gtrless 0. \tag{8.11}$$

If the production function is Cobb–Douglas and the utility function Stone–Geary, condition (8.11) reduces to:

$$\alpha\gamma \frac{\varepsilon}{1-\varepsilon} \frac{F_N}{Y} + \gamma\left(1 - \frac{\bar{U}}{U}\right) \frac{F_N}{Y} - \frac{H}{L-L_0} \frac{Y-Y_0}{Y} \frac{\bar{U}}{U} \gtrless 0. \tag{8.12}$$

An unfavorable employment effect of a cut in hours is more likely for high values of (a) the elasticity of output with respect to workers, $\alpha$, and hours, $\gamma$; (b) the elasticity of utility with respect to income relative to that with respect to hours, $\varepsilon/(1-\varepsilon)$; (c) the ratio of the marginal product of a worker and its cost, $F_N/Y$; (d) the level of utility when employed relative to fallback utility when unemployed, $U/\bar{U}$; (e) the proportion of vital income relative to actual income $Y_0/Y$ and the proportion of net leisure relative to hours of work $(L - L_0)/H$. The dynamic model is therefore more complex than the simple static model but yields similar qualitative answers. Since $F_N/Y$ exceeds unity to cover the marginal adjustment cost of employing an additional worker, realistic values of $\alpha$ and $U/U$ suggest that in this case also the employment effect of a reduction in hours is negative. Implausibly high values of $\varepsilon/(1-\varepsilon)$ and $\bar{U}/U$ very close to unity are required to generate favorable employment consequences.

As explained earlier, the solution to the dynamic Stackelberg game between the union and the firm is time inconsistent, in the sense that the union has the incentive to renege on previously agreed contracts. Therefore, the union's announced wage strategy will not be credible.

We now show how to obtain a time-consistent feedback Stackelberg solution for this game using dynamic programming. (See Simon and Cruz, 1973, for the general discrete time case.) Van Der Ploeg (1985) develops this solution in continuous time for the case in which there are convex costs in adjusting the capital stock. Let $V^F = V^F(N, t)$ be the maximum value function for the firm, and $V_t^F$ and $V_N^F$ represent the derivatives with respect to time and employment, respectively. Recall that $V_N^F = \psi$, then the Bellman equation for the firm is:

$$rV^F - V_t^F = \max_X \ [F(N, H) - WHN - g(X) + \psi(X - \delta N)]. \qquad (8.13)$$

Equation(8.13) implies:

$$-g'(X) + V_N^F = 0, \qquad (8.14)$$

so that $X = f(\psi)$, $f' > 0$, which is the result obtained previously (see equation (8.4)). Differentiating (8.13) with respect to $N$, one obtains again equation (8.6). For the union, the Bellman equation is:

$$\rho V^U - V_t^U = \max_W \{N[U(WH,H) - \bar{U}] + M\bar{U} + \mu[f(\psi) - \delta N]\}. \qquad (8.15)$$

If no additional constraint is imposed, equation (8.15) would imply that, for a given level of $N$, $W$ is set to infinity, assuming non-satiation for the individual and $U > \bar{U}$. In this case, though, the firm would be forced to shut down. In order for the firm to continue its operations, it is necessary to impose some constraint on the wage. We could, for instance, assume that the wage rate is set at such a level that the firm is left with a share of output (net of adjustment costs) at least equal to $K$, which is the minimum to induce the firm to keep producing.[7] This is what McDonald and Solow (1981) call the 'fair share' solution.

Formally, we assume that:

$$F(N, H) - WHN - g(f(\psi)) \geq K[F(N, H) - g(f(\psi))] \qquad (8.16)$$

In this case, the maximization in equation (8.15) implies:

$$U_Y - \eta = 0; \quad \eta\{(1 - K)[F(N, H) - g(f(\psi))] - WHN\} = 0; \quad \eta \geq 0 \quad (8.17)$$

where $\eta$ is the Lagrange multiplier associated with the constraint. The union will always have the incentive to set the wage rate as high as possible. Therefore, (8.16) holds with strict equality and it is easy to show that $W = W(\psi, N, H)$ with:

$$W_\psi = -\frac{g'f'(1 - K)}{HN} < 0; \quad W_N = \frac{(1 - K)F_N - WH}{HN} \leq 0;$$

$$W_N = \frac{(1 - K)F_H - WN}{HN} \leq 0. \qquad (8.18)$$

After substitution for $W$, the path over time of $N$ and $\psi$ is determined by equations (8.5) and (8.6). The same solution is obtained if constraint (8.16) is initially imposed on the Stackelberg leader in the case of binding contracts, and if it is assumed that the constraint is biting. The system of differential equations represented by (8.5) and (8.6) has a saddle path structure if:

$$\delta[-(1 - K)g'f' + r + \delta] - g'\left[-F_{LL} + \frac{(1 - K)F_L - WH}{L}\right] < 0. \qquad (8.19)$$

If it is assumed that the production function is Cobb–Douglas and the adjustment cost quadratic, then the inequality in (8.19) is always satisfied. In order for a (unique) equilibrium to exist with a positive level of employment, the condition $\alpha + K > 1$ must hold, but it can be easily shown that this inequality is always satisfied in the steady state. This latter condition guarantees also that a cut in hours will necessarily have a negative effect on employment.

These results can be illustrated graphically in Figure 8.1. The DD curve represents the long-run demand for labor obtained by eliminating $\psi$ from equations (8.5) and (8.6), with $\dot{N}$ and $\dot{\psi}$ set to zero. EE is the wage income–employment locus derived from equation (8.16) when the share constraint is binding. Both the EE and DD curves are downward sloping in the positive quadrant and approach the vertical axis asymptotically. Moreover, the DD curve intersects the N axis to the left of the EE curve and the former is steeper than the latter. The steady state combination of WH and N, under the time-consistent solution, is represented by C. Assume that the optimal (but time-inconsistent) solution occurs at a point such that the share constraint is not binding, like point B where the union indifference curve in the steady state is tangential to DD. In

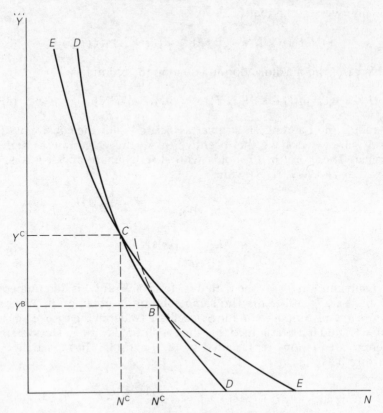

**Figure 8.1** Steady state equilibrium for open-loop and feedback policy

this case, the level of employment is greater and the wage lower than their respective values under the time-consistent policy. When the level of hours is cut, both $DD$ and $EE$ will shift downward, but the downward shift of $DD$ will exceed that of $EE$, causing a decrease in employment. Under the assumption of binding contracts the result, as discussed above, is ambiguous and depends upon the direction of the inequality in (8.12).

Using a solution concept originally introduced by Friedman (1971), it has been noted by several authors (see Barro and Gordon, 1983, and Backus and Driffill, 1986, among others) that the time-inconsistent optimal policy may be supported by a reputational mechanism, even in the absence of binding contracts, when the game is repeated an infinite number of times. Assume, for instance, that the union has always adhered in the past to the time-inconsistent open-loop policy, so the firm believes that it will continue to do so in the future. However, if the union departs from such a policy in any period, then the firm will expect the time-consistent feedback policy to be adopted for the infinite future. The incentive to renege for the union is intuitively given by the fact that the wage rate can be increased above the level dictated by the open-loop policy, while employment takes time to adjust downward. This implies that for an initial period the union's utility will be greater than it would have been under the time-inconsistent optimal policy. The punishment is represented by the loss in credibility by the union so that the wage will be expected from then on to be set at the highest possible level.

When the minimum share constraint is not binding (like at point B in Figure 8.1), as the system approaches its steady state, the level of utility under the open-loop optimal policy tends to be greater than the one under the feedback policy. In general, the value of the rate of time preference for the union, $\rho$, and the length of the punishment, which here we have assumed to be infinite, will determine if the gain from cheating is or is not compensated by the loss of credibility. In our case, if $\rho$ is sufficiently close to zero, so that the loss in the discounted value of future utility is given in an overwhelming weight, the open-loop optimal policy will be chosen even in the absence of binding contracts.

## 8.4 The Employment Effects of a Reduction in Standard Hours when Actual Hours Are Endogenous

So far it has been assumed that the maximum length of the working week was determined exogenously. We now return to the simple static monopoly union model but we assume that firms are free to choose the actual number of hours worked, while the level of standard hours, $H^S$, is determined by the central authority. We retain the assumption of a Cobb–Douglas technology, with a fixed level of capital stock. Suppose now that labor costs comprise a fixed cost, $C$, associated with each worker in addition to the wage cost.[8] Up to the maximum level of standard hours, workers are paid the standard wage rate, $W$. For $H$ greater than $H^S$, they receive an overtime wage of $\theta W$, where $\theta > 1$. Labor costs per person can, therefore, be written as:

$$C + WH^S + \theta W(H - S^S) \quad \text{for } H > H^S \tag{8.20a}$$

and

$$C + WH \quad \text{for } H \leqslant H^S. \tag{8.20b}$$

Assume that the optimum occurs in the region $H > H^S$.[9] Then it can be shown that optimal employment and the optimal number of hours for a profit-maximizing, perfectly competitive firm are respectively:

$$N = b^{1/1-\alpha} \left[ \frac{C + (1-\theta)WH^S}{\alpha - \gamma} \right]^{\gamma - 1/1 - \alpha} \left[ \frac{\theta W}{\gamma} \right]^{-\gamma/1 - \alpha} \tag{8.21a}$$

$$H = \left[ \frac{C + (1-\theta)WH^S}{\alpha - \gamma} \right] \frac{\gamma}{\theta W}. \tag{8.21b}$$

The second-order conditions for a maximum require $\alpha < 1, \gamma < 1$ and $\alpha > \gamma$. For an economically meaningful solution where $L$ and $H$ are positive, we require that $[C - (1 - \theta)WH^S] > 0$. The following results follow from equations (8.21a) and (8.21b):

$$N_{H^s} > 0; \; N_W \lesseqgtr 0 \text{ as } [C\gamma + (1 - \theta)WH^S] \gtreqless 0; \; N_\theta \gtreqless 0 \text{ as}$$

$$\left[ C + \left( 1 - \frac{\theta}{\gamma} \right) WH^S \right] \lesseqgtr 0; \; N_C < 0; \; H_{H^s} < 0; \; H_w < 0; \; H_\theta < 0; \; H_C > 0. \tag{8.22}$$

In order to understand the signs of the partial derivatives, it is useful to decompose the total effect of changes in the exogenous variables into a substitution effect and a scale effect. For instance, for any given level of $N$ and $H$, increases in $\theta$, $W$ and $H^S$ decrease the marginal cost of workers relative to hours, while an increase in $C$ increases it. At the same time, any increase in costs decreases optimal output and therefore employment. This explains why, for instance, $N_W$ and $N_\theta$ have ambiguous signs, since here the substitution and scale effects run counter to each other. Assume that fixed costs represent 15–25 per cent of total labor cost.[10] Then, for realistic values of the overtime premium ($\theta$ in the range 1.3–1.5) and of the number of overtime hours (5–30 per cent of normal hours), we would expect $N_W$ and $N_\theta$ to be negative. Finally, the results that $N_{H^s}$ and $H_{H^s}$ are respectively positive and negative are quite important to our discussion. *Ceteris paribus*, a decrease in the standard week will depress employment and increase overtime. The policy implications are clear. Unless the cut in $H^S$ is accompanied by a fall in the standard wage rate, $W$, or by a decrease in the overtime premium, $\theta$, or by a drop in fixed costs, $\acute{C}$, the direct employment effect will be unfavorable. A cut in $C$ will also generate, *ceteris paribus*, a decrease in the number of hours actually worked, while the opposite effect results from a fall in $W$ or $\theta$.

To obtain the total effects of a change in the level of standard hours on employment, the model for the firm's demand for workers and hours must be embedded in a model of wage determination. Given the complexity of the problem, we assume that the overtime premium and the fixed cost per worker are exogenous. The level of the basic wage, $W$, is again set by a monopoly union. The effect of a reduction in standard hours on $W$ and $N$ is ambiguous and cannot be summarized in a simple expression even when we adopt a simple specification of the utility function. However, it is possible to get a feeling for the results by assigning plausible numerical values to the various parameters. For simplicity, assume that $L_0$ and $Y_0$ are the same proportion of $L$ and $Y$, respectively. The range of values assigned to the elasticity of output with respect to employment, $\alpha$, is between 0.7 and 0.9. The elasticity of output with respect to hours, $\gamma$, is constrained to be less than $\alpha$ for the second-order conditions for profit maximization to be satisfied. The overtime premium is assumed to be 30–50 per cent of the standard wage. Fixed costs are taken to be 15–25 per cent of total wage costs. In this exercise we also impose the restriction that actual hours of work exceed standard hours (assumed to be between 7 and 8) by a plausible margin. For all the cases in which the second-order conditions for utility maximization are satisfied, one finds that the employment effects of a reduction in standard hours are always negative. Under no conditions would shortening the standard working week increase employment. The overtime effect is positive: as standard hours are reduced, firms demand more overtime from their present workforce. A contemporaneous cut in the fixed component of wage costs could be used to mitigate or reverse the negative employment impact. The fall in C would also tend to shorten, *ceteris paribus*, the actual length of the working day.

## 8.5 An Efficient Bargaining Model

It is well known that the wage–employment outcome of the model outlined in the previous sections is not efficient, in the sense that at least one party can be made better off without decreasing the level of utility of the other. Therefore, it is interesting to analyze the consequences of a change in hours in the context of a model where the agents bargain about both the position of the wage schedule and the level of employment. For simplicity we return to the case of a static model with no overtime. We will analyze both the case in which hours are fixed exogenously and the case in which hours are chosen optimally in the initial stage, before the imposition of an exogenous reduction. A reason to assume that hours are exogenously determined throughout is because it is not at all clear, at least for the British institutional setting, that bargaining over hours occurs at the same level as negotiations over pay and possibly employment (see Daniel and Millward, 1984, Ch. 8). The assumption, instead, of an initial optimal length of the working day is more in keeping with the spirit of an efficient bargaining model.

As an illustration we shall use the well-known Nash Cooperative solution (see McDonald and Solow, 1981). In this case the wage, employment (and hours) outcome can be obtained as a solution to the following problem:

$$\max \phi = [F(N, H) - YN]N[U(Y, L) - \bar{U}], \tag{8.23}$$

where it has been assumed that the fallback level of profits is zero. The necessary conditions for a maximum relative to $N$ and $W$ yield the following equations:

Contract curve (CC): $$\frac{U(Y, L) - \bar{U}}{U_Y(Y, L)} = Y - F_N(N, H). \tag{8.24}$$

Equity locus (EL): $$Y = \frac{1}{2}\left[\frac{F(N, H)}{N} + F_N(N, H)\right]. \tag{8.25}$$

If hours are also chosen optimally, then it must be true that $F_H U_Y = N U_L$. As is well known, in the context of this model, the number of workers employed by the firm exceeds the number that would be employed by a profit-maximizing competitive firm. It is also easy to show that the hours chosen in the initial stage will exceed (fall short of) the competitive level if the elasticity of utility with respect to income is greater (smaller) than the elasticity with respect to leisure.

For a given number of hours the Contract Curve and the Equity Curve locus can be plotted in Figure 8.2. If hours are cut, $EL$ unambiguously shifts to the left, whereas $CC$ can shift either to the right or to the left, leaving the effect on $N$ and $Y$ uncertain. Figure 8.2 shows a rightward shift of the contract curve that is not enough to compensate for the leftward shift of the equity locus, so that employment decreases. Formally, the effect of a cut in $H$ on employment will be negative (positive) if

$$\frac{dY}{dH}\bigg|_{EL}^{N=\bar{N}} \text{ is greater (smaller) than } \frac{dY}{dH}\bigg|_{CC}^{N=\bar{N}}.$$

It can be easily proved that $\dfrac{dY}{dH}\bigg|_{EL}^{N=\bar{N}} \gtreqless \dfrac{dY}{dH}\bigg|_{CC}^{N=\bar{N}}$ if:

$$\eta_H^{U-\bar{U}} + \eta_Y^{U-\bar{U}}\eta_H^{F} \frac{F_N}{Y} - \eta_H^{U} - \frac{1}{2}\eta_Y^{U}\left[\eta_H^{F}\frac{F_N}{Y} + \eta_H^{F}\frac{F}{YN}\right] \gtreqless 0. \qquad (8.26)$$

The above condition holds for any given initial level of hours. When bargaining over hours is permitted initially, the optimality condition relative to $H$ implies that the first term on the left-hand side of equation (8.26) equals $-\eta_Y^{U-\bar{U}}\eta_H^{F}F/YN$. In any case, the cut in $H$ always has ambiguous employment effects.[1] When the utility function is Stone–Geary, equation (8.26) becomes:

$$-\frac{\dfrac{H}{L-L_0}}{\dfrac{Y}{Y-Y_0}}\frac{\bar{U}}{U} + \frac{\varepsilon}{1-\varepsilon}\gamma\frac{F_N}{Y} + \frac{\gamma}{2}\left[1-\frac{\bar{U}}{U}\right]\left[\frac{F_N}{Y} + \frac{F}{YN}\right] \gtreqless 0. \qquad (8.27)$$

Here, the likelihood of an unfavorable employment effect increases with $\gamma$, $\varepsilon$ and the ratio of $Y$ to $Y_0$, with the profit rate (through $F/YN$) and with the proximity of the $N$, $Y$ pair to the labor curve (through $F_N/Y$, which is less than 1 in our case). A positive employment effect is more likely when there is a high ratio of hours of work to leisure time, and when the utility, when unemployed, is a high proportion of the level of utility when in employment. Equation (8.27) can be easily modified in the case of initial optimal hours.

Also in this case plausible parameter values imply that it is likely that a reduction in hours is going to decrease the number of workers hired by

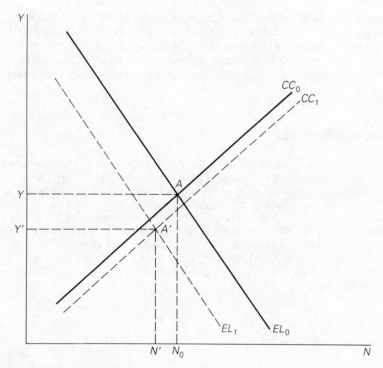

**Figure 8.2** Equilibrium $Y$ and $N$ in the efficient bargaining model (for given $H$)

the firm. For the conclusion to be reversed it is necessary for the utility enjoyed by the individual when unemployed to be very close to his or her utility when employed.

## 8.6 Conclusion

A major problem characterizing many European economies in the 1980s is the high level of unemployment. An important related policy issue is whether or not a reduction in hours can alleviate this unemployment. In order to examine this issue, we used two popular models of the trade union – the monopoly union model and the efficient bargaining model. The analysis was carried out in a static context for both models, but the monopoly union model was also extended into a differential game to see if the employment predictions were robust to a dynamic specification. The overwhelming conclusion of the analysis is that the employment effects of a reduction in hours are at best ambiguous, and in our view likely to be negative. Cuts in hours as predicted by these models are likely to generate unfavorable employment consequences. However, these may be mitigated by policy measures reducing labor costs for firms, by increases in productivity or by the introduction of extra shifts (for example, four shifts could operate instead of three where hours are reduced from 8 per day to 6, permitting greater capacity utilization). These issues deserve further investigation. An intriguing question remains as to why trade unions are pressing for shorter hours when the employment effects and possibly the effect on union utility may well be negative.

## Acknowledgements

This paper is a substantially extended version of the paper 'The Employment Effects of a Shorter Working Week', *Economica*, 54 (May 1987), pp. 237–48. The major innovations are contained in Section 8.3, which discusses the effects of a cut in hours in the context of a differential Stackelberg game.

We would like to thank for their comments the participants of the Economics Workshop at Essex University and of the Conference on Employment, Unemployment and Hours of Work held in Berlin, September 1986.

We are also grateful to A. Alesina, L. Calmfors, J. Driffill, S. Satchell, G. Tabellini and R. Van. Der Ploeg for useful discussions and suggestions. Any mistakes are ours.

## Notes

1  Thus collective bargains might indicate a reduction of hours during periods of growth in labor productivity, as during the four periods of reduction in standard hours in Britain since the 1890s (see Kane, 1982, Ch. 2).

2  This is done partly for simplicity, but also because a stated aim of some unions is to reduce normal hours while simultaneously abolishing overtime in order to increase employment (see TUC, 1984, pp. 3–5). It should be noted that the assumption of no overtime is reasonable for many workers; for example, the *Employment Gazette* shows that on average approximately two-thirds of manufacturing workers were not doing overtime during the last decade.

3  For a fixed *daily* real wage, a cut in hours depends upon the sign of $F_{NH}$. If the production function is multiplicatively separable, as denoted by $g(h)f(N)$, then $F_{NH} > 0$ and, therefore, $N_H > 0$. If the *hourly* real wage is kept fixed, $N_H|_{W=\bar{W}} \gtreqless 0$ as $\eta_H^F \gtreqless 1$, where $\eta$'s denote elasticities. If, instead, output is a function of person-hours, $F = F(HN)$, then it is easy to show that, given $Y$, $N_H \gtreqless 0$ as $|\eta_Y^H|_{H=\bar{H}}| = -F/F''HN \gtreqless 1$. For a given $W$, instead, the reduction in hours will always have favorable employment consequences. However, it is quite restrictive to assume that output is a function of person-hours.

4  Notice that, if it is assumed that the wage elasticity of the demand for labor is constant, then it is easily checked by integration that the production function must be of the Cobb–Douglas form (apart from an additive constant that must be set equal to zero if we assume that application of zero inputs yields no output). In this case, for a perfectly competitive firm whose output is a function of person-hours, $\eta_Y^N|_{H=\bar{H}}$ must be greater than 1 in absolute values, which implies that $N_H > 0$. Therefore, it is inconsistent to

assume that the wage elasticity is constant and greater than 1 and, at the same time, that $N_H$ is negative as it is done in Hoel (1984).

5   The statement concerning $Y_0$ holds for acceptable combinations of parameter values.

6   The qualitative conclusions reached above are robust with respect to a more complex specification of the fallback utility for the union in which $\bar{U}$ is assumed to be a geometric average of the utility when in alternative employment and when receiving unemployment benefits with weights determined by the probability of finding new employment. Suppose that both the expected alternative wage and the perceived probability of remaining unemployed depend upon the exogenous number of hours. If the elasticity of both income and employment with respect to hours is expected to be identical across firms, then it is easy to show that the absolute value of $\eta_H^N$ becomes smaller but the condition under which a reduction in hours increases employment does not change. It can also be shown that, if the capital stock can be chosen optimally, in the basic model, then it is more likely that the cut in hours will have adverse employment effects. A longer version of the paper containing the details of these extensions is available from the authors on request.

7   The results to be discussed below do not change if we assume that $K$ is the minimum share of output before deductions of adjustment costs.

8   See, for example, Ehrenberg (1971a). Fixed labor costs comprise hiring and training costs, welfare payments, etc.

9   If we start from an initial corner solution with $H = H^S$ and we move to a new corner solution when $H^S$ changes, we return basically to the comparative statics results of Section 8.2.

10   Hart (1984b, p. 17) shows that fixed non-wage labor cost in the UK was 20.5 per cent of total labor costs in 1981.

11   This and the other qualitative results described here are robust to the specification of the sharing rule in the efficient bargaining model.

# COMMENT

## GEORGE SHELDON

Booth and Schiantarelli's paper addresses an important employment policy issue: can a reduction in working time create more jobs and thus serve to alleviate the high rate of unemployment plaguing most European countries today? An answer is sought in four union models of employment and wage determination. The distinguishing feature of the union model approach lies in the attempt to predict not only the employment reaction of firms to an exogenous reduction in working hours but also the parallel wage demands of unions, which modify the direct employment effect.

Booth and Schiantarelli begin with a static monopoly union model. In this approach it is assumed that firms are perfect competitors, whereas the labor force is fully unionized and behaves like a monopolist. The union sets the wage so as to maximize the utility of its members subject to the firms' demand for workers, and the firms choose the level of employment that maximizes their profits subject to the wage set by the union. Working hours are exogenous for both parties. Although firms and the union both act unilaterally in setting the value of their respective choice variables, the union is the more powerful of the two in that it fully anticipates the employment reaction of the firms when it sets the wage. Thus in the final analysis, the union, in fixing the wage, ultimately sets the level of employment as well.

This simple monopoly union model has been used before by Calmfors (1985) to investigate the employment effects of shortening the workweek. Booth and Schiantarelli choose Calmfors' approach as their base model and then build upon it by offering us three innovative variations.

To start, they modify the simple monopoly union model by making it dynamic. Utility and profits are now maximized intertemporally. As the behavioral assumptions of the union model would lead one to believe, this modification creates a dynamic game setting in which the union acts the part of a Stackelberg leader. By framing the monopoly union model in a dynamic context, the authors are able to consider the firms' employment adjustment costs, thus adding further realism to the analysis.

Booth and Schiantarelli then turn back to the static model, developing the latter in yet another direction. Firms now have two choice variables: the level of employment and actual working hours. Actual working hours differ from standard working hours, which are still assumed to be exogenous for both the union and the firms, by the amount of overtime work. The introduction of overtime is an important addition, since it allows for the fact that firms may thwart any positive employment effects of cutting working hours by substituting hours for workers.

As a final variation, the authors re-adopt the assumption of fully exogenous working hours and then view wage and employment determination in the context of an efficient bilateral bargaining model. This is done in order to counter the argument that the wage–employment outcome in the monopoly union model is not Pareto-optimal.

The models do not generate unambiguous predictions with regard to the employment effects of shortening working hours when specified in a general-function form. In an interesting attempt to overcome this indeterminacy, the authors choose specific parameterizations for production and for the union utility function and then assign the parameters values that are either drawn from other empirical work or deemed plausible. In so doing, they are able to conclude that a cut in hours will likely lead to negative employment effects.

Booth and Schiantarelli obviously cover a lot of ground in their paper. One might therefore be inclined to say that no stone was left unturned. Yet, despite the apparent breadth and forcefulness of their analysis, I should nevertheless hesitate to draw any very general policy implications from the results. The sources of my scepticism are twofold:

1 A number of rather restrictive assumptions are made at different points in the paper, which to my mind limit the policy implications of the models.
2 The methods employed, and therefore the conclusions drawn, are essentially partial equilibrium in nature.

I wish to elaborate on these points.

For one it is assumed throughout the paper that the size of the labor force is given. Hence any model-generated changes in employment are necessarily mirrored in opposite changes in unemployment. In reality, though, these effects are usually not symmetric. An increase in employment opportunities often encourages people in the non-active population to enter the labor force, as is known from the discouraged-worker effect. Thus, unemployment need not fall even if shortening working hours is successful in creating additional jobs.

Moreover, by assuming that all workers have identical utility functions, the authors ignore the possibility that some workers may be unsatisfied with a working time reduction and try to moonlight, thereby offsetting any positive employment effects a reduced workweek might generate. For example, Galler and Wagner (1983), after polling the working-hour preferences of West German workers, conclude that reducing the hours of work by just 2 per cent or more would create involuntary underemployment and thus induce those affected to seek additional work, possibly thwarting any positive job effects.

It is also assumed throughout that the stock of capital and the level of technology are fixed. This is a reasonable simplification for a short-run analysis, but it seems odd that the authors would hold fast to this assumption in an intertemporal wage and employment model with an infinite time horizon. By so doing, they ignore the possibility of substitution between capital and labor and – to my mind – unnecessarily restrict the dynamic model's policy implications.

One would expect that these neglected channels of influence would have a negative impact on employment. Since the models presented in the paper already suggest that a reduction in working hours would worsen the employment situation, incorporating these additional effects in the analysis would probably not change the authors' results qualitatively. This does not necessarily hold true in the following instances, however.

In accordance with the partial equilibrium characteristics of the analysis, the models neglect to consider the consequences in other markets of shortening working hours. For example, changes in the real wage will affect investment according to the elasticity of substitution between capital and labor. Moreover, as long as the elasticity of employment with respect to real wages is greater than $-1$, real take-home pay and hence consumption will increase despite a negative impact on employment. These demand effects will feedback on the system and perhaps alter the picture the models in the paper give us.

In the monopoly union model of wage and employment determination, the union sets the wage and the firms react by choosing the level of employment. Since the price of output is assumed to be fixed, this implies that unions determine not only nominal wages but real wages as well. Now, unless wages are perfectly indexed, it will be a rare union indeed that has the power to fix real wages. And if unions do not possess this power, then it is possible to show that a reduction in working hours can encourage additional employment even in cases where the union is able to hold nominal take-home pay constant. What is required to establish this point (see Franz, 1984; Linde, 1983) is the assumption that working hours and workers are multiplicatively separable and that the price elasticity of demand is greater than $-1$, i.e. inelastic. The result also seems intuitively plausible since it is to be expected that full wage compensation will not offset the employment-increasing effect of a working-hour reduction as long as the added costs can be passed on to the consumers in the form of higher prices.

Another point seems to be worth making. If labor organizations in Europe are currently pressing for a shortened workweek, as the authors correctly point out at the outset of their paper, then it does not seem very consistent to analyze this union policy in a theoretical framework in which working hours are always viewed as being exogenous to the union. To justify this approach, the authors point out that bargaining over hours occurs at a different level than negotiations over pay in Great Britain. For the Federal Republic of Germany, however, this does not hold true, as contractual settlements in the metal and printing industries demonstrate (see Franz, 1983, p. 637). And in Switzerland, unlike in the models presented, wages are typically negotiated at the firm level. In short, the general applicability of the analysis seems somewhat limited when viewed from other institutional settings.

At the end of Section 8.2, the authors point out that, for a plausible range of parameters, union utility may actually decline as a result of shortening working hours. This leads them to conclude that in these instances unions would not be acting rationally in seeking a reduction in hours. This is somewhat of a *non sequitur* since if working hours are truly exogenous then unions cannot affect them. And if they have no influence on working time, it seems all the more irrational for them to develop an hours policy in the first place. Hence, I see no room for a union working-hours policy in the models presented.

In closing, I should like to re-pose the question appearing in the title of the paper: not what *do*, but rather what *can* union models tell us about the employment effects of reducing working hours? The introduction of a union model into the analysis basically serves to predict the direction that the wage response of labor to a shortened workweek will take. This is an important point to consider since the employment effect of a reduction in hours very much depends on the reaction of wages. Union models are apparently not able to provide us with a definite answer. But cannot casual empiricism? I am not in a position to speak for the UK, but as far as German-speaking countries are concerned I know of no instance where a union has ever pressed for a reduction of both hours and (nominal) wages. Unions are not in a position to enforce real wage demands, so we need not consider them here. But the sign of the nominal wage response to a cut in working hours is basically known from observation and thus can be assumed as being given and negative. If we accept this proposition, then the indirect employment effect of a reduction in hours transmitted through the induced variation in wages will necessarily be positive (i.e. shortening the workweek indirectly reduces employment) since the sign of the employment response to a wage change (the slope of the labor demand curve) has to be negative for profit maximization to hold. The remaining indeterminacy applies then to the sign of the direct effect of reducing working hours on employment. This effect along with the other channels of influence touched upon in this comment therefore appear to be the issues that future work will need to address.

# CHAPTER 9

# The Demand for Workers and Hours: Micro Evidence from the UK Metal Working Industry

ROBERT A. HART AND NICHOLAS WILSON

## 9.1 Introduction[1]

The principal objective in this paper is to investigate empirically the effects of changes in annual scheduled working hours and relative factor prices on the demand for workers and average annual hours (total and overtime). A model is derived from simple micro demand theory of a cost-minimizing firm and relates to the seminal work of Rosen (1968) and Ehrenberg (1971a). It is tested using random samples of cross-sectional, plant-level data of enterprises in the UK metal working industry. In general we obtain a set of results that are consistent with the underlying theory.

Apart from large-scale macroeconometric models, there are three main alternative approaches to the study of the firm's workers/hours allocation from the one adopted here. These are: (i) implicit contract models (e.g. FitzRoy and Hart, 1985; Rosen, 1985); (ii) efficiency wage models (e.g. Hoel and Vale, 1986); and (iii) union bargaining models (e.g. Calmfors, 1985; Booth and Schiantarelli, 1987). Each type of model has strengths and weaknesses relative to the others. The primary reason for the present choice is that, of all the alternatives, this model framework has perhaps developed furthest towards differentiating explicitly between endogenous overtime and exogenous standard working hours. In reality, a significant proportion of firms employ overtime schedules – and this is certainly true of our sample – and accordingly they possess an important means at the intensive margin of reacting to standard[2] hours and relative factor price changes.

The structure of the paper is as follows. Section 9.2, which is in two parts, presents the underlying theory. Section 9.2(a) contains a brief outline of well-established results from a fairly general labor demand formulation for a cost-minimizing firm. In order to emphasize, in particular, the distinction between standard and overtime hours, a simple specific example from the general model background is developed in Section 9.2(b). A number of alternative specifications are mentioned in both subsections with the aim of establishing the sensitivity of key results to differing modeling assumptions. The general approach in Section 9.2(a) reflects the subsequent empirical specifications. These are outlined – together with a short data description – in Section 9.3. No attempt is made to discriminate among competing forms of cost and production functions by imposing and testing varying parameter and other constraints. Rather, we undertake the more modest task of testing simple log-linear versions of the general labor demand functions. We should add, however, that our data provide the possibility of undertaking a broader and more sensitive set of tests of the basic theory than in much of the earlier related work. Empirical results are given in Section 9.4. An assessment of our findings is carried out in Section 9.5 with a particular emphasis on the relationships between employment and hours of work.

## 9.2  Theory

### 9.2(a)  A General Framework[3]

Consider a competitive firm that seeks to combine its factor inputs in order to minimize the costs of fulfilling a given production requirement. In order to keep matters as simple as possible without losing essential detail, it is assumed that the capital stock and state of technology are fixed and that the firm operates a single-shift system. Also, for convenience, we omit other variables that control for specific labor market and other features of the firm.[4]

Per period total labor costs, $C_L$, are given by

$$C_L = [w(h) + z]N, \tag{9.1}$$

where $w(h)$ is the total wage cost per worker per period for $h$ hours of work, $z$ is the average per-period quasi-fixed labor cost and $N$ is the size of the workforce.

Given information costs associated with attempts to allocate labor efficiently on the basis of complex contractual agreements, it is assumed that, as a second-best solution, the wage is predetermined (see, for example, Hall and Lazear, 1984). In common with the vast majority of work in this field, we assume initially that $w(h)$ is adequately approximated by a piecewise linear schedule in which the premium rate for overtime working is paid at some constant proportion $a$ ($<1$) of the standard rate $w_s$. This may be written

$$w(h) = \begin{cases} w_s h_s + a w_s(h - h_s) & \text{for } h > h_s \\ w_s h & \text{for } h \leqslant h_s \end{cases} \tag{9.2}$$

where $h_s$ is per-period standard, or scheduled, hours.

Quasi-fixed costs are also given by a standard expression; thus

$$z = (q + r)Z, \tag{9.3}$$

where $Z$ are once-over hiring and training costs, $q$ is the firm's quit rate and $r$ is a suitable discount rate. Other fixed and variable non-wage labor costs are ignored.

Output, $Q$, is related to labor services, $L$, through the production function $Q = f(L)$ with $f'(L) > 0$, $f''(L) < 0$. Following well-known arguments, we allow for the fact that the marginal contribution to labor services of an additional hour differs as between the employment of a new worker or extending the average worktime of an existing worker. Accordingly the labor services function, $L$, takes the form

$$L = G(N, h) \quad G_N, G_h > 0. \tag{9.4}$$

The firm's objective is to find the optimum combination of workers and hours (denoted by $\bar{h}$ and $\bar{N}$) that satisfies a given output requirement at minimum cost.

Suppose that, in equilibrium, $\bar{h} > h_s$. Making the appropriate substitution of (9.2) into (9.1) and minimizing (9.1) subject to (9.4) produces – assuming the second-order necessary conditions for a minimum are satisfied – the equilibrium labor demand equations

$$\bar{N} = \bar{N}(Z, q, r, h_s, w_s, a, Q)$$

$$\bar{N}_i < 0 \ (i = 1, 2, 3), \ \bar{N}_j > 0 \ (j = 4, 5, 6), \ \bar{N}_7 > 0 \tag{9.5}$$

$$\bar{h} = \bar{h}(Z, q, r, h_s, w_s, a, Q)$$

$$\bar{h}_i > 0 \ (i = 1, 2, 3), \ \bar{h}_j < 0 \ (j = 4, 5, 6), \ \bar{h}_7 \geqslant 0. \tag{9.6}$$

A rise in per-worker costs ($Z$, $q$ and $r$), *ceteris paribus*, increases costs at the extensive relative to the intensive margin and induces a substitution of $\bar{h}$ for $\bar{N}$. Relative cost changes in the opposite direction occur for *ceteris paribus* rises in standard hours as well as standard and overtime wages. While a positive scale response of the equilibrium workforce would be expected (i.e. $\bar{N}_7 > 0$), scale invariance of equilibrium average hours (i.e. $\bar{h}_7 = 0$) is a feature of a fairly broad class of labor services function belonging to (9.4): one such function is featured in our example in the next subsection.

From the perspective of the current working time debate in West Germany and elsewhere in Europe, the results in (9.5) and (9.6) with respect to $h_s$ are of considerable interest. A cut in standard hours is predicted to reduce employment and increase labor utilization. Marginal costs at the extensive margin rise because a smaller proportion of a marginal worker's average total hours can be purchased at the cheaper standard rate, $w_s$. On the other hand, increased overtime working in

(9.2) can be obtained at constant marginal cost. Two critical assumptions – both of which concern the linear wage schedule in (9.2) – produce the associated $\bar{h} - \bar{N}$ substitution effect. The first concerns the fact that we have assumed so far that the relevant segment of the schedule is that for which $\bar{h} > h_s$. The second concerns the choice of schedule itself.

In the first instance, suppose that the firm is working initially in equilibrium at the maximum per-period standard hours with no over-time (i.e. $\bar{h} = h_s$). Now, the second segment of (9.2) is relevant to the cost function (9.1) and the solution to the minimization problem may yield the outcome that a fall in $h_s$ *increases* $\bar{N}$ since the working time reduction may be binding. We analyze this type of outcome in greater detail in the next subsection.

In the second instance, it may be regarded as being more appropriate to model the wage schedule whereby the overtime, or premium, wage function is assumed to be positively related to total hours and negatively related to standard hours. For example, there may exist a range of premium wage rates – for weekday, Saturday, Sunday and holiday working – combined with an uneven workforce distribution of overtime working owing to supply constraints.

Santamäki (1983) has analyzed the implications for the above demand model by replacing the schedule in (9.2) by one that incorporates a continuous premium wage function $\phi$ for per-period hours. This takes the form

$$w(h) = \begin{array}{ll} w_s h_s + \phi(h, h_s) w_s (h - h_s) & \text{for } h > h_s \\ \\ w_s h & \text{for } h \leqslant h_s \end{array} \qquad (9.7)$$

where $\phi(h, h_s) > 1$ and for $h > h_s$, $\phi_h > 0$, $\phi_{h_s} < 0$.

Incorporating (9.7) into the cost-minimization problem, assuming $\bar{h} > h_s$, Santamäki shows that the solution no longer yields an unam-biguous sign $(\partial \bar{h} / \partial h_s)$. Intuitively, this would be expected; costs now rise at *both* extensive and intensive margins with relative rises depending on precise functional specifications. For example, Santamäki shows that if $\phi(h, h_s) = b(h/h_s)$ $(b > 1)$ in (9.7) then minimization yields $\partial \bar{h} / \partial h_s > 0$, which is *opposite* in sign to the equivalent result in (9.6).

Finally, it is worth reporting briefly on the equivalent results for a profit-maximizing firm. Analytical details can be found in Calmfors and Hoel (1988) and FitzRoy and Hart (1985).

Setting output price to unity, the problem in this case can be expressed

$$\max_{N, h} \pi = F[G(N, h)] - C_L,$$

where $\pi$ is profit and $C_L$ incorporates $w(h)$ in (9.2). The most important point to note is that, at least for employment, there are *both* substitution *and* scale effects of changes in standard hours and factor prices. If $\bar{h} > h_s$, the negative employment response to a reduction in $h_s$ in (9.5) still holds; indeed, the $\bar{h}$–$\bar{N}$ substitution effect is *reinforced* by a negative scale effect owing to an increase in unit labor costs. Factor responses to changes in quasi-fixed costs are in the same direction as in the cost-minimizing model. There is some ambiguity with respect to $w_s$ and $a$ (i.e. variable costs), however. For example, while an increase in the overtime premium ($a$) produces, as under cost minimization, an $\bar{N}$–$\bar{h}$ substitution effect, this is *offset* in the profit-maximizing case by a negative scale effect.

If initial equilibrium is at the corner solution ($\bar{h} = h_s$) under profit maximization, a reduction in $h_s$ produces an ambiguous employment response. The possible positive employment effect comparable to the cost-minimizing case (i.e. through moving from one corner solution to another) is offset by a countervailing negative scale effect.

In general, the employment responses to a reduction in standard hours are *less* favorable under profit maximization compared to cost minimization.

### 9.2(b)  An Illustrative Example

With the aim of underlining several of the results discussed above, we concentrate here on a particular example. While retaining the cost functions (9.1)–(9.3), we consider a class of labor services function belonging to the general expression in (9.4) that is multiplicatively separable in $N$ and $h$. This may be written

$$L = N^{1-\alpha}g(h),  \tag{9.8}$$

where $0 \leqslant \alpha < 1$, $g(0) = 0$, $g'(h) > 0$, $g''(h) < 0$. Incorporating (9.8) into the cost-minimization problem produces equilibrium hours that are scale invariant, i.e. $\partial Q/\partial \bar{h} = 0$ (see Ehrenberg, 1971).

Our specific formulation for $g(h)$ follows FitzRoy and Hart (1985). Letting $s$ represent set-up time, we have

$$g(h) = (h - s)^\varepsilon  \quad 0 < \varepsilon < 1  \tag{9.9}$$

where, for $h > s$, $g'(h) > 0$, $g''(h) < 0$.

Replacing (9.4) by (9.8) and (9.9), we chose to illustrate the solutions to the minimization problem diagrammatically.[5]

Combining (9.8) and (9.9), the isoquant with respect to the labor services function is represented by the curve $LL$ in Figures 9.1 and 9.2. Its slope is given by

$$\frac{dN}{dh} = -\frac{\partial L}{\partial h}\bigg/\frac{\partial L}{\partial N} = \frac{-\varepsilon N}{(1-\alpha)(h-s)} < 0.  \tag{9.10}$$

Differentiating (9.10) with respect to $h$ gives $d(dN/dh)/dh > 0$ and so the locus is convex to the origin.

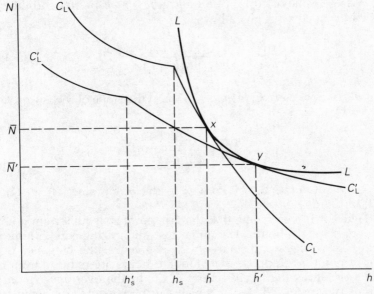

**Figure 9.1**

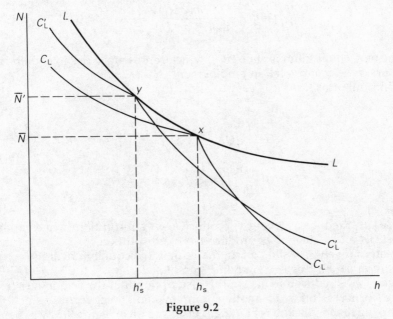

**Figure 9.2**

The isocost curve, $C_L C_L$ is kinked at $h_s$. For $h > h_s$, substituting (9.2) into (9.1) gives labor costs, $C_L = [w_s h_s + a w_s (h - h_s) + z] N$ and the slope of the isocost curve is given by

$$\frac{dN}{dh} = \frac{-a w_s N}{w_s h_s + a w_s (h - h_s) + z} < 0. \tag{9.11}$$

For $h < h_s$, costs are $C_L = (w_s h + z) N$ and the slope of the isocost curve is given by

$$\frac{dN}{dh} = \frac{-w_s N}{w_s h + z} < 0. \tag{9.12}$$

Both segments of $C_L C_L$ are convex to the origin since, in (9.11) and (9.12), $d(dN/dh)/dh > 0$.

In Figure 9.1, we assume that the firm employs equilibrium hours in excess of standard hours. The initial cost-minimizing equilibrium combination of workers and hours $(\bar{N}, \bar{h})$ is given at the tangency of $LL$, $C_L C_L$, at point $x$.[6] Suppose that standard hours are reduced from $h_s$ to $h'_s$; this produces the isocost curve $C'_L C'_L$. In the overtime region, the slope of the isocost 'flattens', which can be shown by differentiating (9.11) with respect to $h_s$ to obtain

$$\partial\left(\frac{dN}{dh}\right)\bigg/\partial h_s = \frac{a w_s^2 N (1 - \alpha)}{[w_s h_s + a w_s (h - h_s) + z]^2} < 0. \tag{9.13}$$

The new equilibrium is at point $y$, which represents a rise in equilibrium hours, $\bar{h}' - \bar{h}$, and a fall in employment, $\bar{N} - \bar{N}'$.

In similar fashion, it is easy to show that

$$\partial\left(\frac{dN}{dh}\right)\bigg/\partial l > 0 \quad l = z, s$$

$$\partial\left(\frac{dN}{dh}\right)\bigg/\partial m < 0 \quad m = w_s, a. \tag{9.14}$$

Rises in 'fixed' costs ($z$ and $s$) produce $\bar{h} - \bar{N}$ substitution, while variable cost ($w_s$ and $a$) increases produce $\bar{N} - \bar{h}$ substitution.

Alternatively, consider a firm that is in initial equilibrium at the corner solution $\bar{h} = h_s$; this is shown in Figure 9.2 at point $x$, the kink of $C_L C_L$. Again, $h_s$ is reduced to $h'_s$. On the assumption that the firm moves from one corner solution to another, employment must *increase* since the working time reduction is binding. This is shown in Figure 9.2 by a change in equilibrium from $x$ to $y$, representing an employment gain $\bar{N}' - \bar{N}$.

Given the shape of isocost curves, the outcome in Figure 9.2, assuming initial $\bar{h} = h_s$, might be considered to be reasonably likely in many situations. It could be the case, however, that the reduction in $h_s$ is so large that an interior solution is reached, in which case $\bar{h} > h_s$ and employment–hours outcomes are ambiguous.

If the firm begins in equilibrium at an interior solution $h < h_s$, a reduction in $h_s$ to $h'_s$ may have *no* effect on equilibrium $\bar{h}$, $\bar{N}$; this would be the case if $\bar{h} < h_s$. Suppose that the firm is free to vary hours in this range. Clearly a rise in $a$ would have no effect on equilibrium manhours. It is easy to show, however, that changes in $z$, $s$ and $w_s$ produce the same hours–employment substitution effects as in (9.14) (see also Rosen, 1968).

The above example provides results that are largely in line with the more general framework of the previous subsection. Alternative functional forms of $g(h)$ to that in (9.9) can provide divergent outcomes. Recent interest, for example, has been shown in special forms of the function

$$g(h) = g[h_s, (h - h_s)],$$

that is, in which standard and overtime hours are separated in the production models as well as in the wage function (see Santamäki, 1984; Hart and McGregor, 1988). As mentioned earlier, however, this present paper stops short at attempting to discriminate among alternative model specifications.

## 9.3 Data and the Specification of Estimating Equations

Our data refer to a random sample of 52 enterprises in the UK metal working industry (UK Standard Industrial Classification 310–70) with a size range of 50–3,000 employees. They are based on results of a plant-level survey conducted in 1984/5 (Wilson, 1985) and cover five separate years of information, 1978–82. The interview schedule consisted of nine main sections. The first asked for basic factual information about each enterprise. Further sections requested details of the product, prevailing market conditions and market structure, production methods, the nature of the production process and technology. Detailed information on the composition of the labor force, turnover, training and working practices was obtained from personnel records. This included data on unionization and collective bargaining arrangements, pay and incentives schemes, wage and non-wage labor costs.

In particular, information on the variables of relevance to Section 9.2 formed a part of this survey and so we are in a position to test the basic labor demand theory while at the same time controlling for an important set of enterprise-specific variables.

Our log-linear stochastic specification of (extended versions of)

(9.5) and (9.6)[7] takes the form

$$\ln Y_{jit} = \beta_{0j} + \beta_{1j} \ln h_{sit} + \beta_{2j} \ln(Z/v)_{it} + \beta_{3j} \ln q_{it}$$

$$+ \beta_{4j} \ln Q_{it} + \sum_{k=1}^{12} \gamma_{kj} \ln X_{kit} + e_{jit} \quad (9.15)$$

$$(j = 1, 2, 3; \ i = 1, 2, ..., 52; \ t = 1, 2, ..., 5)$$

where $Y_{jit}$ refers to the $j$'th input factor in the $i$'th enterprise at time $t$, $h_{sit}$ refers to average annual actual hours worked minus overtime hours,[8] $(Z/v)_{it}$ is the ratio of average non-wage to wage costs,[9] $q_{it}$ is annual quits divided by total employment, $Q_{it}$ is output, $X_{kit} > s$ are the set of control variables, $e_{jit}$ is an error term and the $\beta$'s and $\gamma$'s are parameters to be estimated. The three input factors are $Y_1 = N$, $Y_2 = h$ and $Y_3 = (h - h_s)$.

The 12 variables[10] in the control vector ($X$) are as follows:

$$X = (K, LOST, PUN, COMP, STOC, BATCH, FLOW,$$
$$MALE, SHIFT, RAS, IND1, IND2), \quad (9.16)$$

where $K$ = capital stock, $LOST$ = annual working days lost per worker, $PUN$ = percentage shopfloor unionized, $COMP$ = concentration index ($= 1/$(no. of competitors)), $STOC$ = stocks and work in progress, $BATCH$ = dummy for predominantly batch production, $FLOW$ = dummy for predominantly flow production, $MALE$ = percentage male workers, $SHIFT$ = percentage shopfloor working shifts, $RAS$ = ratio of advertising expenditure to sales, $IND1$ = product group dummy, $IND2$- = product group dummy.

It will suffice to comment briefly on a few of the variables included in (9.16). The capital stock, $K$, has been included in several extended versions of the basic model in Section 9.2(a) (see Brechling, 1965; Calmfors and Hoel, 1988; Hart, 1987). It might be expected that *a priori*, $\partial N/\partial K < 0$, $\partial \bar{h}/\partial K > 0$ and $\partial(h - h_s)/\partial K > 0$, although Brechling argues that, in practice, it is often difficult to interpret the actual role played by $K$ in this type of equation. The main point is that it is clearly important to include $K$ in the regressions, especially given the cross-section dimension of the data. The choice of the variable $LOST$ is motivated by Ehrenberg's (1971a) study and it is taken as a proxy for the absentee rate. The outcome with respect to $PUN$ is of interest given official union opposition to high levels of overtime working over this, largely recessionary, period. Finally, we might expect high average total and overtime hours to be associated with $MALE$ and $SHIFT$.

The results shown in Section 9.4 are obtained from three main types of regression equation based on the structure in (9.15).

### (i) OLS CROSS-SECTION

For the demand equations with respect to $Y_{1it}$ and $Y_{2it}$ (i.e. workers and

170

average total hours) five separate OLS cross-section regressions are estimated for $t = 1$ (1978) through to $t = 5$ (1982). Note, in particular, that the respective signs of the coefficients with respect to $h_{sit}$ (i.e. $\beta_{11}$ and $\beta_{12}$) are *ambiguous* since our enterprises consist of *both* those working some and those working no overtime[11] (see the discussion in relation to Figures 9.1 and 9.2). These are denoted 'overtime' and 'non-overtime' enterprises henceforth.

## (ii) TOBIT CROSS-SECTION

For the demand equation with respect to $Y_{3it}$ (i.e. overtime hours), five separate TOBIT cross-section regressions are estimated for $t = 1$ through to $t = 5$. This estimator is appropriate because, for some enterprises in each year, $Y_3 = 0$. In the cases of these regressions, we expect $\beta_{13} > 0$ from the arguments associated with Figure 9.1.

## (iii) GLS POOLED CROSS-SECTION/TIME-SERIES

The five separate cross-section equations under (i) were also pooled and GLS estimates derived. The estimator was based on the assumed error structure (see Kmenta, 1971, pp. 509–12, for full details):

$$E(e^2_{jit}) = \sigma_{ji}; \ E(e_{jit}e_{jpt}) = 0(i \neq p); \ e_{jit} = \rho_{ji}e_{ji,t-1} + u_{jit} \qquad (9.17)$$

$$u_{jit} \sim N(0, \sigma^2_{uji}) \text{ and } E(e_{ji,t-1}u_{jpt}) = 0 \text{ (all } i, p).[12]$$

Pooled estimates were also obtained for the demand equations in (i) using *separate* samples of overtime and non-overtime enterprises.

Finally, some mention should be given to possible simultaneity problems.

Ehrenberg and Schumann (1982) present arguments – connected with fringe benefit payments – why the ratio of fixed to variable labor costs, $Z/v$, may be endogenously determined with overtime hours.

If we admit arguments from outside the immediate cost-minimization theory, then the quit rate, $q$, may also be regarded as an endogenous variable. For example, Hoel and Vale (1986) provide an analysis of the effects of cuts in the standard workweek based on the efficiency wage theory. In their model, the quit rate plays a central role and it is endogenously determined. The firm is treated as a wage setter and its optimizing behavior includes reacting to potential increases in quit threats and/or the cost of quits by an upward adjustment of the wage rate. Hours reductions increase quit costs – since, effectively, they shorten the expected period over which specific investments are discounted – and thus may be expected to produce wage reactions as firms try to reduce the quit rate.

From the discussion in Section 9.2(a) and 9.2(b), output $Q$ is treated as *either* an exogenous *or* an endogenous variable depending on cost-minimizing or profit-maximizing assumptions. At an enterprise level of aggregation, the assumption of exogeneity might be thought to be reasonable.

From the control variables in (9.16), $K$ and *SHIFT* may well be regarded as endogenously determined. In the latter case, Calmfors and Hoel (1985) present a theoretical analysis of shiftworking treated as an endogenous utilization variable within the cost-minimizing/profit-maximizing workers–hours demand structure outlined in Section 9.2.

Two-stage regressions were undertaken in which instrumental variable estimates of $Z/v$, $q$, $Q$, $K$ and *SHIFT* were obtained and then these were incorporated into the final estimating equations. In the event, the results were in reasonable accord with those obtained under (i)–(iii) above and so for space considerations they are not included.

## 9.4 Results

The main results with respect to (9.15) are shown in Tables 9.1, 9.2 and 9.3.

The results in Table 9.1 (the worker equation) are generally very supportive of the theoretical predictions summarized in equation (9.5). The standard hours variable, $h_s$, is insignificant but, as discussed in Section 9.2, its true role is better evaluated after separating overtime and non-overtime enterprises (see below). The labor cost ratio, $Z/v$, and the quit rate, $q$, display the correct negative sign throughout with generally stable coefficients. The outcome with respect to the labor cost ratio is tempered, however, by an unsatisfactory performance of this variable in the hours equations (see below). Output, $Q$, is comprehensively strong. Of the control variables, it will suffice to comment on ony a few points of interest. Perhaps contrary to *a priori* expectations, the capital stock is everywhere significantly positive: further discussion on why this outcome might occur can be found in Brechling (1965, p. 202). Of the remaining controls, STOC and RAS play the most significant roles, although it is perhaps difficult to give hard and fast reasons for their respective positive and negative influences.

The estimated $h_s$ elasticities are less than unity in the $h$-equations in Table 9.2. A fall in standard hours produces a less than proportional fall in total hours. The coefficient magnitudes – between 0.75 and 0.88 – are reasonably similar to (the average of) those obtained by Neale and Wilson (1985) using time-series regressions for 40 separate UK industries, 1948–77. In line with the comments of these authors, our results are suggestive of the possibility that the proportion of overtime hours to total hours may rise with a fall in standard hours. The equivalent results from the TOBIT regressions in Table 9.3 are consistent with this: these produce $h_s$ elasticities between $-5.3$ and $-7.8$.

In 1980, for example, the average annual values of $h$ and $h_s$ were 1850 and 1750, respectively. If $h_s$ is reduced by 175 hours, or 10 per cent, then $h$ is predicted to fall *less* than proportionately; in fact, $h$ reduces by 141 hours (i.e. $1850 [(1575/1750)^{0.754} - 1]$). This suggests that, as a partial offset, overtime has risen. From the theory, the average non-overtime enterprise would be expected to make up the standard hours deficiency

**Table 9.1**
Worker Equations: OLS Cross-Section and GLS Pooled
Cross-Section/Time-Series, 1978–82

| Independent variables | 1982 | 1981 | 1980 | 1979 | 1978 | Pooled regressions |
|---|---|---|---|---|---|---|
| $h_s$ | −0.561 | 0.052 | 0.461 | 0.411 | 0.287 | −0.167 |
|  | (−0.835) | (0.070) | (0.653) | (0.575) | (0.521) | (−0.784) |
| $Z/v$ | −0.285 | −0.358 | −0.169 | −0.519* | −0.393* | −0.280* |
|  | (−1.483) | (−1.518) | (−0.741) | (−2.327) | (−2.228) | (−3.891) |
| $q$ | −0.009 | −0.111 | −0.077 | −0.108 | −0.060 | −0.039* |
|  | (−0.169) | (−1.674) | (−1.284) | (−1.652) | (−1.388) | (−2.419) |
| $Q$ | −0.701* | −0.485* | −0.551* | −0.699* | 0.649* | −0.619* |
|  | (9.058) | (4.888) | (6.083) | (7.337) | (6.900) | (20.780) |
| $K$ | 0.187* | 0.349* | 0.368* | 0.214* | −0.241* | 0.276* |
|  | (3.122) | (3.940) | (4.732) | (2.318) | (2.799) | (10.869) |
| LOST | −0.109* | −0.080 | −0.073 | −0.052 | 0.098 | −0.067* |
|  | (−2.188) | (−1.032) | (−0.924) | (−0.840) | (1.448) | (−3.516) |
| PUN | 0.001 | 0.003 | −0.000(3) | 0.024 | 0.011 | 0.028 |
|  | (0.840) | (0.044) | (−0.165) | (0.389) | (0.189) | (1.450) |
| COMP | −0.072 | −0.077 | −0.043 | −0.052 | −0.039 | −0.050* |
|  | (−1.602) | (−1.256) | (−0.762) | (−1.018) | (−0.858) | (−3.379) |
| STOC | 0.292* | 0.285* | 0.317* | 0.465* | 0.204* | 0.267* |
|  | (2.799) | (2.356) | (2.103) | (2.810) | (1.810) | (7.170) |
| BATCH | −0.380* | −0.179 | −0.195 | −0.155 | −0.076 | −0.249* |
|  | (−2.451) | (−0.858) | (−0.957) | (−0.867) | (−0.457) | (−5.524) |
| FLOW | −0.067 | −0.003 | −0.046 | −0.093 | −0.075 | −0.094 |
|  | (−0.411) | (−0.014) | (−0.204) | (0.466) | (0.431) | (−0.968) |
| MALE | −0.004 | −0.003 | −0.005 | −0.002 | −0.004 | −0.004* |
|  | (−1.104) | (−0.054) | (−1.071) | (−0.454) | (−0.982) | (−3.716) |
| SHIFT | −0.001 | −0.0003 | 0.0002 | −0.002 | −0.002 | 0.002 |
|  | (−0.148) | (−0.059) | (0.027) | (−0.349) | (−0.426) | (1.087) |
| RAS | −0.055* | −0.058 | −0.060 | −0.038 | −0.046 | −0.072* |
|  | (−1.798) | (−1.294) | (−1.434) | (−0.945) | (−1.348) | (−6.391) |
| IND1 | 0.318* | 0.222 | 0.272 | 0.044 | 0.249 | 0.336* |
|  | (1.847) | (0.946) | (1.284) | (0.197) | (1.439) | (5.537) |
| IND2 | −0.002 | −0.030 | −0.015 | −0.093 | −0.0072 | 0.059 |
|  | (−0.148) | (−0.173) | (−0.092) | (−0.599) | (−0.535) | (1.029) |
| CONSTANT | 2.941 | −1.587 | −4.489 | −4.918 | −3.891 | −0.072 |
|  | (0.576) | (−0.288) | (−0.834) | (−0.902) | (−0.921) | (−0.044) |
| $\bar{R}^2$ | 0.94 | 0.89 | 0.91 | 0.92 | 0.94 |  |
| F | 53.32 | 27.58 | 31.70 | 39.30 | 49.39 |  |

*Notes:* $t$ ratios in parentheses under coefficients; *indicates significant at 5 per cent level.

by increasing its workforce.[13] The average overtime enterprise, on the other hand, would expect a workforce reduction accompanied by a more-than-offsetting rise in overtime hours. Supporting evidence with respect to the workforce predictions is presented in Table 9.4 below. As for overtime hours, a 10 per cent reduction in $h_s$ in 1980 would produce an average rise in annual overtime per worker of 125 hours (i.e.

**Table 9.2**
Total Hours Equations: OLS Cross-Section and GLS Pooled
Cross-Section/Time-Series, 1978–82

| Independent variables | 1982 | 1981 | 1980 | 1979 | 1978 | Pooled regressions |
|---|---|---|---|---|---|---|
| $h_s$ | 0.825* | 0.848* | 0.754* | 0.746* | 0.875* | 0.769* |
|  | (6.718) | (8.786) | (10.017) | (10.107) | (10.594) | (28.360) |
| $Z/v$ | −0.029 | −0.055* | −0.050* | −0.029 | −0.014 | −0.035* |
|  | (−0.831) | (−1.771) | (2.064) | (−1.242) | (−0.517) | (−4.252) |
| $q$ | −0.007 | −0.008 | 0.003 | −0.004 | 0.003 | −0.001 |
|  | (−0.787) | (−0.983) | (0.538) | (−0.597) | (0.518) | (−0.408) |
| $K$ | −0.006 | −0.008 | −0.004 | 0.002 | 0.004 | 0.002 |
|  | (−0.825) | (−1.158) | (−0.753) | (0.437) | (0.721) | (0.922) |
| LOST | −0.002 | 0.004 | 0.006 | 0.014* | 0.002 | 0.005* |
|  | (−0.270) | (0.443) | (0.772) | (2.201) | (0.217) | (2.093) |
| PUN | −0.0007* | −0.014 | −0.0003 | −0.011 | −0.005 | −0.010* |
|  | (−2.359) | (−1.392) | (−1.471) | (−1.671) | (−0.594) | (−4.027) |
| COMP | −0.001 | −0.007 | −0.003 | −0.002 | 0.001 | −0.001 |
|  | (−0.117) | (−0.841) | (−0.506) | (−0.456) | (0.122) | (−0.729) |
| STOC | 0.012 | 0.022 | 0.029* | 0.002 | −0.003 | 0.105* |
|  | (0.617) | (1.360) | (1.795) | (0.184) | (−0.151) | (2.122) |
| BATCH | 0.037 | 0.033 | 0.005 | 0.007 | 0.002 | 0.019* |
|  | (1.290) | (1.181) | (0.253) | (0.372) | (0.079) | (3.378)* |
| FLOW | 0.090* | 0.073* | 0.038 | 0.026 | 0.008 | 0.053* |
|  | (3.005) | (2.455) | (1.682) | (1.240) | (0.302) | (3.555) |
| MALE | 0.001* | 0.001* | 0.0003 | 0.0003 | 0.0002 | 0.002* |
|  | (1.806) | (1.754) | (0.750) | (0.760) | (0.371) | (1.729) |
| SHIFT | 0.0002 | −0.0002 | 0.0003 | 0.001 | 0.0003 | 0.003* |
|  | (0.361) | (−0.256) | (0.531) | (0.903) | (0.504) | (1.860) |
| RAS | 0.0004 | 0.005 | −0.0003 | 0.004 | −0.002 | 0.002 |
|  | (0.067) | (0.867) | (−0.065) | (0.932) | (−0.393) | (0.168) |
| IND1 | −0.502 | −0.038 | −0.031 | −0.022 | −0.013 | −0.025* |
|  | (−1.623) | (−1.238) | (−1.351) | (−0.912) | (−0.490) | (−3.105) |
| IND2 | −0.0001 | 0.003 | −0.001 | 0.007 | 0.017 | 0.006 |
|  | (−0.004) | (0.113) | (−0.064) | (0.414) | (0.844) | (0.925) |
| CONSTANT | 1.280 | 1.083 | 1.856* | 1.845* | 0.025 | 1.727* |
|  | (1.370) | (1.481) | (3.252) | (3.242) | (1.465) | (8.636) |
| $\bar{R}^2$ | 0.54 | 0.72 | 0.75 | 0.75 | 0.72 |  |
| F | 5.07 | 9.69 | 11.07 | 11.13 | 9.78 |  |

Notes: $t$ ratios in parentheses under coefficients; *indicates significant at 5 per cent level.

$100[(1575/1750)^{-7.713} - 1])$. Thus, we do not predict that overtime increases will more than compensate for standard hours losses. The estimated overtime response is quite substantial, however.

Of the remaining 'key' variables in both sets of hours equations (see Tables 9.2 and 9.3), the labor cost ratio is the most disappointing, displaying an incorrect and largely significant negative sign. This outcome may reflect, in part, our inability to distinguish from the data

**Table 9.3**
Overtime Hours Equations: TOBIT Cross-Section, 1978–82

| Independent variables | 1982 | 1981 | 1980 | 1979 | 1978 |
|---|---|---|---|---|---|
| $h_s$ | −7.814* | −5.310 | −7.713* | −6.676* | −5.294* |
| | (−1.965) | (−1.558) | (−2.483) | (−1.926) | (−1.658) |
| $Z/v$ | −1.346 | −2.803* | −2.259* | −2.524* | −1.290 |
| | (−1.180) | (−2.426) | (−2.189) | (−2.264) | (−1.259) |
| $q$ | −0.314 | −0.339 | 0.132 | −0.218 | −0.032 |
| | (−1.071) | (−1.119) | (0.512) | (−0.681) | (−0.130) |
| $K$ | 0.182 | 0.124 | 0.164 | 0.363 | 0.458* |
| | (0.832) | (0.489) | (0.788) | (1.570) | (1.904) |
| LOST | −0.393 | −0.141 | −0.143 | −0.491 | −0.082 |
| | (−1.391) | (−0.427) | (−0.458) | (1.673) | (−0.223) |
| PUN | −0.008 | −0.427 | −0.458 | 1.673 | −0.223 |
| | (−0.742) | (−1.114) | (−0.029) | (−1.212) | (−1.257) |
| COMP | −0.076 | −0.319 | −0.018 | −0.118 | −0.032 |
| | (−0.286) | (−1.095) | (−0.072) | (−0.473) | (−0.124) |
| STOC | 0.216 | 1.110* | 0.396 | 0.082 | −0.827 |
| | (0.358) | (1.897) | (0.603) | (0.136) | (−1.257) |
| BATCH | 1.066 | 1.453 | 0.948 | 1.795* | 1.226 |
| | (1.159) | (1.475) | (1.101) | (2.001) | (1.260) |
| FLOW | 2.689* | 2.888* | 1.900* | 2.171* | 1.416 |
| | (2.699) | (2.682) | (2.017) | (2.181) | (1.437) |
| MALE | 0.019 | 0.036 | −0.002 | 0.0003 | 0.016 |
| | (0.908) | (1.587) * | (−0.113) | (0.016) | (0.770) |
| SHIFT | 0.033 | 0.007 | 0.037 | 0.020 | 0.033 |
| | (1.327) | (0.227) | (1.551) | (0.773) | (1.234) |
| RAS | −0.035 | 0.257 | −0.160 | 0.097 | 0.019 |
| | (−0.199) | (1.248) | (−0.896) | (0.491) | (0.097) |
| IND1 | −2.411* | −2.269* | −1.656* | −1.344 | −1.861 |
| | (−2.300) | (−1.993) | (−1.749) | (−1.189) | (−1.787) |
| IND2 | 0.554 | −0.069 | 0.878 | 1.176 | 0.950 |
| | (0.746) | (−0.085) | (1.236) | (1.500) | (1.212) |
| CONSTANT | 55.849* | 35.369 | 56.083* | 44.131 | 35.421 |
| | (1.847) | (1.372) | (2.380) | (1.655) | (1.454) |

*Notes: t* ratios in parentheses under coefficients; *indicates significant at 5 per cent level.

set between the quasi-fixed and variable components of total non-wage labor costs. The performance of the quit rate is also unsatisfactory, being generally insignificant.[14]

Of the control variables in Tables 9.2 and 9.3, the working days lost variable (LOST) has a significant positive impact on hours in only one year (1979), although it is significant in the pooled *h*-equation in Table 9.2. The union variable (PUN) is associated with lower average total and overtime hours, as might be expected. Also in line with expectation, the proportion of males in an enterprise (MALE) is (in large part) positively associated with both total and overtime hours. Finally, enterprises with a predominantly flow-production technology ( *FLOW* ) appear to require, as might be anticipated, higher average total and overtime hours.

Recall from the theory in Section 9.2 that a fall in $h_s$ is predicted, *ceteris paribus*, to produce a reduction in $\bar{N}$ within enterprises that work significant levels of overtime and an increase in $\bar{N}$ within enterprises that work only standard hours. This is an important dichotomy and, in order to provide a simple test, we divided our enterprises into those that employed some overtime in one or more years in the sample and those that employed none at all during this time. This provided us with respective sample sizes of 43 and 9 enterprises. Accordingly, given the small latter sample, we estimated pooled regressions for each sample over the entire time period. Results are presented in Table 9.4: in order to save space, only those estimates with respect to the variables relevant to Section 9.2 are shown, although, of course, the regressions included the full set of control variables.

In accord with the theory, the results indicate that a fall in $h_s$ would reduce $\bar{N}$ in overtime enterprises and increase $\bar{N}$ in non-overtime enterprises. Our definition of non-overtime enterprises is rather strict. In those cases where overtime working is relatively low – and especially if there is any form of guaranteed element – then such enterprises may be effectively at the 'kink' of their cost functions as in Figure 9.2. We experimented by extending the definition of 'non-overtime' enterprises to include those with relatively little recourse to overtime working.[15] This provided somewhat less significant results than those reported in Table 9.4. The remaining variables in the N-equations in Table 9.4 perform, with one exception, strongly in line with expectations.

Contrary to theory, a fall in $h_s$ produces a fall in $h$ – albeit a less than

**Table 9.4**
Worker and Total Hours Equation for Overtime and Non-Overtime Enterprises: Pooled GLS, 1978–82

| Independent variables | Overtime enterprises | | Non-overtime enterprises |
|---|---|---|---|
| | $N$ | $h$ | $N$ |
| $h_s$ | 0.411* | 0.802* | −0.494 |
| | (1.959) | (29.946) | (−1.369) |
| $Z/v$ | −0.482* | −0.004 | −0.438* |
| | (−5.611) | (−0.374) | (−2.658) |
| $q$ | −0.039* | −0.002 | 0.059 |
| | (−2.303) | (−1.197) | (1.606) |
| $Q$ | 0.527* | — | 0.188* |
| | (14.529) | | (2.247) |

*Notes: t* ratios in parentheses under coefficients; *indicates significant at 5 per cent level.

proportional fall – in the overtime enterprises. A number of factors may help to explain this outcome. First, for those enterprises with relatively low incidences of overtime working, there may be little recourse, or opportunity, to effect a substantial substitution between internal and external margins. Secondly, if only a proportion of employees work overtime then, for those who work only standard hours – owing perhaps to supply or technical constraints – the enterprise may have less opportunity to extend the utilization of its existing workforce. Thirdly, if actual overtime schedules are better approximated by functions such as (9.7) where premium payments are positively related to total hours then the outcome in Table 9.4 may be compatible with theoretical prediction.

## 9.5 Hours and Employment

Although, inevitably, some anomalies occur, our results are generally quite supportive of the underlying theory. In this concluding section we wish to comment in particular on our findings with respect to changes in scheduled hours on employment and overtime.

This work allows us to make some pertinent comments with respect to the working time debate that has featured prominently in Europe (and Australasia) in recent years. On the basis of our evidence, there is little reason for expecting that reductions in annual hours will be translated into more jobs. Any employment increase in those enterprises that are constrained, for whatever reason, to employ little or no overtime, is likely to be offset by a substitution out of employment and into more overtime working by other enterprises.

Interestingly, our results are very supportive of two large establishment-level questionnaire-type surveys into shorter weekly hours in 218 establishments in the UK engineering, pharmaceutical, printing and construction industries carried out in 1981 and 1982/3[16] (White, 1983; White and Ghobadian, 1984). A cut of 1 hour in the standard workweek took place in those industries in 1981. Clear evidence was found that the reduction in weekly standard hours either left employment more or less unchanged or resulted in lower employment. Further, average overtime hours were observed to increase. It should be added that the study period covered a time of general output stability/slight growth in the industries in question.

The results also indicate that large empirical discrepancies tend to exist in the predictions concerning working time changes between partial labor market analyses such as the present contribution and large-scale econometric models.[17] Our belief is that, while there are clear strengths and weaknesses in both approaches, the failure of the latter studies to model the labor market other than in a relatively crude fashion is a decisive deficiency. Besides, more theoretical macro-approaches (e.g. Hoel, 1986; Strøm, 1983) tend to produce predictions broadly on a par with those of the theory in Section 9.2.

## Appendix: The Distribution of Overtime Working in the Complete Sample

Table 9A.1 presents frequency distributions of average annual overtime working for the full 260 observations (i.e. 52 enterprises × 5 years) in our complete sample. It clearly establishes the necessity of accommodating overtime working, at least as far as the UK metal working industry is concerned.

**Table 9A.1**

| Average annual overtime hours | Absolute frequency | Relative frequency |
| --- | --- | --- |
| 0 | 48 | 18.5 |
| 1 and less than 20 | 14 | 5.4 |
| 20 and less than 40 | 27 | 10.4 |
| 40 and less than 60 | 25 | 9.6 |
| 60 and less than 80 | 26 | 10.0 |
| 80 and less than 100 | 12 | 4.6 |
| 100 and less than 120 | 17 | 6.5 |
| 120 and less than 140 | 12 | 4.6 |
| 140 and less than 160 | 12 | 4.6 |
| 160 and less than 180 | 13 | 5.0 |
| 180 and less than 200 | 15 | 5.8 |
| 200 and less than 220 | 14 | 5.4 |
| 220 and less than 240 | 9 | 3.5 |
| >240 | 16 | 6.2 |
| | 260 | 100.0 |

## Acknowledgements

We would like to thank Olaf Hübler and Bill Wells for their comments. The data for the empirical part of the paper derive from the ESRC-sponsored project on Work Organisation, Participation and Economic Performance carried out by John Cable and Nick Wilson.

## Notes

1  For a comprehensive review of theoretical and empirical work in the entire area referred to in the Introduction, see Hart (1987).
2  The word 'standard' is used for convenience. Alternatives include 'normal' and 'scheduled' hours. The essential point is that such hours can be treated as exogenously given to the typical firm.
3  Full derivations for the cost-minimization model presented here can be found in Ehrenberg (1971a) and Hart (1984a).
4  For a similar model that includes multiple shifts and a variable capital stock see Calmfors and Hoel (1988). Further see Hart (1987) for a wide review of

this type of model in which other types of economic variables are also featured. Our approach here is to add the most obvious control variables in a somewhat *ad hoc* manner at the empirical stage.

5  For close variations to these developments see Brechling (1965), Rosen (1968) and Calmfors and Hoel (1988).

6  We assume, therefore, that the second-order necessary condition to achieve a minimum is satisfied. It can be shown that (see Hart, 1987, Ch. 5) this requires $\varepsilon - (1 - \alpha) < 0$, or higher returns to workers than hours. Empirical evidence (for a review, see Hart, 1987, Ch. 6) is mixed.

7  Excluding the discount rate, $r$, which is assumed (heroically) to be constant across enterprises and through time.

8  Both part-time and short-time working are negligible in our sample and so problems of interpretation that would be associated with these variables are minimal.

9  Variable costs, $v$, refer to average wage *earnings* and so $v$ acts as a composite variable for $w_s$ and $a$ in (9.5) and (9.6).

10  Four of the variables are, in fact, dummies (see (9.16)). In order to conform with the notation in (9.15) the original dummies can be regarded as taking the values of 1 or e so that logging produces the required '0–1' values.

11  The relative importance of overtime within the enterprises in our data set is shown in a simple table in the Appendix (p. 178).

12  There is some inconsistency between the methodology in (iii) on the one hand and in (i) and (ii) on the other, since the latter do not accommodate the possibility of heteroskedastic error structures.

13  In 1980, 10 enterprises worked no overtime whatsoever, while 42 worked some overtime.

14  Note the absence of $Q$ in both sets of hours results. The variable proved to be completely insignificant and so the equation equivalent to a scale-invariance interpretation of hours demand – see Section 9.2(b) – was adopted.

15  Defined (somewhat arbitrarily) as those enterprises that never exceeded 50 hours of overtime per worker in any year within the five-year period: this provided an additional 4 enterprises in the 'non-overtime' subset.

16  The second survey was a follow-up investigation that attempted to quantify the *ex post* effects of shorter hours through a detailed examination of production and accounting data.

17  For reviews of European models, see van Ginneken (1984) and Hart (1987).

# COMMENT

## OLAF HÜBLER

Hart and Wilson have presented a very thoughtful and interesting investigation into the relationship between workers, standard hours and overtime. Hart has been working on these topics for several years, and has published new ideas, methods and empirical results in a number of papers. In comparison with these earlier papers, this investigation by Hart and Wilson contains five new points: detailed analysis of standard hours effects concentrated on a particular specification; the use of microeconomic data from firms instead of aggregated industry data; TOBIT estimation of cross-section data for the overtime equations; separate estimation for firms with and without overtime; and pooled cross-section/time-series GLS estimation. In the theoretical section Hart and Wilson follow the cost-minimization approach, which was previously extended by Hart in several stages. However they also discuss other approaches and these introduce alternative implications. Hart and Wilson's main message is their skepticism about the positive employment effects of a reduction in standard hours.

My comments involve some additions to the theory as well as suggestions concerning modifications of method. My first point concerns the question of varying productivity and intensity of labor utilization, which Hart and Wilson do not discuss. The discussion in the literature has concentrated on the question of whether the elasticity of output with respect to hours is larger than that with respect to the number of workers. From a theoretical viewpoint one might expect the elasticity of output with respect to hours to be greater than that with respect to workers. The arguments that support the hypothesis of increasing returns to hours are: (i) some non-wage costs tend to concentrate within standard working time (set-up time, pauses), and (ii) increasing hours may reduce the per-unit cost of capital services because of proportionately lower increases in depreciation and interest charges.

In particular, the results of Hart and McGregor (1988) contrast with these theoretical arguments when they separate the hours variable into its standard and overtime components. Based on a pooled cross-section/time-series model of West German manufacturing data, they find significantly lower returns to premium hours compared to workers. However, Hart (1984b, p. 94) has emphasized that it is difficult to produce a convincing theoretical argument to support a systematic correlation between firm efficiency and working hours. I believe it is necessary to consider the relation between the individual worker's effort and working hours. Perhaps then we can explain a systematic relationship.

My own hypothesis runs as follows. A relationship exists between these two variables but this relation is non-linear. First, effort increases with working hours until we reach an optimal labor intensity; later on, if the hours are further expanded, effort decreases. The increased effort can be explained by points (i) and (ii) above. Another explanation arises from the efficiency wage hypothesis. The overtime premium increases workers' efforts when overtime work starts, but there are physiological restrictions. Overtime work leads to fatigue and exhaustion, with attention and concentration diminishing.

The normal pattern of work intensity with respect to working hours is first increasing and then decreasing. But a short-run rise at any time is possible – for example induced by pressure from superiors to complete a time-limited contract. However, the implication of such short-run expansion of work intensity is an excessive reduction of intensity in the following time period compared with the normal shape, especially if there is no or limited time for relaxation.

If this pattern of work intensity is accepted, then it is possible to explain the theoretical anomaly of the empirical result that total hours decrease with the reduction of standard hours. In a model with profit maximization, with a Cobb–Douglas production function where the number of workers ($N$) and average hours ($h$) are the input factors and with varying labor intensity represented by a parabolic function, it can be shown that there exists a relevant range in which a marginal reduction of standard hours ($h_s$) decreases the total hours ($h$). A sufficient condition for this result is that the output elasticity with respect to workers ($\alpha_N$) is greater than that with respect to hours ($\alpha_h$) and $h^* < h$ where $h^*$ is the hours representing optimal labor intensity. If we assume constant (optimal) labor intensity, then $\partial h / \partial h_s < 0$ follows from $\alpha_N > \alpha_h$. This result is in accordance with Hart and Wilson's. However, if the total hours are in the range of over-optimal intensity, then we have a positive partial derivative. All empirical studies support this result. In contrast to Santamäki's approach (1986), it is not necessary to assume that the premium for overtime working has to vary with the ratio of total to standard hours, although the positive sign $\partial h / \partial h_s$ can be strengthened by this assumption.

My second point concerns the question of heterogeneous labor. Hart and Wilson assume that all employees work the same number of hours. But in practice there are differences. Different groups within the heterogeneous workforce could be relevant to observations of varying working time: the willingness to work overtime differs between young and old employees, legal and union rules relating to overtime are based on the age of the workers or on their seniority, non-wage labor costs vary with tenure and with skill differentials, workers' degree of substitution for capital varies with work qualifications, workers' effort for a given working time differs between skilled and unskilled, between promoted and non-promoted, between motivated and unmotivated workers. We should therefore introduce variables into the equations for workers and for total and overtime hours relating to the proportions of skilled and unskilled workers, young and old employees, workers with short and long tenure. If the coefficients of the other exogenous variables are affected by these new variables, it would be necessary to construct interaction variables (for example between non-wage costs and tenure) or to estimate split regressions for heterogeneous labor. In the latter case, we would have to pay attention to the truncation problem. The procedure of separate regressions has to be preferred if unobserved variables vary systematically with the type of labor.

However, it is not possible to separate firm data in this way because firms have both skilled and unskilled workers, persons with short and long tenure, promoted and non-promoted employees. One way to handle this problem is to classify firms by whether they have predominantly one or the other kind of labor and to eliminate those firms that have more or less the same percentage of the different kinds. Another way is to use individual data. My own calculations using data from the German Socio-economic Panel reveal that the differences in estimated overtime from split regression with short and long tenure are remarkable. For example, the non-wage cost effects of overtime are significant for workers with short tenure but not for workers with long tenure. This can be explained in the following way. Fixed costs for on-the-job training are necessary in the first phase of employment in a new firm and therefore firms are particularly keen for new employees to work more overtime in this phase than later in order to recoup the investment as soon as possible.

In my third comment I consider different kinds of overtime working. Hart and Wilson have not defined overtime hours. Following Ehrenberg (1971a, p. 55), observed overtime includes all hours for which premium pay is received. But I think this definition is too narrow. In an unpublished report on overtime by the West German government three kinds of overtime are distinguished: paid definite overtime hours; unpaid definite overtime hours; transitory overtime hours with leisure compensation. Of course, the first type is the most relevant, but German unions want to prohibit paid overtime hours. Their thesis is that overtime hours with leisure compensation serve to force firms to transform an increased demand for goods into more jobs. In addition, they expect a reduction in annual working hours to lead to more jobs. So I think it is useful to separate the effects of these three kinds of overtime hours.

Transitory overtime involves a temporary redistribution of individual working hours and so fixed costs per hour of one worker are the same with and without transitory overtime hours. Firms thus have no opportunity to improve the fixed cost/hour ratio. If transitory overtime hours are involved, what happens during the leisure compensation time? Three possibilities exist: reduction of output; recruitment of new workers; intensification of labor utilization. If firms could choose they would normally prefer the third kind of overtime, especially for workers with high fixed non-wage costs. The type of leisure compensation would determine the degree of increased labor utilization. In general, I suppose that transitory overtime hours increase with fixed non-wage costs but to a lesser extent than paid overtime hours. The strongest effect is expected for unpaid hours because the fixed costs per hour are lower and there is no premium rate for overtime working. But it is necessary to distinguish between the overtime effects of the diverse non-wage components.

My fourth comment pertains to the pooled cross-section/time-series estimations. Hart and Wilson follow Kmenta's approach, in which the assumptions are heteroskedasticity between the firms, no autocorrelation between the firms' data but a first-order autoregressive process of the time-series observations. The authors do not give a substantial explanation why they use these assumptions. In many circumstances these are likely to be a reasonable set of assumptions, but we can test in each case whether the model is correct or not. Although it is not always necessary for cross-sectional heteroskedasticity and timewise autocorrelation to exist, we have to prove, too, whether the disturbances of different firms are contemporaneously correlated. Perhaps the most restrictive implicit assumption of the Hart–Wilson model is that the coefficients are constant for all firms and over time. In the econometric literature some well-known models include varying intercepts over individuals. This is not so relevant for the Hart–Wilson model because they consider enterprise-specific influences which are incorporated by the control variables. However, there exist time effects that are common to all firms. If we compare the sequential cross-section regressions (Table 9.1), we can observe cyclical effects. Global indicators for the United Kingdom such as the number of unemployed persons ($U$) shed some light on the possibilities. Thus, we have:

| Year | 1982 | 1981 | 1980 | 1979 | 1978 | 1977 |
|------|------|------|------|------|------|------|
| $U$ (in 1,000) | 2770 | 2395 | 1513 | 1234 | 1343 | 1359 |

As examples, the employment effect of standard hours changes increases with a reduction in the unemployment rate, and the negative influence of the ratio of average non-wage to wage costs on employment is strengthened by a decrease in unemployment. In times of upward adjustment (1978), both standard hours and the number of workers increase but the first effect is stronger than at the peak of the cycle (1979). Then the expansion of hours adjustment is limited but further employment increase can be observed (1980). In periods of downward adjustment, the speed of (standard) hours reduction is greater than that of employment (1981). At the bottom of the cycle (1982), the rate of layoffs is strengthened because standard hours and workers' effort increase.

The modeling implication of these cyclical effects is to incorporate interaction variables between global indicators such as $U$ and the variables included by Hart and Wilson. However, I do not believe it is possible to capture all time-varying effects with this procedure, as the vector $X$ (see equation 9.16) cannot control all firm-specific effects. From this it seems sensible to specify a pooled model with a varying intercept over firms and time. Hart and Wilson's equation (9.15) might take the form

$$\ln Y_{jit} = \beta_{0j} + \mu_{ji} + \lambda_{jt} + \beta_{1jt} \ln h_{sit} + \beta_{2jt} \ln(Z/v)_{it}$$
$$+ \beta_{3jt} \ln q_{it} + \beta_{4jt} \ln Q_{it} + \sum_{k=1}^{12} \gamma_{kj} \ln X_{kit} + e_{jit}$$

where $\beta_{ljt} = \bar{\beta}_{lj} + \beta_{lju} \ln U$ for $l = 1, 2, 3, 4$. So the suggested modifications are systematically varying coefficients with respect to global indicators as well as firm- and time-specific intercepts. Further, for model specification, one has to choose between a fixed and a random intercept. In other words, a choice has to be made between the dummy variable and the error component model. A mixed model is also possible. However, two facts point in favor of the dummy variable model: the vector of the control variables is correlated with $\mu_{ji}$, and the number of time periods is small.

My last point is a short one. I think it is very useful that the authors have carried out different estimations for enterprises with and without overtime. However, they neglect a potential selectivity bias. In order to correct for this the hazard rate as a new exogenous variable should be introduced.

# CHAPTER 10

# Labor Demand and Standard Working Time in Dutch Manufacturing, 1954–1982

ERIK R. De REGT

## 10.1 Introduction

Since the 1970s many European industrialized countries have faced high and persistent unemployment, even though the economy has recovered somewhat in recent years. One of the policies often advocated is 'work sharing' or the redistribution of the available scarce jobs among the employed and unemployed by a reduction of the normal length of the working week. The effectiveness of such policies crucially depends, amongst other things, on whether hours actually worked vary proportionally with standard working time and on the possible productivity gains resulting from such reductions. This paper first provides the theoretical basis for these statements and then gives some indicative answers to these questions for the Dutch manufacturing sector.

The paper is organized as follows. Section 10.2 presents the static model of labor demand and elaborates on the substitution between the number of workers and average working time. Section 10.3 outlines the dynamic structure of labor demand and the expectational model. Section 10.4 contains the estimation results: first, the output model is briefly discussed; then the equation for the number of workers is presented; and, finally, some results for overtime behavior are listed. Section 10.5 concludes with some final remarks.

## 10.2 A Static Model of Labor Demand

The static model of firm behavior describes a representative cost-minimizing firm, facing a known demand for its product. The firm produces a single product with two production factors: capital and labor. The services obtained from these inputs depend not only on the homogeneous stocks involved – the capital stock and the number of workers – but also on the utilization of these stocks – the operating time of capital and the working time of workers. Varying working or

185

operating time influences production costs, which include quasi-fixed costs of labor, wage costs and costs of capital services.

We start with a discussion of the model specification. Then comparative static results are presented for the short-run model, with a fixed capital stock. Finally, the properties of the long-run factor demand equations are reviewed.

### 10.2(a)   Model specification

In labor demand models it is increasingly recognized that labor services depend not only on the number of workers, but also on the working time of each worker employed. This has led authors such as Ball and St Cyr (1966) and Ehrenberg (1971a) to specify labor services according to

$$L = L(N, H) \quad 0 < L_N, L_H \tag{10.1}$$

where $L$ represents labor services, $N$ the number of workers and $H$ hours worked per employee. Partial derivatives are denoted by subscripts, e.g. $L_N = \partial L / \partial N$. By assumption workers are homogeneous and work the same number of hours.

To obtain a relation between output and labor services, equation (10.1) is generally substituted in a neoclassical production function. Considering only capital and labor as inputs, the typical production function used is (see, for example, Hart, 1984a):

$$Y = F(K, L) = F[K, L(N, H)], \tag{10.2}$$

where $Y$ is the production volume and $K$ the homogeneous capital stock. However, there seems to be a serious omission in this specification. The flow of capital services is proportional to the capital stock, which ignores the operating time of the capital stock – the number of hours a plant (or a machine) is in operation. But, obviously, given a fixed capital stock, capital services fall when the duration of operations is reduced. The production function should not fail to incorporate this.

The problem is easily remedied by introducing capital services, instead of the capital stock, as an input in the production function, (see, for example, Fair, 1969; Nadiri and Rosen, 1969; and Winston and McCoy, 1974). Analogous to labor services, the flow of capital services, $M$, can be modeled as a function of the capital stock, $K$, and the operating time of machinery. As shiftwork will not be considered in the present paper, the operating time of capital and working time of labor are of identical length. Hence, the production function can be written as

$$Y = F[M(K, H), L(N, H)] \quad 0 < F_M, F_L, M_K, M_H, L_N, L_H \tag{10.3}$$

where $F(M, L)$ is a well-behaved concave production function. In this specification, working time, $H$, is used as a conversion factor: it transforms the inputs from stocks to flows (compare Leslie and Wise,

186

1980). Accordingly, we are able to impose more structure on the general production function $Y = G(K, N, H)$ used by Feldstein (1976) and Bernanke (1986).

In the present analysis, equation (10.3) is further specialized by two additional assumptions. First, $F(M, L)$ is postulated to be linear homogeneous. Second, following the arguments by Ehrenberg (1971a), labor services and capital services are specified to be multiplicative separable functions. More specifically, the production function (10.3) is reduced to

$$Y = F[Ke_K(H), Ne_N(H)], \quad 0 < e_K', e_N'  \qquad (10.4)$$

where the function $e_N(H)$ is sometimes labeled efficiency hours. Efficiency hours have a constant marginal product in terms of labor services, whereas this does not necessarily apply to hours worked, $H$. What can plausibly be said about efficiency hours $e_N(H)$? Following arguments presented by Feldstein (1967, 1976) and Lewis (1969), among others, increasing returns to hours may prevail for short workweeks, for example owing to non-productive hours such as morning start-up times. Eventually, however, lengthening the workweek will have diminishing returns because of increased worker fatigue and boredom.

Similar arguments could apply to the productivity function of hours in capital services, $e_K(H)$, albeit less forcefully. But, unless there are fixed factor proportions in technology $F(\cdot)$, there seem to be no *a priori* reasons to include the same functional form for $e_K(H)$ and $e_N(H)$.

Although the restrictions imposed on the production function seem quite restrictive, a variety of implications can be derived, as will be shown below. However, before the comparative static analysis can be conducted, the cost structure should be introduced.

With respect to capital costs, it is simply assumed that the familiar user costs per unit of capital, $P_K$, are given and known. Possible links between the user costs of capital and the working or operating time, as suggested by Bosworth (1981) and Nadiri and Rosen (1969), are ignored, virtually without changing the qualitative conclusions.

More attention is paid to the specification of labor costs. The firm must obviously pay each worker on its payroll. However, the wage payment per employee, $P_N(H)$, may vary with the actual working time per worker. For the subsequent analysis it is useful to distinguish between standard, or contractual, hours, $H^c$, on the one hand, and hours actually worked, $H$, on the other. Standard hours are considered to be exogenous, for example set on the basis of collective bargaining. Standard working hours are remunerated according to the basic hourly scale wage rate, $W$. But if hours worked, $H$, deviate from contractual hours, $H^c$, the wage payment is adjusted simultaneously. Deardorff and Stafford (1976) have shown that, if the wage schedule is to compensate for the disutility of additional, or reduced, hours, the average wage rate should be roughly U-shaped. This condition is met by our parameterization

$$P_N(H) = WH^c o(H/H^c), \qquad (10.5)$$

187

where

$$o(h) \geqslant h, o(1) = 1; \ o'(h) > \ < 1 \text{ for } h > \ < 1; \text{ and } 0 \leqslant o', o''.$$

The function $o(h)$, with $h = H/H^c$, summarizes the relation between hours worked and their remuneration. Rewriting (10.5) as

$$P_N(H) = WH^c + (1 + \theta)W(H - H^c)$$

with $\theta = [O(h) - h]/(h - 1)$, it is easily checked that for overtime hours, $H > H^c$, an overtime premium $\theta > 0$ is added to the scale wage rate to induce workers to substitute leisure for income and to supply additional hours.

Equation (10.5) also specifies wage costs if short-time prevails, i.e. when hours worked fall below standard hours, $H < H^c$. Although the remuneration per worker, $P_N(H)$, is falling, the average hourly wage costs, $P_N(H)/H$, are rising with a reduction of hours below standard working time. The following rationale can be given: explicit or implicit labor contracts between firms and workers often specify that hours paid for do not fall below some fallback level, sometimes equal to standard hours (see Fair, 1969). Moreover, in many industrialized countries, including the Netherlands, legislation provides workers on temporary short-time with partial unemployment benefit. As a consequence, the firm's wage payments are reduced, though often less than proportionally.

With respect to the wage costs, notice that (10.5) is a continuous function of hours $H$. This is at variance with papers such as Hart (1984a) and Rosen (1968), who consider kinked cost curves, the kink arising at standard hours $H^c$, and concentrate on overtime hours. However, such a piece-wise linear cost equation may lead to the occurrence of a corner solution at standard working time (see Bodo and Giannini, 1985).

To conclude our discussion of the cost structure, it is well documented since the seminal papers by Becker (1964) and Oi (1962) that firms face quasi-fixed labor costs besides their variable wage costs. These non-wage labor costs vary only with the number of workers, not with average working time. They consist of such things as fringe benefits, training and administration costs or clothing expenditure; see Hart (1984b) for an extensive discussion. In the present paper, quasi-fixed labor costs are assumed to be proportional to the number of workers, involving a fixed payment, $V$, per worker. It will be included in our definition of the remuneration of labor. Thus (10.5) is replaced by

$$P_N(H) = V + WH^c o(H/H^c). \tag{10.6}$$

This concludes the specification of the static model. The production

188

function (10.4) is supplemented with a cost equation

$$C = P_K K + P_N(H)N, \tag{10.7}$$

where labor costs per worker are defined in (10.6).

### 10.2(b) Workers versus hours

Apart from the specification of capital services in the production function, the model is more or less similar to short-run labor demand models studied by Ehrenberg (1971a), Hart (1984a), Rosen (1968) and others. As in our production function, fluctuations in working hours also influence capital services and the question arises how this affects the traditional choice between workers and working time.

Thereto, let us first consider a short-run model of labor demand where the capital stock, $K$, is predetermined. The cost-minimization problem of the firm then simplifies to

$$\min_{N,\,H} C = P_K K + P_N(H)N \tag{10.8}$$

subject to (10.4).

The formal optimization problem is solved in an appendix to the working paper version obtainable from the author. The working paper also discusses the second-order conditions and derives the comparative static results presented in Tables 10.1 and 10.2 below. The first-order conditions reduce to the output constraint (10.4) and

$$\frac{F_M K e'_K(H)}{F_L N e'_N(H)} + \frac{e'_N(H)}{e_N(H)} = \frac{P'_N(H)}{P_N(H)} = \frac{Wo'(H/H^c)}{V + WH^c o(H/H^c)}. \tag{10.9}$$

The firm chooses the number of workers and their hours of work in order to equate the ratio of marginal productivities to the ratio of marginal costs. Equation (10.9) is considerably simplified if hours worked do not influence capital services ($e'_K = 0$): the first term on the left-hand side vanishes, and $H$ remains the only endogenous variable in the equation.

The second-order condition for minimum costs essentially sets an upper bound to the elasticity of working time in the production function. For space considerations it is not reported. Except for $e'_K = 0$, the upper bound tends to be a downward-sloping function of the elasticity of substitution between capital services and labor services in the production function (10.4), $\sigma$.

The demand functions for workers and hours per worker as implied by the first-order conditions (10.4) and (10.9) are, respectively,

$$N = N^0(Y, K, V/W, H^c)$$
$$H = H^0(Y, K, V/W, H^c). \tag{10.10}$$

189

**Table 10.1**
Sign distribution: short-run labor demand functions

| Exogenous variable | Condition | Endogenous variable | |
|---|---|---|---|
| | | N | H |
| $Y, -K$ | $\sigma < 1$ and $e_k > 0$ | $+$ [a] | $+$ |
| | $\sigma = 1$ or $e_k = 0$ | $+$ | $0$ |
| | $\sigma > 1$ and $e_k > 0$ | $+$ | $-$ |
| $V/W$ | | $-$ | $+$ |
| $H^c$ | $H < H_0$ | $-$ | $+$ |
| | $H > H_0 \geqslant H^c$ | $+$ | $-$ |

[a]The second-order condition is not sufficient to ensure the sign mentioned; a lower upper bound for the working time elasticity in the production function is required.

No unique sign distribution of the partial derivatives can be derived, although it is possible to present casuistry, as shown in Table 10.1.

As a reference point, consider first the traditional model specification, with $e_k = 0$. The results for the substitution between workers and hours for this model are well known (see Hart, 1984a, or Rosen, 1968). An increase of quasi-fixed costs, $V$, relative to the hourly wage rate, $W$, raises marginal costs of workers relative to marginal costs of hours. Hence, more hours are used to reduce the number of workers. Moreover, working hours are invariant to scale, owing to the multiplicative separability of labor services (see Ehrenberg, 1971a).

The continuous specification of labor costs in (10.6), however, slightly modifies the impact of a mandatory reduction in standard working time, $H^c$. Typically an adverse impact on hours worked is predicted if overtime prevails. In our model, however, the positive correlation between hours worked and standard working time is retained even in the overtime range, unless actual hours exceed some critical level $H_0 \geqslant H^c$ (for an exact definition of $H_0$ see the working paper). This qualification is not too surprising: owing to the concave wage cost schedule (10.6), marginal costs of hours are increasing at the margin; hence the introduction of additional overtime hours is less favorable compared to linear costs schedules.

The above predictions relate to the model with $e_k = 0$. In our more general specification, allowing for working time to influence capital services, $e_k > 0$, the signs of the partial derivatives of the demand functions (10.10) with respect to the cost variables $V$, $W$ and $H^c$ remain unchanged, but one result is challenged. Working time $H$ is no longer necessarily invariant to scale in the short-run model, even though a multiplicative separable specification for labor, and capital, services is used. If the elasticity of substitution is greater than 1, hours might even decline as output is increased, whereas a positive impact occurs for values of the elasticity of substitution below unity.

## 10.2(c)  *Capital versus labor*

Let us now abandon the assumption of a fixed capital stock, and focus on long-run capital–labor substitution. If, in addition to labor, capital is a variable factor, the cost-minimization problem of the firm becomes

$$\min_{K, N, H} P_K K + P_N(H)N$$

(10.11)

subject to (10.4).

The first-order conditions for minimum costs can be rearranged to (10.4), (10.8) and

$$\frac{F_M e_K(H)}{F_L e_N(H)} = \frac{P_K}{P_N(H)}.$$

(10.12)

For a given level of working time, (10.12) characterizes the traditional choice between capital and labor: the marginal rate of substitution is equated to the ratio of marginal costs.

The second-order conditions again set an upper bound to the elasticity of output with respect to working time, and this critical value is a decreasing function of the elasticity of substitution, $\sigma$.

The long-run demand factor functions corresponding to the first-order conditions (10.4), (10.8) and (10.12) are

$$K = K^*(Y, P_K, V, W, H^c)$$
$$N = N^*(Y, P_K, V, W, H^c)$$
$$H = H^*(P_K, V, W, H^c).$$

(10.13)

These demand functions are homogeneous of degree zero in the prices $P_K$, $V$ and $W$. Moreover, they illustrate that working time is invariant to scale in the long run. This is due to the multiplicative separable specification of both capital services and labor services in the production function (10.4).

Table 10.2 presents the signs of the partial derivatives of the demand system (10.13) for the specification with $e_K^t > 0$ and given the second-order conditions (the sign distribution for the limiting traditional case $e_K^t = 0$ is identical to the distribution for $\sigma = 1$).

First, a *ceteris paribus* increase in the user costs of capital, $P_K$, is considered. As expected, the capital stock is reduced and the number of workers is increased, but the impact on hours worked is uncertain and depends critically upon the value of the elasticity of substitution. As Winston and McCoy (1974, p. 424) argue,

If the elasticity is less than one ... it pays to economize on capital stock by using it more of the time. More specifically, a higher relative capital price increases the importance in costs – the relative share – of capital, thereby increasing the incentive for high capital utilization ... If the

**Table 10.2**
Sign distribution: long-run factor demand functions ($e_K > 0$)

| Exogenous variable | Condition | Endogenous variable | | |
|---|---|---|---|---|
| | | K | N | H |
| $Y$ | | + | + | 0 |
| $P_K$ | $\sigma < 1$ | − | +[a] | + |
| | $\sigma = 1$ | − | + | 0 |
| | $\sigma > 1$ | − | + | − |
| $V$ | | +[a] | − | + |
| $W$ | $\sigma < \sigma_1$ | +[a] | −[a] | − |
| | $\sigma = \sigma_1 > 1$ | + | − | 0 |
| | $\sigma > \sigma_1$ | + | − | + |
| $H^c$ | $H < H^c,\ \sigma < 1$ | ? | − | + |
| | $\sigma \geqslant 1$ | + | − | + |
| | $H = H^c,\ \sigma < 1$ | − | − | + |
| | $\sigma = 1$ | 0 | − | + |
| | $\sigma > 1$ | + | − | + |
| | $H^c < H < H_1, \sigma \leqslant 1$ | − | ? | + |
| | $\sigma > 1$ | ? | ? | + |
| | $H = H_1$ | − | + | 0 |
| | $H_1 < H$ | −[a] | + | − |

[a]The second-order condition is not sufficient to ensure the sign mentioned; a lower upper bound for the working time elasticity in the production function is required.

elasticity is greater than one … it pays to economize on labor (as the now-larger share of costs) even though it means using the capital stock less of the time.

An increase in labor costs $V$ or $W$ induces a similar substitution effect, but of opposite sign. Moreover, simultaneously a second substitution occurs, as workers are substituted for by hours, or vice versa, as described in Table 10.1. Therefore, an increase in the quasi-fixed costs per worker reduces the demand for workers as both substitution effects operate in the same direction. Furthermore, hours worked are raised as the hours for workers substitution effect dominates the capital for labor substitution impact.

The opposite is true for an increase in the scale wage rate, $W$: the capital for labor substitution tends to dominate the picture. The capital stock is increased and demand for workers is almost always reduced. The effect on working time, however, typically depends on the value of the elasticity of substitution: the capital for labor substitution impact changes sign at $\sigma = 1$; but, since workers are simultaneously substituted for hours within labor services, the negative sign dominates up to some critical value $\sigma_1 > 1$ (see the working paper for an exact definition of $\sigma_1$).

Finally, consider a *ceteris paribus* reduction in standard hours. As $H^c$ affects only the wage structure, the total impact is essentially some combination of the substitution effects mentioned above. As for the short-run model, it can be proved that there is a critical level, $H_1 \geqslant H^c$, above which hours worked are increased. As a consequence, the demand for workers is increased only as long as the number of hours worked is not too high. The impact on the capital stock is ambiguous, although an increase seems likely.

## 10.3   A Dynamic and Recursive Labor Demand Model

### 10.3(a)   Dynamic adjustment

To test some of the comparative static results presented in Table 10.2, it is necessary to pay attention to the dynamic structure of the model, as it is obvious that the time-series of factor demand do not adjust instantaneously. In theoretical models, dynamic aspects of factor demand schedules are generally accounted for by the introduction of adjustment costs for capital or labor. In labor demand models, adjustment costs consist of hiring and firing costs. Nickell (1987) provides a recent survey of dynamic labor demand models. In this section we sketch some of the implications for labor demand of such an adjustment cost model. For space considerations, the discussion will be brief; additional details can be obtained from the working paper version, but see also Nickell (1984b) for a more or less similar approach.

The following assumptions characterize the model. The hypothesis of a cost-minimizing firm is maintained. Thus, in an intertemporal context, the present value of costs is minimized given an expected future stream of output. The modeling of output expectations is dealt with in Section 10.3(b). The linear homogeneous production function (10.4) is retained, adding a time trend $t$ to cope with technical progress. The capital stock is built recursively and is subject to a constant rate of decay. With respect to costs, the firm faces external and convex adjustment costs for investment and workers, besides investment expenditures and labor remuneration (10.6).

At the beginning of period $t$ the firm minimizes the present value of costs over an infinite planning horizon, with respect to investment (capital stock), the number of workers and working time, but given the expected future output stream. Apart from the (marginal) adjustment costs, the first-order conditions for period $t + s$, $s = 0, 1, \ldots$, are obviously similar to those of the long-run static model of Section 10.2, at least if user costs of capital have been defined appropriately as a function of the price of investment goods. In order to solve the non-linear dynamic model, log-linear approximations have been introduced. The 'target' factor inputs $k^*_{t+s}$, $n^*_{t+s}$, $h^*_{t+s}$ where small letters denote logs in the sequel, are defined by equation (10.13): these values are solutions to the static long-run model, thus in absence of adjustment costs and given expected values of the exogenous variables of the model. Linearizing the dynamic first-order conditions around these target values, a second-order matrix difference equation is obtained. Subsequently, the variable production factor, hours worked, is substituted out using the log-linearized production function constraint

$$0 = \eta^f(k_{t+s} - k^*_{t+s}) + (1 - \eta^f)(n_{t+s} - n^*_{t+s}) + \eta^e(h_{t+s} - h^*_{t+s}), \qquad (10.14)$$

where $\eta^f$, $1 - \eta^f$ and $\eta^e$ are the elasticities of the production function with respect to capital, workers and hours, respectively. The equation for the quasi-fixed factors capital and workers in period $t + s$ can now be written compactly as

$$-ARz_{t+s+1} + [B + A(I + R)]z_{t+s} - Az_{t+s-1} = Bz^*_{t+s}, \quad s = 0, 1, \ldots, \qquad (10.15)$$

where $z_{t+s} = (k_{t+s}, n_{t+s})'$ and $z^*_{t+s} = (k^*_{t+s}, n^*_{t+s})'$. $I$ is the $(2 \times 2)$ identity matrix, whereas the matrices $A$, $B$ and $R$ contain parameters of the model: $A$ summarizes the influence of adjustment costs; $R$ is a diagonal matrix with the expected real discount rates as its elements; and the elements of $B$ are, essentially, functions of the parameters of the static model, such as $\sigma$, $\eta^f$ and $\eta^e$. Although it is hardly likely that these parameters are all time invariant, this assumption is made to keep the analysis tractable. Moreover, tests for structural breaks will be used in the empirical analysis.

Although it is tempting to use (10.12), (10.14) and (10.15) as the appropriate model to implement, this is incorrect: (10.15) only describes, approximately, the decision rule made at the beginning of period $t$ for factor demand in period $t + s$; setting $s = 0$, it is immediately clear that $z_t$ depends on $z_{t+1}$. Hence, a forward solution of (10.15) is needed. The extraction of the stable forward solution that satisfies the transversality conditions is fairly standard (see Sargent, 1978b). It can be shown that the optimal strategy at time $t$ is given by

$$z_t = Vz_{t-1} + \sum_{s=0}^{\infty} (VR)^s(I - VR)(I - V)z^*_{t+s}, \qquad (10.16)$$

where $V = (v_{ij})$ is the unique stable root of the matrix equation

$$-ARV^2 + [B + A(I + R)]V - A = 0. \qquad (10.17)$$

Notice that (10.16) can be rewritten as a partial adjustment equation with a forward-looking target.

Equation (10.16), together with (10.14) and (10.12), finally defines the intertemporal and interrelated factor demand model. However, since we do not intend to get involved in the simultaneous determination of investment and employment in our empirical analysis, and since it is difficult to obtain satisfactory series for the capital stock, the latter is to be eliminated from the model, using its optimal decision rule (10.16).

After tedious algebra (compare Nickell, 1984b, for a more or less similar approach), we finally obtain a recursive model for workers and hours of the type

$$\det(I - VL)n_t = \det(I - V)_{t-1}n_t^*$$

$$+ \sum_{s=0}^{\infty} \{\beta_{1s}(_{t-1}z_{t+s}^* - _{t-1}z_{t+s-1}^*)$$

$$+ \beta_{2s}(_{t-1}z_{t+s-1}^* - _{t-2}z_{t+s-1}^*)\} \qquad (10.18a)$$

$$\eta^e(1 - v_{11}L)(h_t - _{t-1}h_t^*) = (1 - v_{11}L)(y_t - _{t-1}y_t)$$

$$- [(1 - \eta^f)(1 - v_{11}L) + \eta^f v_{12}L](n_t - _{t-1}n_t^*)$$

$$+ \sum_{s=0}^{\infty} \gamma_{1s}(_{t-1}z_{t+s}^* - _{t-1}z_{t+s-1}^*)$$

$$+ \gamma_{20}(_{t-1}z_{t-1}^* - _{t-2}z_{t-1}^*), \qquad (10.18b)$$

where $L$ is the lag operator, and where $z_{t+s}^*$ is replaced by $_{t-1}z_{t+s}^*$ to indicate that expectations about $t+s$ are formed at the end of $t-1$. Moreover, the coefficients $\beta_{1s}$, $\beta_{2s}$, $\gamma_{1s}$ and $\gamma_{20}$ can be expressed explicitly as functions of the elements of $V$ and $R$ (see the working paper for details). Hence, (10.18) corresponds to a very tight specification of the labor demand equations.

As the capital stock is eliminated from the labor demand equations, additional lags appear in (10.18): (10.18a) is a second-order difference equation; whereas, even though hours are a variable production factor, (10.18b) also exhibits a one-period lag. As expected, however, (10.18) guarantees $n_t = _{t-1}n_t^*$ and $h_t = _{t-1}h_t^*$ in a long-run steady state. The ultimate terms in (10.18) consist of forecast revisions, whereas the penultimate terms refer to expected growth rates of the target variables. Finally, (10.18b), which incorporates the production function constraint, shows that hours worked also depend on the output forecast error $y_t - _{t-1}y_t$ and on the deviation of the number of workers from its target level, $n_t - _{t-1}n_t^*$.

## 10.2(b)  Expectations

Before the model in (10.18) can be estimated, the unobservable target variables $_{t-1}z_{t+s}^*$ must be eliminated. These targets have been defined as solutions of the long-run static model in Section 10.2. Hence they are implicitly given by (10.12). Assuming log-linear equations, for simplicity, we can write

$$(_{t-1}z_{t+s}^*, \, _{t-1}h_{t+s}^*)' = G_{t-1}x_{1t+s}, \qquad (10.19)$$

where, if $x_{1t}$ is the vector of relevant exogenous variables in (10.12), $_{t-1}x_{1t+s}$ is the corresponding expected value for period $t + s$ formed at the end of period $t - 1$. The matrix $G$ summarizes the partial derivatives of Table 10.2, where cross restrictions between the elements of $B$ and $G$ are likely to exist, as both depend on the parameters of the static model.

We now need a model to generate the expectational variables $_{t-1}x_{1t+s}$, and we will follow the approach used by Nickell (1984b), among others. Suppose the model for $x_{1t}$ takes the form of the stochastic difference equations

$$x_{1t} = W_{11}(L)x_{1t} + W_{12}(L)x_{2t} + u_{1t}$$
$$x_{2t} = W_{21}(L)x_{1t} + W_{22}(L)x_{2t} + u_{2t} \qquad (10.20)$$

where $x_2$ are additional variables that determine $x_1$, $W_{ij}(L)$ are matrix lag-polynomials and $u_1$ and $u_2$ are innovations. In a more concise notation (10.20) can be stacked to

$$X_t = WX_{t-1} + U_t, \qquad (10.21)$$

where $W$ is the appropriate matrix of coefficients (see Sargent, 1978, for example). As $E(U_{t+s} \mid X_{t-1}) = 0$, the forward expectations at time $t-1$ are given by

$$_{t-1}x_{1t+s} = E_1 W^s X_{t-1}, \qquad (10.22)$$

where $x_{1t} = E_1 X_t$, and $E_1 = (I0)$ a matrix where the dimension of $I$ equals the length of the $x_1$ vector.

The final, tightly specified, model for labor demand then consists of the equations (10.18), (10.19), (10.20) and (10.22). Efficient estimation of the model would require simultaneous estimation of the system, taking into account the implied cross-equation restrictions. Given the difficulties already faced, this procedure will not be followed. Instead, a two-stage procedure is used: first, the equations of the expectational model (10.20) are estimated: then the fitted values, calculated according to (10.22), are used as exogenous variables in the employment and hours equations. Moreover, the tight specification in (10.18) and (10.19) is considerably weakened, since the parameter restrictions, both within and between equations, will be ignored.

## 10.4 Empirical Results

The above model is estimated for the Dutch manufacturing sector, with annual data covering the period 1950–1984 (a data appendix is included in the working paper version).

For all equations we first specified a general unrestricted form, and then, by sequentially imposing and testing restrictions, a parsimonious representation of the data-generating process has been searched. Hendry (1983) and Gilbert (1986) give a more detailed exposition of the modeling strategy.

The misspecification tests used include: an F-test ($Z_1$) against the maintained general model; the modified Lagrange multiplier test ($Z_2$, see Harvey; 1981, p. 171) for first-order autocorrelation of the residuals; an ARCH test ($Z_3$, see Engle, 1982) for heteroskedasticity calculated as $F$-statistic; the Chow (1960) test ($Z_4$) for post-sample stability (two observations have been retained for this purpose); and, finally, a second Chow test ($Z_5$) for a structural break in 1974 after the first oil shock.

### 10.4(a)  Output expectations

First, consider the expectational model (10.20). As the vector $x_1$ contains all exogenous variables of Section 10.2, the expectations model is bound to become fairly large. However, we feel that in the short run fluctuations in expected output play a dominant role in explaining employment fluctuations. Therefore, we focus on the choice of a proxy for expected output. Expectations for the other variables will simply be replaced by a distributed lag of their past observations.

For output the problem remains to choose the variables included in $x_2$. Although it has been assumed that firms are price takers in their factor markets, it seems unrealistic to make the same assumption for the output market. Therefore, supply factors, such as real factor costs, should be included. This has the additional advantage that the model distinguishes between substitution and output effects of relative price shocks. On the other hand, demand indicators cannot be ignored. In this category we consider the money stock, the price level relative to foreign competitors and real, or nominal, interest rates. Finally, Nickell (1984b) has argued that $x_2$ includes a number of variables that can be observed only by firms, but not by the investigator. However, share prices should provide an estimate of discounted future earnings and, therefore, should incorporate some information contained in the unobservable variables. Hence, share prices are included in the output expectations model as well.

Considering the variables mentioned, we end up with a large number of variables in the expectations model. To restrict the analysis, we decided a priori to use a maximum of three variables in the $x_2$ vector. After some experimenting, we finally included in the log-linear model, beside output $y$, real labor costs $p_N$, the real share price $s$ and real money supply $m_1$. Initially, for each equation an unrestricted form was specified with two lags for each variable, plus a constant and a time trend. Unfortunately, no matter which of the above explanatory variables was included, no satisfactory results in terms of within-sample parameter stability could be obtained for the output equation. Eventually, we added a second time trend $t_{75}$, starting in 1975, to cope with the structural break after the first oil shock.

The final estimation results are presented in Table 10.3. An economic interpretation of the estimation results is not obvious. However, the test statistics reported in the table do not indicate serious misspecifications. Thus, we seem to have found a reasonably simple and stable model of the output-generating process. To illustrate its implications, notice that

## Table 10.3

Estimation results: output model (OLS, 1952–1982)

| | Dependent variable | | | |
|---|---|---|---|---|
| | $\Delta y_t$ | $\Delta s_t$ | $\Delta pN_t$ | $\Delta m_t$ |
| constant | 9.211 (1.678) | −3.537 (1.879) | −2.866 (0.715) | 1.065 (0.202) |
| $t*10^{-2}$ | 7.684 (1.353) | 8.307 (3.470) | | |
| $t75\,10^{-2}$ | −4.820 (0.753) | | | |
| $\Delta y_{t-1}$ | 0.276 (0.138) | | | |
| $\Delta s_{t-1}$ | 0.077 (0.026) | 0.389 (0.117) | −0.284 (0.177) | −0.159 (0.052) |
| $\Delta pN_{t-1}$ | | 2.067 (0.313) | | |
| $\Delta m_{t-1} - \Delta pN_{t-1}$ | | | | |
| $\Delta y_{t-1} + \Delta m_{t-1} - \Delta pN_{t-1}$ | −1.014 (0.181) | | | |
| $y_{t-1}$ | | | | |
| $s_{t-1}$ | | −0.507 (0.086) | −0.043 (0.024) | 0.452 (0.157) |
| $pN_{t-1}$ | −0.455 (0.104) | −1.476 (0.545) | | |
| $pN_{t-2}$ | 0.244 (0.065) | | | |
| $m_{t-1}$ | | | 0.115 (0.030) | 0.542 (0.111) |
| $y_{t-1} - pN_{t-1}$ | | | 0.372 (0.096) | −0.773 (0.154) |
| $m_{t-1} - y_{t-1}$ | | −1.160 (0.264) | | |
| $SSR*10^{-2}$ | 0.645 | 14.912 | 0.908 | 3.695 |
| $\bar{R}^2$ | 0.820 | 0.729 | 0.470 | 0.524 |
| F-test against maintained | $Z_1(3,20) = 0.24$ | $Z_1(4,20) = 0.26$ | $Z_1(6,20) = 0.26$ | $Z_1(6,20) = 0.44$ |
| First-order autocorrelation (LM) | $Z_2(1,22) = 1.99$ | $Z_2(1,23) = 2.31$ | $Z_2(1,25) = 0.31$ | $Z_2(1,25) = 0.02$ |
| Heteroskedasticity (ARCH) | $Z_3(1,29) = 1.45$ | $Z_3(1,29) = 0.01$ | $Z_3(1,29) = 0.78$ | $Z_3(1,29) = 3.09$ |
| Post-sample stability (Chow) | $Z_4(2,23) = 2.12$ | $Z_4(2,24) = 2.01$ | $Z_4(2,26) = 0.02$ | $Z_4(2,26) = 2.40$ |
| Structural break 1974 (Chow) | $Z_5(8,15) = 2.47$ | $Z_5(9,15) = 0.58$ | $Z_5(9,17) = 1.48$ | $Z_5(9,17) = 0.27$ |

*Notes:* Standard errors in parentheses; SSR, residual sum of squares; and $\bar{R}^2$, coefficient of determination adjusted for degrees of freedom.

the predicted equilibrium growth rates of output are 5.4 per cent prior to the oil shock and 2.7 per cent since. This corresponds quite closely to the average growth rates. Moreover, the one- and two-period ahead forecast errors are generally smaller than 2.5 per cent in absolute value, except immediately after the first oil shock, as the decline in trend growth could not have been anticipated.

## 10.4(b)  Demand for workers

Having generated output expectations, we proceed with the estimation of the labor demand model. As equation (10.18) suggests, two equations have to be estimated: this section presents the estimation results for the demand for workers, measured in full-time equivalents; results for the overtime equation are given in Section 10.4(c).

In the empirical part, some further modifications of (10.18a) have been imposed. First, the infinite sums in (10.18a) are bound to converge, and thus terms beyond some future date are irrelevant for practical purposes. Given our annual data, and in the light of the lack of degrees of freedom, we decided that a lead of two years should be sufficient for output expectations. Secondly, although the theoretical analysis suggests that this variable should not appear in the parsimonious model, the forecast error $y_t - _{t-1}y_t$ is included in the unrestricted model. We are now able to test this hypothesis. Thirdly, as stated before, expectations of exogenous variables other than output have been replaced by a two-year distributed lag of their past observations. However, the available annual data allow for only a limited number of explanatory variables in the unrestricted specification. Therefore, we shall present estimates of a model without relative factor prices. Only the ratio of quasi-fixed to total labor costs, $\bar{v} = V/P_N(H)$, is included as a cost measure in the analysis. Unfortunately, only a very crude proxy for these quasi-fixed costs is available. Fourthly, with respect to normal working time, a further distinction is made between normal hours per week ($h^c$) and the normal number of weeks worked during a year ($h^w$). This enables us to test whether both dimensions of working time have a different impact on employment. Fifthly, annual hours worked are strongly influenced by absenteeism. Therefore, the rate of absenteeism ($\tilde{h}^a$) is included in the unrestricted model. Notice that in logs yearly normal working time, corrected for absenteeism, is approximately given by $h^{cwa} = h^c + h^w - \tilde{h}^a$.

It is possible to construct the empirical counterpart of Equations (10.18a) and (10.19). This is shown in Equation (10.23) below which, bearing in mind the foregoing modifications and including a constant and two time trends, is the unrestricted log-linear model for employment where $^u{}_{nt}$ is a random variable.

$$\Delta n_t = \alpha_0 + \alpha_1 n_{t-1} + \alpha_2 \,\Delta n_{t-1} + \alpha_3 t + \alpha_4 t_{75}$$

$$+ \sum_{i=0}^{1} \sum_{s=0}^{2} \beta_{ist-1} y_{t+s-i} + \beta_0 (y_t - _{t-1} y_t)$$

$$+ \sum_{i=0}^{2} (\beta_{ci} h_{t-i}^c + \beta_{wi} h_{t-i}^w + \beta_{ai} \tilde{h}_{t-i}^a$$

$$+ \beta_{vi} \tilde{v}_{t-i}) + u_{nt}. \tag{10.23}$$

The estimation period is 1954–1982 because two additional years are lost owing to the construction of output expectations. Since the unrestricted form (10.23) contains 24 parameters, only five degrees of freedom remain. Therefore, we should be very careful in sequentially restricting the model: the F-test against the unrestricted model $Z_1$ proves not to be very powerful.

Not surprisingly, a number of restrictions are easily accepted. First, additional lags due to aggregation seem to play no role. This might be because of the use of annual data. Secondly, the number of working

**Table 10.4**
Estimation results: employment equation (OLS, 1954–1982)

| | Dependent variable $\Delta n$ | |
| --- | --- | --- |
| | (1) | (2) |
| constant | 0.123 (2.043) | 2.255 (0.473) |
| $t^* 10^{-2}$ | −4.50  (0.88) | −3.23  (0.31) |
| $t_{75}^* 10^{-2}$ | 2.26  (0.81) | 1.08  (0.14) |
| $n_{t-1}$ | −0.566 (0.080) | |
| $n_{t-1} + h_{t-1}^w - \tilde{h}_{t-1}^a - _{t-1} y_t$ | | −0.627 (0.058) |
| $h_{t-1}^c$ | −0.252 (0.130) | −0.256 (0.110) |
| $h_{t-1}^w$ | −0.645 (0.360) | |
| $\tilde{h}_{t-1}^a$ | 0.981 (0.377) | |
| $_{t-1} y_t$ | 0.817 (0.142) | |
| $_{t-1} y_{t+1} - _{t-1} y_t$ | 0.181 (0.076) | |
| $_{t-1} y_{t+2} - _{t-1} y_{t+1}$ | 0.207 (0.080) | |
| $_{t-1} y_{t+2} - _{t-1} y_t$ | | 0.123 (0.041) |
| $y_t - _{t-1} y_t$ | 0.322 (0.103) | 0.243 (0.070) |
| $\Delta \tilde{v}_t$ | −0.191 (0.086) | |
| $\Delta \tilde{v}_{t-1}$ | 0.134 (0.093) | |
| $\Delta^2 \tilde{v}_t$ | | −0.191 (0.041) |
| $\tilde{v}_{t-1}$ | −0.469 (0.090) | −0.541 (0.055) |
| SSR$^* 10^{-3}$ | 0.647 | 0.795 |
| $\overline{R}^2$ | 0.923 | 0.929 |
| F-test against maintained | $Z_1(10,5) = 0.45$ | $Z_1(15,5) = 0.44$ |
| First-order autocorrelation (LM) | $Z_2(1,14) = 0.95$ | $Z_2(1,19) = 0.16$ |
| Heteroskedasticity (ARCH) | $Z_3(1,27) = 0.33$ | $Z_3(1,27) = 0.63$ |
| Post-sample stability (Chow) | $Z_4(2,15) = 2.41$ | $Z_4(2,20) = 2.95$ |
| Structural break 1974 (Chow) | $Z_5(8,7) = 0.84$ | $Z_5(8,12) = 0.68$ |

*Note:* Standard errors in parentheses.

time variables is reduced as we could not reject the hypothesis that annual working time corrected for absenteeism, $h^{cwa}$, is the appropriate variable. Neither could we reject the hypothesis that absenteeism plays no role, but the former model outperforms the latter in terms of both the residual sum of squares and predictive failure.

Further testing and simplifying the model, we ended up with two alternative parsimonious representations, both with $h^{cwa}_{t-1}$ as one of the explanatory variables. However, as the F-test against the unrestricted model is not very powerful, owing to the lack of degrees of freedom, we might have accepted a hypothesis during the modeling sequence that should have been rejected. Therefore, we have tested at various stages the inclusion of a subset of variables deleted in earlier steps. It then proved that an alternative specification with respect to the working time variables could be worth while considering.

This is illustrated in Table 10.4, where a separate influence of the different components of the annual working time is allowed for. Simultaneously, the lag structure is simplified omitting the insignificant terms. More specifically, column 1 of Table 10.4 suggests that the coefficient of standard weekly hours, $h^c$, might differ from the coefficient of the normal number of weeks, $h^w$. The latter parameter in turn could be more or less equal, in absolute value, to the parameter of absenteeism, $\tilde{h}^a$. Imposing this restriction and further simplifying, we finally obtain the parsimonious representation of column 2. The test statistics do not indicate serious misspecification. For a first difference model the model tracks well, and it has stable parameters, both within and outside the sample period. Moreover, it outperforms the earlier mentioned representations with $h^{cwa}$ as explanatory variable in terms of both residual sum of squares and predictive failure. Therefore, it is our preferred specification.

Rearranging appropriately, the steady state properties of this equation can be summarized by

$$_{t-1}n^*_t = \text{constant} - 0.051(t - t_{75}) - 0.034t_{75}$$
$$\phantom{xxxxxxxxxxxxx}(0.014)\phantom{xxxxx}(0.015)$$
$$+ _{t-1}y_t + 0.39(y_t - _{t-1}y_t)$$
$$\phantom{xxxxxx}(0.11)$$
$$- (h^w_{t-1} - \tilde{h}^a_{t-1}) - 0.41h^c_{t-1} - 0.86\bar{v}_{t-1}$$
$$\phantom{xxxxxxx}(0.17)\phantom{xxxxx}(0.06)\phantom{xxxxxxxxxxxxxx}(10.24)$$

where the standard errors in parentheses have been calculated using an instrumental variable technique proposed by Wickens and Breusch (1986). These results indicate tht the rate of technological progress has slowed down from 5.1 per cent to 3.4 per cent since the first oil shock. Moreover, in line with our earlier assumption of constant returns to scale, there is a unit steady state elasticity of the number of operatives in manufacturing with respect to expected output. However, the output forecast error also has a significant coefficient. Though this is not in line with the theoretical model discussed earlier, two interpretations can be put foward: on the one hand, expected output as generated by our model might not be fully consistent with expectations used by firms; on the other hand, if employment decisions and forecast revisions are made on a quarterly basis, the forecast error might reflect some of these output revisions occurring within the year.

With respect to the hours variables, there is a proportional impact of the normal number of weeks worked corrected for absenteeism. However, the elasticity of employment with respect to standard weekly hours is considerably less. Thus, a *ceteris paribus* reduction of weekly contractual hours leads to a far from proportional increase in the number of workers. Finally, quasi-fixed labor costs have the expected negative impact, with quite a high steady state elasticity.

### 10.4(c) Overtime behavior

Finally, the equation for hours worked is considered. Without loss of generality, the dependent variable is defined as relative overtime hours $h^o = (H - H^c)/H^c \approx \ln H - \ln H^c$. Overtime hours are corrected for average hours lost per operative owing to temporary short-time. This correction is particularly important after the first oil shock. The resulting series typically reflect cyclical behavior.

With respect to the unrestricted model for hours, equation (10.18) indicated that the same variables as used for workers, see (10.23), should be included, with the exception of lagged employment. On the other hand, the recursive structure of the model requires an output forecast error and employment deviation from its target to be added. Moreover, owing to the elimination of the capital stock, the latter two variables also appear in lagged form, as do lagged hours. Since we would be left with only three degrees of freedom, we decided to restrict our general specification. As the estimation results for the employment equation indicate that forecast revisions of output and second-order lags of other explanatory variables play no role whatsoever, these variables have been excluded *a priori*. The unrestricted model for hours then contains 19 variables, including a constant and two time trends. One of these variables is the employment deviation from its target, $n_{t-t-1}n_t^*$. The target variable is constructed using (10.24), which amounts to the method suggested by Hart and Sharot (1978).

The final estimation results for the overtime equation are summarized in Table 10.5. The parsimonious representation of the data-generating process is given in column 1. The test statistics do not indicate misspecification, but the parameter estimates are rather unsatisfactory. For example, no influence could be found for the employment deviation from its target. Moreover, a permanent positive impact of expected output is found. Though this could correspond to the comparative statics of the short-run model of Section 10.2, we suspect spurious correlation. As column 1 incorporates almost all the terms of target employment in equation (10.24), it can be rearranged as in column 2, where insignificant terms have consequently been dropped, with a

**Table 10.5**
Estimation results: overtime equation (OLS, 1954–1982)

| Dependent variable $h^o = (H - H^c)/H^c$ | (1) | (2) |
|---|---|---|
| constant | −1.832 (0.358) | −2.349 (0.163) |
| $t*10^{-2}$ | −1.37  (0.25) | |
| $t_{75}*10^{-2}$ | 1.07  (0.22) | 0.48  (0.06) |
| $t-1y_t$ | 0.254 (0.041) | |
| $t-1y_{t+2} - t-1y_t$ | 0.079 (0.022) | 0.059 (0.013) |
| $y_t - t-1y_t$ | 0.241 (0.033) | 0.132 (0.023) |
| $h^c_{t-1}$ | −0.116 (0.041) | |
| $t-1n^*_t + h^w_{t-1} - h^a_{t-1}$ | | 0.215 (0.015) |
| $\Delta \bar h^a_t$ | 0.493 (0.121) | 0.496 (0.117) |
| $\tilde v_{t-1}$ | −0.067 (0.014) | 0.108 (0.008) |
| SSR*$10^{-3}$ | 0.108 | 0.114 |
| $\bar R^2$ | 0.931 | 0.933 |
| F-test against maintained | $Z_1(10,10) = 0.22$ | $Z_1(12,10) = 0.25$ |
| First-order autocorrelation (LM) | $Z_2(1,19)  = 0.47$ | $Z_2(1,21)  = 0.69$ |
| Heteroskedasticity (ARCH) | $Z_3(1,27)  = 0.10$ | $Z_3(1,27)  = 0.36$ |
| Post-sample stability (Chow) | $Z_4(2,20)  = 1.20$ | $Z_4(2,22)  = 1.02$ |
| Structural break 1974 (Chow) | $Z_5(8,12)  = 1.15$ | $Z_5(8,14)  = 0.46$ |

*Note:* Standard errors in parentheses.

positive influence for target employment. As, apart from cyclical shocks, overtime hours roughly followed the pattern of an inverted U with the peak around 1970, and simultaneously, employment (and its target) increased in the 1960s but declined ever since, the positive sign of target employment in the overtime equation might capture an unexplained part of this pattern of overtime hours.

A possible explanation for this behavior of overtime hours might be that employment was essentially supply determined during the 1960s. The additional use of overtime could then reduce firms' labor shortage. Vacancy data might reveal this kind of reasoning. But, though there seems to be a positive correlation between the vacancy rate and overtime hours, preliminary tests did not improve the estimation result.

Given these qualifications, we should be very careful in drawing conclusions from the overtime equation. The only definite results seem to be: output forecast errors have the expected positive sign, though we had expected a larger coefficient, more or less consistent with the hours elasticity found in (10.24); moreover, an increase in the rate of absentee-ism is temporarily accommodated using more overtime (Table 10.4 already showed that the number of operatives will be adjusted in the next period). The latter results do not correspond to the predictions on absenteeism by Ehrenberg (1971a). Owing to changes in quasi-fixed relative to variable labor costs, a permanent influence on hours worked was to be expected. Notice, however, that the impact of quasi-fixed costs changes sign between columns 1 and 2.

Perhaps these results just indicate that long-run hours are essentially determined by a corner solution at standard hours, whereas overtime hours are used to accommodate temporary shocks.

## 10.5 Concluding Remarks

The object of this paper has been to build and to estimate a model of manufacturing labor demand that explicitly distinguishes between the number of workers and their average working time. On the basis of the theoretical static model we found, as usual, that hours worked per operative are independent of the production volume in the long run. However, quite a different result was obtained in the theoretical short-run model with fixed capital stock: either a positive or a negative relation could exist, the sign depending critically upon the value of the elasticity of substitution between capital labor services. The theoretical model also focused on the impact of standard working time on both dimensions of labor demand.

The dynamic analysis presented subsequently indicates that employment decisions, particularly with respect to the number of workers, are inherently forward looking. Therefore, we have built a small auxiliary multivariate time-series model to generate output expectations. These expectations have been treated as data in the demand functions for labor.

The equation for the number of workers tracks reasonably well. It has some interesting implications: in the steady state there is an elasticity of 1 between the number of workers and the annual normal number of weeks worked, the latter corrected for absenteeism; however, quite large productivity gains occur when standard weekly working time is reduced – a 10 per cent reduction in standard hours increases employment by only 4 per cent. These conclusions, however, are conditional upon the expected output. Moreover, owing to a lack of degrees of freedom, relative factor costs have not yet been included; only quasi-fixed labor costs, as a percentage of total labor costs, have been included, with a fairly important negative impact on the demand for workers.

The estimation results for the overtime equation are rather unsatisfactory. However, they do suggest that output forecast errors play a role and that the rate of absenteeism temporarily affects overtime behavior. Permanent effects of, for example, standard hours appear to be almost absent.

The present study should be extended in several ways. With respect to the output model it is rather unsatisfactory to rely on a structural break in the time trend after the first oil shock. The inclusion of energy prices might be a better alternative. The same remark applies for the labor demand model. The latter should also be extended by including relative factor prices, to account for long-run substitution between capital and labor. Furthermore, a more accurate model of overtime behavior is needed: the inclusion of labor supply factors might be useful. Finally, there is ample room for improvement in the estimation technique, for instance by the introduction of cross-equation restrictions in the estimation procedure and the use of more efficient simultaneous estimation techniques.

# COMMENT

## SEIICHI KAWASAKI

I would like to make a few comments on this paper with respect to its implications for economic policy, model structure, and empirical specifications.

The main purpose of the paper is to estimate a dynamic system of labor demand functions in order to evaluate the effectiveness of 'work-sharing' policy, namely creating more employment by reducing standard working hours. De Regt assumes that mandatory work-sharing policy is effective if the elasticity of employment with respect to standard working hours is significantly large and if the productivity gains resulting from such hour reductions do not totally offset the employment effects of reduced hours. His empirical results show that a 10 per cent reduction of standard working hours increases employment by 4 per cent after the productivity effect is controlled.

How realistic is this 4 per cent increase in employment for policy consideration? One possible problem in this respect is that the model assumes that the standard hours are exogenous. In a short time period, this is acceptable. In a longer time period covering more than 30 years as in this study, however, standard hours are likely to be endogenous. As de Regt says, standard hours are usually determined by collective bargaining between employers and employees. This decision surely involves considerations of all other relevant labor conditions. A closely related matter is that households' decisions also enter into this and other processes. In the long run, we cannot ignore the reaction of the supply side of the labor market. These factors may introduce simultaneous-equation bias to the model, so that the estimated elasticities may not be suitable for the practical policy considerations.

As for the model specification, de Regt basically follows the approach of Nickell (1984b). There exist several alternative models for the estimation of labor elasticities. One approach is to estimate a system of cost share equations utilizing the duality relationship (see König and Pohlmeier, 1987). More traditional is the interrelated demand system of Nadiri and Rosen (1969, 1974; see also Hart and Sharot, 1978). More recently Pindyck and Rotemberg (1983) and Shapiro (1986) estimated dynamic models incorporating rational expectations. De Regt might well have considered the costs and benefits of alternative approaches. He should also explain why Nickell's model might be expected to fit the Dutch economy, because Nickell specified his model according to the characteristics of British manufacturing industries.

De Regt first considers labor demand in the short run and the long run in a static framework and performs comparative static exercises for static models. He then proceeds to construct and to estimate dynamic models. The results of the comparative statics are supposed to hold also in the steady state of the dynamic models. However, this claim is never explicitly proved, although he writes that they are 'obviously similar'. In the static analysis, capital stock plays an important role in the discussion of models. In the empirical section, however, capital is only implicitly treated and its price is excluded from the list of explanatory variables in the estimation. This gives the impression that the early and later parts of this paper are not well integrated.

In the empirical specification of the dynamic labor demand function, de Regt includes the ratio of quasi-fixed to total labor costs. This variable is in fact employers' contributions to social security divided by the sum of total wage costs and social security costs. Although de Regt admits that this is a very crude proxy, this variable probably does not reflect the ratio of quasi-fixed to total labor costs at all. First, there exist many other non-wage labor costs – which often belong to quasi-fixed costs – in addition to social security costs (see Hart, 1984b). Secondly, and more importantly, employers' contributions to social security are likely to represent more variable labor costs than quasi-fixed costs, although they usually consist of both components (see Hart and Kawasaki, 1987). In other words, in most social security systems employers' contributions to social security are proportional to wages, so that this part of costs is per manhour or variable. The employer only pays fixed amounts of contribution per employee if the employee's wage is under a certain minimum wage or over a certain maximum wage; then such costs are per person, or quasi-fixed costs. The division between quasi-fixed and variable costs varies from industry to industry and from time to time, depending on the wage distribution and contribution schemes. In the case of West Germany, there were some significant variations in the composition, although the dominant part is variable labor costs. This situation seems to hold for most OECD countries.

# CHAPTER 11

# The Impact on Labor Supply of a Shorter Workday: A Micro-econometric Discrete/Continuous Choice Approach

JOHN K. DAGSVIK, OLAV LJONES,
STEINAR STRØM AND TOM WENNEMO

## 11.1 Introduction

A shorter workday as a remedy for (mass) unemployment has again appeared on the political agenda. During the recession in the 1930s a shorter workday was considered by many, especially politicians, to be an effective counter to unemployment. In recent years mass unemployment has come back, at least in some western countries, and with that the argument of sharing work as a means to cut unemployment. This proposal has been widely discussed and also analyzed by economists.

The purpose of the present paper is to analyze how a shorter workday might change labor supply decisions. Special emphasis is laid on how responses differ by sex. An expectation held by many is that a shorter workday, say 6 hours a day, is more suitable for couples with children than an option of working 8 hours a day versus not working at all. An increase in the availability of jobs with 6 hours a day as a full, normal load is believed to give married women a stronger incentive to search for a job. Few have given the fate of the male spouses any thought. It is our purpose to demonstrate how a shorter workday also affects labor supply among married men.

Our demonstration is based on a particular econometric model of labor supply for couples. This model assumes that the individual chooses the most attractive job among feasible jobs where offered hours of work and the wage rate are given latent attributes of each job. Given the job, the worker has no freedom to adjust hours of work.

208

The estimated model provides a tool by which we can simulate individual behavior, hours of work distribution as well as expected aggregates.

This simulation model is also used to simulate the effect of changing the choice sets such that the maximum of hours of work is set at 6 hours a day in each job. This restriction is imposed on each individual, but in a way that preserves the overtime opportunities before the change. In 1979 the so-called normal work day was 8 hours. Among married men working in 1979 the average yearly load was 2240 hours. Thus, the yearly equivalence of the '6-hours a day' restriction is set equal to 6/8 of 2240, or 1680 hours.

When the '6-hours-a-day' restriction is introduced, the probability of finding a suitable job is kept constant. Alternatively, we could have kept the expected number of hours worked constant. This last assumption is more in line with a demand side where production depends on manhours and not shift-work and where unemployment is either Keynesian or classical with rigid real wages. In 1979, however, the unemployment rate was under 2 per cent, which is fairly close to a full employment situation.

Our labor supply model differs from other models previously estimated in the following ways (see Killingsworth, 1983; Hausman, 1985; and Arrufat and Zabalza, 1986, for a review and update on econometric labor supply models):

1  The model contains a detailed specification of the tax structure. Individual tax return data have been used when estimating the model. The tax structure together with fixed costs of work imply a non-convex budget set. Global criteria, rather than local, marginal criteria are needed to simulate individual behavior.
2  The labor supply responses of married couples are jointly estimated.
3  Stochastic properties are justified from theoretical arguments.
4  The model assumes unobservable choice alternatives such as type of job.
5  The econometric framework allows for constraints on hours. By varying these constraints it is possible to simulate the labor supply responses of shortening the workday, say from what we observed in 1979–80 to a maximum of 6 hours a day.

The main conclusions are the following. Without wage compensation, the expected, aggregate participation rate for married women increases while for men it is diminished. Expected aggregates related to hours, such as the hours supplied, conditional on being employed, are reduced for both sexes. This effect is stronger for men than for women. The net result of changes in participation and hours supplied, conditional on being employed, is that the total unconditional expectation of hours supplied is reduced. Aggregate elasticities increase for men and are slightly reduced for women.

## 11.2 The Model

### 11.2(a)  Individual decisions

For expository reasons we start with the model for one-person households.

Each person is assumed to choose a type of job from a distribution of jobs unknown to us as econometricians. Associated with each job, $k$, are

- wages, $w_k$
- hours of work, $h_k$
- non-pecuniary attributes.

Let $U(h, C, k, Z)$ denote utility, where $h$ is hours of work, $C$ is consumption, $k$ is job type and $Z$ is a vector of socio-demographic variables affecting utility. The budget constraint is

$$C = w_k h_k + I - T(w_k h_k, I) + S \equiv f(w_k h_k, I, S) \tag{11.1}$$

$$k \in B \tag{11.2}$$

where $B$ is the set of feasible jobs, $T$ is the tax function and $S$ is tax-free transfers. $I$ is non-labor income. The tax function depends on both labor and capital income. The individual's realized wage and hours of work is equal to $(w, h)$ provided $h_{k^*} = h$, $w_{k^*} = w$, where $k^*$ is the optimal job, i.e. $k^*$ satisfies

$$\max_{k \in B} U(h_k, f(h_k w_k, I, S), k, z) = U(h_{k^*}, f(h_{k^*} w_{k^*}, I, S), k^*, Z). \tag{11.3}$$

### 11.2(b)  Stochastic assumptions and econometric model

As already mentioned, we have no information about the choice set $B$ and the attributes of the jobs. We observe only $Z$, $C$, the wage rate and hours of the optimal job. In the version of the model presented in this paper we assume, however, that the individuals have full information and that they choose a job that maximizes utility. Below we present a set of assumptions concerning the latent choice variables.

The utility function is assumed to have the following structure:

$$U(h, C, k, Z) = V(h, C, Z, T_k) + \varepsilon_k(Z), \tag{11.4}$$

where $\varepsilon_k$; $k = 1, 2, \ldots$, are independent draws from the extreme value distribution, i.e.

$$\Pr[\varepsilon_k(Z) \leqslant x] = \exp[e^{-a + b}], \quad a < 0, \tag{11.5}$$

and where $a$ and $b$ may depend on $Z$.

The variables $T_k$; $k = 1, 2, \ldots$, are independent draws from a general distribution. $\{T_k\}$ is independent of $\{\varepsilon_k\}$. For fixed $(Z, T_k)$ $V$ is a deterministic and concave function in $(h, C)$.

The structure (11.4) can be justified from theoretical arguments (see Dagsvik, 1988).

The variable $T_k$ is a heterogeneity variable that may vary across jobs and individuals. It accounts for possible unobservable heterogeneity in the job-specific marginal utilities, $\partial U/\partial C$ and $\partial U/\partial h$ (given $k, Z$). The heterogeneity accounted for by $T_k$ might be due to unobservable characteristics such as non-pecuniary aspects of jobs. In this paper, however, we assume that $T_k$ is degenerate. The general case is treated in Dagsvik (1988).

As mentioned above, each job is characterized by hours of work, $h_k$, wage rate, $w_k$, and other non-pecuniary characteristics. The individuals know their feasible job set $B$ and job characteristics and take them as given in the market. They are either determined from the demand side or from regulations set by the authorities. For the econometrician, both $h_k$ and $w_k$ are unknown and these two latent variables are represented by a joint distribution given in (11.6).

$$G(x, y) = \Pr[h_k \leqslant x, w_k \leqslant y, k \in B]. \tag{11.6}$$

Let $g(x, y)$ be the density function associated with this cumulative distribution. $G(x, y)$ gives the joint probability of finding a job with hours less than or equal to $x$ and with a wage less than or equal to $y$.

For notational convenience we introduce the following marginal and conditional densities:

$$g_1 = \Pr[k \in B] \tag{11.7}$$

$$g_0 = 1 - g_1 \tag{11.8}$$

$$g_2(x, y) = \frac{g(x, y)}{g_1}. \tag{11.9}$$

$g_1$ is the probability that the job $k$ is feasible. In the following we will refer to this fraction of jobs as the fraction of feasible jobs in the market. $g_0$ is the fraction of non-feasible jobs in the market. $g_2(x, y)$ is a conditional joint density, given that the jobs are feasible. This joint density can be written as a product of two marginal densities and we make the assumption that hours are uniformly distributed with density $d$. Thus,

$$g_2(x, \infty) = d; \text{ with } d \int_D dx = 1,$$

and where $D$ is the available set of hours. Moreover, we assume that $w_k$

211

and $h_k$ are stochastically independent, i.e.

$$g_2(x, y) = d g_2^*(y). \tag{11.10}$$

The assumption of uniformly distributed hours of work corresponds to the standard textbook assumption where the worker can freely adjust hours of work. This assumption is maintained here because we do not have observations of variables that characterize the heterogeneity in the labor market constraints. Thus we have basically an identification problem that we 'solve' here by making the assumption that all working hours offered in the market occur with the same frequency. In the future we hope to deal more seriously with this identification problem by resorting to regional labor market indicators.

From the assumption made above it can be proved that the joint density for an optimal and realized supply of hours, $\bar{h}$, and realized wage, $\bar{w}$ (subscript $i$ for individual $i$ is suppressed), is:

$$\begin{cases} \phi(\bar{h}, \bar{w}) = \dfrac{e^{v(\bar{w}, \bar{h})} g_2^*(\bar{w}) g_1 d}{e^{v_0} g_0 + d g_1 \displaystyle\int_D \int e^{v(x, y)} g_2^*(y)\, \mathrm{d}x\, \mathrm{d}y} \\[4pt] \text{for } \bar{h} > 0 \end{cases} \tag{11.11}$$

$$\begin{cases} \phi(0) = \dfrac{e^{v_0} g_0}{e^{v_0} g_0 + d g_1 \displaystyle\int_D \int e^{v(x, y)} g_2^*(y)\, \mathrm{d}x\, \mathrm{d}y} \\[4pt] \text{for } \bar{h} = 0 \end{cases} \tag{11.12}$$

where

$$v(\bar{w}, \bar{h}) = V[\bar{h}, f(\bar{w}\bar{h}, I, S), Z] \text{ and } v_0 = V[0, f(0, I, S), Z].$$

The conditional density of hours given the realized wage is given by

$$\begin{cases} \phi(\bar{h} \mid w_k^* = \bar{w}, \bar{h} > 0) = \dfrac{\phi(\bar{w}, \bar{h})}{\displaystyle\int_{x>0} \phi(\bar{w}, x)\, \mathrm{d}x} = \dfrac{e^{v(\bar{w}, \bar{h})}}{\displaystyle\int_{x>0}^{D^e} e^{v(\bar{w}, x)}\, \mathrm{d}x} \\[4pt] \text{for } \bar{h} > 0 \end{cases} \tag{11.13}$$

An approximation for $\phi(0)$ is

$$\phi(0) = \dfrac{e^{v^*}}{e^{v^*} + \displaystyle\int_D e^{v(\hat{w}, x)}\, \mathrm{d}x} \tag{11.14}$$

where

$$e^{v^*} = e^{v_0} \cdot \dfrac{g_0}{g_1 d},$$

and where $\hat{w}$ is the mean wage (for given $Z$).

212

The smaller the variance of $w_k$, the better is the approximation in (11.14).

To estimate the model we apply (11.13) and (11.14) for the sake of computational convenience. The unknown coefficients are estimated by a maximum likelihood procedure in two steps. First, (11.13) is applied on the data for those working. Second, given the estimates of this first step, the remaining coefficients are estimated by applying (11.14) on all data, inclusive of those not working. In a forthcoming paper we shall report estimates based on the density functions (11.11) and (11.12) (see Dagsvik and Strøm, 1988).

For married couples the model is completely analogous to the single household case. Let

$$U(h_F, h_M, C, k_F, k_M, Z) = v(h_F, h_M, C, Z) + \varepsilon(k_F, k_M, Z) \quad (11.15)$$

be the household's utility where $h_j$ and $k_j$ denote hours and job-type for sex $j$, $j = M$ (male), $F$ (female). The budget constraints are

$$C = \sum_{j=M, F} w_j k_j h_{jk_j} + I - T(h_{Fk_F} w_{Fk_F}, h_{Mk_M} w_{Mk_M}, I) + S \quad (11.16)$$

$$h_{Fk_F} \in D_F, h_{Mk_M} \in D_M.$$

The corresponding densities for hours and wages are deferred to the Appendix.

## 11.2(c) Data

The data are a sample survey that consists of two different, but linked, sets of information about married individuals in Norway in 1979. The first part is a questionnaire providing us with data on hours of work, wage rates and socioeconomic information such as number and age of children, education level, etc. The other part is based on completed tax returns and provides us with information about all sorts of reported income, compulsory deductions, taxes paid and transfers received. The two data sets are linked on the basis of personal identification numbers. The Central Bureau of Statistics has been responsible for collecting and preparing the data sets.

The data based on the tax returns have been used to check the answers on the wage rate and hours worked given in the questionnaire. In a majority of cases (around 90 per cent) the reported wage rate has been used for those working. For the remaining individuals a fitted wage equation has been applied. Note that this is a necessity in the case of individuals observed to be out of work (defined to be less than or equal to 60 hours worked a year).

The fitted wage equation, one for each sex, regresses the log of the wage rate against years of working experience, educational level in years and a variable accounting for possible selectivity biases. All parameters

213

except for the parameter attached to the selection variable were significantly different from zero. The fitted equations imply that the wage rate is a concave function of working experience, with peaks around 31 years for both sexes. The wage rate is increasing with the level of education.

The model requires that utility is compared for different hours of work in order to simulate individual decisions. Thus, we need to predict what tax deductions and therefore effective tax rates would have been if the individuals were working a different number of hours from what they report. This is done by applying an estimated tax deduction function. The reported deductions are regressed against wage income capital income, pensions, age and age squared. All variables have a significant impact on deductions. The main reason why we expect deductions to vary with income is that interest payments on loans are deductible in Norway. The age variable might account for some cohort effects. It is found that the marginal propensity to deduct related to wage income is 0.08 while the marginal propensity to deduct related to capital income is much higher, 0.75. The deduction function is a concave function of age – increasing up to 33.8 years of age and declining thereafter.

### 11.2(d) Estimation results

In this section we report estimation results for married couples where the female is aged 27–66 years. The structural part of the utility function is specified in Table 11.1 (see also equation (11A.5) in the Appendix).

The following notation is used:

$$C = \text{total consumption of the household}$$
$$L = \text{leisure time in hours per year}$$
$$L_F = 8000 - h_F, \quad L_M = 8000 - h_M$$
$$A_F = \text{age of female}$$
$$A_M = \text{age of male}$$
$$BU6 = \text{number of children under 6 years of age}$$
$$BO6 = \text{number of children 6–17 years}$$
$$K = \text{a dummy variable}$$
$$K_F = \begin{cases} 1 \text{ if female is not working} \\ 0 \text{ otherwise} \end{cases}$$
$$K_M = \begin{cases} 1 \text{ if male is not working} \\ 0 \text{ otherwise} \end{cases}$$

The results reported here are preliminary results, since we have used the approximation (11.14) instead of the true density function. Also, the respective integrals in the denominator of (11.13) and (11.14) are approximated by discrete sums of which each step has size 60 hours. A more rigorous estimation procedure will be performed later and the results will be reported elsewhere (see Dagsvik and Strøm, 1988).

**Table 11.1**
Estimated utility function for married couples, female aged 27–56 years,
Norway, 1979

| Variables | Estimates | t-values |
|---|---|---|
| $10^{-4}C$ | 1.6678 | 5.07 |
| $10^{-9}C^2$ | −0.2443 | −2.44 |
| $10^{-6}L_F^2$ | −0.5729 | −6.79 |
| $10^{-2}L_F$ | 0.5828 | 3.29 |
| $10^{-3}L_F \log A_F$ | 0.7458 | 2.40 |
| $10^{-6}L_F L_M$ | 0.1722 | 1.11 |
| $10^{-3}L_F BU6$ | 1.0491 | 6.48 |
| $10^{-3}L_F BO6$ | 0.3113 | 4.69 |
| $10^{-6}L_M^2$ | −1.8975 | −11.61 |
| $10^{-2}L_M$ | 1.9750 | 7.74 |
| $10^{-3}L_M \log A_M$ | 0.9182 | 2.36 |
| $K_F$ | 2.8068 | 33.51 |
| $K_M$ | 10.6040 | 69.49 |

We observe that, except for one parameter, all parameters are significantly different from zero and we also observe that the utility function
is strictly concave in $\{C, L_M, L_F\}$.

These results can probably best be explained by calculating elasticities.
Two categories of elasticities are of interest:

(1) *Job-specific elasticities.* The estimated job-specific utility function is
    used to calculate elasticities for a representative individual, given
    that he or she works.
(2) *Aggregate elasticities.* The estimated hours of work distribution is
    used to simulate aggregates such as expected participation in
    number of individuals, and hours, conditional on working. Aggre-
    gate elasticities are obtained by increasing the wage level of each
    individual by 1 per cent.

Here, we will report only aggregate elasticities.

## 11.2(e)  *Aggregates and aggregate elasticities*

Let $\tilde{\phi}_{js}(x)$ be the marginal probability density of working $x$ hours by
individual $j$, sex $s$. Altogether there are 778 married couples in the
sample, so that $j = 1, \ldots 778$.

The marginal probability of not working is $\tilde{\phi}_{js}(0)$.
Thus,

$$\tilde{P}_{js} = 1 - \tilde{\phi}_{js}(0). \tag{11.17}$$

is the probability of participation. We define the following unconditional

215

marginal densities for $x > 0$.

$$\tilde{\phi}_{js}^u(x) = \tilde{\phi}_{js}(x)\tilde{P}_{js}; \qquad \text{for } x > 0. \tag{11.18}$$

The following expected aggregates can be specified:

*Expected labor supply in number of persons*

$$N_s^T = \sum_{j=1}^{N} \tilde{P}_{js}; \; s = F, M. \tag{11.19}$$

*Expected participation rates*

$$P_s = N_s^T/N; \; s = F, M. \tag{11.20}$$

$N$ is the total number of married persons. (Note that by definition $N_F = N_M = N$.)

*Conditional expectation of total supply of hours of work, conditional on working*

$$H_s = \sum_{j=1}^{N} \int_D x\tilde{\phi}_{js}(x) \, dx; \; s = F, M \text{ for } x > 0 \tag{11.21}$$

*Unconditional expectation of total supply of hours of work*

$$H_s^u = \sum_{j=1}^{N} \int_D x\tilde{\phi}_{js}^u(x) \, dx; \; s = F, M \text{ for } x \geqq 0. \tag{11.22}$$

Aggregate elasticities are calculated by increasing the wage level for

**Table 11.2**
Aggregate labor supply elasticities, Norway, 1979

| Type of elasticity | Male elasticities | | Female elasticities | |
|---|---|---|---|---|
| | Own wage elasticity | Cross elasticity | Own wage elasticity | Cross elasticity |
| Elasticity of expected number of participating persons, $N_s$ | 0.27 | −0.09 | 0.66 | −0.31 |
| Elasticity of conditional expectaion of total supply of hours, $H_s$ | 0.07 | −0.04 | 0.60 | −0.26 |
| Elasticity of unconditional expectation of total supply of hours, $H_s^u$ | 0.33 | −0.13 | 1.20 | −0.54 |

each individual by 1 per cent. The model is used to compute new marginal densities and new aggregates. The elasticities are set out in Table 11.2.

Observe that for each individual the third line will be the sum of the first two lines. For aggregates this is not necessarily true, but the reported aggregate elasticities are very close to fulfilling this condition. Unconditional aggregate elasticities can therefore be decomposed into participation elasticities and conditional hours of work elasticities, given that the individuals work. As expected, females are more responsive to wages than their male spouses. Somewhat surprisingly, however, we find that the participation response accounts for more of the total responses to wage changes among men than among women. All cross effects are found to be negative but weak, except for the impact of male wages on female hours, conditional on working.

## 11.3   The Labor Supply Response to a Shorter Workday

The estimated model is used to simulate the effect of changing the choice set $D$ (see Appendix). Here the choice set will be changed to imply a maximum of 6 hours a day in every job $k$. On an annual basis this maximum is equivalent to 1680 hours as described in Section 11.1. This change of the choice set has a direct impact on the feasible region for hours $D$ (or $D_M$, $D_F$ in the case of married couples). Let $D^*$ denote the new region. When changing the choice set, one also has to say something about availability of jobs. In our econometric context this means statement about the probability distribution $G(x, y)$. Three alternatives are of interest.

(1)   Fraction of feasible jobs, $g_1$, is kept constant.
(2)   The unconditional density $g_1 d$ is kept constant, which means that all jobs for which hours are more than 6 hours a day disappear.
(3)   The expected demand for hours is kept constant, i.e.

$$g_1 d \int_D x \, dx = g_1^* d^* \int_{D^*} x \, dx,$$

where $g_1^* d^*$ is the new unconditional density.

Only alternative 1 will be shown here.

The results meet the expectation of more women participating in the labor market if jobs are changed towards a shorter maximum workday (see Table 11.3). The number of women wanting to participate in the labor market increases by 17.0 per cent. Before the change of the choice set the female participation rate was 70.3 per cent. After the change it increases to 82.3 per cent. The male labor supply, in contrast, is negatively affected by the introduction of the '6-hours-a-day' restriction. The expected number of participating males is calculated to decrease by

217

**Table 11.3**
Changes in labor supply aggregates if a restriction of 6 hours a day is imposed as a maximum load, Norway, 1979, percentages

| Type of aggregate | Male response | Female response | Total response |
|---|---|---|---|
| Expected number of participating persons, $N_s^T$ | −5.7 | +17.0 | +3.9 |
| Conditional expectation of total supply of hours, $H_s$ | −32.3 | −21.9 | −29.5 |
| Unconditional expectation of total supply of hours, $H_s^u$ | −36.7 | −11.6 | −28.8 |

5.7 per cent which corresponds to a decrease in the participation rate from 92.8 per cent to 87.2 per cent. This decrease, however, is not strong enough to prevent the overall participation rate from increasing. The expected number of married couples wanting to participate is calculated to increase by 3.9 per cent.

The main reasons for these changes in behavior of married couples are in the first place that the increase in available 'full-time' jobs of a shorter daily length makes it easier for married women to combine housework with market activities. The decrease in male participation is harder to explain, but it is probably a mixture of a misspecified rationing constraint, of young males switching roles from market activities to housework and of older males leaving the labor force as their younger wives increase their market activities. Notice that the age of the married females is 27–66 years of age, while on average the male is 2–3 years older. A minor, but still significant, group of married men in the sample is close to or above retirement age, which in 1979 was 67.

As should be expected, the negative impact on hours is substantial, especially among men: the total unconditional expectation of supplied hours is calculated to decrease by 28.8 per cent. Of course, a full assessment of the impact on the labor market of a shorter workday requires a general equilibrium model. An important question would then be the impact on wage levels in different labor markets, and the amount of labor used corresponding to these new equilibria. The answer will depend on different aspects of the demand side, such as production technology, the extent of shift-work, etc. What we have focused on in this paper is only the supply side. However, one can ask whether a shorter workday will make the labor market tighter or not. Our results indicate an ambiguous answer. The total supply response in expected number of persons participating indicates a less tight labor market, especially in those markets that are dominated by female workers. The impact on total labor supply in expected hours is on the other hand negative, indicating a tighter labor market and upwards pressure on hourly wage levels. According to our elasticity results this will induce more women to take part in the labor market and both men and women to increase their supply of hours worked. Thus, after the change in the normal working hours, a new equilibrium might occur in the labor market characterized by a higher real wage level and fewer hours of work supplied by the entire population, but with more females participating.

We end this section by showing the impact on the hours of work

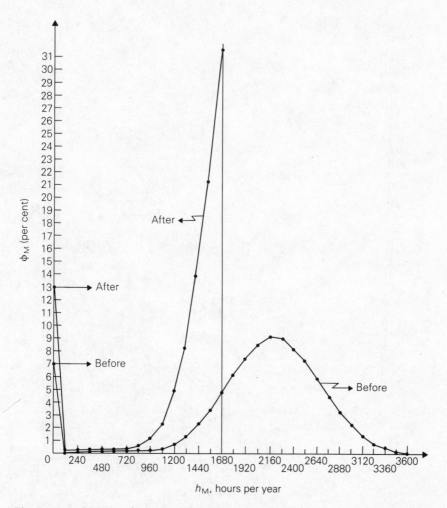

**Figure 11.1** Hours of work distribution for married men, Norway, 1979, 'before' and 'after' a '6-hours-a-day' restriction is imposed on hours of work in each job

219

distribution and wage elasticities of changing the choice set. In Figures 11.1 and 11.2 the estimated hours of work distribution for men and women, respectively, are displayed. We observe that the one-peaked and symmetical distribution of hours worked among males is turned into a skewed and truncated distribution as a consequence of the '6-hours-a-day' restriction. The hours of work distribution for married women is more uniform before the change. The restriction to 1680 hours a year does not change the form of the distribution in the same drastic way as for men; uniformity is to some extent preserved. The reason is of

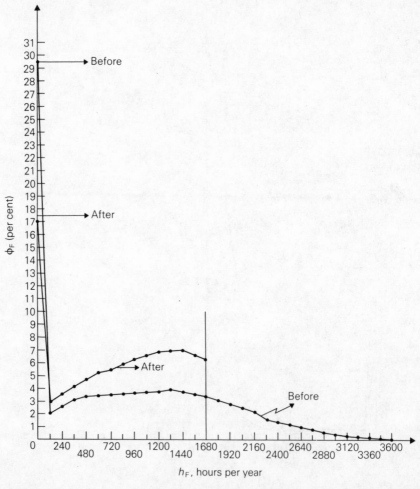

**Figure 11.2** Hours of work distribution for married women, Norway, 1979, 'before' and 'after' a '6-hours-a-day' restriction is imposed on hours of work in each job

**Table 11.4**
Aggregate labor supply elasticities after a '6-hours-a-day' restriction is imposed on working hours in each job

| Type of elasticity | Male elasticities | | Female elasticities | |
|---|---|---|---|---|
| | Own | Cross | Own | Cross |
| Elasticity of expected number of participating persons, $N_s$ | 0.46 | −0.11 | 0.39 | −0.15 |
| Elasticity of conditional expectation of total supply of hours, $H_s$ | 0.05 | −0.01 | 0.45 | −0.17 |
| Elasticity of uncondi-tional expectation of total supply of hours, $H_s^u$ | 0.50 | −0.12 | 0.81 | −0.31 |

course that a substantial number of women were working fewer than 1680 hours a year even before the imposed restriction.

Table 11.4 gives the aggregate wage elasticities calcaulated on the basis of the hours of work distribution occurring after the change of the choice set. We observe that the own-wage elasticity of men's participation is increased and thereby makes the elasticity of the aggregate, unconditional expectation of hours worked larger. In the case of women all aggregate elasticities are lower. Thus, a shorter workday makes both participation rates and wage elasticities more equal between sexes.

## Appendix

Let $\phi(\bar{h}_F, \bar{h}_M, \bar{w}_F, \bar{w}_M)$ denote the density of the couple's realized hours of work and wages, respectively. We have

$$\phi(\bar{h}_F, \bar{h}_M, \bar{w}_F, \bar{w}_M) = \frac{\exp[v_1(\bar{w}_F\bar{w}_M, \bar{h}_F, \bar{h}_M)]g_{11}g_2(\bar{w}_F, \bar{w}_M)d_Fd_M}{R(D)} \quad (11A.1)$$

$$\text{for } \bar{h}_F > 0, \bar{h}_M > 0$$

$$\phi(0, \bar{h}_M, \bar{w}_M) = \frac{\exp[v_1(\bar{w}_M, 0, \bar{h}_M)]g_{01}g_{2M}(\bar{w}_M)d_M}{R(D)} \quad (11A.2)$$

$$\phi(\bar{h}_F, 0, \bar{w}_F) = \frac{\exp[v_1(\bar{w}_F, \bar{h}_F, 0)]g_{10}g_{2F}(\bar{w}_F)d_F}{R(D)} \quad (11A.3)$$

$$\phi(0, 0) = \frac{\exp(v_1(0, 0)g_0}{R(D)} \quad (11A.4)$$

221

where

$$v_1(\bar{w}_F, \bar{w}_M, \bar{h}_F, \bar{h}_M) = v[\bar{h}_F, \bar{h}_M, f(\bar{h}_F\bar{w}_F, \bar{h}_M\bar{w}_M, I, S), Z]$$

for $\bar{h}_F > 0, \bar{h}_M > 0$.

$$v_1(\bar{w}_M, 0, \bar{h}_M) = v[0, \bar{h}_M, f(0, h_M\bar{w}_M, I, S), Z]$$

$$v_1(\bar{w}_F, \bar{h}_F, 0) = v[\bar{h}_F, 0, f(h_F w_F, 0, I, S), Z]$$

$$v_1(0, 0) = v[0, 0, f(0, 0, I, S), Z]$$

$$R(D) = g_{11}d_M d_F \iiiint_{\substack{x_1 \in D_F, x_2 \in D_M \\ x_1 > 0 \, x_2 > 0}} \exp[v_1(y_1, y_2, x_1, x_2)] g_2(y_1, y_2) \, dx_1 \, dx_2 \, dy_1 \, dy_2$$

$$+ g_{01}d_M \iint_{\substack{x_2 \in D_M \\ x_2 > 0}} \exp[v_1(y_2, 0, x_2)] g_{2M}(y_2) \, dx_2 \, dy_2$$

$$+ g_{10}d_F \iint_{\substack{x_1 \in D_F \\ x_1 > 0}} \exp[v_1(y_1, x_1, 0)] g_{2F}(y_1) \, dx_1 \, dy_1 + g_0 \exp v_1(0, 0),$$

$g_2(w_F, w_M)$ is the wage density among the feasible jobs for the couple

$g_{2F}(w_F)$ is the wage density for the female given that the jobs are feasible

$g_{2M}(w_M)$ is the wage density for the male given that the jobs are feasible

$g_{11}$ is the probability that a job combination $k$ is feasible for the couple

$g_{01}$ is the probability that a job is feasible for the male

$g_{10}$ is the probability that a job is feasible for the female, and

$g_{00} = 1 - g_{10} - g_{01} - g_{11}$.

The conditional density of the hours given realized wages is

$$\phi(\bar{h}_F, \bar{h}_M \mid \bar{w}_F, \bar{w}_M, \bar{h}_F > 0, \bar{h}_M > 0)$$

$$= \frac{\exp[v_1(w_F, w_M, h_F, h_M)]}{\displaystyle\iint_{\substack{D_F \ D_M \\ x_1 > 0, \, x_2 > 0}} \exp[v_1(w_F, w_M, x_1, x_2)] \, dx_1 \, dx_2},$$

which demonstrates that this conditional distribution is independent of the distribution of offered hours and wages.

The marginal distribution of hours of work is given by

$$\phi(\bar{h}_F, \bar{h}_M) = \int \int \phi(\bar{h}_F, \bar{h}_M, y_1, y_2) \, dy_1 \, dy_2.$$

Now let

$$\exp \bar{v}(h_F, h_M) = \int \int \exp[v_1(y_1, y_2, h_F, h_M)] g_2(y_1, y_2) \, dy_1 \, dy_2$$

$$\text{for } h_F > 0, \, h_M > 0$$

$$\exp \bar{v}(0, h_M) = \frac{g_{01}}{g_{11} d_F} \int \exp[v, (y_2, 0, h_M)] g_{2M}(y_2) \, dy_2$$

$$\text{for } h_F = 0, \, h_M > 0$$

$$\exp \bar{v}(h_F, 0) = \frac{g_{10}}{g_{11} d_M} \int \exp[v_1(y_1, y_F, 0)] g_{2F}(y_1) \, dy_1$$

$$\text{for } h_F > 0, \, h_M = 0$$

and

$$\exp \bar{v}(0, 0) = \frac{g_{00} \exp v_1(0, 0)}{g_{11} d_M d_F}.$$

Then we can write

$$\phi(\bar{h}_F, \bar{h}_M) = \frac{\exp[\bar{v}(\bar{h}_F, \bar{h}_M)]}{\displaystyle\int\int_{D_F D_M} \exp[\bar{v}(x_1, x_2)] \, dx_1 \, dx_2}. \tag{11A.5}$$

Note that the function $\bar{v}$ depends on the parameters of the wage distribution, $g_2$. As indicated in Section 11.2(d), we have assumed that this dependence can, approximately, be accounted for by replacing the actual wages by their means, respectively.

Now let $\phi^*(\bar{h}_F, h_M)$ denote the supply density after the choice sets $D_F, D_M$ have been changed to $D_F^*, D_M^*$. If we keep the fraction of suitable jobs constant, $g_{00}, g_{01}, g_{10}$ and $g_{11}$ remain constant so that only $d_F$ and $d_M$ change to $d_F^*, d_M^*$ because

$$d_F \int_{D_F} dx = d_F^* \int_{D_F^*} dx = d_M \int_{D_M} dx = d_M^* \int_{D_M^*} dx = 1.$$

223

Let

$$\gamma_F = \frac{\int_{D_F} dx}{\int_{D_F^*} dx}, \quad \gamma_M = \frac{\int_{D_M} dx}{\int_{D_M^*} dx}.$$

Then we get from (11A.5) that

$\phi^*(\bar{h}_F, \bar{h}_M) =$

$$\frac{\exp \bar{v}(\bar{h}_F, \bar{h}_M)}{\iint\limits_{\substack{D_F^* D_M^* \\ x_1, x_2 > 0}} \exp[\bar{v}(x_1, x_2)]\, dx_1\, dx_2 + \gamma_M \int\limits_{\substack{D_F^* \\ x_1 > 0}} \exp[\bar{v}(x_1, 0)]\, dx_1 + \gamma_F \int\limits_{\substack{D_M^* \\ x_2 > 0}} \exp[\bar{v}(0, x_2)]\, dx_2 + \gamma_F \gamma_M \exp \bar{v}(0}$$

(11A

# COMMENT

## KLAUS F. ZIMMERMANN

One can straightforwardly consider the consequences of a shorter workday in the context of labor demand models. It is much more difficult to do so for labor supply models. Clearly, the authors have entered a promising field of frontier econometric work.

Despite many fancy developments, mainstream labor supply econometrics fails to account for the following problems:

(a) Cross-sectional variation in actual hours worked usually has a very peculiar shape, with one or more extreme peaks. This is poorly explained by traditional models, which typically produce a smooth and unimodal distribution of predicted hours.
(b) The assumption that the gross wage rate is exogenous is questionable, especially since the wage is likely to depend on the number of hours worked.
(c) Labor supply decisions should be analyzed in a quantity–quality framework: demand for and supply of job characteristics have to be considered.
(d) Institutional arrangements and other supply constraints should not be ignored, especially in periods of increased unemployment.

From this follows:

(a) Labor supply decisions should be modeled as choices among wage–hours–job characteristics bundles. This involves decisions about a feasible set of discrete alternatives, jobs, and their characteristics.
(b) The utility-maximizing individual is now concerned with discrete and continuous choices at the same time, and these choices should both flow from the same underlying utility-maximization decision. Hence, a discrete/continuous choice model of the consumer is needed. Recent contributions on these lines include Rosen (1976), Hanemann (1984), Dickens and Lundberg (1985), Lundberg (1985), and Gustman and Steinmeier (1986).

The authors fail to discuss their approach in the context of this literature. Also, in too many places the reader is left to guess what actually has been done. Surprisingly, Figures 11.1 and 11.2 show that the model predicts hours (larger than 0) as smooth and unimodal as in the traditional models. (Unfortunately, actual hours are not shown in these diagrams.) It is assumed that offered wages and hours are statistically independent and hours offered are uniformly distributed (equation (11.10)). Data on job characteristics are not available so that they are treated as unobservables. (See equation (11.4) and the discussion below.) It is therefore difficult to trace out the specific merits of the paper. Some conceptual issues are discussed first. Then problems of application are addressed.

The authors assume that the individual households are maximizing equation (11.4), whereas consumption, $C$, is replaced by use of the budget constraint (11.1). This is a discrete/continuous utility function, and a discrete choice has to be made. ($k^* \in B$; $k = 1, 2, \ldots,$) among various alternative conventional utility functions. However, the choice set $B$ is latent. Not even the number of alternatives (which may vary between individuals) is known. (There are, at least, two alternatives – to work or not to work – and this is reflected by equations (11.7) and (11.8).) The only imposed information is that $h = h_{k^*}$ and $w = w_{k^*}$, where $k^*$ is the optimal job. This implies that individuals are not rationed; they are choosing jobs with optimal wage–hours combinations. Hours offered in the model are uniformly distributed and $w_k$ and $h_k$, wages and hours, are stochastically independent (equation (11.10)). $T_k$ disappears from equation (11.4), where only the error term depends on $k$. Hence, the essentials of the outlined model are assumed away.

As Table 11.1 indicates, the deterministic part of (11.4) is

$$U(C, L_F, L_M) = \alpha_C C^2 + \alpha_F L_F^2 + \alpha_M L_M^2 + \beta_C C + \beta_F L_F + \beta_M L_M + \gamma_{FM} L_F L_M$$

$$+ \delta_{FA} L_F \log A_F + (\delta_{FBU} BU6 + \delta_{FBO} BO6) L_F + \delta_{MA} L_M \log A_M$$

$$+ \delta_F K_F + \delta_M K_M. \tag{1}$$

This is a special case of a general quadratic direct utility function with consumption, $C$, and male leisure, $L_M$, and female leisure, $L_F$, as arguments and various taste-shifters. Equation (1) is a second-order Taylor series expansion of any arbitrary utility function concerning $C$, $L_F$ and $L_M$, where consumption and leisure are assumed to be additive separable. The chosen utility index represents a local approximation of preferences, and implies rather complicated labor supply functions and messy expressions for the Slutsky conditions

$$\left. \frac{\partial h}{\partial w} \right|_U = \left. \frac{\partial h}{\partial w} \right|_S - h \frac{\partial h}{\partial S}.$$

The labor supply functions are

$$h_i = \frac{1}{\Delta} [\gamma_{FM} w_j - 2\alpha_j w_i)\mu + w_i^2 2\alpha_C \Omega_i - 2w_M w_F \alpha_C \Omega_j + 2\Omega_i \alpha_i - \Omega_j \gamma_{FM}], \tag{2}$$

where $i, j = F, M$ and $i \neq j$, $\mu = 2\alpha_C S + \beta_C$, $\Omega_M = T(2\alpha_M + \gamma_{FM}) + \beta_M + \delta_{MA} \log A_M$, $\Omega_F = T(2\alpha_F + \gamma_{FM}) + \beta_F + \delta_{FA} \log A + \delta_{FBU} BU6 + \delta_{FBO} BO6$, $T = 8000$, and $\Delta = 4(\alpha_C \alpha_F w_M^2 + \alpha_C \alpha_M w_F^2 - \alpha_C \gamma_{FM} w_M w_F + \alpha_F \alpha_M) - \delta_{FM}^2$. Second-order conditions require $\Delta > 0$.

The role of $K_F$ and $K_M$ in equation (1) is, however, not quite clear and is explained nowhere in the paper. Potentially, these variables are more than taste-shifters and define a choice set of the family with four elements. But to call (1) for this reason a job-specific utility function would be misleading.

Equation (11.4) contains a stochastic part that reflects the fact that the utility index, which is deterministic for the household, is only partly observed by the researcher. The random utility model captures unobserved components of heterogeneous preferences and the attributes of the opportunity set of the jobs. The authors assume a Weibull or extreme value distribution and independent draws of the error term. The Weibull distribution is quite flexible, approximates the normal distribution closely and is easy to fit, but exhibits the IIA property and excludes the possibility of any correlation between the random errors $\xi_k$. An alternative is the generalized extreme value distribution.

The application contains several puzzles or leaves open questions. However, the authors are cautious enough to stress the preliminary nature of the analysis in several parts of the paper. The density functions (11.11) and (11.12), as with their analogues in the Appendix, do not depend on $k$. For computational convenience, the conditional densities are used instead of the joint densities. These functions are independent of the distribution of offered hours and wages and are applied separately in a two-step procedure. No statistical evidence is reported suggesting that the asymptotic properties of the estimates are still valid, which is crucial because the sample separation is between working and non-working families. No information is given how the probabilities of getting feasible job offers for the couple are fixed and they seem not to vary between households.

Some model specification tests would have been useful; for instance, whether the separability assumption between leisure and consumption is appropriate. However, it is acknowledged that tests about the stochastic specification seem to be too fancy for a preliminary investigation. The parameter estimates in Table 11.1 show that the utility function is strictly quasi-concave in consumption and male and female leisure. The consistency with utility maximization could have been checked by examining the properties of symmetry and negative definiteness of the Slutsky matrix. In particular, the compensated wage responses of labor supply have to be non-negative. This is not in general true for the chosen utility index (1) and can only be proved numerically given the range of the exogenous variables, so that results may differ between households.

One may feel that the Taylor series approximation is no longer valid for drastic restrictions on hours worked as imposed in the simulation of a shorter workday. More crucial, however, is that the assumption of a uniform distribution of offered hours and the probabilities of getting feasible job offers are kept fixed. Changes in the offer distributions are at the heart of such policy measures.

Discussants usually fail to relate fairly the outcome of a paper with the general state of research. This certainly qualifies the critical comments on the paper, which is a step in the right direction.

# CHAPTER 12

# Hours Reductions within Large-scale Macroeconomic Models: Conflict between Theory and Empirical Application

## J. D. WHITLEY AND R. A. WILSON

## 12.1 Introduction

This paper is concerned with two related but separate issues. First we explore the apparent contradiction that, while pressure continues to mount for a reduction in normal hours to alleviate the problems of mass unemployment in Western Europe, most theoretical analyses by economists suggest that reductions in normal hours will have precisely the reverse effect and will result in an increase in actual hours worked and a reduction in employment. It is argued in Section 12.2 that the main explanation for this apparent conflict lies in the fact that much of the theoretical work has concentrated upon the demand side, within a partial equilibrium framework, whereas the demand for a cut in the normal working week rests upon the observed tendency for average hours to follow the secular downward trend in normal hours. We argue that this long-term decline in normal and average hours primarily reflects supply-side forces resulting in a shift in the choice between income and leisure as real incomes have risen. Consequently, although it may be acceptable to regard normal hours as exogenously determined in the short term, this is not acceptable in the medium to long term, when they will be affected by both demand and supply side forces (albeit through the filter of a complex institutionalized bargaining process). In assessing the effects of a change in normal hours it is important to clarify the mechanism by which such a change may come about. For this reason we argue that a satisfactory treatment of this question ideally requires a complete demand/supply sub-model for hours integrated within a full macroeconomic model.

The second issue we examine follows on naturally from the first, and this is to explore the extent to which sub-models exist within current UK macroeconomic models. This is done in Section 12.3. Our exploration reveals the very limited nature of most treatments of hours of work within UK macro-models. In the light of these difficulties we then go in Sections 12.4 and 12.5 to provide an assessment of what insights such models can give on the question of how hours reductions might affect employment, despite these limitations. Section 12.6 contains our conclusions.


## 12.2 Work Sharing and Employment: The Debate

Since the middle of the last century there has been a steady reduction in the length of the working week (see, for example, Bienefeld, 1972; Williams, 1984; and Blyton, 1985). The historical evidence suggests that average hours have tended to follow the path of normal hours, albeit with a lag and with a strong cyclical pattern around the trend (Wilson, 1986). It is this 'stylized fact' that lies behind much of the pressure to reduce normal hours as a means of bringing about a reduction in average hours and thereby increasing employment.

There has been a long-running debate concerning the determinants of secular changes in the length of the working week, although debate is perhaps too strong a term to describe the rather incoherent and disparate nature of the discussion that has been conducted on this subject over many years. The link between the length of the working week and employment has been a central issue in this debate since the last century and the current interest in work sharing as a means of reducing unemployment has a very long history (Culliver, 1984; Evans, 1975). In recent years, with the dramatic rise in unemployment and the apparently paradoxical situation of continued high levels of overtime working in many industries, the pressure from unions to reduce hours worked as a means of alleviating the worst symptoms of the recession has increased.

Authors from different specialisms have focused on various aspects of the determinants of hours. On the one hand, one can identify what might be loosely described as an 'institutionalist' approach, which emphasizes the importance of institutional factors, custom and practice, etc. On the other hand, there are the more economic explanations based on theories of a rational response of individuals and firms to the costs and benefits of alternative actions. Other contrasts in the literature arise between: those who stress supply-side and those who emphasize demand-side influences; those who concentrate upon explaining normal weekly hours and those who are interested in overtime hours, and so on. The perspectives obtained from these different approaches may have much to do with the apparent disagreement about the effectiveness of reductions in hours worked as a means of reducing unemployment.

The stylized facts to be explained by the various competing hypotheses are as follows:

1 The long-term trend reduction in both normal and average hours.
2 The tendency for overtime working to remain at *relatively* high levels despite the trend in normal and average hours.
3 The discontinuous nature of the reduction in normal hours, while average hours have trended more smoothly, albeit with a strong cyclical pattern.[1]
4 The common pattern of standard or normal hours across most sectors of the economy and the tendency for changes to be synchronized across sectors.

Bienefeld (1972) and Lewis (1971) explain the long-run trend developments in the UK and US, respectively, largely by supply-side factors. The gradual secular reduction in both average and normal hours over time arises, it is argued, from the desire of workers to take at least some (about one-half according to Bienefeld) of the potential increase in economic growth in the form of greater leisure. Discontinuity in movements in normal hours is explained by the supply-siders (for example, Blyton, 1985) in terms of the pressure from employees being greatest when real wages are rising strongly and when unemployment is low (when there are fears of rising unemployment in the future). The synchronicity of changes in hours is explained in terms of organizational convenience and the effects of collective bargaining at the national level, among other factors (Carter and Maddock, 1984). The presence of persistent overtime working either reflects indivisibilities in continuous-process plants or is a means of paying selected workers a bonus. (For a more extensive discussion see Whitley and Wilson, 1986b.)

The demand-side approach, in contrast, concentrates upon the micro-economic theory of the demand for hours using comparative statics. Work by Hart (1984a), Ehrenberg (1971a,c) and Santamäki (1983, 1984) has focused on the cost-minimization problem facing employers when making decisions on the appropriate combination of factor inputs required to meet a given output in a partial equilibrium framework. The main conclusions of this body of work are that (employers') desired hours are a *negative* function of both normal hours and the basic wage rate, although there are some exceptions (e.g. Bodo and Giannini, 1985). Explanations for the persistence of overtime working include: the growing importance of quasi-fixed labor costs (Ehrenberg, 1971a, c; Ehrenberg and Schuman, 1972); the higher productivity of overtime hours; and finally, some of the factors used in the supply-side explanation. The main distinction between the demand- and the supply-side approaches is that the former stresses the importance of costs and benefits associated with different working patterns, while the latter emphasizes institutional or non-economic factors. For further discussion see Leslie and Wise (1980), Bosworth and Westaway (1986) and Whitley and Wilson (1986b).

Much of the empirical work on this subject for the UK has concentrated upon the demand side and has been conducted within the framework of the so-called 'short-term employment function'. The long-run supply-side influences on hours, and in particular the choice between income and leisure, have by and large been ignored or subsumed within an 'exogenously' determined variable 'normal hours'. The literature has therefore tended to concentrate upon the determinants of overtime hours and the cyclical pattern of average hours around the underlying trend for normal hours, rather than attempting to explain the latter.

It seems clear that changes in hours in the long term reflect both demand and supply factors, but few, if any, empirical models have been set up within a full demand/supply framework to consider these issues. There has, however, been some theoretical analysis along these lines, explictly concerned with the effects of hours reductions on employment, although most of these still take *normal* hours as exogenous. For example, authors such as Hoel (1984), Calmfors (1985), Calmfors and Hoel (1988), and Booth and Schiantarelli (1985) have developed theoretical supply/demand/bargaining models to analyze the impact of cuts in hours on employment. Leslie (1978) has attempted to introduce supply-side considerations more explicitly into an empirical factor demand model. However, such considerations have not figured very highly in the empirical work, or indeed in the hours equations subsumed within most UK macroeconomic models.

The results of the theoretical supply/demand models are generally ambiguous regarding the impact of hours reductions on employment. The outcome varies between the different authors depending upon the precise specifications adopted for the various components of the model such as the workers'/unions' utility function and the underlying production function.

From the discussion so far it would seem appropriate that, if such issues are to be examined within the framework of a macroeconomic model, then ideally a full supply/demand model for hours worked is required, where both normal and average hours are determined endogenously. In practice, such an ideal is not attained in any of the macro-models considered here. The general rule is that, if a model of hours is included, it takes the form of the models referred to earlier, with actual hours dependent on normal hours and some form of cyclical variable. Such relationships contrast sharply with the microeconomic demand perspective, as outlined above. The latter predicts a negative partial relationship between average and normal hours as employers substitute hours for workers. This substitution mechanism is absent in most of the empirical models, although this may simply reflect the fact that, historically, other factors influencing hours, such as the size of the basic wage, may have altered in such a way as to swamp this negative partial effect. This implies, however, that such relationships may be misspecified, particularly from the point of view of conducting simulations involving changing normal hours.

Such equations could be regarded as a 'reduced form' of a simultaneous demand/supply model. Strictly speaking, of course, it is not a reduced form if, in the period covered by the model, variables such as normal hours appearing on the right-hand side as regressors are not truly exogenous but depend upon demand- and supply-side factors. The use of such models to simulate the effects of changing hours on employment therefore begs two questions. First, whereas the case for regarding normal hours as exogenous in the short run seems reasonable, the sort of changes envisaged for this variable over the medium term may invalidate this assumption. If in a full specification both normal and average hours should be determined endogenously, it is not clear that a variable such as normal hours can be regarded as *causing* changes in actual hours in the typical equations as estimated in most empirical studies. Second, even if normal hours could be considered to be weakly exogenous to the rest of the system (and this is consistent with the variable being dominated by long-run supply-side factors), this does not imply that normal (or, indeed, average) hours can be used as a policy lever that the government is able to manipulate. This is essentially the same sort of criticism made of simulations of the impact of changes in the real wage on employment as advanced in Andrews *et al.* (1985).

On balance the evidence from case studies in the UK of particular industries such as those by White (1982) and White and Ghobadian (1984) and a close examination of the French 'experiments' in this area (see the discussion in Jones, 1985) leave us very skeptical about the short-term impact of normal hours reduction on employment. Nevertheless, in the longer term it seems clear that the leisure–income 'trade-off' will again come into play. However, past hours reductions have *not* been designed to achieve increases in employment, but have rather been won as concessions from employers in place of improvements in pay. It seems likely therefore that any further reductions in hours must be negotiated between workers and employers and cannot be imposed by dictum by the state if they are to be successful in reducing unemployment.

## 12.3  Macroeconomic Models and the Treatment of Hours

The preceding section outlined some of the main elements in the debate about the impact of a change in the standard working week upon the demand for labor. In the main, this has taken place within a partial equilibrium framework. Having noted the main empirical findings related to developments in average weekly hours, we now consider the effects of changed hours of work within a wider macroeconomic context. This leads us into a discussion of the main UK models and the importance of various linkages between hours and employment and the remainder of the economy.

As noted in the previous section, there have been several pieces of work in the theoretical literature that have examined these linkages. Examples are publications by Strøm (1983), Hoel (1986), Calmfors (1985), and Calmfors and Hoel (1988). These typically assume that the initial change in actual hours of work can be accomplished and then concentrate upon the effects on employment, both direct and indirect. Where links with the macro-economy are made, emphasis is typically placed upon the nature of the system in which the hours reduction is set, that is, whether it is characterized by classical or Keynesian unemployment, and the specification of the production function (including differential impacts between sectors). An important element in these theoretical models is the nature of the relationship between the economy in question and the rest of the world (for example, the openness of the economy, and features determining the behavior of the exchange rate).

Although these theoretical studies provide many insights into the issue of hours reduction and employment, they are unable to draw any strong conclusions once the model is made sufficiently general. Thus Calmfors and Hoel conclude that 'it is only in very simple models that a reduction of working time increases employment unambiguously ... in more complex models, a reduction of working time is quite likely to be counterproductive as an employment-promoting measure'. They go on to argue that 'to predict the outcome would seem to require detailed knowledge about the relative importance of Keynesian and Classical unemployment ... as well as the structural parameters of production functions'. Clearly empirical models do not suffer from this shyness since they employ quite explicit estimates of the necessary parameters required to derive employment effects due to hours reductions. How useful they are in this respect depends on the sophistication and relevance of the various linkages embedded in them. By examining a range of UK macroeconomic models we show that their contrasting implications for the effects of hours reductions emanate from the extent to which various key mechanisms identified in the literature on hours reduction are present. In this section we outline a fairly general framework, abstracting from dynamic considerations, within which hours reductions can be considered and then proceed to fit the UK models into this framework. The likely consequence on employment of hours reductions can then be predicted from knowledge of the model structure. These are then compared with the actual simulation results from the models in Section 12.5.

A GENERAL FRAMEWORK

As noted in Section 12.2, the typical relationship for hours of work can be written:

$$H = h(HN, CYC),$$ (12.1)

where $HN$ are normal hours of work and $CYC$ is some measure of cyclical deviations from trend, which will in turn be some function of output, $Q$. Employment demand functions in the models take the

233

following very general form:

$$E = f(Q, H, We/p), \qquad (12.2)$$

where $Q$ is output, $E$ is numbers employed, $We/p$ is the real wage per worker (or the relative price of labor to capital). Some of the theoretical debate has considered special cases where labor services ($L = EH$) has hours and employment as perfect substitutes. In general, in most of the empirical literature, capital does not appear in the employment demand equation explicitly, although its effects are often proxied by a time trend. A common assumption with respect to labor supply is that it is perfectly elastic over a given range (we consider later how this is modified in some of the UK models).

The first relationship represents one of the key elements in the work-sharing debate. Where normal hours ($HN$) appear in the models, they are assumed to be exogenous. A key question is what happens to actual hours in response to a fall in normal hours. Although often couched in terms of demand, econometric relationships based on (12.1) reflect both demand and supply influences and, as noted above, can be regarded as a reduced form. They typically produce a positive relationship between $H$ and $HN$. To the extent that $HN$ can be regarded as truly exogenous, then the main issue as far as the work-sharing debate is concerned is the degree to which actual hours respond. We describe this as the 'overtime leakage' ($\gamma$). If actual hours fall in the same proportion as normal hours then the overtime leakage is zero, whereas if actual hours are unchanged the overtime leakage is 100 per cent.

The second relationship can be used to illustrate the potential productivity offset to a change in normal hours. A productivity offset is defined to occur if, for a given level of output, total labor input varies in response to a change in normal hours through improved efficiency. The degree of the productivity offset in the models (which we call $\beta$) can be inferred from knowledge of the parameter on $H$ in (12.2) and the size of the substitution effect ($We/p$).

We can now differentiate between three main classes of model. In the first there is a direct link between hours and employment in the employment demand function (that is, the parameter on $H$ is non-zero and negative). In this model we would expect a positive *first-round* employment effect from a reduction in normal hours, for given output, as long as the overtime offset is weak (that is, actual hours also fall).

In the second class of model the parameter on $H$ is zero and the linkage between $E$ and $H$, for given output, depends solely on any change in relative factor prices ($We/p$). Since our subsequent analysis suggests that relative prices are likely to rise, we would expect a negative first-round effect on employment in this case.

In the third class of model neither actual hours nor relative prices enter the employment demand relationship and hence the employment response depends exclusively on an induced change in the level of output. There is therefore a zero first-round effect on employment and the implied productivity offset is 100 per cent. Thus only in the first class of model will a positive first-round effect be observed. The causes of second-round effects owing to changes in output are common to all three classes of model and are now considered.

The prediction of lower output owing to the pressure of higher costs is one that has been stressed in many studies of the potential employment impact of hours reductions. Higher unit labor costs can originate from three sources for a given level of output:

- higher overtime costs owing to greater use of overtime
- a combination of an (initially) fixed weekly wage and higher employment levels
- a higher weekly wage owing to labor market pressures.

Assuming that the overtime premium remains unchanged, the addition to overtime costs is uniquely determined by the overtime leakage ($\gamma \Delta HN$). Higher overtime costs will then generate an increase in unit labor costs. The second element depends on whether income is shared and on the size of the productivity offset. The standard case that we examine here is that income is not shared, and that the standard weekly wage initially remains constant as the hourly wage rises in proportion to the fall in hours. Given that unit labor costs are expressed as a product of wages and employment per unit of output, the overall effect depends on the class of model as defined earlier. Models with a strong productivity offset will generate a smaller increase in unit labor costs than models that are initially most favorable to employment generation (that is, those with a weak productivity offset).

The third element arises from any second-round effects on weekly wages through labor market pressure. Phillips curve mechanisms often relate wage inflation to labor market disequilibrium as proxied by the level of unemployment. Any initial impact of an hours reduction on employment should, in principle, be neutral in its effect on the excess demand/supply of labor, since this is simply a voluntary shift between hours and employment. However, in most of the models considered, such a policy will have a positive impact on employment, which will imply a reduction in demand-deficient unemployment, thus driving up wage inflation. Therefore there may be an upward bias to the inflation effects of an hours reduction as estimated in such models.

Any increase in unit labor costs that emerges from the above considerations is translated into prices in most of the UK models via cost mark-up. Increased domestic prices then lower export competitiveness and most of the discussion of potential output loss has concentrated on this effect. However, the exchange rate mechanism is critical in this respect. Models of the Scandinavian type (such as Ball, Burns and Laury, 1977) imply that the nominal exchange rate depreciates in such a way as to restore the previous loss of competitiveness. Thus the output loss from this source is transitory, but higher domestic inflation is generated. In other models a permanent change in competitiveness may result.

Finally, we note that many of the UK models contain a role for the effects of inflation upon domestic demand, most notably consumption. Thus we can conclude that the second-round effects on output are all likely to produce a negative effect.

## 12.4   The UK Macroeconomic Models

The main UK macroeconomic models covered in this survey are those of the Cambridge Growth Project (CGP), the Bank of England (BE), the London Business School (LBS), the National Institute of Economic and Social Research (NIESR) and Her Majesty's Treasury (HMT). The Liverpool University Research Group in Macroeconomics and the City University Business School were excluded as neither includes hours of work.

The CGP model is based on annual data, whereas the others are quarterly based models. All are used regularly in the UK for forecasting and policy analysis, and the BE and HMT models are a direct input into the policy process by the authorities. The CGP model is by far the largest by virtue of its high degree of disaggregation (39 industrial sectors). Disaggregation by sector is very limited in all of the other models, which distinguish only between the public and private sectors of the economy, and between the manufacturing and non-manufacturing sectors. LBS and HMT lie more in the middle ground between monetarist and Keynesian models. Both CGP and NIESR occupy the Keynesian end of the spectrum. Some of the models adopt a rational expectations framework. In the LBS and NIESR models forward-consistent expectations are only partial. In the LBS model they appear in the financial market, whereas in the NIESR model they influence the behavior of the goods and labor markets and exchange rate behavior.

Empirical macroeconomic models are not constant over time; their structure and implied properties change as modifications to parameter values, and the form of the equations, are made. Indeed, had this survey been made on an earlier vintage of the models there would have been very little to say regarding the consequences of changing hours of work. The versions of the models analyzed here are those that were deposited at the ESRC Macroeconomic Modelling Bureau at Warwick towards the end of 1985. The Bureau produces regular accounts of the models, their forecasts and their properties, and two volumes in this series have already appeared under the general heading of *Models of the UK Economy*, by K. F. Wallis (ed.) *et al.* The vintage of models used here is analyzed in their third volume in the series (Wallis *et al.*, 1986). Further information on model features relevant to the exercise is given in Whitley and Wilson (1986b).

In the remainder of this section we outline how these models treat hours of work using the framework described in Section 12.3. A summary account is given in Table 12.1, where we also include details of our own earlier study (Whitley and Wilson, 1986a), using the CGP

**Table 12.1**
Model Features

| | WW | CGP | HMT | A | BE | LBS | NIESR |
|---|---|---|---|---|---|---|---|
| Relationship between actual and normal hours | ✓ | | × | × | ✓ | ✓ | × |
| Direct link between employment and hours | ✓ | ✓ | ✓ | × | ✓ | × | × |
| Indirect link between employment and hours (factor prices) | × | ✓ | ✓ | × | ✓ | ✓ | ✓ |
| Non-income sharing (hourly wage rises) | ✓ | ✓ | ✓ | ✓ | ✓ | ✓ | ✓ |
| Overtime cost effects | ✓ | × | × | × | × | ✓ | × |
| Phillips curve and pressure of demand | unemployment | unemployment | output | unemployment | unemployment | unemployment | unemployment |
| Phillips long-run trade-off | ✓ | × | × | × | ✓ | × | × |
| Sectoral modeling of hours/employment | all | all | non-manufacturing | all | manufacturing | manufacturing | manufacturing |
| Labor supply | exogenous | exogenous | exogenous | exogenous | exogenous | females – endogenous | exogenous |

Notes:
(a) A ✓ symbol indicates that such an assumption or relationship is included within the relevant model, an × symbol, that it is not.
(b) The models are as follows:
  WW – Whitley and Wilson (1986), using an earlier version of the CGP model
  CGP – Cambridge Growth Project model
  HMT – Her Majesty's Treasury model
  A – Allen (1980), using an earlier version of the HMT model
  BE – Bank of England model
  LBS – London Business School model
  NIESR – National Institute of Economic and Social Research model.
The versions of CGP, BE, LBS, HMT and NIESR models used are described in more detail in Wallis *et al.* (1986).

**Table 12.2**
Model Properties

| | Real wage elasticity of employment | | Output elasticity of employment | | Overtime leakage (%) | | Productivity offset (%) | |
|---|---|---|---|---|---|---|---|---|
| | S–R | L–R | S–R | L–R | S–R | L–R | S–R | L–R |
| CGP (whole economy aggregate) | −0.16 | −0.34 | 0.35 | 1.0 | 37 | — | 75 | 35 |
| LBS : manufacturing | −0.45 | −0.73 | 0.36 | 0.84 | 100 | 100 | 100 | 100 |
| : non-manufacturing | −0.17 | −1.10 | 0.49 | 1.0 | n/a | n/a | n/a | n/a |
| BE : manufacturing | −0.02 | −0.05 | 0.35 | 1.0 | 13 | 50 | — | — |
| : non-manufacturing | −0.078 | −0.10 | 0.11 | 1.0 | n/a | n/a | n/a | n/a |
| HMT : manufacturing | −0.01 | −0.33 | 0.5 | 1.0 | n/a | n/a | n/a | n/a |
| : non-manufacturing | −0.03 | −0.11 | 0.4 | 1.0 | n/a | n/a | — | — |
| NIESR : manufacturing | −0.45 | −1.31 | 0.53 | 1.54 | n/a | n/a | 100 | 100 |
| : non-manufacturing | — | — | 0.06 | 0.58 | n/a | n/a | n/a | n/a |
| A : average, non-government | n/a | n/a | unknown | unknown | 40 | 40 | 30 | 30 |
| WW : average, all industries | n/a | n/a | 0.33 | 0.66 | n/a | 20 | 18 | 18 |

*Notes* S–R denotes the short-run impact, i.e. effect after 4 quarters or 1 year
L–R denotes the long-run effect
n/a denotes not applicable

model, and a study conducted by Allen (1980) using an earlier version of the HMT model.

## 12.4(a) Cambridge Growth Project (CGP)

The GCP model contains an explicit relationship between actual hours worked and normal hours for each of the non-government sectors of the model with normal hours exogenous. The employment equation contains terms in the level of output, the real wage, investment, hours, a time trend and aggregate unemployment and hence falls into the first class of model under Section 12.3. The implicit assumption in the CGP model is that of non-income sharing, but there is no additional labor cost element due to the short-run increase in overtime working. Prices are cost determined and the initial increase in employment conditional on lower hours worked will combine with the (initially) unchanged wage to generate higher costs and prices. Additional effects on wages occur through the wage equation. This is a target real wage relationship so that higher prices will, in the long run, increase nominal earnings proportionally, leaving real wages unchanged apart from a very weak pressure of demand effect. Thus real wage effects in the employment equation will be merely temporary. Higher domestic prices influence the exchange rate through relative prices, but the real exchange rate can vary so that the simulation of lower hours is likely to result in a lower real exchange rate. Our analysis of this model leads us to predict that it is unlikely to produce strong indirect influences on employment (for example, through changes in aggregate output) that will counteract the initial direct impact on employment from lower hours. Although the model includes cost effects through non-income sharing there is no additional overtime cost element, the pressure of demand (that is, unemployment) effects are weak in the wage equation, and the exchange rate depreciates to offset some of the cost competitivenesss.

These predictions are tested against the actual simulation response in Section 12.5. Our own earlier work (Whitley and Wilson, 1986a) used the basic CGP macroeconomic framework, but with a rather different treatment of factor demands that allows for overtime cost effects. It also examined the sensitivity of the results to different assumptions about income sharing, productivity offset and overtime leakage.

## 12.4(b)  London Business School (LBS)

Actual hours of work are effectively exogenous in this model, so that any change in normal hours has an equal and opposite impact on overtime working (thus the overtime leakage is 100 per cent). Actual hours of work do not enter the employment demand equation, and employment in manufacturing depends on output, real wage costs (including overtime) and real input prices, thus placing this model in the second class as outlined in Section 12.3. The inclusion of overtime costs implies that any change in normal hours of work will have a negative impact effect on employment through this cost term, there being no direct link between employment and hours. Overtime costs are not included in employment in private non-manufacturing. Thus we would expect, for given output, a weaker adverse employment response in non-manufacturing. There is some endogeneity of female labor supply to both real wages and demand. Since there is no direct positive employment response to a change in hours in the LBS model, any effect on labor costs must occur through an increase in the effective wage rate.

There are separate equations for earnings in manufacturing and non-manufacturing. The equations are based on union/firm bargaining theory where real wages are determined by variables on both sides of the bargain. In the absence of any direct relationship between hours and employment, any first-round impact on earnings must come from the allowance for higher overtime costs, so that a reduction in normal hours will increase effective earnings and hence labor costs with proportional effects in both the short and long run. The labor cost effect associated with a 5 per cent reduction in normal hours is $1\frac{1}{2}$ per cent. The equation for non-manufacturing earnings has similar arguments to those of manufacturing, but is additionally influenced by earnings in manufacturing. It is this variable that transmits the wage impact of higher overtime onto the non-manufacturing sector with an impact elasticity of 0.13 and a long-run effect of 0.22. The exchange rate in the LBS model is determined within the sub-model dealing with the financial sector where rational expectations are assumed. It corresponds to a portfolio type of exchange rate model and thus it is not a simple monetary exchange rate model.

Our analysis of the LBS model suggests that it is extremely unlikely to generate a positive employment response from lower normal hours of work. This essentially arises from the absence of any effect on actual hours worked (that is, complete overtime leakage) but also because there is no direct link between hours and employment. All the effects identified are cost effects, which, with the implicit assumption of non-income sharing, will tend to reduce employment demand.

## 12.4(c)  Bank of England (BE)

The BE employment demand equation for manufacturing is derived in terms of person-hours and its determinants include manufacturing output, the real wage and a time trend. The split between employment and hours is made in a subsidiary equation where employment is determined by normal hours. Since in the BE model the demand for labor services is in terms of man-hours with a long-run elasticity of unity with respect to output, there is a zero productivity offset. Employment in other private industries is determined in terms of heads, with output and the real wage the main determinants. We would expect any employment effects from an hours reduction to arise from indirect effects such as from output and real wages, as there is no hours equation for this sector.

Prices are cost determined in the BE model and so, for given wage costs, will rise in proportion to the direct employment impact. The overtime element is captured in a term measuring costs per hour, which enters trade competitiveness (through export prices). Wages in manufacturing themselves depend on unemployment, prices, public sector earnings and tax rates. The long-run Phillips curve is not vertical. Effects on costs are therefore likely to lead to a more damped result on earnings than in some of the other models. Incomes are not shared and the hourly wage rises to preserve the weekly wage, but this is defined as inclusive of higher overtime, whereas for LBS the weekly wage rises additionally owing to the extra overtime effects. Earnings in other private industries are related to unemployment and earnings in the other sectors of the economy. The exchange rate in the BE model depends on the relative velocity of circulation of money, relative prices, and the current account of the balance of payments.

The lack of any productivity offset in the BE model makes it likely that the direct (positive) effects on employment will be quite large (despite the overtime leakage). Recognized cost features exist in the determination of domestic prices and additional overtime costs appear in export prices. The weakness of relative price effects on employment and of unemployment on wages make it likely that the main offset to the initial positive effects on employment operate through lower output. Any impact on non-manufacturing occurs indirectly and thus we would expect this sector to be less affected by any change in normal hours than the manufacturing sector where more direct linkages are specified.

### 12.4(d)  Her Majesty's Treasury (HMT)

The CGP models hours linkages fairly uniformly across the industrial sector of the economy, whereas in the LBS and BE models' effects are concentrated upon the manufacturing sector. HMT, in contrast, omits any linkage of hours to employment in this sector (either directly or through costs) and hours of work enter the model only through private non-manufacturing employment. Employment in manufacturing depends on expected manufacturing output (modeled by a vector autoregressive process), real wage costs, real capital costs and real material prices. It therefore belongs to the second class of models identified in Section 12.3. The distinction in the non-manufacturing sector is that employment is modeled in terms of full-time equivalents. Full-time equivalents are defined as numbers employed adjusted for the proportion working a 40-hour week. Thus this model implies the absence of productivity offset in response to a change in hours worked, but no explicit assumption is made regarding overtime leakage in the absence of a normal hours variable. Wages in the HMT model are determined for the private sector as an aggregate. A distinctive feature is the inclusion of output rather than unemployment as the demand term. Other variables included in the equation are public sector employment and tax rates. Public sector employment is included to proxy a labor supply effect. The exchange rate in the HMT model depends on relative money supplies, price competitiveness, the real value of North Sea oil reserves and relative short-term interest rates.

Our prior expectation is that the HMT model will deliver a strong positive employment response to lower actual hours of work – since normal hours are not considered and with no overtime leakage there is a bias towards employment optimism. The cost effects on output are likely to be diluted as they are concentrated in the non-manufacturing (non-traded) sector and the absence of an unemployment term in the wage equation implies little wage push from this source. We also expect the positive employment effects to appear almost exclusively in the non-manufacturing sector for the reasons outlined above.

### 12.4(e)  National Institute of Economic and Social Research (NIESR)

The NIESR model includes forward-consistent expectations in the labor market. Thus employment in manufacturing depends upon expected output and the expected real wage. The latter variable is omitted from the non-manufacturing equation. The long-run real wage elasticity for manufacturing is the highest among all the models. There is a separate hours equation for manufacturing, which relates actual hours to the level of output and a time trend, but there is no normal hours variable in the equation and, although its effects may be implicit in the time trend, no overtime effects can be identified from the model structure. There is no direct linkage between hours and employment, although both depend on output. Thus any external influence on hours has no immediate effect upon employment in the formal model. The main role for hours in the model is the relation between hours, hourly wages and weekly wages. Average weekly wages are defined as the product of basic wages and average hours with the latter proxying total average hours in the economy. Thus there is an implicit assumption of non-income sharing. Since this model lies in the second class of models, the sole effects on employment in this model come from changes in the wage rate.

The exchange rate is also a forward-looking variable that is determined by relative (real) interest rates (exogenous), its own expectation and changes in the trade balance. In practice, the exchange rate is highly dependent on the terminal conditions for the expected exchange rate. The absence of a normal hours variable means that the NIESR and HMT models have to be treated differently from the other models. In the simulation experiment we expose the model to a step change in actual hours. Our expectation is that the absence of a direct employment effect from lower hours is likely to produce an overall negative effect on employment.

## 12.5  Simulation Results

### 12.5(a)  Methodology

The properties of the models are derived from simulation analysis. A base run of the model is first computed, usually the published forecast. In the first instance a new solution run is then calculated by perturbing an appropriate exogenous variable (normal hours) by a given amount with no other changes to the model. The effects of this shock are then derived by comparing the results of this simulation with the base run. Both solutions include all the residual adjustments and exogeneity assumptions in the base run. In this section, we expose the models to a shock in normal hours of 5 per cent with no other modifications. To the extent that the models are approximately linear the results can be scaled to represent an alternative level of shock. However, if the chosen shock is outside the sample experience of the models we can be less confident of the results in this respect. The simulations are conducted around a base that begins in the range 1985(3)–1986(1) for the quarterly models and 1984 for the CGP model. The longest common simulation period is four years.

We argued in Section 12.2 that normal hours might best be viewed as endogenously determined by a combination of demand- and supply-side forces. In any case, they cannot be regarded as a policy instrument and the underlying assumption in using the models in the way described above is that the reduction in hours is negotiated between workers and employers. Following the arguments of Andrews *et al.* (1985) this is therefore an 'if only' experiment and the simulation results do not themselves provide support for a reduction in normal hours of this form. They should therefore be viewed as descriptions of the models rather than an indication of the effects of hours policy, although they do provide policymakers and labor market participants with a guide to the orders of magnitude of the employment effects that might be achieved through negotiated hours reductions.

There is, however, one particular policy assumption embedded within the simulations, that is, the response of the authorities to the change in hours. It is assumed that interest rates are fixed (real interest rates in NIESR) so that any changes in government borrowing are accommodated by money finance. It was shown in Wallis *et al.* (1985) that the assumptions regarding monetary policy were important in respect of a direct change in government spending. We do not examine alternative assumptions here as (a) this is not possible over the whole range of models and (b) since there is no initial change in government borrowing the PSBR effects are of the second-round variety and hence results are less sensitive to the policy assumption.

Having simulated the models by perturbing the normal hours variable alone, we then attempt to derive results under a standard framework. A common feature of this standardization is the assumption that the impact effect of lower normal hours produces a productivity offset of 18 per cent and an overtime leakage of 20 per cent. These are achieved by appropriate residual adjustments to the relevant hours and employment equations. However, the ultimate impact on employment from these effects can vary according to the nature of the feedbacks in the models. The precise values chosen correspond to those used in our earlier study (Whitley and Wilson, 1986a), where we also examined the sensitivity of a different version of the CGP model to alternative values of these various offsets.

## 12.5(b)  Basic simulation results

The results from perturbing normal hours by 5 per cent in the models with no further adjustments are shown in Table 12.3. In all the models lower normal hours result in a fall of GDP, but this is negligible. In the LBS model actual hours of work are exogenous and thus the reduction in normal hours is completely matched by an increase in overtime working. In both the CGP and BE models actual hours fall by around one-half of the change in normal hours after four years, but much less initially. All the models produce higher prices as a result of cost pressures; this increase is the greatest for LBS and HMT and least for BE. The lower level of international price competitiveness leads to a fall in the nominal exchange rate (although this is very small for LBS and BE). The real exchange rate is unchanged after four years in the HMT model in contrast to a real fall in the other models, hence the greater output loss for HMT.

There is no net employment effect in the LBS model, but in all the other models the change in hours leads to higher employment. Both CGP and BE produce an increase in employment of around 100,000 jobs in the first year of the simulation. The HMT results are much greater initially, but similar in size to those of CGP and BE after four years. Table 12.4 gives the broad sectoral breakdown of the employment change. The employment increase in BE is entirely concentrated in manufacturing (since the production function for the non-manufacturing sector has no allowance for hours), whereas the CGP effects are greater in non-manufacturing. The HMT hours effects are defined to occur initially only in non-manufacturing and there is a net loss of jobs in manufacturing. The results for the CGP model are very much in line with our expectations based on knowledge of the structure of the model. Cost effects are quite weak. This reflects the lack of overtime leakage in the long run and a substantial productivity offset. In addition there is little induced wage inflation as a result of unemployment being reduced. Furthermore, where cost effects emerge there is some partial compensation of the exchange rate for lost price competitiveness and so the reduction in output is moderated.

The LBS results also correspond with our prior expectations. The small fall in employment reflects the higher costs associated with overtime working and, as predicted, these are weaker in non-manufacturing than in manufacturing. Results from the BE simulation

**Table 12.3**

Model Simulations: percentage difference from base run

| Model | | GDP Year 1 | 4 | 7 | Prices Year 1 | 4 | 7 | Employment Year 1 | 4 | 7 | Exchange rate Year 1 | 4 | 7 | Average hours 1 | 4 | 7 |
|---|---|---|---|---|---|---|---|---|---|---|---|---|---|---|---|---|
| CGP | (1) | -0.1 | -0.2 | -0.1 | 0.5 | 2.9 | 5.3 | 0.5 | 1.3 | 1.7 | — | -1.3 | -3.3 | -1.9 | -3.1 | -3.4 |
| LBS | (1) | -0.1 | -0.3 | -0.4 | 0.5 | 1.5 | 2.3 | — | — | -0.2 | 0.1 | -0.4 | -0.4 | — | — | — |
| | (2) | -0.4 | -2.2 | -3.4 | 0.4 | 2.0 | 2.4 | 0.7 | -0.1 | -0.8 | 6.5 | 10.0 | 16.9 | -4.0 | -4.0 | -4.0 |
| | (3) | -0.1 | -1.6 | -2.9 | 0.9 | 3.9 | 6.1 | 1.4 | 0.7 | — | 4.0 | 5.5 | 10.7 | -4.0 | -4.0 | -4.0 |
| | (4) | -0.3 | -2.9 | -4.8 | 0.5 | 1.9 | 0.7 | 2.7 | 1.1 | -0.2 | 14.4 | 21.5 | 37.4 | -4.0 | -4.0 | -4.0 |
| HMT | (1) | — | -0.8 | ... | 1.3 | 2.9 | ... | 2.9 | 1.5 | ... | -0.8 | -2.9 | ... | -5.0 | -5.0 | ... |
| | (2) | -0.1 | -0.9 | ... | 1.6 | 6.3 | ... | 2.9 | 1.6 | ... | -0.9 | -3.5 | ... | -4.0 | -4.0 | ... |
| | (3) | — | -0.8 | ... | 1.7 | 8.5 | ... | 3.7 | 2.3 | ... | -1.2 | -5.6 | ... | -4.0 | -4.0 | ... |
| BE | (1) | — | -0.2 | ... | 0.1 | 0.9 | ... | 0.3 | 0.4 | ... | — | — | ... | -1.4 | -2.6 | ... |
| | (2) | -0.1 | -0.4 | ... | 0.3 | 1.9 | ... | 0.9 | 0.7 | ... | — | — | ... | -3.9 | -3.9 | ... |
| | (3) | — | -0.5 | ... | 0.4 | 2.2 | ... | 1.7 | 1.4 | ... | — | 0.4 | ... | -3.9 | -3.9 | ... |
| NIESR | (1) | 0.1 | -0.4 | ... | 0.1 | -0.7 | ... | -0.1 | 2.9 | ... | 0.5 | -1.3 | ... | -3.7 | -0.3 | ... |
| | (2) | 0.1 | -0.9 | ... | 0.4 | 9.1 | ... | 0.7 | -1.5 | ... | 2.7 | -1.9 | ... | -3.7 | -3.9 | ... |
| | (3) | 0.1 | -0.8 | ... | 0.9 | 12.4 | ... | 1.5 | -1.4 | ... | 3.6 | -9.9 | ... | -3.9 | -3.9 | ... |
| A | | — | -1.1 | ... | 3.4 | 10.2 | ... | 2.9 | 1.6 | ... | -3.6 | -9.9 | ... | n/a | n/a | ... |
| WW | | -1.1 | -1.1 | -0.7 | 7.8 | 14.2 | 17.0 | 1.4 | 2.5 | 3.0 | -0.1 | -7.1 | -7.7 | -2.7 | -3.4 | -4.1 |

*Notes:* (1) indicates a standard model with no modifications

(2) an adjusted model with a 20 per cent overtime leakage and 18 per cent productivity offset

(3) as (2) but allowing for an impact on government employment

(4) as (3) but introducing common effects in non-modeled sector

— indicates an insignificant effect

... indicates that simulations were not conducted

n/a indicates not applicable.

**Table 12.4**

Sectoral employment effects: difference from base run, thousands

| Model | | Manufacturing Year 1 | 4 | 7 | Non-manufacturing Year 1 | 4 | 7 | Government Year 1 | 4 | 7 | Total economy Year 1 | 4 | 7 |
|---|---|---|---|---|---|---|---|---|---|---|---|---|---|
| CGP | (1) | 8 | 103 | 148 | 105 | 192 | 267 | — | — | — | 113 | 295 | 415 |
| LBS | (1) | −1 | 2 | −36 | 4 | −5 | −12 | — | — | — | 3 | −3 | −48 |
| | (2) | 184 | 152 | 127 | −15 | −180 | −354 | — | — | — | 169 | −22 | −227 |
| | (3) | 188 | 188 | 178 | −19 | −179 | −358 | 180 | 180 | 180 | 350 | 188 | — |
| | (4) | 148 | −84 | −234 | 340 | 184 | 6 | 180 | 180 | 180 | 668 | 280 | −48 |
| HMT | (1) | −21 | −108 | … | 712 | 470 | … | — | — | — | 691 | 362 | … |
| | (2) | −19 | −120 | … | 723 | 514 | … | — | — | — | 704 | 394 | … |
| | (3) | −26 | −125 | … | 725 | 497 | … | 180 | 180 | … | 879 | 551 | … |
| BE | (1) | 71 | 117 | … | — | −16 | … | — | — | … | 71 | 101 | … |
| | (2) | 182 | 180 | … | 1 | −27 | … | — | — | … | 182 | 153 | … |
| | (3) | 182 | 171 | … | 4 | −41 | … | 180 | 180 | … | 358 | 310 | … |
| NIESR | (1) | −25 | −122 | … | 8 | −37 | … | — | — | … | −18 | −149 | … |
| | (2) | 143 | −229 | … | 11 | −95 | … | — | — | … | 154 | −325 | … |
| | (3) | 128 | −324 | … | 13 | −145 | … | 180 | 180 | … | 321 | −295 | … |
| A | (1) | n/a | n/a | … | n/a | n/a | … | 69 | 69 | … | 370 | 100 | … |
| WW | (1) | 67 | 116 | 160 | 123 | 323 | 375 | 139 | 178 | 191 | 329 | 617 | 726 |

*Notes:* see Table 12.3

also accord with our earlier predictions. The cost effects are fairly weak so that output changes very little and the employment effects are concentrated in the manufacturing sector. The effects on employment are much weaker than for the CGP simulation however, despite the lack of any productivity offset in the BE model. This can be broadly explained by the smaller long-run overtime leakage in the CGP model and the fact that direct hours effects are limited to manufacturing in the BE case, whereas the CGP model incorporates effects throughout the industrial sector of the economy. The constrast in the LBS results with both those of BE and CGP reflects the absence of any direct employment effect in the former (complete productivity offset).

The short-run effects on employment are substantial in HMT, as expected from the zero productivity offset. The decay over time reflects the build-up of cost pressures, which reduces employment in manufacturing. The higher employment response is partly due to the assumption in the simulation that average hours in non-manufacturing are reduced in proportion to normal hours (zero overtime leakage). The study by Allen (1980) was based on an earlier version of the HMT model where there were no explicit hours mechanisms or real wage effects upon employment. Allen imposed both productivity and overtime offsets upon the model, under alternative assumptions regarding income sharing.

The NIESR simulation is not directly comparable with the other experiments since no change in normal hours occurs, and actual hours are endogenous in this model. In this case, a once-and-for-all adjustment to the level of hours was made (via the equation residual) but hours rapidly return to their original level. However, the induced cost effects lead to a reduction of employment of 150,000 jobs after four years.

## 12.5(c)  Standardized simulations

In the next set of simulations we attempt to standardize the models in respect of assumptions regarding the overtime leakage and productivity offsets. These simulations are identified as simulation (2) for the respective models in Tables 12.3 and 12.4. These modifications are made initially only for those sectors in the models where there is already some link between hours and employment (that is, manufacturing for NIESR, LBS and BE and non-manufacturing for HMT).

### (i)  COMMON OVERTIME LEAKAGE AND PRODUCTIVITY OFFSET

The standard version of the BE model allows for interaction between normal hours, actual hours and employment (in manufacturing) with a 50 per cent overtime leakage, but with no productivity offset. In simulation (2) we impose an adjustment equivalent to overtime leakage of 20 per cent and an addition to employment that implies a permanent productivity effect in manufacturing of 18 per cent of the equivalent

247

hours reduction (this amounts to around 180,000 jobs). The effects of these revised assumptions are, of course, potentially offsetting since we now assume that a smaller overtime leakage is accompanied by a larger productivity offset. The overall impact is to increase costs so that prices rise more rapidly than in the standard model simulation, with a slightly greater reduction of output. The employment effects are considerably larger, however, but remain concentrated in the manufacturing sector.

In the HMT model we have reduced the scale of the effective hours reduction in order to allow for an implicit overtime leakage and included a productivity offset. In this model the direct effects are concentrated within the non-manufacturing sector. The employment consequences are similar to those in the standard model simulation, although there is a greater increase in prices.

In the standard version of the LBS model there was no direct effect on employment through hours, and a complete overtime leakage was assumed. One problem encountered with revising the latter assumption is that the overtime cost effect in the LBS model acts perversely when actual hours are decreased by less than normal hours. This is owing to the weighting of actual and normal hours in the overtime cost calculation, where lower actual hours can lead to a smaller overtime cost. We therefore retained the overtime cost effect from the standard simulation, but added a direct employment effect corresponding to a 20 per cent actual leakage and an 18 per cent productivity offset in manufacturing. The interesting feature of the results is the much greater loss of output – over 3 per cent more than in the standard case after seven years. Employment effects are positive initially but are reversed over time. This results from a positive impact in the manufacturing sector, which is gradually offset by a very strong downward trend in non-manufacturing. These results reflect the operation of the financial sector of the model, with its assumption of forward-consistent expectations. A sharp appreciation of the exchange rate occurs very early on in the simulation, which produces a fall in manufacturing production. Despite the rise in the exchange rate, prices still rise and the increase in earnings in manufacturing drives up earnings in non-manufacturing so that the output and real wage effects are unambiguously negative for non-manufacturing (where there is no direct link between hours and employment). A sharp fall in employment therefore results.

In the standard NIESR model we noted that there was no direct relationship between hours and employment. In simulation (2) we assume an effective hours reduction equivalent to our assumptions for the other models. We also introduce a direct employment response, as for LBS but for manufacturing only. As for the LBS model, we observe only a temporary increase in overall employment. Here the exchange rate appreciates only in the short term. Forward expectations of a lower level of competitiveness (and hence lower output) are translated into current output through lower investment and stockbuilding. Lower output results in both sectors, but the manufacturing sector suffers more. In addition, the increase in real earnings in manufacturing leads to lower employment in this sector, but there is no such mechanism for the other private sector.

## (ii) COMMON SECTORAL TREATMENT

Two further sets of simulations attempt to impose a common treatment across all sectors. These involve, first, imposing an effect on the government sector (simulation 3) and, second, imposing effects on other sectors where there is no existing link between hours and employment (simulation 4). In both cases modifications are made to employment and hours that are consistent with the offsets and leakages in (i). In the case of government employment, an exogenous addition of 180,000 jobs is made.

For the BE model the introduction of an exogenous effect on government-sector employment adds to the total employment response, but with little impact on the overall level of macroeconomic activity or employment in the other sectors. For the HMT model the total employment effect is also increased. In the case of the NIESR model the immediate effect is to increase the employment impact, but this gain is soon dissipated, while inflation is increased and there is a substantial decline in the exchange rate.

In order to consider the effects of standardizing hours effects across *all* sectors of the economy we attempted to use the LBS model as an example and adopt the same adjustments to the non-manufacturing sector as in manufacturing. Thus we include a residual adjustment of 360,000 jobs ($3\frac{1}{2}$ per cent). These results are shown as simulation (4). The resultant fall in GDP is greater than in the other simulations with this model, but in contrast the inflationary impact is reduced. This is a consequence of the sharp appreciation of the exchange rate. The forward expectations in the model bring forward this appreciation into the early part of the simulation. Initial employment effects are increased, but there is a net decline in employment after seven years. This crowding out of employment arises from lower exports owing to the higher exchange rate, rather than as a consequence of weaker price competitiveness owing to poor performance in terms of productivity or labor costs. The effect on exports can be clearly seen in the sectoral employment results where manufacturing employment declines by the fourth year of the simulation. Now, however, there is a positive employment effect in non-manufacturing. These results illustrate the importance of the sector in which hours and employment linkages are modeled. However, such modifications apparently do not remove the discrepancies between the LBS results and those from models where these effects are already modeled throughout the economy (for example, CGP, Whitley and Wilson, 1986a). The main contrast is that the employment effects in the LBS model do not increase over time as in the other models. It should be noted, however, that the LBS results depend critically on the modeling of the financial sector (especially the exchange rate mechanism), which is to a large extent imposed rather than estimated. In particular, it is not easy to understand why the exchange rate should appreciate as a result of lower hours of work and higher labor costs.[2] The LBS result is clearly at variance with the other models in this instance. The assumptions underlying our earlier study (Whitley and Wilson, 1986a) make it more comparable to rows (3) and (4) of the simulation results for the other models and thus explain some of the apparently higher estimates from this study. Some of the remainder is the result of changes in the CGP model (notably the introduction of relative factor prices), as can be seen from the comparison with the CGP results.

## 12.6 Conclusions

We began this paper by highlighting the apparent conflict between the advocates of reductions in normal hours as a means of reducing unemployment, and the conclusions of many economists that such a policy is likely to have precisely the reverse effect to that desired. From the discussion in Section 12.2 it is clear that this division of views centers upon an important difference in emphasis between the two sides. Much of the economic analysis of this issue has been conducted in terms of the short-run implications for labor demand, whereas the advocates of work sharing have had in mind the longer-term relationship between average hours and employment. We have argued that the latter is primarily a reflection of supply-side factors, which have resulted in much of the labor-displacing effects of technological change taking the form of reductions in hours worked rather than increased unemployment. We concluded that there is a need for a fully specified supply/demand model for both normal and average hours of work if the effects of reductions in normal hours are to be properly assessed within a macroeconomic framework.

It is apparent from our review of the empirical literature, however, that most researchers have developed equations to explain average hours worked that are essentially reduced forms, with average hours in the short run being explained in terms of cyclical movements around an exogenously determined trend represented by normal hours. It is this type of specification that is most common with UK macro-models (if indeed hours are explicitly considered at all). In practice, the evidence suggests that normal hours have been determined in the long run by a complex interaction of both supply and demand forces. Normal hours cannot therefore be regarded as a truly exogenous variable within a macroeconomic model, nor can such a variable sensibly be taken as a policy lever that can be manipulated by the government. Nevertheless, the empirical relationships established between employment, hours and normal hours do tell us something about the trade-offs that have been established through the medium of collective bargaining in the past.

The use of such relationships embedded within a full macroeconomic model can therefore provide some guide to the potential scope for reducing unemployment through *negotiated* reduction in hours. Such simulations are thus of value to the main actors in the labor market in demonstrating the orders of magnitude of changes in hours that might be required to make a serious dent in unemployment, while at the same time highlighting the importance of cost and competitiveness effects. In this spirit in Section 12.4 of the paper we went on to examine the effects of changing hours worked using simulation techniques on various UK macroeconomic models.

Although we argued in Section 12.3 that the nature of the standard simulation results could be largely inferred from a knowledge of the mechanisms relating hours, employment and wages in these models, we found that attempts to standardize effects such as overtime leakage and productivity offset do not lead to any consensus over the effects of lower hours on employment. Standardization does increase the likelihood of a positive employment response at first, with a median estimate in the range of 150–200,000 jobs (after one year). This arises as higher incomes drive up domestic demand, whereas the offsetting cost effects take time to work through. Thereafter the results diverge considerably. It is notable that models with forward-looking expectations (LBS and NIESR) generate a negative employment response after three–four years. In the case of LBS this occurs as the exchange rate appreciates sharply in contrast to the results for other models. In the instance of NIESR the exchange rate does not adjust to lower competitiveness and goods markets react to this expectation, thus lowering output immediately. Allowing for an exogenous impact on government employment does not alter the qualitative conclusion, although the initial positive employment impact is increased. Sectoral implications depend very much on where hours/employment mechanisms are modeled, since it is in these sectors that the employment gains tend to be greatest, with the remaining sector experiencing a loss in output even in the short run. This explains some of the contrast in the results between those of CGP and Whitley and Wilson, on the one hand, and the other models on the other hand. In the former, effects are spread throughout the private sector and hence employment effects are positive in both manufacturing and services.

Standardizing initial hours effects across both sectors of the LBS model does not significantly alter the qualitative conclusion derived from this model. It should be noted that the distribution of employment effects is changed, with manufacturing employment now falling and non-manufacturing employment increasing. This reflects the far greater exchange rate appreciation, and hence contraction of the traded sector, whereas there are now compensating direct employment effects in non-manufacturing to counter the adverse output consequences in this sector.

Although the differences in the results are narrowed when we standardize the direct effects across the models, there remain significant areas of disagreement regarding the total (that is, direct and indirect) effects. In turn these effects appear to be largely connected with the presence of forward expectations and the behavior of the exchange rate.

In models where the exchange rate moves very little (BE) or depreciates gently (CGP) with no forward expectations, there is the suggestion that the resulting loss of competitiveness on trade is fairly weak. However when forward expectations of future losses in competitiveness are introduced (as in the NIESR model) output falls sharply. Similar large output losses arise when the exchange rate *appreciates* despite lower competitiveness (LBS). Thus there are some genuine differences between model structures, which generate the employment results given in Tables 12.3 and 12.4. Our earlier results (Whitley and Wilson, 1986a) are more in line with those of the CGP and BE models where forward expectations are absent. Given the relative novelty of such effects in UK macro-models we would not be tempted to substantially revise our earlier conclusions. In particular, we view the LBS results as implausible.

The main qualification that we would make is in the nature of the exercise itself. We have abstracted from an explanation of the mechanism that causes normal hours to change in this paper. Yet it is clear from the discussion in Section 12.2 that a satisfactory analysis of the effects of hours reductions on employment requires a much more explicit model of *both* normal and average hours of work that distinguishes demand *and* supply factors. This seems to us to represent a major gap in the present literature and should be a top priority for future research.

## Acknowledgements

We are grateful to the ESRC and the Manpower Services Commission for general financial support. Axel Mittelstädt and other participants at the conference on Employment, Unemployment and Hours of Work, Berlin, 1986, provided many helpful comments, as did Derek Bosworth and Ken Wallis. Any remaining errors are our own.

## Notes

1 Aggregation effects across collective agreements may tend to blur the discontinuity in the change in normal hours.
2 One possible explanation for this result might be that the relative *cost* competitiveness weakens far more substantially than relative *price* competitiveness.

# COMMENT

## AXEL MITTELSTÄDT

Whitley and Wilson have given us a stimulating paper on reductions in working hours and employment creation. The theoretical discussion is lucid, the presentation of empirical results transparent. In particular, standardizing the simulations for several macroeconomic models for the United Kingdom is of great use. Such a procedure may help narrow the range of disagreements about how reduced hours affect employment. Nevertheless, as the authors correctly note, the empirical results still need to be treated with caution and perhaps with some suspicion.

My comments are in three parts: the first concerns the theoretical discussion; the second deals with the empirical findings; and the last suggests further lines of research.

As regards the theoretical discussion, two regimes of economic conditions may be distinguished, one marked by low unemployment, rapid real wage growth, strong productivity gains and related real income aspirations, the other by high unemployment, weak real wage growth, small productivity gains, downward revisions of real income expectations and high real interest rates.

In the first set of economic conditions, reductions in average and normal working hours are likely to be influenced by the employee's desire to take part of the potential benefits of economic growth in the form of greater leisure. The academic literature seems quasi-unanimous about this point. Hence, when rates of unemployment are low and labor shortages emerge, workers are strongly inclined to curtail working hours. Without income sharing, this raises the rate of increase in the relative price of labor. More labor-saving investments are then forthcoming, creating room for further gains in labor productivity and real wages. Further reductions in normal working hours can be expected.

How will average hours respond in such a setting? In the theoretical framework, employers' desired hours are partly a negative, function of normal working time. Hence, desired hours go up when normal working hours are reduced. But, as Robert Hart has pointed out, employers' desired hours also depend upon the real wage increases, which reduce desired hours. Thus, when normal working hours decline and real wages rise, employers' desired hours may fall, rise or remain unchanged depending upon the relative size of these two elasticities. The long-run decline in both normal and average working hours suggests that the real wage effect has dominated the normal hours effect. There is therefore no real conflict between theory and practice, contrary to what Whitley and Wilson suggest in their paper.

In the second set of economic conditions, real income expectations are weak. Given high unemployment, employees are likely to ease their demands for reductions in average working time, especially when consumer indebtedness is high and real interest rates are high or rising.

253

Consequently, supply-side forces influencing reductions in working time are likely to be strong in periods of strong economic growth and weak in periods of weak economic expansion. On the demand side, the real wage effect reinforces supply-side forces: if real wages move procyclically, reduced real wage growth will lead employers' desired hours to fall less rapidly than before. This may help lower the speed at which hours are cut in a recession. In contrast, the income effect goes in the opposite direction: average hours are high in periods of strong growth and low in periods of weak growth.

How have average hours behaved in a setting of weak output growth after the first oil price shock? A look at the seven largest OECD countries reveals a picture of great diversity both within and across countries. In some countries the falling trend in real wage growth in the 1970s and early 1980s coincided with a lower speed of reduction of average hours. This happened in West Germany until 1982, in France until 1979, Italy until 1980, in Canada from 1976 to 1983 and in Japan from 1974 to 1978. A combination of reduced real wage growth and reduced cuts in average working hours may point to comparatively strong supply-side forces and/or real wage effects: given lower real income expectations, employees may accept a lower speed of hours reduction or may even press for such a deceleration in the form of more overtime work. Remember in this context that both strike activity and absenteeism have fallen in the 1970s and early 1980s. At the same time, lower real wage increases mean smaller reductions in employers' desired hours. In contrast, in the United States beginning in 1972 the fall in average hours accelerated even though real wage growth ceased and real wages started to decline. The same phenomenon is observed for France (beginning in 1979) and Japan (beginning in 1978). Such a constellation suggests that both the real wage effect and supply-side influences are weak. In the case of France, discretionary cuts in normal working time and extended holidays have played a part in these developments.

Let me now turn to the second part of my comments: the empirical results. Whitley and Wilson rightly state that capturing the different demand and supply effects discussed above requires a full demand/supply framework where both normal and average hours are determined endogenously. In the various UK models, however, actual hours are made a function of normal hours and a form of cyclical variable, a procedure that amounts to a reduced form of a simultaneous demand/supply model. In these circumstances, it is obviously difficult to determine whether further cuts in normal or average hours will have the same effect unless they come about through the same mechanisms as in the past.

The standardized simulations are subject to two basic assumptions: first, the overtime leakage is 20 per cent and the productivity offset 18 per cent. What do the simulations tell us? Each of the four models used for *standardized* simulations indicates a rise in employment in the first year following a permanent cut in normal working time of 5 per cent. In two cases, the initial employment gains diminish over time, but remain positive, while in the other two cases they are transformed into losses after four years. Hence, the models (notwithstanding their different features) agree on the direction of the *short-run* employment change, but they differ with respect to the *medium-term employment consequences*. Naturally, policymakers are mostly interested in sustainable employment gains.

Several questions come to mind: which are the principal mechanisms through which a short-run rise in employment is generated? Note that there is no income sharing, i.e. hourly basic wages rise when working time is cut. Furthermore, the results indicate short-run output losses resulting in decreases in productivity (relative to baseline). Consequently, the unit labor cost position deteriorates over the short run. Second, three of the models identify manufacturing as the sector where the bulk or even the entire short-term employment gain takes place. Hence, employment increases precisely in the sector where increased unit labor costs translate into higher selling prices. Once again, this seems to be a counter-intuitive result. Finally, current rates of return on capital in UK manufacturing are still low, especially relative to real interest rates. Given this constellation, is it not possible that short-run cost-induced gains in productivity are larger than assumed in the paper? In other words, is the assumption about the productivity offset sensitive to the assumption about no-income sharing?

Let me finish my comments by suggesting two lines for further research. First, the standardized simulations for the UK may be re-run assuming a cut in normal working hours with income sharing. The assumptions about the productivity offset and overtime leakage would then, of course, be different. Second, in the European context, simulating cuts in normal working time simultaneously enacted by several countries could shed some light on the employment-creating potential of reduced working hours. The OECD has recently developed a new supply block for the seven largest countries. Unfortunately, in its present form this model is not capable of adequately dealing with the above issue. We intend looking into this matter, however, and hopefully we may soon make a contribution to the ongoing debate about cuts in working time as a means of achieving sustainable gains in employment.

# CHAPTER 13

# Part-time Employment in the United States

RONALD G. EHRENBERG, PAMELA ROSENBERG
and JEANNE LI

## 13.1 Introduction

It is well documented that part-time employment has grown as a share of total employment in most European countries since the early 1970s (see, for example, OECD, 1985). To the extent that this growth reflects voluntary behavior by workers it has important implications for economic welfare, because it allows an increased number of workers to be employed at any given level of aggregate demand. Put another way, explicit or even implicit work-sharing arrangements allow for easier absorption of a growing labor force into employment.

For the most part, explanations for the growth in part-time employment have focused on the supply side of the labor market and the changing industrial composition of employment. The growing shares of married women with children in the labor force, of older workers phasing into retirement, and (at least in the United States) of students who need to work to help finance their education, coupled with the growth in the share of service sector employment, have all been thought to contribute to part-time employment growth. (See, for example, OECD, 1983, 1985; Owen, 1979.)

Recently, though, attention has shifted to the demand side of the labor market and the role that relative costs play. In theory, *ceteris paribus*, part-time employment should expand relative to full-time employment if the hourly labor cost (wages and hour-related fringes) of part-time workers falls relative to that for full-time workers, or if the quasi-fixed cost (non-hour-related fringes and hiring and training costs) of part-time workers falls relative to that of full-time workers (see FitzRoy and Hart, 1986). Numerous studies for various OECD countries in fact show that part-time workers' wages and fringe benefits are often lower than those for full-time workers, and that the part-time workers are sometimes not eligible for employer-financed social insurance programs or redundancy payments.[1]

To say that part-time workers are less costly than full-time workers, however, is *not* an explanation for the trend in the use of part-time employees that has occurred. Rather, one must show that the relative

256

cost advantage of part-time workers has increased over time *and* that variations in the relative cost advantage are associated with variations in the usage of part-time employment. Somewhat surprisingly, few researchers have tried to do this, and even these only indirectly.[2]

This paper addresses this issue, albeit in a slightly different way, focusing on data from the United States. We begin in the next section by analyzing data on part-time employment in the United States. After controlling for cyclical factors, an increasing trend in the usage of part-time employment is observed. Moreover, it is clear from the component of part-time employment that is increasing that this is a demand-side, not a supply-side phenomenon.

The following two sections attempt a *partial* test of several demand-side explanations. Although, we have no data on how part-time/full-time wage and fringe benefit differentials have varied over time, we can estimate how they vary across industries at a point in time. We do this in Section 13.3 using data from the March 1984 *Current Population Survey* (*CPS*), a sample of approximately 122,000 individuals aged 14 and older. These estimated differentials are then entered in Section 13.4 as explanatory variables in a simple structural model of the inter-industry determinants of part-time employment and we attempt to estimate their effects. That is, we try to infer if there is an inter-industry relationship between the relative cost advantage of part-time employees and their usage.[3] If such a relationship exists, evidence that the relative cost advantage has been increasing over time could then be used to estimate the importance of relative costs in explaining the trend in the usage of part-time employees that has occurred.[4]

Section 13.3 also focuses on a potential demand-side influence that has been ignored to date, namely employers' alleged desire in the United States to maintain non-union work environments. It is often asserted (though the evidence does not always support this assertion) that part-time employees, who tend to have shorter expected tenure with a firm than otherwise comparable full-time employees, are less likely to be union members or vote for a union than their full-time counterparts.[5] *Ceteris paribus*, the greater the differential in the probability of being a union member between part-time and full-time workers in an industry, the greater the advantage that will accrue to employers trying to 'keep out' unions from hiring part-time workers.

We present two efforts to see if this influence may have contributed to the growth of part-time employment in the United States. First, we trace if government policy in the United States has made it increasingly difficult for part-time workers to join unions in recent years. Second, we estimate part-time/full-time probability of union membership differentials by industry, with the goal of including such differentials in our inter-industry cross-section model of part-time employment variation. Unfortunately, these differentials prove in the main to be statistically imprecise, so we are unable to include them in the inter-industry model.

A brief concluding section summarizes our findings and their implications for public policy and future research.

257

## 13.2 Trends in Part-time Employment in the United States, 1955–1984

The definition of what constitutes a part-time employee varies widely across countries, which makes international comparisons difficult. A person is classified as working part-time in the United States if he or she works less than 35 hours per week during the *CPS* survey week. This is a much higher cut-off point than exists in most OECD nations and, unlike them, bases part-time status on current week hours rather than usual weekly hours.

Part-time employees are further broken down into those employed part-time for non-economic reasons and those employed part-time for economic reasons. The former are voluntary part-timers; this category includes individuals who work part-time because of family or school responsibilities. The latter are involuntary part-timers; this category includes people who are temporarily part-time owing to cyclical or seasonal factors, or to temporary firm-specific fluctuations in demand, but who would prefer a full-time job. Changes in the part-time employment for non-economic reasons category reflect supply behavior, while changes in the total, and especially in the part-time for economic reasons category, probably reflect demand factors.

Appendix Tables 13A.1–13A.5 of our paper (pp. 277–81) present background data on the growth of part-time employment in the United States. Table 13A.1 contains annual data for 1963–84 on the percentage of employees who worked part-time for the total employed workforce, for youths aged 16–19, and for adult males and adult females. These raw data do not control for cyclical factors and they suggest that since 1980 only the percentage of teenagers who work part-time has increased.[6] This lack of increase in the overall part-time employment rate in the United States in recent years has been noted by other observers, as has the relatively low incidence of part-time employment among adult males (OECD, 1985).

Table 13A.2 contains annual data for 1955–84 on the percentage of employees employed part-time; the data are presented separately for part-timers for economic and non-economic reasons. The latter category, which represents voluntary part-time employees, almost doubled during the period, peaking around 1980. The former fluctuated substantially from year to year, suggesting that trends in it will be obscured when one ignores cyclical factors. Similar data are presented in Table 13A.3 for various demographic groups (teenagers, adult males, adult females, Whites, and non-Whites), starting in 1968 when these more detailed data were first published. Although the failure to control for cyclical factors may distort things, there does appear to be an increasing trend in part-time employment for economic reasons for each group, suggesting that demand-side forces may be important.[7]

Might part of the apparent trend in part-time employment be an artifact of the 35-hour cut-off point (which is higher than many European countries) for the classification of part-time employees? If, through collective bargaining or unilateral employer adoption, standard workweeks for some regular full-time employees were reduced over time from, say, 40 hours to 32 hours a week, these workers would be classified as part-time in recent years. As a result, average weekly hours of part-time employees would be higher in recent than in earlier years. In fact, Table 13A.4 does indicate that average weekly hours of part-time employees in each of the demographic groups increased over the 1968–84 period. The increases probably are not sufficiently large, however, to support the contention that the apparent trends in part-time employment primarily reflect some full-time employees now working fewer than 35 hours a week.

Finally, by way of background, Table 13A.5 presents data for 1968 and 1984 on the shares of adult males, adult females and teenagers in total and part-time employment. In spite of the increasing proportion of employed teens who work part-time, the teenage share of part-time employment declined over the period because the share of teens in the United States labor force declined. Part-time employment, for both economic and non-economic reasons, continues to be primarily an adult female phenomenon in the United States.

Of course, all of the above conclusions come from visual inspections of data that do not control for cyclical factors. To be a bit more precise, Table 13.1 presents estimates of the time-trends in the percentage of non-agricultural workers who are employed part-time in the United States, which we obtained from models that included the adult unemployment rate to control for cyclical factors. Separate estimates are presented for part-time workers for economic and non-economic reasons and the time-trends are estimated over a variety of periods (1955–84, 1963–84, 1968–84 and 1973–84) to see how sensitive the results are to the starting date. Results are also presented for various demographic groups during the 1968–84 period.

This table does suggest the importance of controlling for cyclical factors, of varying the starting date and of disaggregation. Over the 1973–84 period, the trends in the percentage employed part-time for economic reasons and part-time for non-economic reasons were positive and negative (but not statistically significant), respectively, with the former clearly dominating.[8] Since the positive trend in total part-time employment (after controlling for cyclical forces) coincides with a non-positive trend in part-time employment for non-economic reasons, demand-side forces *must* be responsible for the increase in total part-time employment. It is interesting to note, however, that if one starts the analyses in 1955 a positive trend in part-time employment for non-economic reasons emerges while there is no trend in part-time employment for economic reasons. The growth of part-time employment in the early years of the longer period obviously was influenced by supply-side forces.

Focusing on the 1968–84 period, one sees from the bottom panel of the table that, while adult males are increasingly working part-time voluntarily, adult females are decreasingly doing so. Similarly, the increasing

**Table 13.1**

Estimated Time-Trends in the Percentages of Non-agricultural Workers
Employed Part-time in the United States

|  | Part-time for: | |
|---|---|---|
|  | *Economic reasons* | *Non-economic reasons* |
| *All workers* | | |
| 1955–84 | .011 (0.7) | .208 (4.2) |
| 1963–84 | .042 (2.1) | .140 (2.4) |
| 1968–84 | .083 (3.4) | .024 (0.5) |
| 1973–84 | .113 (3.8) | −.055 (1.4) |
| *1968–1984* | | |
| Males age 20+ | .039 (1.7) | .052 (4.0) |
| Females age 20+ | .035 (0.6) | −.117 (2.4) |
| Both sexes 16–19 | .202 (3.0) | .122 (0.9) |
| Whites | .088 (4.3) | .055 (1.3) |
| Non-whites | .091 (1.1) | −.164 (3.4) |

*Source:* Obtained from models that used annual data, included the adult male unemployment rate to control for cyclical factors, and that corrected for autocorrelation using the Prais–Winsten method. See Tables 13A.1–13A.5 for the underlying data.

*Note:* Absolute value of *t* statistic in parentheses

probabilities observed (after controlling for cyclical factors) that teenagers and adult males involuntarily work part time are not matched by an analogous trend for females. The female share of all part-time employment increased during the period (Table 13A.5) only because of the increased share of women in the labor force.

The bottom line of this section is that in recent years in the United States there *has* been a positive trend in the proportion of people employed part-time and that the data suggest this has been due to employer, not employee, decisions.

## 13.3 Part-time Employee/Full-time Employee Wage, Fringe Benefit and Union Membership Differentials

The previous section suggests that there has been a trend towards increased employment of part-time workers vis-à-vis full-time workers in recent years in the United States and that this trend is probably due to demand-side factors. Do these factors include a growing cost advantage of part-time workers caused by increases over time in differentials in part-time/full-time wages, fringe benefits and probability of being a union member? Time-series data are not available to answer this question directly. Instead, in this section, we estimate the extent to which these differentials vary across industries at a point in time. In the next section, we then see if these estimated differentials can help explain inter-industry variations in the usage of part-time employment.

The March 1984 *Current Population Survey* is a national probability sample of roughly 122,000 individuals aged 14 and older. We restricted our attention to employed wage and salary workers who were working during the survey week and were *not* self-employed, and stratified the sample into 46 industry subsamples. Recalling that part-time employees are defined as those who work less than 35 hours during the survey week, Table 13.2 presents background data on the number of individuals in each subsample and the percentage of these employees classified as part time. The percentages vary widely across industries, from about 2 per cent in the petroleum and coal products industry to 40 per cent in retail trade.[9]

For each industry, we used the individual observations to estimate wage equations of the form

$$\log W_{ji} = a_{0i} + \sum_{k=1}^{m} a_{ki} X_{kj} + a_{pi} P_j + e_{ji}, \ i = 1, 2, \ldots 46. \qquad (13.1)$$

Here $W_{ji}$ is the hourly earnings of individual $j$ in industry $i$, the $X_{kj}$ are a set of variables available in the *CPS* data to control for human capital, cost-of-living and other factors that influence wages, $m$ is the number of these variables, $P_j$ is a dichotomous variable that takes on the value of 1 if the individual is a part-time employee and zero otherwise, $e_{ji}$ is a random error term, and the $a$'s are parameters to be estimated. The estimate of $a_{pi}$ is an estimate of the extent to which part-time workers in the industry $i$ are paid less than full-time workers in the industry.[10]

The control variables used include years of schooling completed, proxies for years of potential labor force experience (age minus years of school minus five) and experience squared, the number of children in the family, and dichotomous variables for marital status, gender, race, veteran status, hispanic ethnicity, being a student, residence in a standard metropolitan statistical area, and residence in various census regions. As is well known, the effects of some of these variables on earnings (children, experience, education, marital status) are often found to vary with gender, so some specifications interact gender with these variables. Finally, some specifications use part-time status in the survey week as an explanatory variable, while others use usual part-time employment status.

The estimates of the part-time/full-time wage differentials that we obtained from these models are displayed in Table 13.3. As noted there, the differentials in the columns headed *RW1* and *RW3* (*RW2* and *RW4*) are based on the survey week (usual) part-time/full-time dichotomy, and those in the columns headed *RW1* and *RW2* (*RW3* and *RW4*) are from the models without (with) interaction terms. As might be expected, the four sets of estimates are highly correlated (in the range of .90 to .98) across industries. This suggests, and the next section confirms, that the estimated effects we will obtain from the inter-industry analyses will be relatively insensitive to the relative wage differential measure that we use.

**Table 13.2**
Distribution Across Industries of the
March 1984 Current Population Survey Sample

| Industry code | Number of observations | Percentage part-time | Industry description |
|---|---|---|---|
| 1 | 971 | 24 | Agriculture |
| 2 | 707 | 5 | Mining |
| 3 | 3238 | 14 | Construction |
| 4 | 456 | 8 | Lumber and Wood Products |
| 5 | 319 | 5 | Furniture and Fixtures |
| 6 | 324 | 4 | Stone, Clay, Glass and Concrete |
| 7 | 512 | 4 | Primary Metals |
| 8 | 789 | 5 | Fabricated Metals |
| 9 | — | — | Not Specified Metals |
| 10 | 1551 | 4 | Machinery, except Electrical |
| 11 | 1336 | 3 | Electrical Machinery |
| 12 | 623 | 2 | Motor Vehicles and Equipment |
| 13 | 323 | 3 | Aircrafts and Parts |
| 14 | 455 | 3 | Other Transportation Equipment |
| 15 | 395 | 5 | Professional and Photographic Equipment and Watches |
| 16 | 84 | 7 | Toys, Amusements and Sporting Goods |
| 17 | 257 | 14 | Miscellaneous Manufacturing |
| 18 | 1061 | 11 | Food |
| 19 | 35 | 11 | Tobacco |
| 20 | 427 | 9 | Textiles |
| 21 | 836 | 12 | Apparel |
| 22 | 405 | 4 | Paper and Allied Products |
| 23 | 1076 | 20 | Printing, Publishing and Allied Industries |
| 24 | 715 | 3 | Chemicals and Allied Products |
| 25 | 113 | 2 | Petroleum and Coal Products |
| 26 | 440 | 9 | Rubber and Miscellaneous Plastic Products |
| 27 | 182 | 20 | Leather and Leather Products |
| 28 | 2507 | 13 | Transportation |
| 29 | 989 | 6 | Communications |
| 30 | 974 | 3 | Utilities and Sanitation |
| 31 | 2444 | 10 | Wholesale Trade |
| 32 | 10217 | 40 | Retail Trade |
| 33 | 1834 | 9 | Banking and Other Finance |
| 34 | 1978 | 12 | Insurance and Real Estate |
| 35 | 927 | 71 | Private Household Services |
| 36 | 1902 | 23 | Business Services |
| 37 | 744 | 17 | Repair Services |
| 38 | 1501 | 30 | Personal Services, except Private Household |
| 39 | 638 | 37 | Entertainment and Recreation Services |
| 40 | 2675 | 20 | Hospitals |

*Continued*

**Table 13.2** (*Continued*)

| Industry code | Number of observations | Percentage part-time | Industry description |
|---|---|---|---|
| 41 | 2055 | 32 | Health Services, except Hospitals |
| 42 | 5542 | 26 | Educational Services |
| 43 | 952 | 33 | Social Services |
| 44 | 1910 | 20 | Other Professional Services |
| 45 | 108 | 13 | Forestry and Fisheries |
| 46 | 3329 | 6 | Public Administration |

*Source:* Authors' computations from the March 1984 *CPS* extract (see the text for sample restrictions).

**Table 13.3**
Estimated Part-time/Full-time Wage Differentials: by Industry

| Industry code | RW1 | RW2 | RW3 | RW4 |
|---|---|---|---|---|
| 1 | −.199 (2.0) | −.229 (2.1) | −.155 (1.6) | −.179 (1.7) |
| 2 | −.201 (1.9) | −.259 (1.6) | −.148 (1.4) | −.153 (0.9) |
| 3 | −.153 (4.7) | −.196 (4.8) | −.147 (4.5) | −.185 (4.5) |
| 4 | −.077 (0.8) | −.281 (2.2) | −.068 (0.7) | −.288 (2.2) |
| 5 | −.002 (0.0) | −.047 (0.2) | −.107 (0.2) | −.011 (0.1) |
| 6 | −.147 (1.0) | −.012 (0.7) | −.131 (1.0) | −.086 (0.6) |
| 7 | .142 (1.3) | .125 (0.8) | .145 (1.3) | .139 (0.8) |
| 8 | −.031 (0.3) | −.066 (0.6) | −.033 (0.3) | −.077 (0.7) |
| 9 | [a] | [a] | [a] | [a] |
| 10 | −.200 (2.1) | −.143 (1.4) | −.171 (1.8) | −.110 (1.1) |
| 11 | −.238 (2.6) | −.159 (1.5) | −.230 (2.6) | −.141 (1.3) |
| 12 | −.044 (0.3) | −.029 (0.2) | −.072 (0.6) | −.052 (0.3) |
| 13 | −.213 (1.7) | −.306 (2.1) | −.233 (1.8) | −.309 (2.1) |
| 14 | −.302 (1.5) | −.566 (2.4) | −.264 (1.4) | −.530 (2.3) |
| 15 | −.326 (3.1) | −.273 (2.4) | −.330 (3.2) | −.260 (2.2) |
| 16 | .057 (0.2) | .057 (0.2) | .109 (0.3) | .109 (0.3) |
| 17 | −.321 (2.5) | −.414 (2.9) | −.338 (2.6) | −.435 (3.0) |
| 18 | −.170 (2.9) | −.289 (4.1) | −.177 (3.0) | −.296 (4.2) |
| 19 | [a] | [a] | [a] | [a] |
| 20 | −.069 (1.0) | −.198 (1.9) | −.071 (1.0) | −.203 (1.9) |
| 21 | −.165 (3.0) | −.180 (2.4) | −.178 (3.2) | −.184 (2.5) |
| 22 | −.245 (1.6) | −.419 (2.3) | −.211 (1.4) | .322 (1.8) |
| 23 | −.306 (4.1) | −.290 (3.8) | −.269 (3.6) | −.240 (3.1) |
| 24 | −.083 (0.8) | −.115 (0.9) | −.054 (0.5) | −.077 (0.6) |
| 25 | .444 (1.5) | .444 (1.5) | .361 (1.2) | .361 (1.2) |
| 26 | −.091 (1.0) | −.081 (0.8) | −.081 (0.9) | −.045 (0.4) |
| 27 | −.058 (0.6) | −.064 (0.5) | −.049 (0.5) | −.046 (0.4) |
| 28 | −.226 (6.2) | −.237 (5.9) | −.203 (5.5) | −.209 (5.2) |
| 29 | −.298 (3.7) | −.277 (3.3) | −.261 (3.3) | −.250 (3.0) |
| 30 | −.415 (4.6) | −.428 (4.7) | −.349 (3.8) | −.363 (3.9) |
| 31 | −.172 (3.2) | −.168 (3.0) | −.157 (2.9) | −.151 (2.7) |

*Continued*

263

**Table 13.3** (*Continued*)

| Industry code | RW1 | RW2 | RW3 | RW4 |
|---|---|---|---|---|
| 32 | −.123 (7.3) | −.117 (6.8) | −.088 (5.2) | −.081 (4.6) |
| 33 | −.086 (1.9) | −.078 (1.7) | −.065 (1.5) | −.056 (1.3) |
| 34 | −.300 (4.7) | −.264 (4.1) | −.266 (4.2) | −.299 (3.5) |
| 35 | .323 (4.7) | .283 (4.1) | .330 (4.8) | .294 (4.3) |
| 36 | −.213 (5.0) | −.211 (4.9) | −.186 (4.3) | −.185 (4.2) |
| 37 | −.346 (3.8) | −.370 (3.7) | −.337 (3.7) | −.358 (3.4) |
| 38 | −.065 (1.3) | −.050 (0.9) | −.052 (1.0) | −.032 (0.6) |
| 39 | −.111 (1.4) | −.102 (1.3) | −.093 (1.1) | −.085 (1.1) |
| 40 | −.047 (1.8) | −.041 (1.6) | −.034 (1.4) | −.027 (1.1) |
| 41 | −.052 (1.5) | −.048 (1.3) | −.040 (1.1) | −.036 (1.0) |
| 42 | −.177 (9.1) | −.179 (9.1) | −.150 (7.6) | −.151 (7.6) |
| 43 | −.124 (2.5) | −.127 (2.5) | −.107 (2.1) | −.110 (2.1) |
| 44 | −.247 (4.0) | −.200 (3.1) | −.192 (3.0) | −.141 (2.2) |
| 45 | −.369 (2.1) | −.227 (1.1) | −.358 (1.9) | −.264 (1.3) |
| 46 | −.255 (7.1) | −.263 (7.0) | −.239 (6.6) | −.246 (6.6) |

*Notes:* Absolute value of $t$ statistics in parentheses.
"Sample size too small to compute difference.

| Correlations: | RW2 | .91 | | |
|---|---|---|---|---|
| | RW3 | .98 | .90 | |
| | RW4 | .90 | .98 | .90 |
| | | RW1 | RW2 | RW3 |

*Source:* Authors' computations from within-industry wage equation estimates. RW1 and RW3 are based on part-time status in the survey week, while RW2 and RW4 are based on usual part-time status. RW1 and RW2 are from models without interaction terms, while RW3 and RW4 are from models that interact gender with number of children, marital status, education and experience. See the text for details.

Most striking, the estimated differentials are primarily negative (part-time workers *do* get paid less) and vary widely across industries. For example, 40 of the 44 RW1 coefficients are negative, with 25 of these being statistically significantly different from zero. The mean of the negative differentials is about −.18, with the largest close to −.41. All of the estimated positive differentials are statistically insignificantly different from zero, save for that for private household workers. As noted earlier, because of the unique nature of this industry, we exclude it from the inter-industry analyses reported in the next section.

The March 1984 *CPS* data also contained information on whether an employee was covered by a health insurance plan to which an employer contributed and on whether the employee was covered by a pension plan. As a result, it was possible for us to estimate equations similar to equation (13.1) in which the dependent variables were dichotomous (1.0) variables indicating an employee's coverage under these types of plans. Estimates of the coefficients of $P_j$ in these linear probability

**Table 13.4**

Estimated Part-time/Full-time Fringe Differentials: By Industry (absolute value of $t$ statistics)

| Industry code | Employer contributes to a health insurance plan for the employee (1,0) RH1 | | RH2 | | Employee is covered by a pension plan (1,0) RP1 | | RP2 | |
|---|---|---|---|---|---|---|---|---|
| 1 | −.170 | (4.6) | −.172 | (4.3) | −.078 | (3.1) | −.075 | (2.7) |
| 2 | −.320 | (4.6) | −.559 | (5.2) | −.381 | (4.3) | −.575 | (4.3) |
| 3 | −.265 | (10.8) | −.321 | (10.3) | −.181 | (7.6) | −.228 | (7.5) |
| 4 | −.246 | (3.1) | −.351 | (3.3) | −.069 | (0.7) | −.264 | (2.3) |
| 5 | .020 | (0.2) | .025 | (0.2) | .018 | (0.2) | −.153 | (0.9) |
| 6 | −.449 | (3.9) | −.509 | (4.0) | −.349 | (2.5) | −.446 | (2.9) |
| 7 | −.240 | (3.2) | −.514 | (4.7) | −.111 | (1.1) | −.271 | (1.8) |
| 8 | −.130 | (1.9) | −.228 | (2.3) | −.193 | (2.2) | −.287 | (2.4) |
| 9 | [a] | | [a] | | [a] | | [a] | |
| 10 | −.397 | (7.8) | −.447 | (8.2) | −.278 | (4.0) | −.288 | (3.9) |
| 11 | −.455 | (7.3) | −.503 | (6.8) | −.350 | (4.6) | −.376 | (4.1) |
| 12 | −.116 | (1.2) | −.296 | (2.4) | .048 | (0.4) | .191 | (1.2) |
| 13 | −.343 | (3.8) | −.320 | (3.1) | −.478 | (3.6) | −.399 | (2.6) |
| 14 | −.161 | (1.6) | −.271 | (2.3) | −.438 | (3.6) | −.448 | (3.2) |
| 15 | −.271 | (2.9) | −.297 | (3.0) | −.280 | (2.4) | −.206 | (1.6) |
| 16 | −.248 | (1.1) | −0.94 | (0.3) | −.077 | (0.3) | −.085 | (0.3) |
| 17 | −.280 | (3.1) | −.383 | (3.9) | −.175 | (1.9) | −.171 | (1.7) |
| 18 | −.247 | (5.9) | −.312 | (6.3) | −.212 | (4.3) | −.306 | (5.3) |
| 19 | [a] | | [a] | | [a] | | [a] | |
| 20 | −.135 | (1.7) | −.133 | (1.1) | −.106 | (1.1) | −.124 | (0.9) |
| 21 | −.105 | (2.0) | −.199 | (2.9) | −.095 | (1.9) | −.142 | (2.1) |
| 22 | −.398 | (4.6) | −.496 | (4.5) | −.338 | (2.9) | −.517 | (3.4) |
| 23 | −.410 | (10.4) | −.398 | (9.7) | −.274 | (6.6) | −.274 | (6.3) |
| 24 | −.356 | (4.8) | −.386 | (4.6) | −.413 | (4.3) | −.463 | (4.3) |
| 25 | −.463 | (2.3) | −.463 | (2.3) | −.426 | (1.2) | −.426 | (1.2) |
| 26 | −.269 | (3.8) | −.265 | (3.2) | −.257 | (3,0) | −.264 | (2.6) |
| 27 | −.188 | (2.0) | −.289 | (2.1) | −.088 | (1.0) | −.036 | (0.8) |
| 28 | −.384 | (14.3) | −.421 | (14.4) | −.290 | (9.7) | −.306 | (9.3) |
| 29 | −.441 | (9.2) | −.415 | (8.1) | −.367 | (5.9) | −.359 | (5.4) |
| 30 | −.610 | (9.7) | −.598 | (9.3) | −.647 | (8.4) | −.642 | (8.3) |
| 31 | −.389 | (12.1) | −.408 | (12.2) | −.262 | (7.2) | −.270 | (7.1) |
| 32 | −.265 | (25.4) | −.266 | (25.0) | −.121 | (13.0) | −.120 | (12.7) |
| 33 | −.465 | (13.5) | −.472 | (13.6) | −.257 | (6.2) | −.257 | (6.1) |
| 34 | −.446 | (13.4) | −.438 | (13.0) | −.269 | (7.6) | −.273 | (7.6) |
| 35 | −.037 | (2.2) | −.050 | (3.0) | −.019 | (1.3) | −.027 | (1.9) |
| 36 | −.381 | (14.3) | −.368 | (13.4) | −.206 | (7.7) | −.193 | (7.0) |
| 37 | −.334 | (6.3) | −.287 | (4.8) | −.104 | (2.3) | −.098 | (1.9) |
| 38 | −.240 | (8.6) | −.244 | (8.5) | −.118 | (5.0) | −.112 | (4.5) |
| 39 | −.374 | (8.9) | −.382 | (9.0) | −.187 | (4.6) | −.190 | (4.7) |
| 40 | −.348 | (15.5) | −.361 | (15.8) | −.298 | (12.0) | −.302 | (12.0) |
| 41 | −.312 | (13.5) | −.309 | (13.2) | −.190 | (8.6) | −.189 | (8.4) |
| 42 | −.419 | (29.1) | −.423 | (29.3) | −.396 | (27.9) | −.397 | (27.9) |

*Continued*

265

**Table 13.4** (*Continued*)

| Industry code | Employer contributes to a health insurance plan for the employee (1,0) | | Employee is covered by a pension plan (1,0) | |
| --- | --- | --- | --- | --- |
| | RH1 | RH2 | RP1 | RP2 |
| 43 | −.342 (10.7) | −.352 (10.9) | −.263 (8.4) | −.263 (8.4) |
| 44 | −.370 (12.8) | −.360 (12.1) | −.239 (7.9) | −.233 (7.5) |
| 45 | −.544 (3.9) | −.543 (3.6) | −.570 (4.6) | −.580 (4.2) |
| 46 | −.411 (13.1) | −.425 (13.2) | −.429 (15.0) | −.428 (14.5) |

*Notes:* Absolute value of *t* statistics in parentheses.
"Sample size too small to compute differentials.

*Correlations:* (RH1, RH2) = .85      (RP1, RP2) = .90

*Source:* Authors' computations obtained from within-industry employer contribution to health insurance and employee pension plan coverage equations. RH1 and RP1 (RH2 and RP2) are based on survey week (usual) part-time status. Results are for models without gender interactions; differentials from models with such interactions were correlated at .97 or higher level. See text for details.

function models will thus indicate the differential in the probability that a part-time worker was covered by these plans, *ceteris paribus*.

The estimates of these coefficients appear in Table 13.4. To conserve space, only the estimates from models without interaction terms are presented (estimates from the models that included interaction terms were very highly correlated with these). In all cases these estimates are negative and in virtually all cases statistically significantly so. Part-time employees do have lower probabilities, *ceteris paribus*, of being covered by a health insurance plan that an employer contributes to or by a pension plan. The mean part-time/full-time differentials across industries in these two probabilities are − .31 and − .25, respectively. As Table 13.4 indicates, however, the probabilities vary widely across industries.

Finally, for approximately one-quarter of the sample, the March 1984 *CPS* contained information on whether the individual was a union member.[11] For the subsample of individuals for which this information was present, one can estimate equations similar to equation (13.1), using a dichotomous (1, 0) variable for union membership as the dependent variable. The estimated coefficient of $P_j$ in each industry from these regressions will be an estimate of the differential in the probability of

*Notes:* Absolute value of *t* statistics in parentheses.
"Sample size too small to compute meaningful differentials.
'Magnitude of coefficient too large to be believable and probably due to the very small number (4) of part-time workers in the sample.

*Source:* Authors' computations obtained from within-industry probability of union membership equations. RU1 (RU2) based on survey week (usual) part-time status. See the text for details.

**Table 13.5**

Estimated Union Membership Proportion and Part-time/Full-time Probability of Membership Differentials: by Industry

| Industry code | Number of observations with membership data | Proportion/number union/union | Estimated differentials | |
|---|---|---|---|---|
| | | | RU1 | RU2 |
| 1 | 176 | .03/5 | − .026 (0.8) | − .026 (0.8) |
| 2 | 172 | .20/34 | − .254 (1.3) | − .118 (0.3) |
| 3 | 672 | .26/175 | − .145 (2.9) | − .215 (3.2) |
| 4 | 113 | .29/33 | − .221 (0.9) | − .122 (0.4) |
| 5 | 64 | .13/9 | − .128 (0.7) | [a] |
| 6 | 85 | .29/25 | − .340 (1.5) | − .340 (1.5) |
| 7 | 132 | .45/59 | .665(2.1)[b] | − .051 (0.0) |
| 8 | 164 | .26/43 | − 0.66 (0.4) | − .092 (0.5) |
| 9 | — | — | [a] | [a] |
| 10 | 400 | .20/80 | − .089 (0.6) | − .228 (1.4) |
| 11 | 309 | .20/62 | . 043 (0.3) | − .047 (0.3) |
| 12 | 161 | .57/92 | .233 (0.7) | .066 (0.1) |
| 13 | 83 | .25/21 | − .834 (2.5) | − .718 (1.8) |
| 14 | 108 | .20/22 | − .091 (0.4) | − .091 (0.4) |
| 15 | 84 | .08/7 | − .122 (0.4) | − .122 (0.4) |
| 16 | 19 | .26/5 | [a] | [a] |
| 17 | 56 | .23/13 | − .135 (1.3) | − .361 (1.5) |
| 18 | 253 | .36/91 | .038 (0.4) | − .110 (1.0) |
| 19 | 8 | .63/5 | [a] | [a] |
| 20 | 94 | .17/16 | − .199 (1.4) | − .267 (1.3) |
| 21 | 171 | .25/43 | .059 (0.6) | − .105 (0.7) |
| 22 | 95 | .54/51 | − .379 (1.3) | − .681 (2.0) |
| 23 | 255 | .12/31 | − .070 (1.0) | − .066 (2.0) |
| 24 | 168 | .17/29 | − .248 (1.1) | − .206 (0.8) |
| 25 | 28 | .36/10 | [a] | [a] |
| 26 | 97 | .18/17 | .192 (1.4) | .136 (0.8) |
| 27 | 33 | .21/7 | [a] | [a] |
| 28 | 565 | .44/249 | − .187 (3.0) | − .234 (3.5) |
| 29 | 239 | .43/103 | − .155 (0.9) | − .157 (0.9) |
| 30 | 208 | .32/67 | − .116 (0.6) | − .261 (1.3) |
| 31 | 520 | .08/42 | − .032 (0.7) | − .023 (0.5) |
| 32 | 2310 | .07/162 | .007 (0.5) | .004 (0.3) |
| 33 | 463 | .02/9 | − .023 (1.0) | − .023 (1.0) |
| 34 | 420 | .05/21 | − .048 (1.4) | − .047 (1.4) |
| 35 | 191 | .01/2 | − .015 (1.1) | − .015 (1.1) |
| 36 | 414 | .04/16 | − .029 (1.2) | − .029 (0.8) |
| 37 | 152 | .06/9 | − .060 (0.9) | − .076 (1.0) |
| 38 | 346 | .10/35 | − .118 (3.1) | − .135 (3.5) |
| 39 | 153 | .14/21 | − .035 (0.5) | − .109 (0.2) |
| 40 | 688 | .15/103 | − .067 (1.8) | − .056 (1.4) |
| 41 | 439 | .08/35 | − .017 (0.6) | − .024 (0.8) |
| 42 | 1369 | .32/438 | − .224 (7.1) | − .224 (7.1) |
| 43 | 229 | .09/21 | − .125 (3.0) | − .125 (3.0) |
| 44 | 439 | .05/22 | − .007 (0.3) | − .002 (0.1) |
| 45 | 30 | .00/0 | [a] | [a] |
| 46 | 780 | .26/203 | − .105 (1.6) | − .112 (1.8) |

union membership for part-time and full-time workers in the industry, *ceteris paribus*.

These estimated coefficients for each industry, as well as the size of the subsample available to conduct the analyses, and the proportion of employees who are union members in the subsample are found in Table 13.5. While over 80 per cent of the estimated differentials are negative, only 8 are statistically significant, perhaps because of the relatively small sample sizes.

Table 13.6 summarizes the patterns of signs and statistical significance of the part-time/full-time employee wage, fringe benefit and unionization differentials that we have obtained in this section. The fringe benefit and, arguably, wage differentials appear to be sufficiently precisely estimated to use as inputs in the inter-industry analyses that will be presented in the next section. The union membership differentials clearly are not, however, and we omit them from the subsequent analyses.

In concluding this section, it is nevertheless interesting to ask whether government policy in the United States has made it increasingly difficult for part-time workers to join unions in recent years? If so, this might encourage employers to increase their usage of part-time employees.

Union elections in the private sector in the United States are governed by the National Labor Relations Board (NLRB) and it is to the NLRB that disputes over whether part-time employees should be included in

**Table 13.6**
Patterns of Estimated Differentials

| Equation | Number of differentials estimated | Number that are negative | Number negative and statistically significant |
|---|---|---|---|
| Wage | | | |
| RW1 | 44 | 40 | 25 |
| RW2 | 44 | 40 | 27 |
| RW3 | 44 | 40 | 23 |
| RW4 | 44 | 40 | 24 |
| Health insurance | | | |
| RH1 | 44 | 43 | 41 |
| RH2 | 44 | 43 | 41 |
| Pension | | | |
| RP1 | 44 | 42 | 35 |
| RP2 | 44 | 42 | 38 |
| Union membership | | | |
| RU1 | 41 | 33 | 8 |
| RU2 | 42 | 36 | 8 |

*Source:* Authors' computations from coefficient estimates in Tables 13.3, 13.4 and 13.5.

proposed bargaining units and thus eligible to vote in union elections are brought. The *stated* policy of the NLRB has remained roughly constant over time; it has always attempted to determine bargaining units on the basis of a 'community of interest'.[12] That is, employees who share similar interests in wages, hours and other conditions of employment are placed in the same bargaining unit.

Part-time employees are generally included in a bargaining unit with full-time employees whenever the part-time employees perform work within the unit on a regular basis, for a sufficient period of time, during an appropriate calendar period. In determining in a specific case whether part-time employees share a sufficient community of interest to be placed in the same bargaining unit as full-time employees, the NLRB considers a number of factors including: the similarity (with full-time employees) and regularity of part-time employees' hours of work, the similarity (with full-time employees) of part-time employees' wage and benefit packages, common supervision for both types of employees, the similarity of their qualifications, training skills and job functions, the frequency of their contact and interchange while performing their job duties, the history of collective bargaining in the firm and the extent of union organization, the desires of both part-time and full-time employees, and the organizational structure of the firm.

Of course, to say that the *stated* policy of the NLRB has remained roughly constant over time is not to say that the *actual* policy has remained constant. To investigate if the latter has changed, we searched through NLRB decisions during the 1976–1984 period, finding 52 that dealt with part-time workers. About 60 per cent of these decisions resulted in part-time workers being included in a larger bargaining unit or allowed to set up their own unit for a bargaining election.

Given the small number of decisions each year (four to five), not surprisingly the proportion of times part-time workers were included in other units or allowed to set up their own unit fluctuated from year to year. None the less, to see if there were any trends in board decisions during the period, we estimated linear probability function models in which a dichotomous ((1, 0) part-time worker included or allowed to set up own unit) variable was regressed on a time-trend term. No significant trend showed up in the data even when higher order trend terms (i.e. a quadratic term) were included to allow for non-linearities. We thus found no evidence that changes in NLRB policy in recent years have encouraged the growth of part-time employees relative to full-time employees. That is, it does *not* appear that the NLRB is increasingly making it more difficult for part-time workers in the United States to join unions.

## 13.4 Inter-industry Variations in Part-time Employment in the United States

Given that estimates of the part-time employee/full-time employee wage ($RW$), at least partially employer-financed health insurance coverage probability ($RH$), and private pension coverage probability ($RP$) differentials vary widely across industries, our goal in this section is to see if the variations in these differentials help to explain the pattern of inter-industry variations in part-time employment in the United States. To do this, we embed them in a simple model of the demand and supply of part-time employment.

On the demand side, the ratio of part-time to full-time employees ($E_P/E_F$) is postulated to be a function of the relative costs of the two groups, as measured by the above differentials, and the production technology in use in an industry. Since the latter is not directly observable, it is proxied by a vector of variables ($Y$) that indicate the share of an industry's workforce in each of seven major occupational groups. A negative value for each of the differentials indicates a cost advantage for part-time workers; the larger (in absolute value) the differential is, the greater the cost saving from part-time workers. Thus, we expect the coefficients of $RW$, $RH$, and $RP$ all to be negative.

$$(E_P/E_F) = D(R\overline{W}, R\overline{H}, R\overline{P}, Y). \qquad (13.2)$$

On the supply side, the larger in absolute value these differentials are the less attractive is the relative reward to being a part-time worker and thus the smaller the fraction of workers who will want to work part time. The relative supply of part-time workers will also depend upon the characteristics of workers 'attached' to the industry (13.2). For example, *ceteris paribus*, married women with children, students and older workers phasing into retirement may all find part-time employment attractive. Similarly, unions may try to discourage their members from working part time if they perceive that widespread use of part-timers may discourage new workers from joining unions. Thus, we have on the supply side

$$(E_P/E_F) = S(R\overset{+}{W}, R\overset{+}{H}, R\overset{+}{P}, Z). \qquad (13.3)$$

Linear versions of the system in (13.2) and (13.3) were estimated using the estimates of $RW$, $RH$ and $RP$ obtained in the last section, and mean values (by industry) of the other variables obtained from the May 1984 CPS. The analyses reported below use 43 observations, dropping only the two industries whose sample sizes were too small to estimate the part-time/full-time wage differentials (see Table 13.3) and also the private household services industry (industry 35). Restricting the sample further to only those industries for which we estimated negative values of $RW$, or still further to those for which these estimates were negative and statistically significant, did not lead to more precise estimates of the model.

Table 13.7 contains estimates of the model when survey week part-time status is used to classify workers, and $RW1$, $RH1$ and $RP1$ are used as explanatory variables. The complete list of other demand ($Y$) and supply ($Z$) side variables included in the model is found in this table, along with their definitions. All results presented in the table are for unweighted regressions; weighting by the square root of the number of individuals in each underlying industry sample (Table 13.2) did not appreciably change the sign pattern or significance of the coefficients.

Column 1 presents OLS estimates of the structural demand curve. While the relative wage differential variable performs as expected, with larger part-time employee wage rate savings leading to increased use of part-time employees, the coverage by pension plan differential perversely appears to have a positive coefficient, implying that the less likely it is that part-time employees are covered by a pension, the fewer part-time employees will be employed. The pattern of occupational share coefficients suggests that industries that employ a relatively large number of blue-collar skilled workers (the omitted reference group in the equation) also tend to employ relatively few part-time employees.

Might the above pattern of results be affected by simultaneous equations bias? To answer this question, the demand (and supply) model is re-estimated by 2SLS. Columns 3, 4 and 5 in Table 13.7 present, respectively, the instrumental variable estimates we obtained for the wage, health insurance coverage probability and pension coverage probability differentials. The explanatory power of the wage differential equation is very low; indeed no individual coefficient is statistically significant. The health insurance and pension coverage probability differential equations are somewhat better. It is interesting to note that females and veterans are both less likely to be covered by either type of plan; females possibly because of coverage under other family members' plans and veterans possibly because of their access to medical care and retirement benefits through veterans' administration programs. Union membership, however, increases the probability of pension coverage, as does the average number of children in each family.

The structural demand and supply equations appear in columns 5 and 6 of Table 13.7. The 2SLS demand estimates in 5 are very similar to the OLS estimates, save that they are slightly less significant. The only cost differential that is significant in the supply curve is the wage differential; as expected, greater (more negative) part-time/full-time wage differentials lead to relatively fewer employees wanting to work part-time. The coefficients of the personal characteristics variables confirm that an increased number of children per worker and an increased percentage of workers who are students both increase the likelihood that employees will want to work part-time. Increases in the percentage of workers who are union members, however, have only an insignificant negative effect on part-time employment.

To assure the reader that the effects of the part-time/full-time wage, health insurance coverage probability and pension coverage probability differentials that we obtained are not unique to our usage of $RW1$, $RH1$ and $RP1$, Table 13.8 presents the coefficients of the differentials in the relative demand equations that we obtained when we used the other

**Table 13.7**

Inter-industry Cross-Section Regressions

| Variable | (1) OLS PTNOW | (2) RW1 | (3) RH1 | (4) RP1 | (5) 2SLS PTNOW | (6) PTNOW |
|---|---|---|---|---|---|---|
| | | | *Instruments* | | | |
| RW1 | −12.022 (2.0) | | | | | |
| RH1 | −7.137 (0.6) | | | | | |
| RP1 | 29.566 (3.1) | | | | | |
| RW1 | | | | | −15.825 (1.3) | 36.469 (2.5) |
| RH1 | | | | | −5.532 (0.3) | −28.817 (1.4) |
| RP1 | | | | | 32.450 (2.8) | 10.951 (0.8) |
| PROF | .279 (2.7) | −.008 (0.8) | .000 (0.0) | −.004 (0.7) | .318 (2.6) | |
| SALES | .298 (2.7) | −.002 (0.3) | .002 (0.4) | .003 (0.7) | .283 (2.4) | |
| ADS | −.154 (1.3) | −.005 (1.1) | −.002 (0.6) | .003 (1.2) | −.140 (1.0) | |
| SERV | .545 (6.4) | .002 (0.5) | .001 (0.2) | .003 (0.9) | .543 (6.1) | |
| AGF | .204 (2.9) | −.001 (0.1) | −.003 (2.1) | −.005 (2.7) | .211 (2.9) | |
| BCU | .433 (1.3) | −.000 (0.0) | −.013 (1.9) | −.018 (2.6) | .553 (1.5) | |
| FEM | | −.041 (0.1) | −.668 (1.6) | −1.513 (3.8) | | 2.723 (0.2) |
| CHILD | | −.112 (0.3) | .232 (0.9) | .572 (2.3) | | 22.445 (2.7) |
| AGE | | −.031 (0.6) | .018 (0.6) | .031 (1.0) | | 2.560 (2.2) |
| MNOW | | .016 (1.7) | .000 (0.1) | −.008 (1.5) | | −.969 (3.1) |
| RACE | | −.007 (0.5) | −.008 (1.1) | −.008 (1.0) | | −0.83 (0.3) |
| VET | | −.010 (0.7) | −.014 (1.7) | −.036 (4.3) | | −.011 (0.0) |
| HISP | | −.003 (0.3) | .004 (0.7) | −.009 (1.6) | | .074 (0.2) |
| EDUC | | .118 (0.8) | −.055 (0.6) | −.014 (0.2) | | −.047 (0.0) |
| STUD | | .005 (0.2) | −.005 (0.4) | −.021 (1.6) | | 1.399 (3.0) |
| A55 | | .013 (0.5) | −.001 (0.0) | .002 (0.1) | | −.658 (1.3) |
| UN | | .002 (0.5) | .000 (0.0) | .004 (2.0) | | −.145 (1.5) |
| $R^2$ | .728 | −.154 | .415 | .598 | — | — |

where:

*PTNOW* = percent of industry employees employed part-time last week

*RW1* = estimated part-time/full-time wage differential (Table 13.3)

*RH1* = estimated part-time/full-time employer contributes to a health insurance plan differential (Table 13.4)

*RP1* = estimated part-time/full-time employee is covered by an employers pension plan differential (Table 13.4)

*RW1* = instrumental variable estimate for *RW1*

*RH1* = instrumental variable estimate for *RH1*

*RP1* = instrumental variable estimate for *RP1*

*PROF* = percentage of workers in the industry who are professionals

*SALES* = sales

*ADS* = administrative support

*SERV* = service

*AGF* = agriculture or farm

*BCU* = blue-collar unskilled

*FEM* = fraction of workers who are female

*CHILD* = average number of children per worker

*AGE* = mean age

*MNOW* = percentage of workers married now

*RACE* = percentage of workers who are White

*VET* = percentage of workers who are veterans

*HISP* = percentage of workers with Spanish surnames

*EDUC* = mean years of education

*STUD* = percentage of workers who are students

*A55* = percentage of workers age 55 and older

*UN* = percentage of workers who are union members

⎫
⎬ omitted group
⎭ is blue-collar
skilled

*Note:* Absolute value of *t* statistics in parentheses.

*n* = 43 for all equations.

**Table 13.8**
Relative Price Coefficients from the Part-time
Worker Employment Share Equations: Various Specifications

| | Part-time last week | | | Part-time usual | |
| | OLS | 2SLS | | OLS | 2SLS |
| --- | --- | --- | --- | --- | --- |
| RW1 | −12.022 (2.0) | −15.825 (1.3) | RW2 | −7.785 (1.8) | −5.964 (0.8) |
| RH1 | −7.137 (0.6) | −5.532 (0.3) | RH2 | −3.260 (0.4) | −5.908 (0.4) |
| RP1 | 29.565 (3.1) | 32.450 (2.8) | RP2 | 22.910 (3.5) | 33.653 (3.3) |
| | | | | | |
| RW3 | −14.273 (2.2) | −18.807 (1.4) | RW4 | −7.192 (1.5) | −3.409 (0.4) |
| RH3 | −12.252 (1.1) | −24.981 (1.2) | RH4 | −1.546 (0.2) | −4.871 (0.3) |
| RP3 | 34.846 (3.5) | 43.894 (3.2) | RP4 | 21.577 (3.2) | 33.451 (2.8) |

*Note:* Absolute value of $t$ statistics in parentheses.
*Source:* Regressions in Table 13.7 and analogous ones for other variable specifications.

estimates of the differentials (i.e. RW2, RW3, RW4, ...). As can be seen there, the pattern of coefficients is very similar across all four specifications, although the specifications based on part-time employment in the survey week 'perform' better than those based on usual part-time employment.

## 13.5 Concluding Remarks

Our analyses of the aggregate time-series data for the United States suggest that there has been a tendency towards increased employment of part-time workers in the United States in recent years, a trend that is observed *after* one controls for cyclical factors. Moreover, this trend has come from an increase in 'involuntary' part-time employment, not from an increase in voluntary part-time employment. Searches for explanations for the recent growth of part-time employment in the US should therefore focus on the demand side of the labor market.

Such a search led us to ask if a growing cost differential between part-time and full-time employees might provide part of the explanation. We addressed this issue by focusing on inter-industry variations in the part-time employment/full-time employment ratio and seeing if variations in the relative cost differential across industries could help explain this part-time/full-time employment variation. In fact, relative wage costs did appear to influence relative employment levels, as predicted, on the demand side of the market.

In contrast, the larger the differential between the probability of pension coverage for full-time and part-time workers in an industry, the smaller the relative demand for part-time employees tended to be. At first glance this result seems inconsistent with our model. However, upon reflection, it may make sense. It is well known that pension coverage tends to reduce turnover and increase employees' expected tenure with firms (see, for example, Mitchell, 1983). The additional costs of pension coverage for part-time employees may be offset by savings in turnover and training costs if in fact this coverage induces them to have longer job tenure, making part-time employees more, rather than less, attractive to employers. To begin to test if this is occurring, one would want to see if the expected job tenure of part-time workers, by industry, is correlated, *ceteris paribus*, with the probabilities of pension coverage that we have estimated. Sadly, however, job tenure data are not available in the March 1984 *CPS*.

Finally, it is worth noting that the relative cost of part-time workers influences the relative supply of them (vis-à-vis full-time workers) as well as the relative demand. Indeed, our estimates, at least for the relative wage cost variable, suggest that supply responses exceed demand responses. Of course, given that some part-time workers are 'involuntarily' part-time, it is not obvious that the structural demand and supply model we have estimated is an entirely appropriate one.

## Notes

1 For example, evidence that part-time workers earn less than full-time workers, either in raw data or, more appropriately, after controlling for personal characteristics, is found in Ballard (1984) for the United Kingdom, Labor Canada (1983) for Canada, and Owen (1979) and Parsons (1974) for the United States. Similarly, evidence on part-time workers' poorer access to fringe benefits, such as health insurance, vacations, sick leave and private retirement plans, are found in Ballard (1984) for the United Kingdom, Labor Canada (1983) for Canada, Nakakubo (1985) for Japan, and Ichniowski and Preston (1986) for the United States. Finally, Disney and Szyszczak (1984) discuss how coverage of part-time workers under various social insurance programs and protective labor legislation has varied over time.
2 Disney and Szyszczak (1984) show that employment of part-time workers in Great Britain expanded most rapidly in periods when they were covered by fewer employer-financed social insurance programs and less protective labor legislation.
3 See Owen (1979) for an earlier effort in this direction. While Owen had estimates of relative wage cost differences, he had no data on fringe benefits.
4 A similar approach was used by Ehrenberg and Schumann (1982) in investigating the growth of overtime hours in the United States.
5 Evidence on the part-time employment–union membership relationship is very weak. For example, in the United Kingdom, Bain and Elsheikh (1979) and Richardson and Catlin (1979) found no strong relationship between part-time employment ratios and unionization percentages across industries. Similarly, Dickens (1983) found in a sample of roughly 1,000 workers who voted in 31 union elections in the United States in the early 1970s that, *ceteris paribus*, part-time workers' were some 6–7 per cent less likely to vote for a union, although this relationship was not statistically significant. Somewhat surprisingly, virtually all studies seeking to explain the well-publicized decline in unionization in the United States have failed to

consider if the growth of part-time employment has played any role. (See, for example, Dickens and Leonard, 1985, and their bibliography.)

6 The latter undoubtedly owing to cutbacks in financial aid for college students that increasingly forced college students in the US to work to help finance their education. For evidence on the increasing hours of work of college students, see Ehrenberg and Sherman (1987).

7 A quick look at Table 13A.1, however, will caution the reader that whether or not one observes an apparent trend may depend heavily on the starting date one chooses. More on this point below.

8 Similar results are reported in Ichniowski and Preston (1986) who use monthly data over the 1973–83 period. Both their results and ours fail to control for minimum wage changes. Matilla (1981) provides some evidence that increases in the minimum wage are associated with increases in the part-time/full-time employment ratio of teenagers, while Ehrenberg and Marcus (1982) find the opposite, at least for teens from low-income families.

9 The percentage is actually as high as 71 per cent for private household service workers. However, because the 'employers' in this industry are typically private individuals (not firms) and most employees work for a number of different people in any one week, we will ignore data from this industry in most of what follows.

10 To be a bit more precise, given two otherwise identical individuals except for their part-time status, $a_{pi} = \log(W_P/W_F)$, where the subscripts P and F refer to part-time and full-time workers respectively. Consequently, the proportional $a$ wage differential of part-time workers is $(W_P - W_F)/W_F = e^{a_{pi}} - 1$. For small $a$ values of $a_{pi} \cdot a_{pi} \approx e^{a_{pi}} - 1$.

11 The *CPS* consists of eight 'rotation groups' and only two of the groups were asked about union membership.

12. The material in this paragraph and the next two are drawn from Morris (1983) and Nash and Blake (1979).

**Table 13A.1**

Percentage of Part-time Employees in the United States Economy, 1963–84

| Year | All individuals 16+ | All individuals 16–19 | Males 20+ | Females 20+ |
|---|---|---|---|---|
| 1963 | 10.7 | 37.8 | 3.6 | 19.5 |
| 1964 | 11.0 | 40.5 | 3.7 | 19.5 |
| 1965 | 11.2 | 40.7 | 3.5 | 19.3 |
| 1966 | 11.7 | 41.2 | 3.6 | 19.6 |
| 1967 | 12.4 | 44.1 | 4.0 | 20.3 |
| 1968 | 12.8 | 44.9 | 4.1 | 20.8 |
| 1969 | 13.3 | 46.1 | 4.4 | 20.9 |
| 1970 | 13.7 | 47.0 | 4.7 | 21.5 |
| 1971 | 13.9 | 47.8 | 4.7 | 21.6 |
| 1972 | 14.0 | 46.2 | 4.8 | 21.6 |
| 1973 | 14.0 | 44.3 | 4.8 | 21.6 |
| 1974 | 14.0 | 44.1 | 4.8 | 21.5 |
| 1975 | 14.3 | 46.4 | 5.0 | 21.4 |
| 1976 | 14.3 | 46.5 | 4.9 | 21.4 |
| 1977 | 14.3 | 45.6 | 5.0 | 21.2 |
| 1978 | 14.3 | 45.6 | 5.0 | 20.9 |
| 1979 | 14.2 | 46.1 | 4.9 | 20.7 |
| 1980 | 14.4 | 47.7 | 5.1 | 20.5 |
| 1981 | 14.2 | 48.4 | 5.0 | 20.5 |
| 1982 | 14.3 | 50.1 | 5.2 | 20.4 |
| 1983 | 14.0 | 49.6 | 5.3 | 20.0 |
| 1984 | 13.7 | 50.2 | 5.1 | 19.5 |

*Source:* Authors' calculations from data in US Bureau of Labor Statistics (BLS), *Labor Force Statistics Derived from the Current Population Survey: A Databook*, Bulletin 2096 (Washington, DC, September 1982), Table A11 (for 1963–81), and *Employment and Earnings*, various issues (for 1982–84).

**Table 13A.2**
Percentage of Part-time Employees in Non-agricultural
Industries, 1955–84, by Reason for Part-time Status

| Year | Part-time for economic reasons | Part-time for non-economic reasons |
|------|--------------------------------|-------------------------------------|
| 1955 | 3.4 | 7.1 |
| 1956 | 3.6 | 7.9 |
| 1957 | 3.9 | 8.2 |
| 1958 | 5.4 | 8.3 |
| 1959 | 4.2 | 8.7 |
| 1960 | 4.5 | 9.0 |
| 1961 | 4.9 | 9.3 |
| 1962 | 4.0 | 9.7 |
| 1963 | 3.8 | 10.1 |
| 1964 | 3.5 | 10.5 |
| 1965 | 3.0 | 10.6 |
| 1966 | 2.5 | 11.4 |
| 1967 | 2.9 | 12.0 |
| 1968 | 2.5 | 12.4 |
| 1969 | 2.6 | 12.9 |
| 1970 | 3.1 | 13.3 |
| 1971 | 3.4 | 13.4 |
| 1972 | 3.3 | 13.5 |
| 1973 | 3.0 | 13.5 |
| 1974 | 3.5 | 13.6 |
| 1975 | 4.6 | 13.8 |
| 1976 | 4.2 | 13.8 |
| 1977 | 4.0 | 13.9 |
| 1978 | 3.8 | 13.9 |
| 1979 | 3.8 | 13.8 |
| 1980 | 4.5 | 13.9 |
| 1981 | 4.9 | 13.7 |
| 1982 | 6.5 | 13.8 |
| 1983 | 6.5 | 13.4 |
| 1984 | 5.7 | 13.1 |

*Source:* Authors' calculations from data in BLS Bulletin 2096, Table A18 (1955–81), *Employment and Earnings,* various issues, thereafter.

**Table 13A.3**
Percentage of Part-time Employees in Non-agricultural Industries, 1968–84,
by Age, Sex, Race and Reason for Part-time Status

| Year | Males 20+ | Females 20+ | All 16–19 | All Whites | All non-Whites |
|------|-----------|-------------|-----------|------------|----------------|
| *Part-time for economic reasons* | | | | | |
| 1968 | 1.7 | 3.3 | 5.9 | 2.1 | 5.6 |
| 1969 | 1.7 | 3.2 | 6.1 | 2.3 | 5.2 |
| 1970 | 2.2 | 3.7 | 6.9 | 2.8 | 6.1 |
| 1971 | 2.4 | 4.2 | 8.0 | 3.1 | 6.2 |
| 1972 | 2.1 | 3.9 | 8.5 | 3.0 | 5.7 |
| 1973 | 2.0 | 3.7 | 7.4 | 2.8 | 5.1 |
| 1974 | 2.4 | 4.2 | 7.9 | 3.2 | 5.9 |
| 1975 | 3.4 | 5.2 | 10.0 | 4.2 | 7.3 |
| 1976 | 2.9 | 4.7 | 10.0 | 3.8 | 6.8 |
| 1977 | 2.7 | 4.7 | 9.6 | 3.8 | 6.3 |
| 1978 | 2.4 | 4.5 | 9.0 | 3.5 | 6.1 |
| 1979 | 2.5 | 4.6 | 8.4 | 3.5 | 5.7 |
| 1980 | 3.3 | 5.1 | 9.8 | 4.2 | 6.5 |
| 1981 | 3.5 | 5.6 | 11.0 | 4.6 | 7.2 |
| 1982 | 5.0 | 7.2 | 14.2 | 6.1 | 9.2 |
| 1983 | 4.8 | 7.4 | 15.4 | 6.1 | 10.3 |
| 1984 | 4.1 | 6.6 | 13.2 | 5.3 | 9.5 |
| *Part-time for non-economic reasons* | | | | | |
| 1968 | 3.6 | 20.2 | 45.1 | 12.5 | 11.5 |
| 1969 | 3.8 | 20.3 | 46.3 | 13.0 | 12.0 |
| 1970 | 4.1 | 20.8 | 47.3 | 13.4 | 11.9 |
| 1971 | 4.1 | 20.8 | 47.9 | 13.6 | 11.5 |
| 1972 | 4.3 | 20.8 | 46.2 | 13.7 | 11.8 |
| 1973 | 4.3 | 20.9 | 44.2 | 13.8 | 11.4 |
| 1974 | 4.3 | 20.8 | 44.1 | 13.8 | 11.5 |
| 1975 | 4.4 | 20.7 | 46.7 | 14.1 | 11.9 |
| 1976 | 4.4 | 20.6 | 46.5 | 14.2 | 10.8 |
| 1977 | 4.6 | 20.4 | 45.7 | 14.3 | 11.1 |
| 1978 | 4.5 | 20.1 | 45.6 | 14.3 | 11.1 |
| 1979 | 4.5 | 19.9 | 45.9 | 14.2 | 10.8 |
| 1980 | 4.7 | 19.7 | 47.6 | 14.3 | 10.9 |
| 1981 | 4.6 | 19.6 | 48.4 | 14.2 | 10.1 |
| 1982 | 4.7 | 19.6 | 50.0 | 14.3 | 9.7 |
| 1983 | 4.8 | 19.0 | 49.8 | 14.0 | 8.9 |
| 1984 | 4.7 | 18.6 | 50.3 | 13.7 | 9.1 |

*Source:* Authors' calculations from data in BLS Bulletin 2096, Table B22 (1968–81), *Employment and Earnings*, various issues, thereafter.

**Table 13A.4**
Average Weekly Hours of Part-time Employees in
Non-agricultural Industries 1968–84 by Age, Race, and Sex

| Year | All | Males 20+ | Females 20+ | All 16–19 | All Whites | All non-Whites |
|------|-----|-----------|-------------|-----------|------------|----------------|
| 1968 | 18.6 | 18.4 | 19.3 | 15.6 | 18.4 | 19.2 |
| 1969 | 18.2 | 19.3 | 19.3 | 15.8 | 18.7 | 19.1 |
| 1970 | 18.3 | 20.1 | 19.2 | 15.9 | 18.2 | 19.6 |
| 1971 | 18.6 | 19.8 | 19.6 | 16.0 | 18.1 | 19.4 |
| 1972 | 18.6 | 19.6 | 19.1 | 16.5 | 18.8 | 19.3 |
| 1973 | 18.4 | 19.0 | 19.6 | 17.0 | 19.2 | 19.0 |
| 1974 | 18.8 | 20.2 | 19.8 | 16.9 | 18.9 | 19.0 |
| 1975 | 19.3 | 21.0 | 19.8 | 16.8 | 19.0 | 19.5 |
| 1976 | 19.2 | 20.8 | 19.6 | 17.1 | 19.0 | 19.8 |
| 1977 | 18.8 | 19.6 | 19.9 | 17.4 | 19.2 | 18.9 |
| 1978 | 19.1 | 20.0 | 19.7 | 17.4 | 19.4 | 19.3 |
| 1979 | 19.3 | 19.8 | 20.2 | 17.6 | 19.8 | 19.7 |
| 1980 | 19.7 | 20.2 | 20.1 | 17.6 | 19.6 | 20.1 |
| 1981 | 20.0 | 20.1 | 20.4 | 17.3 | 19.9 | 20.2 |
| 1982 | 19.6 | 21.0 | 20.4 | 17.0 | 19.9 | 20.1 |
| 1983 | 19.9 | 21.2 | 20.2 | 17.1 | 19.6 | 20.3 |
| 1984 | 20.2 | 20.6 | 20.5 | 17.6 | 19.5 | 20.6 |

*Source:* Authors' calculations from data in BLS Bulletin 2096, Table B22 (1968–81), *Employment and Earnings*, various issues, thereafter.

**Table 13A.5**
Shares of Various Groups in Total and
Part-time Employment, – 1968 and 1984

| Category | Year | Males 20+ | Females 20+ | All 16–19 |
|----------|------|-----------|-------------|-----------|
| Total employment | 1968 | 58.5 | 33.8 | 7.6 |
|  | 1984 | 52.8 | 41.0 | 6.1 |
| Part-time employment | 1968 | 20.7 | 53.1 | 26.2 |
|  | 1984 | 24.5 | 54.8 | 20.6 |
| Part-time employment (economic reasons) | 1968 | 38.3 | 43.8 | 17.9 |
|  | 1984 | 38.3 | 47.6 | 14.1 |
| Part-time employment (non-economic reasons) | 1968 | 17.1 | 55.0 | 27.9 |
|  | 1984 | 18.6 | 57.8 | 23.5 |

*Source:* Authors' calculations from data in BLS Bulletin 2096, Table B22 (1968) and *Employment and Earnings.*

# COMMENT

## CHRISTOPH F. BÜCHTEMANN

Perhaps even more than in the United States, the issue of part-time employment in most Western European countries has shifted into the focus of the debate on employment policy and job creation in recent years. Most European countries – under the issue of increasing 'labor market flexibility' – have recently introduced programs and taken measures to promote part-time employment as well as to lower existing institutional barriers to its further expansion. As the debate on 'labor market flexibility' in Europe is still largely inspired by the so-called 'American employment miracle', it is certainly valuable to be given an account and analysis of the development of part-time employment in the USA as thoroughly as that presented by Ronald Ehrenberg and his colleagues in their paper. This is also the reason why – contrary to common practice – I shall not concentrate on discussing the points made and arguments put forward by these authors but shall confine my comments to some remarks on the development of part-time employment from a European perspective.

### *Growth of part-time employment: differences between Europe and the US*

Let me begin by stating one important difference in the development of part-time employment between the US and most European countries, which is quite significant with respect to its socioeconomic implications and consequences.

On both sides of the Atlantic part-time employment has grown considerably *in absolute numbers* since 1970. Between 1970 and 1985 the number of persons usually working part-time (i.e. fewer than 35 hours per week) has risen by 56 per cent in the United States (see Nardone, 1986; Appelbaum, 1986) and by 20–100 per cent in Western European countries (see De Neubourg, 1985; OECD, 1983). The important difference to be noted, however, is that in the US *both* part-time *and* full-time employment have shown a considerable increase over this period, whereas in most *European* countries full-time employment has rather tended to decline or at least to stagnate. Taking Western Germany as an example: while the number of persons on full-time schedules was roughly the same in 1984 as it was in 1970, the absolute number of persons usually working part-time increased over the same period by almost 1 million or 40 per cent (see Büchtemann and Schupp, 1986). This means that – though starting from a lower level than in US – the increase of the *proportion* of part-time workers within the whole labor force has indeed been much stronger in West Germany (1970: 10 per cent; 1984: 16 per cent) than in the US (1970: 15.2 per cent; 1984: 17.6 per cent; see Nardone, 1986).

The specific constellation of a significant increase in part-time employment with declining (or, at best, stagnating) full-time employment explains some of the importance attached to the issue of part-time employment in the present European debate on employment policy and job creation. Part-time employment, indeed, appears to be the only significant growth sector in most European labor markets (see OECD, 1986), a development that certainly raises the question of its underlying determinants – even more urgently than in the US. Beyond this, in the face of persisting high numbers of unemployed, 90 per cent of whom are looking for full-time jobs, this development has far-reaching implications, especially in the area of social policy and income maintenance. European governments will have to find new institutional solutions if – as is most likely – the trends outlined continue in the future.

## Growth of part-time employment: supply- or demand-side effects?

The contribution of Ehrenberg and his colleagues is particularly valuable for the European debate on part-time employment, as it stresses the importance of demand-side factors underlying the recent growth of part-time work. Just as in the US, most empirical research on part-time employment in Europe has hitherto focused on its supply-side aspects, such as household composition and family time budgets, changing fertility rates and changing attitudes towards female labor market participation (for a summary, see Conradi, 1982). Such strong supply-side orientation, however, should be seen against the background of both the kind of available time-series data on part-time work and the very specific demographic composition of part-time workers themselves.

In the first place, most available empirical data on working time in general and on part-time employment in particular are obtained from population surveys (such as the annual European labour Force Sample Surveys and the annual German 'Mikrozensus'), which usually contain detailed information on the characteristics of workers and their households, but do not shed much light on the demand side of the labor market, such as type of establishment and characteristics of the workplace. In Germany, not even pay and fringe benefit data are available.

Secondly, and perhaps more importantly, the demographic – that is, supply-side – structure of part-time workers in terms of age, sex, family composition and the like contrasts very sharply with the patterns observed for full-time workers. Indeed, at least in most European countries, such supply-side structural differences between part-time and full-time workers appear to be much more pronounced than the structural differences on the demand side, such as concentration in certain industries, skill levels and sizes of establishment. For example, unlike in the US, part-time employment in most European countries still almost exclusively involves female workers. (In West Germany, 94 per cent of all part-timers were women in 1984.) The growth of part-time employment has therefore played a large part in the increase of the overall rate of *female* labor market participation over the last few years.

283

In West Germany, at least 70 per cent of the overall increase in female employment over the period 1970–84 was due to the expansion of part-time employment (see Büchtemann and Schupp, 1986). Reasons for the rising labor force participation of women have traditionally been explored on the supply rather than on the demand side of the labor market.

In Germany as well as in most other European countries, no data have been available until very recently on the reasons (economic and non-economic) for working part-time; certainly, nothing compared to the time-series data that Ehrenberg *et al.* quote in their paper. According to data from the 1984 European Labour Force Survey, the share of persons working part time *because they could not find a full-time job* amounted to only 7 per cent of all part-time workers in Germany, 9 per cent in France and 13 per cent in Britain (Büchtemann and Schupp, 1988; for the US, compare Hanel, 1985). Owing to the lack of time-series data, however, it cannot be said if this proportion of involuntary part-timers has increased over recent years. From the available information, it is perhaps more reasonable to conclude that in Western Europe, unlike the US, workers who under present labor market conditions cannot find full-time employment are much more likely to be found among the (full-time) unemployed than among the part-time labor force. This is in line with empirical evidence showing that in European countries employers seem to be reluctant to hire workers who would prefer full-time permanent jobs for part-time or temporary jobs; to fill part-time vacancies employers evidently take into consideration only those candidates who themselves prefer to work part time.

However, despite the rather low proportion of involuntary part-time workers and notwithstanding the fact that, owing to demographic and socioeconomic developments, there is a growing supply of part-time workers, strong arguments support the assumption that, at least since the middle of the 1970s, *demand factors* rather than supply factors have become more or less *predominant* in inducing the continuous rise in actual part-time employment. Four arguments are given here to support this contention.

(1) The simultaneous growth of part-time employment *and* both male and female *unemployment* in most European countries during the 1970s and 1980s is at odds with the conclusion that the actual expansion of part-time work should be viewed as a response of employers to shortages in the supply of workers seeking full-time employment. This might have been true for the period preceding the 1974/75 recession, but certainly cannot be argued for the last 10–12 years. Similarly, the persistently low skill level of most European part-time jobs does *not* leave any room for the argument that skill shortages might have induced increased offers of part-time jobs. Indeed, the reverse seems to be true: the supply-side qualification structure of part-time workers is significantly better than the skill level of the jobs they are being offered (see Büchtemann and Schupp, 1986; Schoer, 1987).

(2) The persisting strong concentration of part-time workers in a narrow range of industries and occupations on the one hand and the low level of wages as well as of fringe benefits associated with most part-time jobs on the other (see, for Germany, Büchtemann and Schupp, 1986; for the UK, Wallace and Robinson, 1984; for France, Ballard, 1984) can hardly be explained in terms of supply-side forces operating in the labor market unless we regard part-time workers as 'disadvantage-maximizers'.

(3) It can be demonstrated for various European countries that working time *preferences* of both part-time workers and those willing to take up part-time work are quite different from the hours schedules operating in the areas where the expansion of part-time employment over the last few years has actually taken place (see Nerb, 1986; Büchtemann and Schupp, 1988). In West Germany, for example, a series of recent studies have all found that working time preferences of those willing to work part time strongly concentrate on schedules in the range of 25–35 hours per week (see Landenberger, 1983), while the actual expansion of part-time employment has been largely – for 89 per cent of new part-time jobs between 1976 and 1984 – in the range up to 20 hours per week (see Büchtemann and Schupp, 1986).

(4) Recent evidence from both employer surveys and company case studies in Germany has clearly shown that the expansion of part-time employment is largely limited to those industries/companies where the employment of part-time workers permits a better matching of working time with variations in labor utilization. In other words, greater recourse to part-time work is anticipated to have positive effects on both productivity and average labor costs. This motive has been found to be predominant in employers' decisions to offer part-time jobs (see Hoff, 1983; Bielenski and Hegner, 1985; Robinson and Wallace, 1984).

All these empirical arguments point to the conclusion that – as in the US – in European countries such as West Germany and Great Britain forces and factors on the demand side rather than on the supply side of the labor market should be taken into consideration when explaining the growth of part-time employment over the last 10 to 18 years.

## Wages and non-wage labor costs as determinants of the growth of part-time employment

Finally, the roles of relative wages, fringe benefits and unionization in the growth of part-time employment are worth considering. A recent study of female part-time employment in West Germany found some evidence indicating that an analysis of the demand-side determinants of the growth of part-time employment should not exclusively focus on wage levels, but should also consider other factors (Büchtemann and Schupp, 1986, 1987). One of these concerns the German system of compulsory social security contributions, which have to be paid by both employee and employer if weekly hours schedules and monthly gross earnings exceed certain legally fixed hours and earnings thresholds. Social security contributions have been raised several times since the middle of the 1970s and, at about 18 per cent of workers' gross earnings, presently comprise a large part of the employers' overall labor costs. In fact, non-wage labor costs, including social security contributions as well as fringe benefits, make up a much larger part of total labor costs in Germany (as well as in other European countries like Sweden and France) than in the US. Given less pronounced inter-industry wage differentials in Germany than in the US, more weight should be attached to the varying levels of non-wage labor costs, of which social security contributions and company fringe benefits constitute a considerable proportion.

Some results of a West Germany study are worth reporting briefly (see Büchtemann and Schupp, 1986). Contrary to the findings of Ronald Ehrenberg and his colleagues for the US, no significant differences are found between the average gross wages of women with full-time and part-time jobs. This also holds true when controlling for skill level. However, when considering different categories of part-time jobs delineated by their status with respect to the social security system – namely those that fall under the threshold and those above the threshold of compulsory social security contributions – significant differences emerge.

Apart from receiving far fewer fringe benefits (such as paid sick leave, holiday allowances, '13th month salary', and the like) and apart from the fact that the employer does not have to pay any social security contributions in addition to the gross wages, the hourly gross earnings of female part-time workers with schedules below the threshold of compulsory social security contributions are significantly lower than those of both full-time and 'regular' part-time workers above the threshold. This finding can be explained both by the considerably smaller (if not non-existent) wage drift in the segment of marginal part-time workers falling under the thresholds, as well as by the fact that some collective wage agreements in female-dominated, part-time, intensive sectors of activity explicitly exclude workers under the threshold from collective minimum wage regulations (see Büchtemann, 1988). All factors considered, total labor costs per hour for those part-time workers below the threshold can be assumed to be 30–50 per cent lower than those for 'regular' part-time employees. Furthermore, female part-time workers in general and those with jobs not subject to compulsory social security contributions in particular show a significantly lower degree of unionization (11 and 6 per cent respectively) than their full-time counterparts (at 23 per cent) (see Büchtemann and Schupp, 1988). Beyond this, the German income tax system, by allowing a (comparatively low) 10 per cent flat rate of income tax for all part-time jobs not exceeding a certain monthly wage level (*Pauschalierung*), exerts an additional incentive for both employers and part-time workers to provide/engage in rather marginal part-time jobs.

On the basis of available time-series data, it can be shown that rather marginal part-time jobs likely to fall below the threshold of social security contributions have actually expanded much more strongly than regular part-time jobs exceeding 15 or 20 hours per week in recent years. Indeed, a tendency can be observed that, along with the growth in the number of part-time employees, the average weekly hours worked by part-time employees (unlike in the US) have been steadily *decreasing*. Therefore, despite the significant expansion in the *number* of part-time workers in recent times, the actual share of total *hours* worked by part-time employees in the overall labor input has grown much less or has remained fairly constant. Taking into account the considerably lower overall employment costs associated with jobs below the thresholds of compulsory social security contributions, it can be inferred that labor costs, especially non-wage labor costs, are likely to have played an important part in the recent expansion of part-time employment.

This conclusion is reinforced in an international comparative perspective. When comparing, for example, France, West Germany and the UK – three countries in which part-time employment is not highly concentrated in the politically regulated public sector – the relative pace of the recent growth of part-time employment clearly reflects relative hourly labor costs and especially the advantages associated with part-time job arrangements in terms of social security contributions and labor law regulations. (The UK exhibits the largest part-time workforce, with West Germany second and France third; see Büchtemann, 1988.)

Summing up, it seems clear that in Europe, too, investigations into the patterns and determinants of the growth of part-time employment should focus much more than hitherto on demand-side factors. In this context, special attention should be given to aspects of non-wage labor costs rather than to wage levels alone.

Let this brief discussion also be seen as a plea for a differentiated analysis of part-time employment that takes into account the wide range of heterogeneous working time arrangements covered by the concept of part-time employment, with each arrangement having quite different implications for employment, labor market and social policy (for a detailed discussion of these issues, see Büchtemann and Schupp, 1986; 1988).

# CHAPTER 14

# Flexible Staffing Arrangements and Employers' Short-term Adjustment Strategies

## KATHARINE G. ABRAHAM

## 14.1  Introduction

Any viable enterprise must somehow accommodate uncertainty and flux in both output and input markets. In this paper, I explore the use of a hitherto largely neglected mechanism for accomplishing this: the use of workers who provide their services only on an as-needed basis. Reliance on this sort of flexible staffing arrangement offers employers an alternative to adjusting hours, adjusting the size of the regular workforce and/or using inventories as a buffer – approaches that have been the focus of a considerable body of earlier work.[1] I conclude that the use of flexible staffing arrangements constitutes an important component of many US employers' short-term adjustment strategies.

There are at least two sorts of fluctuations that may lead employers to use flexible staffing arrangements. First, if demand varies from period to period, it may make sense to cover some part of peak demand with flexible staffers. Second, it may be appropriate to rely in part on flexible staffing arrangements to deal with labor supply fluctuations due to absences, vacations, leaves, and so on. Section 14.2 develops two simple models designed to illustrate how demand variability and the existence of a stochastic component in regular employees' labor supply affect employers' optimal staffing strategies and, in particular, create a motivation for using flexible staffing arrangements. Empirical evidence on the use of agency temporaries, short-term hires and on-call workers from a new survey of over 400 US employers is presented in Section 14.3. This survey yields unique evidence on the use of these flexible staffing arrangements, on employers' reasons for relying on flexible staffers and on the organizational characteristics associated with flexible staffing use. The survey results support the conclusion that, in the United States, flexible staffing arrangements play an important role in the short-run adjustment process.

In recent years, considerable attention has been given to what anecdotal evidence suggests is an increasing reliance on non-standard

FLEXIBLE STAFFING ARRANGEMENTS

employment relationships by many US employers. While this paper does not speak directly to the question of how and why the use of flexible staffing arrangements has changed over time, it does provide a benchmark for future investigations. Section 14.4 summarizes the paper's main conclusions and suggests some directions for future research, including some thoughts on the changing pattern of flexible staffing use.

## 14.2  Models of Employers' Staffing Decisions

The two simple models presented in this section of the paper provide a starting point for thinking about the role of flexible staffing arrangements in employers' overall staffing strategies. In the first model, demand varies and employers cover peak demand with workers who provide their services on an as-needed basis.[2] In the second, the existence of a stochastic element in the labor supply of workers hired on long-term contracts (vacations, leaves, etc.) provides the motivation for using flexible staffers. Both models imply that flexible staffing arrangements should be an important component of many employers' cost-minimizing staffing plans and suggest several factors that should influence the extent to which they are relied upon. At the end of the section, I briefly discuss how allowing for alternatives to the use of flexible staffers affects these models' implications.

The partial equilibrium nature of the analysis undertaken here should be stressed from the outset. In the models that follow, the relative costs of employing workers under alternative arrangements are taken as fixed. While these models capture important features of individual employers' decisions regarding the use of flexible staffing arrangements, a full understanding of the evolution of flexible staffing patterns will eventually require consideration of the overall demand for different sorts of workers and the supply of labor to different sorts of jobs.[3]

### 14.2(a)  Stochastic Demand for Output

Variability in product demand is one potentially important motivation for using flexible staffing arrangements. This can be illustrated in the context of a simple model of a cost-minimizing firm. Each period, this firm produces output $x$, where $x$ is distributed as $f(x)$. Ignoring discounting, actual output may be thought of as either unpredictable (each period's output drawn from the same $f(x)$ distribution) or predictable (output varying over, say, the course of a year according to some seasonal pattern that is known in advance). At this point I assume that, in the initial period, the firm must make a once-and-for-all decision concerning the number of regular employees, $L_p$, to be hired at a given wage, $w_p$; new regular workers cannot be hired later on and regular workers never leave the firm. I also assume initially that regular workers work a fixed number of hours.

Each regular employee can produce one unit of output per period. If it turns out that $x \leqslant L_p$, the regular workforce can produce all the output required and no temporary workers will be hired. If $x > L_p$, the firm may hire supplemental workers, $L_s$, at a given wage, $w_s$, to make up the shortfall in production capacity. Because these flexible staffers are unfamiliar with the firm's production process, they may be less productive than regular workers; $b$ flexible staffers are required to produce one unit of output, $b \geqslant 1$.

A more complete model might explicitly incorporate other differences between regular employees and flexible staffers, such as differences in expected supervision costs. As already noted, flexible staffers are likely to have less experience with the particular tasks they are performing than regular employees. Moreover, a flexible staffer who expects to be on a job only a short time will not be motivated by the hope of future rewards for good performance and may for that reason be more likely to shirk. For both of these reasons, flexible staffers may require closer supervision than regular employees. The easiest way to allow for these possibilities is to think of $w_p$ and $w_s$ as the total per-hour costs associated with the use of regular employees and flexible staffers, respectively, including not only wages and benefits but also indirect costs such as supervision costs.[4] I assume that it is more expensive to produce a fixed quantity of output using flexible staffers than using regular workers ($bw_s > w_p$), so that some regular workers are hired.

The firm's problem is then to choose the level of regular employment that will minimize its expected production costs:

$$E(C) = w_p L_p + w_s \int_{L_p}^{\bar{x}} b(x - L_p) f(x) \, dx, \tag{14.1}$$

where $\bar{x}$ is the maximum of the output distribution and $b(x - L_p)$ equals the number of supplemental workers hired when $x > L_p$.[5] The first-order condition for a minimum is:

$$w_p = bw_s \int_{L_p}^{\bar{x}} f(x) \, dx. \tag{14.2}$$

Intuitively, the firm equates the cost of expanding production capacity by hiring another permanent employee to the expected cost of producing the marginal unit of output by hiring flexible staffers as needed ($bw_s$ times the probability that flexible staffers are hired). This first-order condition can be rewritten:

$$R = \frac{bw_s - w_p}{bw_s}, \tag{14.3}$$

where $R$ is the fraction of its output distribution the firm chooses to cover with regular workers. As might be expected, $R$ increases with $b$; that is, the lower the relative productivity of flexible staffers, the smaller the expected number hired. Thus, one implication of the model is that the use of flexible staffers should be greater in positions in which firm-specific skills are relatively unimportant for successful job performance. $R$ also decreases with $w_p$ and increases with $w_s$; that is, the lower the relative cost of using flexible staffers, the greater the reliance placed upon them.

Intuition suggests that increases in the dispersion of demand ought to increase the expected ratio of supplemental to regular staff. This intuition can be formalized. Imagine a mean-preserving spread of the original demand distribution such that:

$$\tilde{x} = \mu + (x - \mu)/k, \quad 0 < k < 1, \tag{14.4}$$

and:

$$f(\tilde{x}) = kf(x) \tag{14.5}$$

where $\tilde{x}$ is the new output variable, $\mu$ is the common mean of the new and old output distributions, and $k$ captures the relative dispersion of the new distribution compared to the old, with smaller values of $k$ being associated with greater relative dispersion. Note that $R$, the share of its demand distribution the firm chooses to cover with regular employees, is independent of the dispersion of demand. If $L_p$ is optimal regular employment in the initial situation, optimal regular employment in the new regime is:

$$\tilde{L}_p = \mu + \frac{(L_p - \mu)}{k}, \quad 0 < k < 1. \tag{14.6}$$

The expected level of temporary employment in the new regime is:

$$E(\tilde{L}_s) = \int_{\tilde{L}_p}^{\tilde{x}} b(\tilde{x} - \tilde{L}_p)f(\tilde{x}) \, d\tilde{x} = \int_{L_p}^{x} \frac{b}{k}(x - L_p)f(x) \, dx. \tag{14.7}$$

The proportional change in $L_p$ associated with an increase in demand dispersion (decline in $k$) is:

$$\frac{-\partial \tilde{L}_p/\delta k}{\tilde{L}_p} = \frac{(L_p - \mu)}{\mu + (L_p - \mu)} * \frac{1}{k}, \tag{14.8}$$

and the proportional change in $E(L_s)$ turns out to be simply

$$\frac{-\delta E(\tilde{L}_s)/\delta k}{E(\tilde{L}_s)} = \frac{1}{k}. \tag{14.9}$$

If $L_p$ is less than the mean of the demand distribution ($R \leqslant 1/2$), increases in the dispersion of demand reduce $L_p$ and increase $E(L_s)$, so $E(L_s)/L_p$ clearly increases. But even if $L_p$ is greater than the mean of the demand distribution ($R > 1/2$), so long as $\mu$ is positive – which it must be for any observed demand distribution – the percentage increase in $L_p$ will be less than $1/k$, so $E(L_s)/L_p$ increases. Thus, increases in the dispersion of demand of the sort considered here unambiguously raise the expected ratio of supplemental to regular employment.

## 14.2(b)  Stochastic Labor Supply by Regular Workers

The preceding discussion assumes that regular employees supply a fixed flow of labor services to the firm. But any manager could tell you (though perhaps not in precisely these words!) that there is a stochastic element in employees' labor supply. Overstaffing is one way to accommodate vacations, leaves, absences due to illness, etc.; relying on supplemental workers to fill in for regular employees as needed is another, possibly complementary, strategy.

Let us represent the stochastic nature of regular employees' labor supply as follows:

$$L_p = gL, \tag{14.10}$$

where $L_p$ is the actual quantity of labor supplied, $L$ is the number of regular workers hired, and $g$ is distributed as $f(g)$, $0 \leqslant g \leqslant 1$. This means that the density of the labor supply distribution can be written:

$$f(L_p) = f(g) * (1/L).^6 \tag{14.11}$$

Note that there is no reason to use flexible staffers unless $g$ varies from period to period. If individual employees' labor supply varied but the aggregate quantity of labor supplied by regular employees within a relevant grouping did not, one could simply hire $1/g$ times as many regular employees as actually needed and have exactly the right number at work in every period. In general, however, $g$ will vary from period to period. For example, absences are typically higher on Mondays and Fridays than on other days of the week, and more vacations are scheduled during the summer than at other times of year.

I assume that regular employees must be paid whether they work or not. As in the previous model, I also assume that the cost per effective unit of labor supplied by supplemental workers is higher than for regular employees (here, $bw_s > w_p/E(g)$), so that some regular employees are hired.[7]

To highlight the implications of stochastic variation in the quantity of labor supplied by regular employees, output is taken as fixed. The firm's objective is to choose $L$ to minimize expected production costs:

$$E(C) = w_p L + w_s \int_0^x b(x - L_p) f(L_p) \, dL_p. \tag{14.12}$$

Substituting for $L_p$ and $f(L_p)$ from equations (14.10) and (14.11) above:

$$E(C) = w_p L + w_s \int_0^{x/L} b(x - g * L) f(g) \, dg. \qquad (14.13)$$

Differentiating with respect to the number of regular employees hired, $L$, yields the first-order condition for cost minimization:

$$w_p = b w_s \int_0^{x/L} g f(g) \, dg. \qquad (14.14)$$

Given our assumptions, this condition implies that the firm will choose to hire more than $x$ regular employees.[8] Flexible staffers are used to fill in when $g * L$ is less than $x$. Thus, overstaffing and the use of supplemental workers are complementary approaches to dealing with variation in regular employees' labor supply. As in the model with variable demand, decreases in $b$, increases in $w_p$ and decreases in $w_s$ all lead the firm to reduce the number of regular employees hired and to increase its reliance on flexible staffers. Though intuition suggests that increases in the variability of the firm's absenteeism rate should raise the relative use of supplemental workers, this does not in fact hold as a general proposition.

### 14.2(c)  Alternatives to the Use of Flexible Staffing Arrangements

A model in which employers' only choices are to use regular employees who work a fixed number of hours or to use flexible staffers is, of course, unrealistic. Some of the alternative approaches to dealing with variability/uncertainty in product demand and labor supply have already been mentioned: varying the hours worked by regular workers; hiring and firing regular workers as conditions change; and/or using inventories as a buffer.

For many employers, varying regular employees' hours of work, particularly through scheduling of overtime, is an important instrument for absorbing demand fluctuations and for handling absences, vacations, leaves, and so on. The ability to vary regular employees' hours is not, however, a perfect substitute for the use of flexible staffing arrangements. Standard arguments imply that marginal productivity of hours worked by the regular workforce during a given time period will eventually decline. For a firm with a given regular workforce, beyond a certain point it will be cheaper to accommodate higher-than-usual demand or higher-than-usual absenteeism by using supplemental staff rather than by increasing regular workers' hours.

Adjusting the size of the regular workforce is another approach to accommodating changing circumstances. If there is a change in demand or in employees' labor supply behavior (for example, an increase in expected absenteeism) that is expected to persist for an extended period of time, one would expect an employer to make changes in the size of the regular workforce. But one would not expect an employer to hire additional regular staff to meet short-term needs; any wage savings associated with using additional regular staff rather than flexible staffers would be more than offset by the fixed costs of increasing and then decreasing the size of the regular workforce. Hiring costs include the costs of screening potential new hires plus the costs of any initial on-the-job training provided. The costs of reducing the size of the regular workforce will depend upon the method chosen for accomplishing that end. Attrition takes time; moreover, the wrong employees (from the employer's perspective) may choose to leave. Layoffs may also be costly, both because of government regulations (for example, US employers who lay off workers may incur increased unemployment insurance costs) and because of firms' own previous strategic decisions (for example, a no-layoff firm that resorts to layoffs may experience deterioration of employee morale and commitment). So long as the costs of adjusting the size of the regular workforce exceed the costs associated with taking on and releasing flexible staffers, there will be circumstances under which it is optimal to rely on flexible staffers.

In certain goods-producing industries, inventories may be used to buffer fluctuations in demand or, possibly, in regular employees' labor supply. The degree of reliance on inventory buffer stocks will depend, *ceteris paribus*, on the costs associated with holding them. A strategy of holding sufficient inventories to cover all possible contingencies is likely to be very expensive. Thus, even in industries producing reasonably standardized and storable products where the use of inventory buffer stocks is feasible, there is likely to be a role for flexible staffers. A similar argument can be made concerning the strategy of lengthening delivery or waiting times during busy periods. Some lengthening of the customer queue may be optimal; however, if delivery or service lags become too long, customers will seek other sources of supply. Thus, beyond a certain point, it will pay to hire flexible staffers.

## 14.3  Empirical Evidence on the Use of Flexible Staffing by US Employers

The theoretical discussion just concluded suggests that flexible staffing arrangements can play an important role in employers' accommodation of variations in demand and/or in the labor supply of regular employees. Flexible staffers should be concentrated in jobs that require little firm-specific knowledge or skills, and the duration of flexible staffing assignments should be sufficiently short that adjusting the size of the regular workforce is not a cost-effective alternative. The theoretical discussion also implies that the use of flexible staffing arrangements should be greatest in organizations where the relative costs of using flexible staffers are low, demand is highly variable, and alternative methods of accommodating fluctuations are costly. To shed light on these propositions, this section of the paper presents new empirical evidence on US employers' use of flexible staffing arrangements.

## 14.3(a)   The Flexible Staffing Survey

The data analyzed here come from an employer survey that I recently conducted in collaboration with the Bureau of National Affairs (BNA). The survey questionnaire included questions on responding organizations' use of agency temporaries, short-term hires, on-call workers and contracting out. The analysis in this paper focuses on the first three of these arrangements, all of which involve bringing people other than regular employees onto the organization's premises to do work that in principle might be done by regular employees. My objectives were to document the reliance upon these arrangements and the factors responsible for their use.

For purposes of this study, respondents were given the following definitions:

*Agency temporaries:* Individuals employed through a temporary help agency to work for your organization. Examples: accountants, clerical help, laborers, maintenance workers, nurses.

*Short-term hires:* Employees hired on the company payroll either for a specific period of time or for a specific project. Examples: employees hired during the Christmas season, students hired for the summer, employees hired for a one-time project or event. This classification includes freelancers hired by the hour or day, but does not include individuals in an 'on-call' pool.

*On-call workers:* Individuals in a pool of workers who are called in on an as-needed basis. Examples: laborers supplied by a union hiring hall, retirees who work for a few days a month.

All questions on the survey pertained to calendar year 1985.

The survey questionnaire was sent during May 1986 to 799 human resource executives at private firms, some corporate-level personnel and some with division or plant-level responsibility. All were members of a standing panel previously solicited for participation in a short quarterly survey on absence and turnover rates and in an annual survey on personnel department activities and budgets. A follow-up letter including another copy of the survey form was sent to those executives we had not heard from by the end of June 1986. Replies from 469 respondents were received by the end of July 1986. The questions about on-call work generated some confusion; follow-up telephone interviews were conducted to clarify the answers to these questions.[9] Altogether, 442 surveys were usable in at least some of our analyses, a usable response rate of 55 per cent.[10]

The replies do not mirror the industry distribution of employment, but are skewed towards manufacturing, finance, insurance and real estate, and health care, and away from trade and services other than health care.[11] In addition, almost all the responding organizations had more than 50 employees at year-end 1985 and many are part of even larger corporations.[12] While the non-random nature of the survey sample mandates caution in generalizing from the survey findings, evidence described at the end of this section suggests that the pattern of flexible staffing use reported by survey respondents is not out of line with that of US employers overall.

### 14.3(b)  Use of Temporary Workers, Short-Term Hires and On-Call Workers

The top panel of Table 14.1 reports the percentages of responding organizations that use flexible staffers. Overall, 93 per cent of respondents use at least one of the three flexible staffing arrangements.

While previous studies have suggested that many US employers use flexible staffers, particularly agency temporaries, to my knowledge none has yielded estimates of how *intensively* these arrangements are used.[13] For each type of flexible staffing, the survey described here collected two pieces of information that together permit an estimate of use intensity: the total number of assignments during calendar year 1985; and the typical duration of calendar year 1985 assignments (which can be expressed as a fraction of a year). For each organization for which both of these pieces of information were reported, their product yields an estimate of person-years worked by flexible staffers. This person-years number was then divided by regular employment as of year-end 1985 and the resulting ratio multiplied by 100 to yield a use intensity measure that is a rough proxy for the average percentage addition made by flexible staffers to the regular workforce's labor input over the course of the year.[14]

The second panel of Table 14.1 reports estimates of how intensively flexible staffers are used. These estimates indicate that average use intensity among users of each of the individual categories of flexible staffing amounts to between a 0.5 per cent and 1.0 per cent addition to their regular employment, with combined use for organizations using at least one of the three arrangements averaging a 1.5 per cent addition. Since 93 per cent of all respondents said that they used flexible staffers, this number implies an average use intensity across all sampled organizations of approximately 1.4 per cent.

The use intensity distribution is markedly skewed. For most organizations, use intensities are small: 45 per cent of user organizations had use intensities for all three categories of flexible staffers combined of less than 0.5 per cent and another 21 per cent had use intensities of less than 1.0 per cent. But for a minority of user organizations, use intensities are very large: 8 per cent had use intensities in excess of 5.0 per cent and 2 per cent had use intensities in excess of 10.0 per cent.

**Table 14.1**

Percentage of Organizations Using Flexible Staffers and Intensity of Their Flexible Staffing Use

| | Agency temporaries | Short-term hires | On-call workers | All three combined |
|---|---|---|---|---|
| Percentage of organizations using flexible staffers[a] | 77 | 64 | 36 | 93 |
| Overall mean use intensity among users[b,c] | 0.82 | 0.85 | 0.62 | 1.49 |
| Mean use intensity[b,c] among top 25% of users | 2.84 | 2.43 | 2.03 | 4.50 |
| Mean use intensity[b,c] among top 10% of users | 5.86 | 4.16 | 3.92 | 7.91 |
| Percentage of users with use intensity in range:[c] | | | | |
| 0.01–0.49 | 76 | 55 | 75 | 45 |
| 0.50–0.99 | 11 | 23 | 11 | 21 |
| 1.00–1.99 | 4 | 11 | 9 | 16 |
| 2.00–4.99 | 4 | 8 | 3 | 10 |
| 5.00–9.99 | 3 | 3 | 1 | 6 |
| 10.00–14.99 | 1 | 0 | 0 | 1 |
| 15.00 and over | 1 | 0 | 1 | 1 |
| Sample size | 265 | 221 | 107 | 329 |
| Total number of users | 339 | 282 | 161 | 413 |

[a]The percentages in this row are based on 442 total responses.

[b]The use intensities reported in this row represent the contribution of the given category of flexible staffers, expressed in person-years of work divided by the number of regular employees times 100.

[c]These estimates are based upon answers from respondents who provided complete information on flexible staffing use intensity. These responses were weighted in inverse proportion to the response rate in the relevant use category (use agency temporaries only, use both agency temporaries and short-term hires, and so on). In defining use categories, those who used only former regular employees as on-call workers were distinguished from other on-call users.

An important assumption underlying the discussion in Section 14.2 was that flexible staffers cost more per hour to employ than comparably productive regular employees; otherwise, I reasoned, there would be an incentive for employers to employ only flexible staffers, at least in certain types of jobs. Testing this assumption turns out to be very difficult. The data in the top panel of Table 14.2 pertain to the direct hourly costs associated with using flexible staffers. The answers imply that temporary help agencies' per-hour charges typically equal or exceed the per-hour wage and benefit costs associated with regular employees in comparable positions; however, a substantial share of users of short-term hires and on-call workers report lower per-hour wage and benefit costs for those flexible staffers than for regular employees in comparable positions.

**Table 14.2**
Selected Characteristics of Flexible Staffing Use

|  | Agency temporaries | Short-term hires | On-call workers |
|---|---|---|---|
| *Percentage of users reporting direct costs of flexible staffers compared with regular employees:*[a] | | | |
| Generally higher | 42 | 6 | 11 |
| Generally about the same | 30 | 33 | 46 |
| Generally lower | 27 | 60 | 43 |
| Sample size | 330 | 273 | 156 |
| *Percentage of users reporting typical assignment duration:* | | | |
| Up to 1 week | 26 | 2 | 54 |
| 1 week to 1 month | 41 | 9 | 27 |
| 1 to 3 months | 25 | 73 | 11 |
| 3 to 6 months | 5 | 13 | 4 |
| More than 6 months | 2 | 3 | 4 |
| Sample size | 307 | 269 | 139 |
| *Percentage of users reporting assignments that are:* | | | |
| Managerial/administrative | 1 | 5 | 6 |
| Professional/technical | 29 | 38 | 35 |
| Office/clerical | 96 | 75 | 63 |
| Sales | 3 | 5 | 4 |
| Production/service | 29 | 44 | 36 |
| Sample size | 336 | 277 | 159 |
| Total number of users | 339 | 282 | 161 |

[a]The question asked about agency temporaries was, 'Is your hourly cost for agency temporaries generally higher or lower than the pay and benefits costs for regular employees in comparable positions?' The questions about short-term hires and on-call workers substituted 'your hourly pay and benefits cost' for 'your hourly cost'.

Unfortunately, it was not possible to collect information either on flexible staffers' relative productivity or on the relative costs of supervising them, as would have been required to construct direct estimates of per-unit production costs. The data in the second panel of Table 14.2, which show that flexible staffing assignments are typically quite short, are consistent with per-unit production costs being higher for flexible staffers than for regular workers. If using flexible staffers reduced per-unit production costs, I would expect flexible staffing assignments to be longer than they typically are.[15]

The discussion in Section 14.2 also implied that the use of flexible staffers should be more prevalent in jobs requiring little firm-specific expertise than in jobs where firm-specific skills are important. The data in the bottom panel of Table 14.2 are at least consistent with this implication. Substantial numbers of organizations assign flexible staffers to office/clerical, professional/technical and production/service positions, but very few make use of flexible staffers in either managerial/administrative or sales positions.[16]

### 14.3(c)  Reasons for Using and Perceived Importance of Flexible Staffing Arrangements

Let me turn next to the question of whether employers' reasons for using flexible staffers are consistent with the theoretical models developed in Section 14.2. The choices made by survey respondents from a list intended to capture a variety of possible motivations suggest that the theoretical discussion does capture important elements of the decision to use flexible staffers. As shown in Table 14.3, among those using at least one of the three flexible staffing arrangements 90 per cent checked at least one factor that might be put under the broad heading of variability in demand – 'special projects', 'seasonal needs' or 'provide a buffer for regular staff against downturns in demand'. While only 22 per cent of the user population checked 'provide a buffer against downturns in demand', 42 per cent of the top 10 per cent of users indicated that this

**Table 14.3**

Percentage of Respondents Reporting Various Reasons for Use of Agency Temporaries, Short-Term Hires and On-Call Workers

|  | Agency temporaries | Short-term hires | On-call workers | Any of the preceding |
|---|---|---|---|---|
| Special projects | 70 | 56 | 51 | 77 |
| Seasonal needs | 24 | 53 | 39 | 52 |
| Provide a buffer for regular staff against downturns in demand | 14 | 8 | 20 | 22 |
| Any of the above | 79 | 84 | 73 | 90 |
| Fill vacancy until a regular employee is hired | 61 | 15 | 34 | 60 |
| Fill in for absent regular employee | 74 | 42 | 68 | 80 |
| Either of the above | 88 | 48 | 72 | 89 |
| Identify good candidates for regular jobs | 16 | 14 | 9 | 23 |
| Special expertise possessed by flexible staffer | 12 | 13 | 34 | 29 |
| Prefer not to hire regular employees for some ongoing jobs | 15 | 10 | 13 | 20 |
| Other | 2 | 10 | 9 | 11 |
| Sample size | 338 | 282 | 158 | 412 |
| Total number of users | 339 | 282 | 161 | 413 |

was one of their reasons for using flexible staffers. In addition, 89 per cent of users included at least one factor that might be put under the broad heading of fluctuation in the labor supply of regular employees – 'fill vacancy until a regular employee is hired' or 'fill in for absent regular employee'.

How important are flexible staffers in employers' overall staffing strategies? The fact that flexible staffing arrangements account for less than 2 per cent of employment at responding firms over the course of the year might at first blush suggest that they are of little strategic importance. But on further reflection, it is obvious that flexible staffers could account for an even smaller part of total average employment but still absorb a substantial fraction of the day-to-day and month-to-month fluctuation in demand and/or labor supply. Table 14.4 reports respondents' answers to a set of questions concerning the importance of each of a number of strategies for absorbing fluctuations in the responding organization's workload. The strategy most often mentioned as 'very important' or 'somewhat important' for absorbing workload fluctuations was the use of overtime; however, the second and third most frequently mentioned strategies were the use of agency temporaries and the use of short-term hires. Altogether, 36 per cent of the survey respondents said that at least one of the three flexible staffing arrangements was 'very important' for absorbing workload fluctuations and an additional 48 per cent said that at least one was 'somewhat important'. Not surprisingly, heavy users of flexible staffers – those in the top 10 per cent of the overall use intensity distribution – were even more likely to say that at least one of the three flexible staffing

**Table 14.4**
Importance of Various Approaches to Absorbing Fluctuations in Organizations' Workloads

|  | *Percentage of all organizations reporting approach:* | |
| --- | --- | --- |
|  | *Very important* | *Somewhat important* |
| Overtime | 55 | 36 |
| Reduced workweeks | 7 | 18 |
| Temporary layoffs | 18 | 20 |
| Management of inventories | 26 | 15 |
| Agency temporaries | 19 | 46 |
| Short-term hires | 13 | 42 |
| On-call workers | 18 | 17 |
| Any of the above three flexible staffing arrangements | 36 | 48 |

*Notes:* The percentages in this table are based upon 433 responses. Other responses include 'not important', 'not applicable', and 'don't know'; in addition, some respondents did not indicate every approach's importance.

arrangements was 'very important' (78 per cent) or 'somewhat important' (17 per cent) for absorbing workload fluctuations.

## 14.3(d)  Organizational Characteristics Associated with
Flexible Staffing Use

Perhaps the most interesting question concerning US employers' use of
flexible staffing arrangements is what accounts for the tremendous
cross-organization variation in the share of labor input accounted for by
flexible staffers. The theoretical discussion implied that the use of flexible
staffers is likely to be greatest where the relative cost of using flexible
staffers is low, demand is highly variable, and the costs of alternative
shock-absorbing strategies are high. The survey questionnaire was
designed to yield proxies for a number of these organizational characteristics.

The fraction of the organization's workforce represented by a union
can be thought of as one proxy for the relative costs of using flexible
staffers; unions typically oppose the use of flexible staffers and thus
likely raise the costs associated with using them. The survey included
two questions that asked respondents to indicate whether the demand
for their organization's product or service was highly or somewhat
seasonal, and whether it was highly or somewhat variable across years.
The answers to these questions serve as proxies for the variability
in organizations' demand. One might also expect organizations that had
recently experienced either rapid growth or rapid shrinkage to be more
uncertain concerning their future staffing needs and thus to place greater
reliance on flexible staffing arrangements; the absolute value of the
proportional change in the organization's employment between
December 1980 and December 1985 serves as an employment trend
measure.[17] No questions pertaining to the costs of alternative modes of
accommodating demand and/or labor supply fluctuations were included
on the survey questionnaire; however, one might expect these costs to
differ across industries, particularly between manufacturing and non-
manufacturing industries, and possibly across units of different sizes. In
addition, organizations with a stronger emphasis on job security and
long-term employment relationships for their regular employees might
find it more difficult to adjust through hiring and firing and, thus, make
greater use of flexible staffers; to assess this hypothesis, I compared
flexible staffing usage by low-turnover, high-wage, non-union organizations that had not laid off any workers in the past five years to that by
other organizations.

Table 14.5 reports some simple tabulations of the mean characteristics
of high-intensity users, low-intensity users and non-users of flexible
staffing arrangements.[18] High-intensity users have much lower unionization rates than either low-intensity users or non-users. High-intensity
users are also more likely to say that their demand is highly seasonal and
to say that it is highly variable across years. Both the mean absolute
percentage change in employment between 1980 and 1985 and the

**Table 14.5**

Mean Characteristics of High-Intensity Users, Low-Intensity Users, and Non-users of Flexible Staffing Arrangements

| | Top 10 per cent of users | Bottom 50 per cent of users | Non-users |
|---|---|---|---|
| Proportion of non-exempt workforce unionized | 0.097 (30) | 0.264 (154) | 0.229 (25) |
| Demand highly seasonal (yes = 1) | 0.028 (31) | 0.020 (167) | 0.000 (29) |
| Demand somewhat seasonal (yes = 1) | 0.232 (31) | 0.295 (167) | 0.345 (29) |
| Demand highly variable from year to year (yes = 1) | 0.119 (30) | 0.049 (168) | 0.071 (28) |
| Demand somewhat variable from year to year (yes = 1) | 0.707 (30) | 0.624 (168) | 0.750 (28) |
| Absolute value of proportional change in employment, 1980–85 | 0.829 (29) | 0.396 (150) | 0.265 (26) |
| Manufacturing (yes = 1) | 0.638 (31) | 0.633 (170) | 0.620 (29) |
| Number of employees in unit | 715 (31) | 1618 (170) | 647 (29) |
| Low-turnover, no-layoff, high-wage, non-union employer (yes = 1)[a] | 0.148 (30) | 0.061 (142) | 0.043 (23) |

*Notes:* The number of responses on which each estimate is based is shown in parentheses. The estimates in the first and second columns are based upon the observations falling in the relevant percentiles of the use intensity distribution for all three categories of flexible staffers combined, weighted as described in Table 14.1, note (c).

[a]Employers in this category are non-union organizations reporting turnover rates in the bottom quartile of the distribution, no layoffs during the past five years, and wages in the top quartile of the distribution.

proportion of low turnover, no layoff, high-wage, non-union employers were larger among high-intensity users than among low-intensity users or non-users. There were no systematic differences across user groups in the proportion of manufacturing organizations or in mean unit size.

The univariate relationships that emerge from Table 14.5 could, of course, be misleading. The logical next step is to specify an appropriate multivariate model for analysis of the factors affecting flexible staffing use intensity. Let $Y_i$ represent organization $i$'s underlying propensity to use flexible staffing arrangements. Suppose that:

$$Y_i = X_i\beta + \varepsilon_i, \qquad (14.15)$$

where $X$ is a vector of organizational characteristics, $\beta$ is a parameter vector, and $\varepsilon$ is a normally distributed error term. For an organization that does not use flexible staffers, we know only that $Y_i$ is less than or equal to zero. The contribution to likelihood for such an organization is:

$$P1_i = P(X_i\beta + \varepsilon_i \leqslant 0) = F(-X_i\beta/\sigma), \tag{14.16}$$

where $F(\cdot)$ is the cumulative standard normal density and $\sigma$ is the standard deviation of the error term in (14.15). For a user organization that provides valid information on use intensity, the contribution to likelihood is:

$$P2_i = P(X_i\beta + \varepsilon_i = Y_i) = (1/\sigma) * f[(Y_i - X_i\beta)/\sigma], \tag{14.17}$$

where $f(\cdot)$ is the standard normal density. Specifying the contribution to likelihood for an organization that uses flexible staffers but provides no information or incomplete information on intensity of use is slightly more complicated. For a user organization that provides no use-intensity information, we know only that its use intensity is positive; in this case, $Y_i^r$, the lower bound on total flexible staffing use intensity, equals zero. For an organization that uses more than one category of flexible staffer but provides valid information for only a subset of the categories used, $Y_i^r$ equals the intensity of use in that subset of categories. The contribution to likelihood for a user organization with missing or incomplete use-intensity information is:

$$P3_i = P(X_i\beta + \varepsilon_i > Y_i^r) = 1 - F[(Y_i^r - X_i\beta)/\sigma]. \tag{14.18}$$

The log-likelihood for the entire sample is thus:

$$\ln L = \sum_{i=1}^{k_1} \ln P1_i + \sum_{i=k_1+1}^{k_1+k_2} \ln P2_i + \sum_{i=k_1+k_2+1}^{k_1+k_2+k_3} \ln P3_i \tag{14.19}$$

where $k_1$, $k_2$ and $k_3$ are the number of observations on non-users, users with valid use-intensity information and users with missing or incomplete use-intensity information, respectively.[19]

Estimates of the use-intensity model just described are reported in Table 14.6. The column 1 specification includes the proportion of the organization's workforce that is unionized and dummy variables that capture whether the organization's demand was reported to be seasonal or to vary from year to year. The union variable takes on a large and statistically significant negative coefficient; that is, unionized firms make less use of flexible staffing arrangements than non-union firms.[20] Organizations that report their demand to be either highly seasonal or highly variable from year to year make greater use of flexible staffing arrangements than other organizations. The column 2 specification is like that in column 1, but with the absolute value of the proportional change in the

**Table 14.6**

Organizational Characteristics Associated with the Use of Flexible Staffing Arrangements

| | Mean [S.D.] | Dependent variable = overall intensity of flexible staffing use | |
|---|---|---|---|
| | | (1) | (2) |
| Proportion of non-exempt workforce unionized | 0.207 (0.334) | −1.71 (0.67) | −1.72 (0.68) |
| Demand highly seasonal (yes = 1) | 0.028 (0.166) | 2.03 (0.70) | 2.08 (0.70) |
| Demand somewhat seasonal (yes = 1) | 0.319 (0.467) | −0.14 (0.39) | −0.12 (0.41) |
| Demand highly variable from year to year (yes = 1) | 0.059 (0.237) | 2.73 (0.64) | 2.74 (0.66) |
| Demand somewhat variable from year to year (yes = 1) | 0.650 (0.478) | 0.47 (0.56) | 0.47 (0.57) |
| Absolute value of proportional change in employment, 1980–85 | 0.415 (0.812) | — | 0.17 (0.22) |
| Manufacturing (yes = 1) | 0.575 (0.495) | — | 0.05 (0.38) |
| ln (number of employees in unit) | 6.313 (1.244) | — | −0.05 (0.17) |
| Low-turnover, no-layoff, high-wage, non-union employer (yes = 1)[a] | 0.063 (0.242) | — | −0.27 (0.97) |
| Constant | — | 1.47 (0.51) | 1.73 (1.16) |
| ln (likelihood) | — | −658.41 | −657.85 |

Notes: Both models were estimated using a Tobit procedure written by Robert H. Meyer which allows for both lower and upper truncation of the dependent variable. Among the 320 organizations for which all explanatory variables could be constructed, there were 20 non-users, 252 users providing complete use-intensity information, and 48 users providing no or only partial use-intensity information.

[a] Employers in this category are non-union organizations reporting turnover rates in the bottom quartile of the distribution, no layoffs during the past five years, and wages in the top quartile of the distribution.

organization's employment between 1980 and 1985, a manufacturing dummy variable, the logarithm of the number of employees in the unit, and a dummy variable intended to capture the organization's employment philosophy added as a separate control variable. The unionization, seasonal dummy and year-to-year demand variability dummy coefficients in this model are almost identical in magnitude to those in the previous model. Somewhat surprisingly, however, none of the added variables takes on significant coefficients.[21]

## 14.3(e)  Can the Survey Results Be Generalized?

Given the non-random nature of the survey sample, an obvious question is whether the survey findings are at all generalizable. Two specific concerns are, first, that the pattern of answers might have looked significantly different had the industry composition of the sample more closely mirrored that in the economy as a whole, and, second, that the organizations responding to the survey are unrepresentative in ways that are less easy to observe. Weighting the survey responses to correct for the discrepancy between the industry distribution of survey responses and the industry distribution of, alternatively, employment in establishments with 50 or more employees and total employment produced no noteworthy changes in the pattern of use frequency, use intensity, reasons for use or reported importance of use.[22] Of course, it should be kept in mind that the survey did not reach very small firms.

Beyond possible distortions related to the industry distribution of the responding organizations, I was concerned that organizations that did not use flexible staffers might have felt that the survey questionnaire did not apply to them and might therefore have been less likely to reply. For this reason, the short letter accompanying the follow-up mailing to those we had not heard from by the end of June emphasized that we were interested in answers from all organizations, including those that made no use of flexible staffing arrangements. If my concern were warranted, one might expect the answers of those who replied following the first mailing to differ systematically from the answers of those who replied only after receiving this second letter. However, there were only minor differences between early and late responders' answers.[23]

It would be particularly reassuring if estimates of use frequency and use intensity based on the survey data could be shown to correspond to estimates from other sources. Unfortunately, there is little other information on flexible staffing use available; indeed, the paucity of information on flexible staffing usage was the primary motivation for carrying out the survey in the first place. The US Bureau of Labor Statistics does collect information on employment in the temporary help industry that provides one useful benchmark. As reported in Table 14.1, my survey results indicate that 77 per cent of employers used agency temporaries during 1985; agency temporaries added an average of 0.76 per cent to these firms' employment levels over the course of the year, which implies that agency temporaries accounted for an average of 0.58 per cent of total employment during 1985. BLS statistics on non-supervisory employment in the temporary help industry compared to total non-agricultural payroll employment, adjusted for the difference between average weekly hours in the temporary help industry compared to the economy as a whole, imply that agency temporaries accounted for an average of 0.60 per cent of hours worked during 1985.[24] My 0.58 per cent estimate of aggregate agency temporary help use intensity and the 0.60 per cent estimate based on the BLS data are remarkably close.

## 14.4 Conclusions

This paper represents a first look at employers' use of agency temporaries, short-term hires and on-call workers. My starting point was to hypothesize that variability in demand and stochastic variation in regular employees' labor supply should lead many employers to make use of one or more of these flexible staffing arrangements. The models in Section 14.2 developed these hypotheses more formally, and also yielded some additional implications concerning the likely characteristics of flexible staffing assignments and the characteristics of organizations likely to make the greatest use of flexible staffers.

Over 90 per cent of the employers responding to the survey described in Section 14.3 make at least some use of flexible staffing arrangements. On average, flexible staffers add 1.5 per cent to annual average employment at user firms; use intensity at a majority of organizations is well below 1.0 per cent, but it exceeds 10.0 per cent and even 20.0 per cent for a small number of organizations. Office/clerical, professional/technical and production/service assignments are common. Variability in product demand and in regular employees' labor supply are reported by most employers to be among the factors motivating their use of flexible staffers and over 80 per cent of survey respondents indicate that flexible staffers play an important role in absorbing workload fluctuations. Finally, organizations with a low percentage of their non-exempt workforce covered by collective bargaining agreements and organizations that report their demand to be either highly seasonal or highly variable across years make greater use of flexible staffing arrangements than other organizations.

While fluctuations in both output and input markets provide a central motivation for using flexible staffers, this does not imply that other reasons for using flexible staffers are never important. One possible alternative motivation is that flexible staffing arrangements permit employers to do a better job of screening candidates for regular positions.[25] Although very few organizations report this as a reason for their use of flexible staffers, a substantial number say they often or occasionally hire these flexible staffers into regular jobs. Identification of potential permanent hires thus seems to be, at this point, mainly an unanticipated benefit of the use of flexible staffing arrangements.[26]

With better data, one might be able to say more than I have done here about the determinants of flexible staffing use, and also something about whether and under what circumstances firms that incorporate flexible staffing use into their overall staffing strategy outperform firms that do not. Some of the same factors that lead firms to use flexible staffers may also lead to decisions to contract work out; these decisions are another important subject for future study.

Considerable recent interest has been focused on the question of how and why employers' decisions to use flexible staffers and to contract out have changed over time. Answers to questions concerning the relative magnitude of flexible staffing use in 1985 compared with 1980 suggest that agency temporary use, short-term hire use and on-call use have all grown.[27] The cross-section analysis carried out in this paper suggests two demand-side changes that could have contributed to growing use of flexible staffing arrangements: the decline in union coverage among US workers and what some evidence suggests may have been an increase in the variability of demand for many organizations' products and services (see Pindyck, 1984). But other factors seem likely to have been at work as well. Still on the demand side, the growing strength of anti-discrimination legislation and the erosion of the employment-at-will doctrine may have raised the perceived cost of reliance on a hire/fire adjustment strategy. In addition, many observers have pointed to the growing proportion of youth and women in the labor force; if these workers are more willing than adult men to take temporary and on-call positions, the relative wages of flexible staffers may have fallen and thus encouraged their greater use. Slack labor markets may also have contributed to employers' ability to restructure their employment relationships in ways they find advantageous. These hypotheses merit more careful investigation.

Finally, this paper has focused exclusively on employers' decisions concerning the use of flexible staffing arrangements and the role played by flexible staffers within the firm. The broader social implications of employers' reliance on flexible staffing arrangements should also be explored.

## Acknowledgements

This paper has benefited from numerous helpful comments on an earlier draft made by participants in the Employment, Unemployment and Hours of Work conference held at the Science Center, Berlin, 17–19 September 1986, and by workshop participants at MIT, NBER, the University of Michigan, and the University of California, Berkeley. Kelly Eastman provided outstanding assistance with all phases of the research. Both Abraham's and Eastman's work on this project has been supported by the Brookings Institution. Data collection was carried out in collaboration with the Bureau of National Affairs. The views expressed here are those of the author and should not be attributed to the trustees, officers or staff members of the Brookings Institution or the Bureau of National Affairs.

## Notes

1 Most of this earlier work has been concerned with firms' responses to fluctuations in product demand. Hart (1984b) discusses the choice between hours adjustment and employment adjustment, and also cites numerous other studies; see particularly Nickell (1978). Medoff (1979) discusses the allocation of the burden of adjustment to downturns across layoffs, quits and hours reductions in union and non-union settings. Topel (1982)

analyzes the strategic use of inventories as an alternative to varying employment and/or hours.

2  This model is much in the spirit of Piore (1980), who suggests that different employment arrangements are likely to evolve to cover the stable and the unstable components of demand.

3  In a perfectly competitive labor market in which workers' preferences for stable versus unstable work were static and firms' flexible staffing needs were uncorrelated, individual employers would face fixed relative costs of employing workers under alternative arrangements. This need not be true if labor markets are not perfectly competitive, workers' preferences change over time or firms' flexible staffing needs are correlated.

4  Shapiro and Stiglitz (1984) and Bulow and Summers (1986) offer formal analyses in which the relative costs of employing different types of workers diverge from their relative wages. They reason that fear of losing a high-paying job will inhibit worker shirking and that this inhibiting effect will be strongest where workers expect to remain in their jobs for a long time if not fired for poor performance. This reasoning suggests that it may make sense to pay market wages to those with short expected tenures (flexible staffers) and closely monitor their performance, but to pay above-market wages to those with longer expected tenures (regular employees), thereby saving on direct supervision costs. These analyses imply that the per-hour costs of using flexible staffers may exceed the per-hour costs of using regular employees even when flexible staffers are paid lower wages.

5  The firm maximizes expected profits subject to the constraint that

$$L_p + L_s/b \geqslant x$$

for all $x$. Given our assumptions, this implies that

$$L_s = b(x - L_p)$$

when $x > L_p$. This expression for $L_s$ has been substituted in equation (14.1).

6  This is less general but more tractable than writing the firm's labor supply function as $g(L)$, with density $f[g(L)]$.

7  The assumption that regular employees must be paid whether they work or not is appropriate for situations where most of the stochastic variation in regular employees' labor supply reflects paid vacations, paid sick leave or other paid time away from work, but not for situations where most of the stochastic variation reflects unpaid time away from work or unexpected quits. If regular workers are paid only for time actually worked, the optimizing employer uses relatively more regular employees and relatively fewer flexible staffers.

8  If $L$ equalled $x$, equation (14.14) could be rewritten

$$w_p = b w_s E(g),$$

but we have assumed

$$w_p < b w_s E(g).$$

Increases in $L$ lower the value of the right-hand side of equation (14.14). Given our initial assumptions, $L$ must be greater than $x$.

9 Many respondents did not provide the information needed to estimate on-call use intensity. Between mid-July and mid-August of 1986, my research assistant, Kelly Eastman, telephoned all 92 respondents who reported using on-call workers other than former regular employees; useful clarification was obtained from 55 of these 92 respondents.

10 Respondents who did not answer all the yes/no questions about whether they used each of the various flexible staffing arrangements were excluded from all analyses. I also excluded a very few replies from agricultural, mining and construction firms, one reply from a firm located in Puerto Rico, and two replies from firms whose industry and location could not be determined. Two respondents replied twice; in these cases, I used the information from the earlier reply.

11 The industry distribution of survey responses, the industry distribution of employment in establishments with 50 or more employees (excluding agriculture, mining, construction and government), and the industry distribution of total employment (again excluding agriculture, mining, construction and government) are as follows:

|  | Survey responses | 1984 employment in establishments with 50+ employees | Total 1984 employment |
|---|---|---|---|
| Manufacturing | 56.6% | 38.5% | 27.0% |
| Transport/utilities | 6.6 | 7.7 | 6.5 |
| Trade | 2.3 | 19.0 | 30.0 |
| Finance/insurance/real estate | 17.6 | 7.4 | 8.1 |
| Health care | 12.7 | 10.6 | 8.7 |
| Other services | 4.3 | 16.8 | 19.8 |

The numbers in the two right-hand columns come from United States Bureau of the Census (1986).

12 In the letter accompanying the first survey mailing, respondents were instructed that '[i]f staffing practices vary by facility or if you can provide more accurate information for particular facilities than for the company as a whole, please answer for one facility, preferably the largest'. Some replies apply to a single establishment; some apply to a division or subsidiary; and some apply to an entire firm. This makes meaningful comparison of the size distribution of responding organizations with other data difficult.

13 The best earlier study was carried out by Donald Mayall and Kristin Nelson (Mayall and Nelson, 1982; see also Mangum, Mayall and Nelson, 1985). Their data apply to 1981, a year in which use of flexible staffers might be expected to have been low; they collected information on whether firms used agency temporaries, short-term hires and on-call workers, but not on use intensity. Official government statistics provide information on temporary help industry employment but not on where agency temporaries actually work. See Carey and Hazelbaker (1986) for a discussion of these data.

14 Not all users of flexible staffing arrangements provided complete information on their intensity of use. The responses from those that did were weighted in inverse proportion to the response rate in the relevant use category (use agency temporaries only, use both agency temporaries and short-term hires, and so on). In defining use categories, those whose only on-call use consisted of sometimes having former regular employees come in to work were distinguished from other on-call users.

309

15 Mayall and Nelson (1982) and Mangum, Mayall and Nelson (1985) argue that the relative median assignment durations associated with each of the three flexible staffing arrangements reflect differences in their respective cost structures.

16 One might also hypothesize that managerial/administrative and sales personnel are particularly difficult to monitor, so that it is very expensive to use flexible staffers in these positions. It may also be relevant that managerial/administrative and sales personnel are most likely to represent the organization to the outside world.

17 This absolute value measure is more highly correlated with flexible staffing use intensity than the proportional change in employment growth itself.

18 High-intensity users are defined here as those in the top 10 per cent of the use intensity distribution, and low-intensity users as those in the bottom 50 per cent. Qualitatively similar results were obtained with different high-intensity and low-intensity cut-offs.

19 This is just a Tobit model with both lower and upper truncation. See Tobin (1958).

20 In contrast, preliminary analysis indicates that unionized firms are significantly *more* likely to contract work out than non-union firms.

21 Requiring valid values for the four variables added in the column 2 model cuts the sample size available for estimation from 396 to 320; however, a model like that in column 1 estimated using the larger sample yields coefficient estimates very similar to those reported. The qualitative findings reported in Table 14.6 are very robust to changes in model specification.

22 A six-industry classification was used in constructing these weights: durables; non-durables; transportation, communication and utilities; finance, insurance and real estate; health care; and trade and other services. With a larger sample, it would have been possible to use finer industry classifications in constructing the weights, but this was not feasible here.

23 Early responders were slightly more likely than late responders to use short-term hires (68 per cent versus 55 per cent). However, early responders who used either agency temporaries or short-term hires also made slightly less intense use of these flexible staffing arrangements than late responders. In all other respects, the two groups' answers were statistically indistinguishable.

24 Non-supervisory employment in the temporary help industry averaged 691,300 and total non-agricultural payroll employment for the year averaged 97,519,000 in 1985. The ratio of these two numbers would overstate agency temporaries' contribution to total employment, since the payroll survey counts everyone who received any pay during a week as employed, and agency temporaries are more likely than the typical employee to work less than a full week. A reasonable adjustment is to weight each person on the temporary agency payrolls by the ratio of average weekly hours worked by non-supervisory employees in the temporary help industry (30.2 hours) to average weekly hours in the economy as a whole (35.9 hours, assuming that private sector supervisory employees average 40 hours per week and that weekly hours in the public sector average the same as in the private sector).

25 Bull and Tedeschi (n.d.) discuss this possibility. Fine and Gibbons (1986) consider screening of temporary workers in a somewhat different context, in which temporary workers never become permanent workers but the firm keeps some temporary workers on the job longer than others.

26 In response to a question that asked whether flexible staffers were 'often',

'occasionally', 'seldom' or 'never' hired into regular positions, 'often' or 'occasionally' was checked for 62 per cent of 339 organizations using agency temporaries, 55 per cent of 281 organizations making short-term hires and 44 per cent of 151 organizations using on-call workers. The survey questionnaire also included an open-ended question concerning unanticipated benefits and unanticipated drawbacks of using flexible staffers. Identification of potential permanent hires was mentioned as an unanticipated benefit more often than anything else, by 35 of the 81 respondents who cited any unanticipated benefit.

27  Altogether, 40 per cent of the 441 organizations providing information on changes in flexible staffing use intensity reported greater use of agency temporaries in 1985 than in 1980, while only 15 per cent reported less use; the corresponding percentages for short-term hires are 25 per cent and 12 per cent; and for on-call workers, 15 per cent and 4 per cent.

311

# COMMENT

## TOSHIAKI TACHIBANAKI

Katharine Abraham has made an important contribution to the understanding of flexible staffing arrangements which are becoming common
in some industrialized countries. She has constructed a neat theoretical
model in order to investigate why and when flexible staffing arrangements are adopted by employers. The empirical part adopts two
approaches to verify her theory. First, it presents several descriptive
statistics, such as averages or percentage shares. The second more
econometric, orientation uses a Tobit model with lower and upper
truncation. The two empirical approaches are fairly successful in
verifying her theoretical propositions, although they are not highly
sophisticated. We economists are sometimes inclined to apply fancy
econometric techniques to perform empirical research. It is, however,
also true that those fancy econometric techniques do not always produce
results that are different from those found by an informative and less
sophisticated method. Thus, I am willing to accept her empirical
methodologies and to acknowledge that the results are basically successful in verifying the theory. Also, the empirical part is very thoughtful
and careful. Aside form this, I have five comments on the paper.

First, Abraham often argues in the paper that flexible staffing
arrangements, such as agency temporaries, short-time hires and on-call
workers, are important means of dealing with variability in product
demand and labor supply. Her intention is to support this by presenting
several statistics on flexible staffing arrangements. However, she does
not report statistical evidence on alternatives to the use of flexible staffing
arrangements, such as varying the hours worked by regular workers,
hiring and/or firing regular workers and using inventories as a buffer.
Some brief mention of these alternatives is made, but no attempt is
made to ascertain their relative importance. Some readers, including the
reviewer, may suspect that an exaggerated importance is given to
flexible staffing arrangements in the US. There are two reasons for this
conjecture. First, she concludes that flexible staffers add 1.5 per cent to
annual average employment in user firms. Obviously, the contribution
of flexible staffers to the change in total man-hours would have been a
more appropriate basis on which to form a judgment. Secondly, the
great majority of American labor economists are also concerned with the
alternatives to the use of flexible staffing when they investigate changes
in employment and unemployment. In sum, it would be desirable to
assess the *relative* importance of flexible staffing arrangements in order to
convince readers that it is worthwhile investigating the issue of flexible
staffing arrangements. Otherwise, several readers may feel that the
author is concentrating on a very minor issue. She is aware of the
problem and she does present details on the *subjective* evaluations of
employers on flexible staffing. Those evaluations are not sufficient to

convince the reader that flexible staffing arrangements are important *quantitatively*.

Secondly, related to the above comment, I believe that overtime hours may be a substitute for the use of flexible staffing arrangements. An earlier version of this paper, which was presented at the conference, discussed this issue substantially, and contained some interesting results. The current version, however, eliminates the issue of the relationship between overtime hours and flexible staffing for unknown reasons. I personally regret this.

Thirdly, the author presents two separate reasons why employers use flexible staffing arrangements. One is demand variability and the other is stochastic variation in labor supply. When one of these is considered independently of the other, no problem occurs. I wonder what happens if the two reasons are taken into account simultaneously? This is probably more representative of the real world. In the two extreme cases, the net effect of these two gives either (1) no incentive to adopt any flexible staffing or (2) double incentives for flexible staffing. It might be necessary to keep in mind that the author's theoretical development of flexible staffing arrangements works only in a restrictive world.

Fourthly, the author presents a hypothesis that unions typically oppose the use of flexible staffers. This has been supported by a statistically significant negative coefficient on the union variable in the econometric estimation. Why are unions opposed? The author suggests that the costs associated with using flexible staffers in unionized firms provide a possible answer. The reasoning here is not too clear. Suppose that there are no significant differences in variability in sales and in labor supply between unionized and non-unionized firms. Both types of firm have to deal with adjustments in employment. Unions typically oppose the frequent use of changes in employment in order to protect their privileges as 'insiders'. Thus, it is possible to hypothesize that unionized firms have to use flexible staffers more frequently than non-unionized firms because the latter experience no opposition to frequent changes in employment. If the popular 'insider' theory was valid, it would be predicted that unionized firms lay relatively *more* stress on the use of flexible staffers. The statistical analysis, however, does not support this prediction. In other words, the author's interpretation is not the only story and the issue can only be settled by further investigation. At least the author addresses an important open question.

Finally, the paper concentrates on employers' preferences, that is, the demand side of flexible staffers. It would be interesting to inquire into the supply side as well. Important supply questions include: 'Who are hired as flexible staffers?' or 'Are they voluntarily working as flexible staffers?' Obviously, the working of the labor market for flexible staffers is assessed by an interaction of demand and supply. It might be difficult to integrate the supply side at this stage. This is a subject for future work.

# CHAPTER 15

# The Structure and Short-run Adaptability of Labor Markets in Japan and the United States

MASANORI HASHIMOTO and JOHN RAISIAN

## 15.1 Introduction

In contemporary Japan, at least two economic barometers are portrayed as the envy of the United States. First, economic growth rates, as measured by the growth in real gross national product (GNP), have averaged 7.1 per cent per year in Japan during the period 1961–85, compared to 3.1 per cent in the United States – an appreciable difference.[1] Second, economy-wide unemployment rates during roughly the same period, 1959–83, averaged 1.7 per cent in Japan, as compared to 6.0 per cent in the United States.[2] Thus, in Japan, the rate of long-term economic growth is more than double, and the rate of unemployment is nearly one-quarter, the respective rates observed for the United States.

There has been much speculation about the factors responsible for the high growth and low unemployment environment of Japan. Japanese labor markets are often described as having unique institutional features that have potential for explaining the observed differential economic growths. Lifetime employment practices, bonus payments and cooperative work environments are mentioned frequently in this regard.

The objective of this research is to uncover some of the empirical details relating to the organization of Japanese and US labor markets, and to highlight some of the common employment practices that prevail in the two countries. In particular, we argue that an important clue for understanding the fundamental differences of economic performance between the countries is contained in the way employment, hours of work and worker compensation vary with short-run demand disturbances. We will document some of the empirical regularities that are observed as demand conditions change, focusing on the manufacturing sectors of the two countries. We maintain that Japanese workers

314

accumulate greater amounts of firm-specific capital than their US counterparts. If this hypothesis has merit, an explanation for this phenomenon becomes the next important link of inquiry. We will offer a plausible hypothesis in this vein based on lower 'transaction costs' prevailing in Japanese organizations.

## 15.2 A Closer Look at Output Growth and Unemployment Rates

We begin by presenting some facts on the economic performance of Japan and the United States as described by output growth statistics and unemployment rates. While economy-wide US growth rates in real GNP normally have been around 3 per cent since 1960, Japanese rates have shifted from double-digit levels of around 11 per cent during the 1960s to rates of around 5 per cent in the 1970s and 1980s. Thus, while overall economic growth continues to be higher in Japan than in the US, the differential in the growths has narrowed appreciably, from an 8 percentage point differential to only 2 percentage points.

In the manufacturing sector, real output growth has averaged 12.1 per cent in Japan over the period 1951–83, comparing favorably to the US rate of 3.1 per cent. In both countries, output growth has trended downward since 1951 – by 0.4 percentage points per year in Japan and by 0.1 percentage points per year in the US.[3] Although the differential has narrowed rather dramatically between the two countries, the relative advantage in output growth as of the early 1980s for the Japanese manufacturing sector remains more pronounced (6 per cent versus 2 per cent in the US) than the advantage for the Japanese economy as a whole (5 per cent versus 3 per cent in the US).

Differential growths in labor productivity (i.e. output per hour or per worker) are mainly responsible for the differences in output growth rates between the two countries, rather than differential labor force growths or growths in hours worked. In Japan, the civilian labor force steadily grew by 1.2 per cent per year after 1960, while in the US the corresponding figure is a higher rate of 2.2 per cent. Thus, as of the early 1980s, the growth in real GNP per labor force participant was around 4 per cent in Japan and 1 per cent in the US. In manufacturing, the growth in real output per hour has remained steady in the US at approximately 2.5 per cent per year since the early 1950s. In Japan, the rate of growth in output per hour has trended downward from around 10 per cent in the 1950s to around 7.5 per cent in the early 1980s. Even with the declining trend in labor productivity growth in Japan, the rate remains three times that of the United States.[4]

Another commonly used measure of labor market performance is the unemployment rate. Reported unemployment rates for the United States are consistently three to four times higher than for Japan. While rates in both countries have been trending upward for the past three decades, the ratio of the rates for the two countries has remained remarkably unchanged. Moreover, the coefficients of variation for the two countries (i.e. the ratios of standard deviations to means) over the period 1959–83 are identical at 0.28; the relative variability is the same for the two countries, with only the means differing substantially.

Why are unemployment rates so low in Japan? One source of the differential magnitudes is differing statistical definitions of unemployment between the two countries. The Japanese unemployment rate data used here are already slightly modified by the US Bureau of Labor Statistics to conform better to the US concept of unemployment – for example, unpaid family workers working less than 15 hours per week are omitted from those counted as employed in Japan, consistent with the treatment of these individuals in the US.[5] However, the treatment of layoffs and the job search period used in the statistical surveys in the development of the underlying data differs substantially in the two countries, and these differences remain uncorrected in our unemployment rate series.

In Japan, persons on layoff awaiting recall are categorized as employed rather than unemployed, being regarded as 'with a job, but not at work'. Even if laid-off individuals in Japan were instead counted as unemployed persons, unemployment rates would increase by only around 10 per cent and not significantly alter the dramatic differential between the countries (see Moy and Sorrentino, 1981).[6] The reason layoffs do not close the gap to a greater degree is that layoffs as a proportion of the labor force typically amount to only 0.2 per cent in Japan, compared to 1.0 per cent in the US – one-fifth the size. This observation may well be affected by the unemployment insurance (UI) framework present in Japan after 1975, where UI compensation is available to workers placed on short-time schedules – i.e. fewer days worked per week (see Sorrentino, 1976, p. 22); in the US, workers are not eligible for UI compensation on the basis of short-time schedules. An alternative adjustment that illuminates the relatively common practice of temporary layoffs in the US is suggested by Ito's results (1984, Table 2); namely, the differential incidence of temporary layoffs between the countries accounts for about 25 per cent of the unemployment rate differential in recent years.

Another significant definitional difference relates to the length of time for which job search activity is applied in the determination of unemployment. In the US anyone who searched for a job during the four weeks prior to the survey date is counted as unemployed, whereas in Japan only those who sought jobs during a single reference week are included among the unemployed. Obviously, the Japanese definition tends to exclude individuals who seek employment infrequently, whereas these same individuals are more likely to be categorized as unemployed in the US. According to Hamada and Kurosaka (1984, Table 2), an adjustment of the Japanese definition to the US concept would raise the unemployment rate for men in 1980 by only a miniscule amount (i.e. 0.5 per cent), but would raise the rate for women by 55 per cent.

A second source of explanation for the overall unemployment rate differential relates to underlying compositional differences. For example, there are pronounced differences in unemployment and labor force activity among youth (aged less than 25). In 1979, half of all unemployment in the US was experienced by individuals less than 25 years of age, though they accounted for only a quarter of the labor force. In Japan, only one-fifth of total unemployment pertained to this age category, while their labor force proportion amounted to one-eighth. Thus, while the overall unemployment rate in 1979 was three times higher in the US than in Japan, the rate pertaining to individuals aged 25 and above was just over twice as high. Not surprisingly, in both the US and Japan, youth are more likely to be unemployed than other members of the labor force. In the US however, the likelihood is much higher. The ratio of the share of unemployment to labor force share for youth is 2.5 in the US in contrast to the Japanese ratio of 1.6. In the US, not only are there twice as many youth in the labor force in relative terms, they are more likely to be unemployed than their Japanese counterparts.[7]

In sum, the statistics on output, productivity growth and unemployment suggest that Japan has indeed enjoyed a relatively high level of economic performance in recent decades. On the output and productivity side, growth remains higher in Japan, though it has gradually converged to growth experienced by the US. With regard to unemployment rates, a significant differential persists, with Japan exhibiting lower rates than the US, even when layoff, length of job search and youth considerations are compensated for.

## 15.3  Labor Force Characteristics

In Japan, workers are commonly grouped into four basic categories: self-employed individuals, family workers, regular employees, and non-regular employees (i.e. temporary workers and day laborers). In recent years, self-employment and family workers have comprised 20 per cent of aggregate non-agricultural employment, a much higher fraction than the US figure of 8 per cent. Furthermore, more than two-thirds of this combined category for Japan are self-employed individuals. Thus, self-employment is more ubiquitous in Japan than in the US.

Among Japanese non-agricultural wage and salary workers (i.e. omitting self-employed and family workers), about 90 per cent are 'regular workers', the remaining 10 per cent being temporary workers or day laborers. Regular workers are employees with employment contracts of unspecified duration. In contrast, temporary workers and day laborers are under contracts having a specified period of employment, though such arrangements can always be renewed. We have no way of identifying this distinction for the US. For example, a student who is hired for a summer job is not distinguishable from a young household head having a permanent job. On the other hand, a fast-growing temporary help industry is identifiable in the US. This industry is made up of establishments engaged in supplying temporary help to other businesses, and currently accounts for 1 per cent of aggregate non-agricultural employment.[8]

Japanese women are more likely to be family workers than are men; in 1983, 14 per cent of female employment was attributable to the family worker category compared to 2 per cent for males. Self-employment percentages were similar for both women (12 per cent) and men (14 per cent). Among female non-agricultural wage and salary workers, about 80 per cent were regular workers, compared to 95 per cent for males. Thus, employed Japanese women are more likely to be family workers, temporary workers or day laborers than men. Also, more than a quarter of working women are on part-time schedules compared to 3 per cent of working men. Thus, Japanese women definitely appear to have a weaker attachment to the labor force as a whole. However, the notion that very few Japanese women are regular full-time workers is inaccurate and misleading.

The structure of employee compensation differs fundamentally between the two countries. In Table 15.1, we present the categories of employee compensation, albeit for production workers in the manufac-

**Table 15.1**
Structure of compensation for production workers in Japanese and US Manufacturing Industries

| Percentage of total compensation attributable to: | Japan | | | United States | | |
|---|---|---|---|---|---|---|
| | 1965 | 1971 | 1978 | 1966 | 1972 | 1977 |
| Direct compensation | 82.8 | 82.5 | 77.0 | 83.0 | 79.5 | 75.2 |
|   Wages and salaries | 64.6 | 61.2 | 56.7 | 82.4 | 79.0 | 74.8 |
|   Bonuses | 18.2 | 21.3 | 20.3 | 0.6 | 0.5 | 0.4 |
| Indirect compensation | 12.3 | 12.3 | 16.1 | 11.4 | 14.4 | 17.3 |
|   Pay for leave time | 3.2 | 3.2 | 4.7 | 5.6 | 6.2 | 6.9 |
|   In-kind payments | 4.2 | 4.1 | 4.0 | — | — | — |
|   Benefits | 4.9 | 5.0 | 7.4 | 5.8 | 8.2 | 10.4 |
| Legally required insurance | 4.8 | 5.2 | 6.9 | 5.5 | 6.2 | 7.4 |

*Notes:* Figures do not always sum precisely to 100 per cent owing to rounding. Wages and salaries include overtime premiums and shift differentials. Payments for leave time include vacation pay, holiday pay and personal leave pay. Pay for sick leave is part of benefits payments. In-kind payments include costs to the employer of goods and services provided free or at reduced costs, such as food or housing, and cash allowances paid in lieu of direct in-kind payments. Benefit payments include employer costs associated with health, life and disability insurance plans and any other benefits provided to the employee.

*Source:* US Bureau of Labor Statistics, *Handbook of Labor Statistics*, 1985, Table 134.

turing sector. As of the late 1970s, the proportions of total compensation going to direct, indirect and legally required insurance components were not that different for the two countries. Direct payments (i.e. wages, salaries and bonuses) constituted 75–77 per cent of total compensation, indirect payments (i.e. paid leave, in-kind payments and the provision of non-pecuniary benefits) amounted to 16–17 per cent, and legally required insurances (e.g. unemployment insurance) accounted for about 7 per cent. However, the division between wages and salaries on the one hand and bonuses on the other is appreciably different between the countries. While bonuses in the US are extremely rare among production workers, they amounted to 20 per cent of total compensation in Japan, and more than a quarter of direct compensation.[9] Over time, the direct compensation component has declined, but this decline is attributable solely to the declining proportion of the wage and salary component. Consequently, bonuses have increased as a fraction of direct compensation. Moreover, the proportion of total compensation going to bonus payments in Japan has remained steady. All other components of compensation have been growing over time in both countries.

Finally, the degree of job attachment represents a major difference between the countries. For example, as of 1979, the median job tenure of a Japanese male worker was eight years, double that of a US male.[10] Nearly half of Japanese male workers had employment tenures of 10 years or more, compared to 30 per cent for US counterparts. Cross-sectional evidence of tenure distributions by age category suggests that a typical Japanese man will hold around five jobs over his working life, whereas his US counterpart will hold 11 jobs.[11]

In the next section, we focus on the job attachment issue as it relates to employment variability over business cycles. We will also assess compensation and hours worked variabilities over business cycles for purposes of comparison and ranking of importance. The overall pattern of short-term adjustments in employment, hours and compensation will be characterized for each of the countries to discern the differences in responses to short-run shifts in demand and production.

## 15.4 Adjustments of Labor Market Measures to Changes in Output

The finding that individuals hold fewer jobs over their working lives in Japan than in the US could reflect two underlying processes. First, workers and firms in the US may be more likely to attach and separate in an effort to realize more efficient and productive matches, leading to greater job mobility in the US. It could also be the case that Japanese labor market participants may be more successful in identifying high-quality matches prior to entering an employment arrangement, thereby necessitating fewer job separations over a lifetime. Regardless of any US–Japanese difference in the efficiency of the job-matching process, we judge that this explanation does not hinge on differential responses to cyclical vagaries. Instead, the observation of greater job instability in the US may be attributable to a greater reliance on employment adjustments by US employers when adapting to changes in demand conditions. It is our objective to investigate the empirical correlations of changes in output and associated adjustments in several labor market measures in an attempt to better understand the underpinnings of the lifetime employment characteristics of the two countries.

All of our evidence in this regard pertains to the manufacturing sectors of the two countries, because of the availability of detailed and comparable series on compensation, hours worked and employment. While the manufacturing activities of the two countries do not dominate economy-wide commerce, they none the less are sizeable sectors, represent similar fractions of their respective workforces, and have been declining in terms of their employment shares at similar rates over the past decade.[12] Short-term variabilities of the real value of manufacturing output are also similar. As already mentioned, Japan has enjoyed an average growth rate in real output of 11.4 per cent over the period 1951–83, far higher than the 3.1 per cent rate of the US. However, the standard deviation of output growth is 7.7 per cent in Japan and 6.1 per cent in the United States, a more or less similar magnitude.[13]

Table 15.2 contains various descriptive and regression statistics on employment, weekly hours worked and real hourly compensation for manufacturing industries covering the period 1951–83. These statistics are computed from time series of data gathered from establishments and available from the US Bureau of Labor Statistics. The data, typically in the form of indexes, are transformed into year-to-year changes in the logarithm of the labor market magnitude. Thus, the transformation approximates the percentage change in the labor market measure from the previous year's level.[14]

Among the descriptive statistics in Table 15.2, the most striking comparative finding is that the variability of employment is higher in the US, and the variability of compensation is higher in Japan. This is evident in the standard deviations of the measures across the countries, but is also more appropriately apparent from output-normalized variabilities of the employment and compensation measures. An output-normalized variability is the ratio of the standard deviation of a labor market measure in question to the standard deviation of the real output measure. It indicates the variability of a labor market measure for a given degree of output variability, thus avoiding possible misinterpretation of the overall variability in a labor market measure.[15] The output-normalized variabilities for employment are 0.67 in the US and 0.46 in Japan; for the hourly compensation measure, the magnitudes are 0.50 in the US and 0.25 in Japan. Thus, employment variability (for a given variability in real output) is nearly 50 per cent greater in the US, while hourly compensation variability is only half as large. Also, weekly hours variability is slightly smaller in the US, by about 10 per cent. In the US, over the period of analysis, employment growth is most variable,

**Table 15.2**

Variabilities and Growths in Labor Market Measures for Manufacturing
Industries: Japan and the United States, 1951–83

| Labor market measure | Descriptive statistics | | | Regression statistics | | |
|---|---|---|---|---|---|---|
| | Indicator | Japan | US | Coefficient | Japan | US |
| Employment | Growth rate | | | Output | 0.3329 | 0.5802 |
| | – Mean | 0.0299 | 0.0061 | | (5.7) | (9.6) |
| | – Standard deviation | 0.0356 | 0.0408 | Constant | −0.0081 | −0.0118 |
| | | | | | (1.0) | (2.9) |
| | Output-normalized variability | 0.4642 | 0.6711 | $R^2$ | 0.51 | 0.75 |
| Weekly hours worked | Growth rate | | | Output | 0.1241 | 0.1606 |
| | – Mean | −0.0019 | −0.0004 | | (4.0) | (9.1) |
| | – Standard deviation | 0.0163 | 0.0114 | Constant | −0.0161 | −0.0053 |
| | | | | | (3.8) | (4.5) |
| | Output-normalized variability | 0.2125 | 0.1875 | $R^2$ | 0.34 | 0.73 |
| Real hourly compensation | Growth rate | | | Output | 0.1175 | 0.0362 |
| | – Mean | 0.0527 | 0.0191 | | (1.4) | (0.8) |
| | – Standard deviation | 0.0381 | 0.0152 | Constant | 0.0393 | 0.0180 |
| | | | | | (3.3) | (6.0) |
| | Output-normalized variability | 0.4967 | 0.2500 | $R^2$ | 0.06 | 0.02 |

*Notes*: All of the measures are converted to year-to-year changes in logarithmic values to approximate annual percentage changes. The output-normalized variability refers to the ratio of the standard deviation of the labor market measure to the standard deviation of the output measure. Magnitudes in parentheses are absolute *t*-values.

*Source*: Data series originate from the US Bureau of Labor Statistics, *Handbook of Labor Statistics*, 1985.

followed by compensation growth and then by hours growth. In Japan, employment and compensation growth exhibit roughly equal variabilities, followed by hours growth.

These descriptive statistics have a shortcoming in that they do not correlate percentage changes in output with the percentage changes in the labor market measures to distinguish a direct association of these measures from either random variability or variability attributable to trends throughout the period. To ameliorate this shortcoming, we regress the percentage change in each of the labor market measures on the percentage change in real output. Estimated regression coefficients (along with $R^2$ statistics) are presented in Table 15.2 alongside the descriptive statistics.

With regard to employment, the output coefficient is positive and significant for each country, though substantially higher for the US. A 10 percentage point decline in the growth of manufacturing output is associated with a 3.3 percentage point decline in the growth rate of Japanese employment and a 5.8 percentage point decline in the growth rate of US employment. Consequently, employment growth in the US is substantially more procyclically affected by short-term movements in output than in Japan.[16,17]

Turning to weekly hours worked, output coefficients are also positive and significant, but in this case the US coefficient is only slightly higher than Japan's. The same 10 percentage point decline in output growth amounts to a 1.2 percentage point reduction in hours growth in Japan and a 1.6 percentage point decline in the US. These magnitudes are approximately one-third of the employment effects in the respective countries.[18,19]

For hourly compensation, neither of the output coefficients is statistically significant by conventional standards, and the US estimate is below that of Japan. Here, a 10 percentage point decline in output growth is associated with declines in compensation growth of 1.2 percentage points in Japan and a meager 0.4 percentage points in the US. In Japan, the output coefficient is similar in size to its counterpart in the hours equation; therefore it, too, is one-third the size of the employment adjustment. In the US, real compensation is virtually unrelated to movements in output.[20] Thus, even though the output-normalized compensation variabilities are rather substantial, especially in Japan, compensation variabilities in fact prove not to be strongly correlated with changes in output variability.

A comparison of the cyclical sensitivities of compensation and productivity (i.e. output per hour) reveals whether or not compensation is insulated from cyclical vagaries. The output coefficient in a regression for productivity growth can be deduced from the estimated output coefficients for the employment and hours specifications. Since the product of measured productivity, weekly hours and employment is a virtual identity to measured total output, it is straightforward to show that the output coefficient in a productivity regression equation is simply one minus the sum of the output coefficients from the employment and hours equations. The implied coefficients amount to .543 for Japan and .259 for the US. Thus, productivity is much more procyclical in Japan than in the US, which is not at all surprising given the greater procyclical sensitivity found for employment and hours in the US. Moreover, the observation that the variability of compensation growth (associated with changes in output growth) is substantially smaller than the variability of productivity growth (for the same changes in output growth) suggests that workers in both countries have a kind of wage 'insurance' that stabilizes compensation, substantially protecting them during downturns in output growth. In Japan, the output coefficient associated with

322

compensation growth is only 22 per cent of the output coefficient associated with productivity growth; in the US this factor amounts to an even lower 14 per cent.

Thus, the regression statistics portray the United States as utilizing quantity adjustments (i.e. employment and, to a lesser extent, hours per week) to a much greater degree than Japan as a way of adapting to short-term changes in output growth. There is a hint that compensation growth in Japan is procyclically impacted by changes in output growth, though the correlation is rather weak. In the US on the other hand, compensation growth is found to be uncorrelated with movements in output growth, strengthening the idea of short-run wage rigidity over business cycles.

Additional evidence on production workers in manufacturing industries is presented in Table 15.3.[21] The underlying data are available only for the period beginning in 1968. Output coefficients associated with various labor market measures are estimated for production workers as well as for all workers in manufacturing when possible to facilitate a comparison of coefficient estimates covering the same time period. In both countries, output coefficients associated with weekly hours worked are larger for production workers than for manufacturing workers as a whole, though the difference is not appreciable. The most notable change from the results of Table 15.2 is the size of the compensation effect for the US production workers: a 10 percentage point decline in output growth is associated with a 2.1 percentage point decline in compensation growth among production workers, compared with a 0.5 percentage point decline among all manufacturing workers during this

**Table 15.3**

Regression Coefficients on Output for All Workers and Production Workers in Manufacturing Industries: Japan and the United States, 1968–83

| Labor market measure | Japan | | US | |
|---|---|---|---|---|
| | All workers | Production workers | All workers | Production workers |
| Employment | 0.2873 | — | 0.5458 | — |
| | (4.2) | | (5.5) | |
| Weekly hours worked | 0.1701 | 0.2044 | 0.1672 | 0.2004 |
| | (2.4) | (2.4) | (6.8) | (6.6) |
| Real hourly compensation | 0.2108 | 0.2321 | 0.0503 | 0.2125 |
| | (1.0) | (1.0) | (0.9) | (2.9) |
| Real hourly wage | — | 0.2712 | — | 0.2117 |
| | | (1.2) | | (3.0) |

*Notes:* Regressions are specified as year-to-year changes in the logarithm of the labor market measure on year-to-year changes in the logarithm of real output in the manufacturing sector. Magnitudes in parentheses are absolute *t*-values.

*Source:* Data series originate from the US Bureau of Labor Statistics, *Handbook of Labor Statistics*, 1985.

period. In Japan, the compensation effect is nearly twice as large for this shorter time period than for the entire period (i.e. a 2.1 versus a 1.2 percentage point decline for a 10 percentage point decline in output), and this effect is not very different for production workers. Finally, compensation can be narrowed for production workers into a real hourly wage variable that includes bonus payments to Japanese workers. Whereas the compensation and wage effects are identical for US production workers, the output coefficient in the Japanese wage equation is slightly higher than that of the compensation equation, perhaps indicating a more cyclically sensitive bonus component.[22]

Thus, in the US, production workers exhibit compensation and hours growth adjustments, about equal in size, that are positively and significantly associated with changes in output growth. Moreover, similar magnitudes of compensation and hours effects are found for Japanese production workers when compared to US production workers, though they are statistically less significant. The key finding, however, is that production workers and non-production workers exhibit very similar adjustments in hours and compensation associated with changing output growths in Japan, whereas compensation of production workers in the US is much more procyclically affected by changes in output growth than is the case for non-production workers.

Further investigation of the nature of wage and compensation adjustments reveals an important insight into the apparent differences in the underlying adjustment process for the two countries. Any overall compensation (or wage) adjustment can be separated into two component adjustments: (1) a change in compensation attributable to a change in hours worked holding output growth constant, and (2) a change in compensation attributable to a change in output growth holding hours worked constant. The former adjustment can be characterized as a short-term trade-off between compensation and worker utilization (i.e. hours worked), established contractually in the labor market, either explicitly or implicitly, for situations where output growth is unchanged. The latter adjustment can be characterized as the short-term adjustment in compensation that is established by employers and employees as demand conditions change in the absence of utilization adjustments. Thus, a reduction in output growth may result in a reduction in compensation growth, with the latter reduction attributable to employees experiencing wealth losses associated with the slack conditions and/or employers choosing a reduction in utilization along the compensation–utilization trade-off.

With regard to the compensation–utilization trade-off holding output growth constant, it is easy to imagine two very different locuses. One pertains to a typical 'salaried' worker who is paid a fixed weekly income independent of any short-term adjustments in hours worked during the course of a week. For this arrangement, hourly compensation and weekly hours worked would exhibit a negative relation, *ceteris paribus*. An alternative arrangement might call for premium wages for increased hours of work during the course of a week – e.g. 'time-and-a-half for

**Table 15.4**

Compensation and Wage Adjustments Attributable to Separate Output and Hours Variations in Manufacturing Industries: Japan and the United States, 1968–83

| Labor market measure | Japan | | US | |
|---|---|---|---|---|
| | All workers | Production workers | All workers | Production workers |
| **Real hourly compensation:** | | | | |
| Output coefficient | 0.6548 | 0.6580 | −0.0994 | 0.1331 |
| | (5.0) | (3.9) | (0.9) | (0.9) |
| Hours coefficient | −2.6100 | −2.0836 | 0.8949 | 0.3964 |
| | (6.3) | (4.7) | (1.5) | (0.6) |
| **Real hourly wage:** | | | | |
| output coefficient | — | 0.7175 | — | 0.1458 |
| | | (4.6) | | (1.0) |
| Hours coefficient | — | −2.1835 | — | 0.3287 |
| | | (5.4) | | (0.5) |

*Notes:* All data are transformed into year-to-year changes in logarithmic values. Output and weekly hours coefficients are regression coefficients when both variables together are specified as right-hand-side variables in a single regression. The left-hand-side variable is either the real hourly compensation measure or the real hourly wage measure. Magnitudes in parentheses are absolute *t*-values.

*Source:* Data series originate from the US Bureau of Labor Statistics, *Handbook of Labor Statistics*, 1985.

overtime'. In this case, hourly compensation and weekly hours worked would exhibit a positive relation, *ceteris paribus*.

To assess the relevance of this distinction, we regress the compensation measure (as well as the wage growth measure) on both real output growth and weekly hours growth simultaneously. The coefficient estimates are reported in Table 15.4. Focusing on the results for production workers, adjustment processes are found to differ dramatically between the two countries. Recall from Table 15.3 that a 10 percentage point reduction in output growth was associated with a 2.3 percentage point reduction in compensation growth in Japan, and a similarly sized 2.1 percentage point reduction in the US. The underpinnings of these overall adjustments are very different, however. In Japan, the same 10 percentage point reduction in output growth is associated with a much greater 6.6 percentage point reduction in compensation growth holding hours growth constant. In the US, compensation growth is found to decline by only 1.3 percentage points holding hours growth constant.

A full characterization of these adjustments is portrayed in Figures 15.1 and 15.2. For Japan, two compensation–utilization trade-offs are

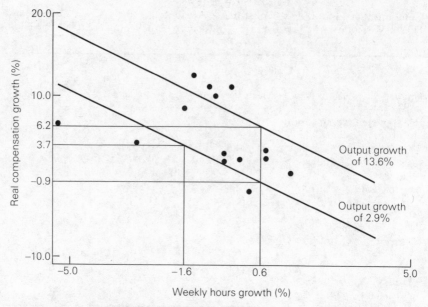

**Figure 15.1** Decomposing real compensation adjustments in Japan

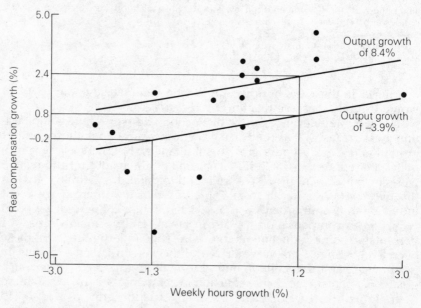

**Figure 15.2** Decomposing real compensation adjustments in the US

depicted for two different output growth situations: the higher output growth represents one standard deviation above the mean and the lower growth is one standard deviation below the mean.[23] For the high-growth situation, expected hours growth is 0.6 per cent and expected compensation growth is 6.2 per cent. The impact of a two standard deviation fall in output growth is then decomposed into the two conceptual effects. If weekly hours (and therefore weekly hours growth) were not to change, compensation growth is projected to fall substantially to −0.9 per cent. However, a concurrent reduction in hours worked to −1.6 per cent (as projected using the appropriate estimates of Table 15.3) has the effect of mitigating the reduction in compensation growth since compensation is projected to rise with reductions in hours; the net decline in compensation is from 6.2 per cent to 3.7 per cent rather than to −0.9 per cent. This observed negative trade-off between compensation and hours suggests that production workers in Japan tend to have salary arrangements, though the salary itself is procyclically responsive to movements in output growth.

In the United States, a two standard deviation reduction in output growth from 8.4 per cent to −3.9 per cent breaks down very differently from the Japanese situation. In the high output growth situation, expected compensation growth is 2.4 per cent and expected hours growth is 1.2 per cent. The reduction in output growth is projected to cause compensation growth to fall to 0.8 per cent holding hours constant. The expected reduction in hours growth from 1.2 per cent to −1.3 per cent has the effect of further reducing compensation growth to −0.2 per cent. Here, the compensation–utilization trade-off is suggestive of wage premiums being prevalent for increased utilization, so that the overall wage adjustment overstates the pure cyclical component – i.e. the change in compensation associated with a change in output growth holding utilization constant.

In these examples, overall compensation growth falls by 2.5 percentage points in Japan (from 6.2 to 3.7 per cent) and 2.6 percentage points (from 2.4 to −0.2 per cent) in the US – virtually identical magnitudes. The pure cyclical effect, however, indicates that compensation would have fallen by 7.1 percentage points (from 6.2 to −0.9 per cent) in Japan and only 1.6 percentage points (from 2.4 to 0.8 per cent) in the US. From this latter perspective, compensation is much more procyclical in Japan. Once again, estimates for all workers in Japanese manufacturing presented in Table 15.4 resemble those of production workers, suggesting no distinction between non-production and production workers. Moreover, the output coefficient in the wage growth equation is somewhat higher than its counterpart in the compensation growth equation, again plausibly attributable to greater procyclical movements in bonus payments. In the US, the findings for all workers in manufacturing reveal a smaller cyclical effect and a more pronounced positive relation between compensation and utilization than for production workers. This latter attribute is puzzling since the typical expectation is that non-production workers in the US are more likely to have salary arrangements and therefore the category of all workers to exhibit less of a positive trade-off.[24]

Additional disaggregations of employment, hours and compensation variabilities using US household data are presented in Table 15.5. Employment is often categorized as full time or part time, with the latter group thought to have less durable employer–employee attachments. For the part-time category, a further distinction is made between voluntarily working part time, and working part time for economic reasons.[25]

According to these data, a 10 percentage point decline in output growth is associated with a 5.4 percentage point decline in overall employment growth. However, the composition of the decline is not uniform among these categories. Surprisingly large reductions in employment growth are found for both full-time and voluntary part-time workers: 7.1 per cent and 6.8 per cent, respectively. Moreover, these declines are similar in magnitude, contrary to the general impression that the latter group has greater employment instability. However,

**Table 15.5**

Regression Coefficients on Output for Other Labor Market Measures in Manufacturing Industries: United States

| Labor market measure | Output coefficient |
|---|---|
| Employment of all workers (1958–83): | |
| Total | 0.5372 |
| | (6.8) |
| Full-time | 0.7125 |
| | (9.2) |
| Voluntary part-time | 0.6762 |
| | (3.5) |
| Part-time for economic reasons | −3.7072 |
| | (8.5) |
| | |
| Weekly hours for production workers (1957–83): | |
| Total | 0.2005 |
| | (8.0) |
| Overtime | 2.2222 |
| | (9.8) |
| Real hourly wage for production workers (1957–83): | |
| Overall average | 0.1711 |
| | (3.6) |
| Straight-time | 0.1094 |
| | (2.4) |

Notes: Regressions are specified as year-to-year changes in the logarithm of the labor market measure on year-to-year changes in the logarithm of real output in the manufacturing sector. Magnitudes in parentheses are absolute $t$-values.

Source: Data series originate from the US Bureau of Labor Statistics, *Handbook of Labor Statistics*, 1985.

employment growth of workers who are part time for economic reasons is projected to increase by 37.1 percentage points with the 10 percentage point decline in output growth. Thus, the overall decline in employment growth is somewhat understated because the hidden countercyclical employment growth of seemingly temporary part-time work dampens the decline in employment growth among full-time and voluntary part-time workers.

The same US household data base contains information on overtime hours for production workers. While a 10 percentage point decline in output growth is associated with a 2 percentage point decline in overall hours growth, it is not surprising to find that overtime hours growth is projected to decline by 22 percentage points.[26]

Finally, employed individuals in US households report a straight-time wage rate as well as information on labor income and hours worked, allowing the calculation of an overall average hourly wage. The results presented in Table 15.5 are consistent with the compensation decomposition results for the US presented earlier. A 10 percentage point decline in output growth is associated with a 1.7 percentage point decline in the overall hourly wage growth and a 1.1 percentage point decline in the straight-time wage growth. The latter effect is akin to a pure cyclical effect, and is lower than the overall effect owing to the loss of premium wages associated with the decline in overtime hours growth.

Interesting disaggregations of short-term adjustments in Japanese employment and earnings measures for men are presented in Table 15.6. A 10 percentage point decline in output growth is associated with a 4.3 percentage point decline in the employment growth of non-production workers and a 5.2 percentage point decline in the employment growth of production workers – not a particularly striking contrast. However, the same 10 percentage point decline in output growth is associated with a relatively small reduction in the employment growth of regular workers amounting to 2.9 percentage points, and a 6.0 percentage point decline in the employment growth of temporary workers and day laborers. Thus, regular workers exhibit more employment stability than non-regular workers over the course of demand disturbances.

Using the Japanese data, wage variability can be separated into base wage and bonus components. For male production workers, a 10 percentage point decline in output growth is associated with a 3.9 percentage point decline in the growth of base earnings, a substantial magnitude by itself (though not statistically significant); but the same reduction in output growth is associated with an 11.9 percentage point decline in the growth of bonus earnings – a much greater procyclical effect. Similar though slightly smaller, output coefficients are observed for non-production workers.

In 1975, an important public policy initiative in Japan fundamentally affected labor markets – the Employment Insurance Law. This shifted the emphasis away from unemployment insurance directly provided by the government to workers dismissed from employment (the usual

**Table 15.6**
Regression Coefficients on Output for Additional Labor Market Measures for
Men in Manufacturing Insustries: Japan

| Labor market measure | Output coefficient |
| --- | --- |
| Employment (1959–83) | |
| Non-production workers | 0.4285 |
| | (3.7) |
| Production workers | 0.5220 |
| | (5.6) |
| Regular workers | 0.2886 |
| | (3.5) |
| Temporary workers/day laborers | 0.6008 |
| | (1.4) |
| | |
| Real Earnings (1965–83) | |
| Non-production workers: | |
| Base | 0.3486 |
| | (1.5) |
| Bonus | 1.1000 |
| | (4.8) |
| Production workers: | |
| Base | 0.3878 |
| | (1.9) |
| Bonus | 1.1900 |
| | (5.0) |

*Notes*: Regressions are specified as year-to-year changes in the logarithm of the labor market measure on year-to-year changes in the logarithm of real output in the manufacturing sector. Magnitudes in parentheses are absolute *t*-values.

*Source:* Data series originate from the *Japanese Yearbook of Labor Statistics*, various years.

conception of such programs) to a system in which subsidies are directed to employers for workers who are put on furlough, enabling employers to offer at least partial compensation during such periods and have the employee remain 'employed' by the firm (see Cole, 1979, and Taira and Levine, 1985, for details). One element of this initiative is a provision allowing for subsidies in circumstances where employers wish to implement short-time schedules – i.e. reduced days during a week or month (see Sorrentino, 1976).

It seems likely that such a scheme would have the effect of reducing 'employment' variability and increasing weekly hours variability, both because of the short-time work schedule provisions in the law and because there is an incentive for employers to retain on their payroll (i.e. 'employ') employees who are working zero hours during an extended furlough. To investigate the empirical impact of this public policy change, the employment and weekly hours regression specifications are modified by adding an interaction variable – the output growth variable times a qualitative variable that is equal to 1 for the years 1975–83 and zero otherwise.[27] This variable represents the change in the output coefficient from the pre-1975 period and is termed the 'output contrast' in the discussion to follow. Inclusion of the output contrast implies that the coefficient on the output growth variable is itself relevant for the pre-1975 period, and that the sum of the output coefficient and the output contrast represents the output coefficient relevant for the period 1975–83.

Coefficient estimates for the pre-1975 and aftermath periods are contained in Table 15.7. Indeed, employment variability is found to

**Table 15.7**

Regression Coefficients on Output for Various Labor Market Measures pre- and post-Employment Insurance Reform in Manufacturing Industries: Japan

| Labor market measure | Output coefficient pre-1975 | Output contrast | Output coefficient 1975–83 |
|---|---|---|---|
| Employment (1951–83) | 0.3197 (5.8) | −0.2357 (2.2) | 0.0840 |
| Hours per week (1951–83) | 0.1346 (5.1) | 0.1863 (3.6) | 0.3209 |
| Employment of male workers (1959–83): | | | |
| Non-production workers | 0.7224 (6.0) | −0.4961 (2.3) | 0.2263 |
| Production workers | 0.8262 (7.9) | −0.3412 (1.8) | 0.4850 |
| Hours worked by male workers (1959–83) | | | |
| Non-production workers: | | | |
| Hours per month | 0.1702 (4.9) | 0.2380 (5.0) | 0.4082 |
| Days per month | 0.0904 (2.4) | 0.1346 (2.6) | 0.2250 |
| Production workers: | | | |
| Hours per month | 0.2121 (5.8) | 0.3437 (6.9) | 0.5558 |
| Days per month | 0.0768 (3.5) | 0.1797 (5.3) | 0.2565 |

*Notes:* All data are transformed into year-to-year changes in logarithmic values. Each of the labor market measures is regressed on the output variable and an interactive variable that is the product of the output variable and a zero–one qualitative variable set to unity if the year of observation is beyond 1974 (labeled the output contrast). The estimated coefficient on the output measure is the pre-1975 time period, and the sum of the coefficients represents the output coefficient for the later period of 1975–83. Magnitudes in parentheses are absolute *t*-values.

*Sources:* Data series originate from the US Bureau of Labor Statistics, *Handbook of Labor Statistics*, 1985, and, for Japanese men, the *Japanese Yearbook of Labor Statistics*, various years.

decline significantly and weekly hours variability to increase significantly after the enactment of the law.[28] Whereas a 10 percentage point decline in output growth is associated with a 3.2 percentage point decline in employment growth in the pre-1975 period, it is associated with a much smaller 0.8 percentage point decline for the post-1974 period. Moreover, the same 10 percentage point decline in output growth is associated with a 3.2 percentage point decline in weekly hours growth during 1975–83, a significantly greater impact than the 1.3 percentage point decline projected for the pre-1975 period. Similar patterns are observed for male employment and hours worked magnitudes using an alternative data source. Here, different dimensions of hours worked are available – hours per month and days per month. Dramatic increases in the magnitudes of the output coefficients in the hours equations are found for the 1975–83 period for both production and nonproduction workers. As an example, a 10 percentage point decline in output growth is associated with a 5.6 percentage point decline in the growth rate in hours per month and a 2.6 percentage point decline in the growth rate of days per month for production workers in the post-1974 period. For the pre-1975 period, the respective declines amounted to 2.1 and 0.8 percentage points, appreciably smaller in magnitude. Similar patterns are found for non-production workers. To summarize, the findings reported in Table 15.7 indicate that Employment Insurance Law decreased employment volatility and increased weekly hours volatility in the Japanese manufacturing sector.[29]

## 15.5 In Search of an Explanation for the Empirical Findings

The Japanese economy in the past few decades has been characterized by high output growth and low unemployment conditions relative to the US. Lifetime employment and bonus payments are often alleged to be contributing factors for Japan's seemingly superior performance during these times. We have attempted to solidify and add to the stock of stylized facts relating to labor market attributes exhibited by the two countries. Specifically, our comparisons highlight the short-term adjustability of labor market magnitudes to changing conditions of output demand and production. Our empirical findings indicate that the US seems to rely on quantity adjustments to a greater degree than Japan as a primary means of adjusting to changing demand conditions (at least in the manufacturing sector). For example, a reduction in output demanded and produced leads to a far greater reduction in employment in the US than it does in Japan according to our estimates; reductions in weekly hours worked are projected to be somewhat greater in the US, though these adjustments are not found to be appreciably different. On the other hand, procyclical hourly compensation adjustments holding weekly hours worked constant are found to be much more pronounced in Japan than in the US, especially the portion of compensation attributable to bonus payments. In the US, much of the procyclical variability in hourly compensation is instead attributable to wage premiums associated with procyclical weekly hours variability rather than pure procyclical compensation variability in the absence of hours variability.

Why do Japan and the United States differ in the use of layoffs and wage flexibility? One promising explanation could indeed have cultural roots. Our reading of the literature, however, suggests that these differential adjustment patterns may relate primarily to the post-World War II era. For example, Japanese turnover rates were reported to be substantial during the early part of this century (see Taira, 1970, Chapter 6). At the same time, US wages are portrayed as being much less rigid prior to World War II than afterwards (see Gordon, 1982). Thus, we are hesitant to limit our scope of explanation solely to cultural and traditional differences between the countries. Instead, we prefer to emphasize economic underpinnings that might play a definitive role.

One economic explanation is based on possible differences in fixed costs of employment (i.e. initial hiring costs or costs that do not vary with labor utilization – e.g. hours per week or days per month).[30] Becker (1962) and Oi (1962) demonstrated that workers with greater fixed employment costs (including costs associated with investment in firm-specific human capital) experience smaller reductions in employment when product demand declines. Rosen (1968) extended these analyses by including hours of work as an operating variable at the disposal of the firm. In his expanded framework, greater reductions in hours of work are also expected for workers having high fixed-cost components. In previous work, we relaxed the wage rigidity presumption and argued that workers who contributed to earlier investments are willing to accept a reduction in their wages when demand has declined (see Hashimoto, 1975, 1979; Raisian, 1979, 1983). The rationale for this behavior on the part of workers is that: (1) previous investment outlays are sunk costs and not relevant for current economic decisions, and (2) workers and the firm have incentives to maintain an attachment in the event that the decline in demand is projected to be temporary, and returns on past investments could resume if recovery were to occur.

Taken together, the analytical frameworks suggest less cyclical employment variability, but greater wage and hours variability, for workers with higher degrees of fixity. If the typical Japanese worker indeed has a higher degree of fixity compared to the typical US worker, our empirical findings are consistent, broadly speaking, with this hypothesis, since employment variability is smaller, and wage variability greater, for Japanese workers compared to their US counterparts. The wage variability differences are especially pronounced when holding hours variability constant, an attribute that is certainly consistent within the conceptual framework.

A principal source of the differential fixities of Japanese and US workers is likely to be differential investments in firm-specific human capital. While the breakdown between direct and indirect compensation costs is shown to be rather similar in the two countries, the proportion of total compensation in the form of bonus payments is much higher for Japanese than for American workers. Hashimoto (1979) argues that Japanese bonus payments largely represent returns to investments in firm-specific human capital – a form of profit sharing. Based on this argument, the bonus proportions evident in Table 15.1 can be viewed as underscoring the relative importance of firm-specific human capital in Japan compared to the United States. A worker who invests in firm-specific capital is in essence purchasing stock in the firm. The return to this stock ownership is expected to fluctuate procyclically independent of the rate at which labor is utilized (i.e. hours of work). This procyclical pattern is much greater in Japan, and is most pronounced in the variability of bonus payments.

Weekly hours variabilities are similar in the two countries; in fact, they tend to be somewhat higher in the US, contrary to the expectation generated from the analytical construct. However, our finding that Japanese workers appear to have salary-style contracts and US workers tend to exhibit hourly-style contracts (at least within the manufacturing sectors) mitigates this inconsistency. Within the analytical construct, there is an implicit presumption that reducing hours of work accomplishes a reduction in employer costs. If workers are salaried, however, the incentive to reduce hours is drastically diminished. Thus, while hours variability would normally be expected to be greater in Japan if workers have embodied in them greater degrees of fixity, a dominance of salary arrangements in Japan would tend to reduce the extent of procyclical hours variability and narrow the cyclical variabilities between the countries.

We have presented other evidence elsewhere that supports the notion that a typical Japanese worker invests to a greater extent in firm-specific human capital (see Hashimoto and Raisian, 1985a,b). Wage-tenure profiles are found to be steeper in Japan, with most of the wage growth attributable to firm-specific tenure rather than to general labor market experience. For example, a Japanese male worker who enters a large firm immediately after the completion of schooling can expect to see his earnings increase by 214 per cent after 20 years of employment, most of which (85 per cent) is attributable to firm-specific tenure. In contrast, a similar individual from the US can expect a 93 per cent earnings growth, less than half of which (39 per cent) is attributable to firm-specific tenure (see Hashimoto and Raisian, 1985a, Table 6). On the basis of the shapes of wage–tenure profiles for the two countries, we also project that Japanese workers invest more than twice as many resources as US workers in the development of income-producing human capital (see Hashimoto and Raisian, 1985b, Table 6).

Why might Japanese workers invest more in firm-specific human capital than their US counterparts? One possible explanation focuses on differential 'transaction' costs that may prevail in the two economies (see Hashimoto and Yu, 1980). By transaction costs, we mean costs that Robinson Crusoe would not have incurred until he met Friday – i.e. the costs associated with exchange and information. In employment relationships, employers and employees require information about business conditions as well as labor market conditions in order to make wise decisions about efficient resource allocation. This information encompasses business and labor market indicators both external and internal to the firm. In particular, a worker who invests in firm-specific human capital must be informed about the value of that capital or be confident that the employer will live up to the spirit of an implicit arrangement calling for returns to prior investment by the worker. If these transaction costs are relatively small, workers are more likely to contract with the firm via an investment in human capital that has specific value to the firm. Alternatively, an employer is more likely to invest in the worker if he/she is reliable and will not engage in haggling and post-contractual opportunistic behavior.

A number of commonly mentioned features relating to Japanese industrial relations might be indicative of a low transaction cost environment in Japan. For example, Japanese employees are often described as identifying with their employers. According to Hanami (1981, p. 47), an employer–employee relationship in Japan is 'accompanied by the feeling that the employee's families are subordinated to, and dependent on, the employer for protection'. While qualitative impressions of this sort do not represent conclusive evidence of the differential transaction cost argument, they do offer clues to the direction one might pursue to obtain explanations. For example, hard facts that do highlight relatively harmonious working conditions in Japan are available from work stoppage statistics (see the *1983 Handbook of Labor Statistics*). In 1979, 1,153 labor disputes were recorded in Japan involving 450,000 workers. The number of days lost by these work stoppages amounted to 930,000, which translates to 2.1 days per affected employee, or 24 days per 1,000 employees economy wide. In the US, there were 4,800 disputes involving 1.7 million workers leading to 33 million working days lost. This translates to a much higher 19.4 days lost per affected employee or 381 days lost per 1,000 employees economy wide.

Much more investigation is required to determine with confidence the reasons why the Japanese and US labor markets are structured and adjust so differently. However, it has been our intent to: (1) provide empirical facts that allow one to judge alternative explanations and consequences better, and (2) interpret and evaluate these facts from the perspective of the human capital framework. In our view, the evidence is mounting that firm-specific investments are more prominent in Japan. The question is 'why?'

## Acknowledgements

We are grateful to John Martin and Naoki Mitani, both of the OECD, to Jacob Mincer, Yoshio Higuchi, Joe Altonji and other participants of the Columbia University Labor Workshop, and to Barbara Brugman for valuable comments on earlier drafts of this work. Also, we commend Nancy Hinsen and Linda Sigel for their patience and reliable clerical support. This paper represents a substantial revision of the version presented at the conference on Employment, Unemployment and Hours of Work, Berlin, 1986.

## Notes

1 See the 1986 *US Economic Report of the President*. The growth rate for European countries taken together amounts to 3.2 per cent during the same period; rates for particular countries include France at 3.9 per cent, Italy at 3.7 per cent, West Germany at 3.2 per cent and the United Kingdom at 2.2 per cent.

2 See the 1985 *US Handbook of Labor Statistics*. Unemployment rates for countries other than the US are adjusted to approximate the US definition of the unemployment rate; this issue is discussed in greater detail subsequently. Among European countries, West Germany and Sweden compare favorably to Japan with unemployment rates averaging 2.0 per cent over the period; other countries include France at 3.2 per cent, the Netherlands at 3.7 per cent, the United Kingdom at 4.7 per cent and Italy at 6.3 per cent.

3 Thus, normal rates of nearly 20 per cent in the early 1950s declined in Japan to rates of around 6 per cent in the early 1980s; whereas rates in the US, running at just over 4 per cent in the early 1950s, declined to around 2 per cent in the early 1980s.

4 While economic growth rates in Japan have consistently been above those of the United States, it is sometimes asserted that the level of productivity in Japan has remained below the level in the US throughout the past three decades. For example, Taira (1983a) has claimed that the level of real GNP per capita is well below that of the US as of the early 1980s – namely, around 70 per cent of the US magnitude. However, in the manufacturing sector, the claim is that Japanese labor productivity is on a par with that of the US, if not a shade above. We speculate that Taira converts nominal GNP to treat GNP for each of the countries, and then uses the exchange rate for the year chosen as a base to convert yen to dollars so as to make cross-country comparisons. Conclusions based on this approach should be interpreted with caution. Real GNP per capita in 1983 was $14,093 (in 1983 dollars) in the US and $9,697 in Japan using this method, seemingly indicating that Japan's level of 'productivity' was 69 per cent that of the United States (see the *1985 Statistical Abstract of the United States*, p. 847). However, the market exchange rates used in converting national currencies do not necessarily reflect relative purchasing power in the two countries; for example, it is obvious that exchange rates can vary for speculative reasons that would not affect living standards directly in either of the countries. While knowledge of the level of productivity could have a bearing on comparing economic performances across the countries, the inability to measure the differences properly causes us to instead focus on rates of growth.

5 This adjustment raises unemployment rates in Japan, but by at most only one-tenth of a percentage point. However, the divergence of rates between countries attributable to this family worker issue is not pertinent, since this adjustment has already been implemented in the data we are using.

6 Taira (1983b) claims that unemployment rates would increase by around 80 per cent in Japan if made consistent with US definitions. He reaches this conclusion using special detailed labor force surveys available only for the

late 1970s. Sorrentino (1984) disputes Taira's finding, however, on the basis of Taira's treatment of persons without a job and waiting to report to a new job within 30 days. This latter group is excluded from the pool of unemployed in Japan, and Taira argues that they should be included for consistency with US concepts. However, in the US survey, persons waiting to begin a new job within 30 days are classified as unemployed only if they are available to begin work immediately. We share Sorrentino's concern that Taira has overcompensated for the impact of this recategorization issue. Also, see Hamada and Kurosaka (1986) for an informative discussion of Japanese unemployment.

7  The presence of youth differences does not necessarily imply that unemployment rates should be adjusted. Indeed, one interpretation is that, while youth have a greater likelihood of being attached to the labor force in the US, the attachment is rather weak with regard to employability. However, an alternative interpretation is that the relatively poor performance of the US labor market as portrayed by the overall unemployment rate differential across countries is more pronounced with regard to youth.

8  One classification readily available for US data is the categorization of employment into part-time and full-time components. In 1983, 81 per cent of total non-agricultural wage and salary workers were full time, though an additional 2 per cent who usually work full time were part time for economic reasons. In Japan, approximately 12 per cent of employees are part-time workers, somewhat lower than the 17–19 per cent figure for the US.

9  Japan's use of bonuses as a significant part of the compensation package is not that unique. As a proportion of total compensation, however, it ranks by far the highest among developed countries. For example, as of 1978, 8 per cent of total compensation and 12 per cent of direct compensation are attributable to bonus payments in West Germany; the analogous statistics for France are 6 per cent and 10 per cent. On the other hand, the United Kingdom and Canada are much like the US in this respect – namely, no pronounced bonus payments.

10  These job tenure contrasts are discussed in detail by Hashimoto and Raisian (1985a).

11  See Hashimoto and Raisian (1985a) for a description of the methodology used to generate the cumulative number of jobs held over a lifetime. Similar statistics were also computed for women in the two countries. Findings indicate that Japanese women will also hold five jobs over their working lives, compared to 10 for US women – almost identical to the statistics computed for men in their respective countries. While women hold a similar number of jobs over the lifetime, the fact that women participate in the labor market fewer years during their lifetimes implies shorter tenures per job. A similar study by the OECD (1984, Chapter 4) was also brought to our attention by John Martin.

12  In 1983, manufacturing's share of total employment was about 20 per cent in the US and 25 per cent in Japan. This share has been declining in the US: since 1960, it has trended downward by 0.3 percentage points per year.

13  In 1951, Japan exhibited a growth rate in manufacturing output of 34 per cent, a definite outlier. Omitting 1951, computation of means and standard deviations for the period 1952–83 reveals a 10.7 per cent average annual growth in Japan and 2.8 per cent in the US, with approximately the same standard deviations of 6.6. per cent in Japan and 6.0 per cent in the US. Growth rates in Japan for this period range from −4.2 per cent to 22.5 per

cent, whereas in the US they range from −9.1 per cent to 11.1 per cent. Furthermore, similar standard deviations attached to these very different means are indicative of a greater likelihood that years of negative growth have been more numerous in the US than in Japan. Indeed, a quarter of the years between 1951 and 1983 were periods of declining growth in US manufacturing, whereas only about 10 per cent of the years during the same time span represented negative growth periods in Japan. This observation suggests that, if labor market adjustments are asymmetric depending upon the occurrence of rising or falling absolute output levels rather than the mere short-term variability of the levels, the presence of differential incidences of positive and negative periods of output growth could provide an explanation for why the countries might choose different methods of adjusting to short-term disturbances in demand conditions. We were aware of this possibility, but we found minimal empirical support for introducing this feature into our statistical framework, especially given the aggregate nature of our data and the use of limited annual time series.

14 The precise percentage change is computed by taking the exponent of the transformed value and then subtracting 1. For percentage changes that are close to zero, the approximation is fairly accurate. The main advantage of such a transformation is the common base that results, easily allowing comparisons across countries.

15 Recall that the standard deviations in the real output measure were not very different for the US and Japan. It is not surprising, therefore, that a comparison of the unadjusted standard deviations and the output −normalized standard deviations yields the same conclusions.

16 Note that the constant term represents an estimate of the percentage change in employment (or any of the other labor market measures) if output were not to change. Obviously, if we were to use the average growth rate in output in the regression equation, we would, upon calculation, obtain the mean growth in employment (or any of the other labor market measures) over the sample period; the mean growth rate is presented with the descriptive statistics in Table 15.2. Inserting output growths that are different from the mean but within the sample range of values provides estimates of the growth in a labor market measure associated with a growth rate in output that is different from the overall sample average. That is, short-term adjustments in the growth of any labor market measure can be projected for any hypothetical change in output based on the underlying correlations estimated between the output and labor market measures.

17 A reduction in output growth and an associated reduction in employment growth does not necessarily imply a reduction in actual employment for the industry as a whole. Our estimates indicate, however, that projected negative employment growths for the industry as a whole do occur when output growth falls below 2.0 per cent in the US and below 2.4 per cent in Japan. These thresholds are determined by taking the ratio of the constant term to the output coefficient and then multiplying by minus 1. The threshold for the US is just slightly below the mean growth rate of 3.1 per cent; for Japan, it is substantially below the mean of 11.4 per cent. Furthermore, it is noteworthy that negative growths in employment for Japan actually occurred six times during our sample period, representing almost one-fifth of the cases; in the US, two-fifths of the sample had negative employment growths.

18 It is interesting to note that hours are trending downward in both countries

independent of changes in output. Hours per week are projected to decline if output growth falls below 13 per cent in Japan and below 3.3 per cent in the US. Both of these magnitudes are slightly above the respective mean output growths of 11.4 and 3.1 per cent. In actuality, hours growth is negative in three-fifths of the sample in Japan, and two-fifths of the sample in the US.

19   In assessing the employment and hours worked adjustments associated with changes in output growth, we became concerned that differences may exist in the reporting of payroll statistics, which would therefore lead to estimated output coefficients that are not strictly comparable. To the best of our knowledge, total weekly hours worked during a sample time frame are reported in a straightforward and consistent fashion by employers for each of the countries. If Japanese employees on layoff are counted as employed at the time of the establishment survey, however, the cross-country comparison of output coefficients for both employment and weekly hours worked per employee could be misleading. In this circumstance, the appropriate output coefficient in the Japanese employment equation to be compared with the US estimate would be higher than is currently estimated, and the analogous coefficient in the Japanese weekly hours equation would be lower, since laid-off employees would be working zero hours per week and the current hours adjustment would be overstated. While we are unable to verify the existence of the extent of this reporting bias with respect to employment and hours effects, recall that Moy and Sorrentino (1981) find that layoffs (which are classified as employment in the Japanese statistics) as a proportion of the labor force amount to only one-fifth the magnitude reported for the US. Thus, such a reporting bias may not be very serious. None the less, we can definitively claim that short-term adjustments in total weekly hours associated with output growth adjustments (i.e. quantity adjustments in general) are larger in the US than in Japan. Total hours effects are easily determined by summing the estimated output coefficients on employment and weekly hours worked. A 10 percentage point decline in output is thus projected to be associated with a 7.4 percentage point decline in total weekly hours growth in the US and a 4.5 percentage point decline in Japan. The Japanese magnitude is based currently on a 3.3 percentage point decline in employment growth and a 1.2 percentage point decline in weekly hours growth. Whether the employment effect should be larger, causing the weekly hours per worker effect to be correspondingly lower, is indeterminant until the reporting methodology is further clarified. It is worth mentioning, however, that this bias is likely to be much more pronounced for the period after 1975 when the Employment Insurance Law was enacted in Japan with the objective of lowering layoff propensities by subsidizing employer payrolls for workers on furlough – added discussion on this issue is provided later in this section.

20   Our estimates project real compensation to decline only when output growth falls below −33 per cent in Japan and −50 per cent in the US, far below any decline that would be expected to occur. Despite these projections, real hourly compensation actually did fall on three occasions in Japan and on four occasions in the US; this is not surprising given the low predictive power of the regression estimates.

21   Production workers make up the bulk of the workforce in the manufacturing industries in both countries. In 1983, approximately two-thirds of employees in each of the countries were production workers.

22 The output coefficient in the real wage equation for Japan is statistically insignificant, however.

23 The circles in the figures represent actual data points.

24 Analysis for all workers in manufacturing (i.e. not just production workers) can be applied to the expanded time span of 1951–83 because of the availability of data. The coefficient estimate on output in this case is $-.0024$ (i.e. less countercyclical than the counterpart of $-.0994$ in Table 15.4) and the estimate on hours worked is .2398 (i.e. smaller than the counterpart estimate of .8949 in Table 15.4 as well as the estimate of .3964 for production workers). We find these results to be far less puzzling. For Japan, estimates for the expanded time period reveal an output coefficient estimate of .3303 (i.e. about half the size of its counterpart of Table 15.4) and an hours coefficient estimate of $-1.7143$ (i.e. also smaller than its counterpart in absolute value terms). While these estimates are less pronounced, they portray decomposition patterns that are none the less consistent with those obtained for the shorter time span.

25 Individuals who are working part time for economic reasons are further categorized into those who usually work full time versus those who usually work part time; normally, one-third of these workers are usually full-time workers and two-thirds are usually part-time workers. They are aggregated here because resulting estimates are virtually identical for these subclassifications.

26 During the period 1957–83, total weekly hours for production workers in manufacturing ranged from 38.9 to 41.4 hours, averaging 40.2 hours. Overtime hours for the same group ranged from 2.0 to 3.9 hours, with an overall average of 3.1 hours.

27 Instead, a specification of the growth rate for the various labor market magnitudes regressed on the output growth variable separately for each of the time periods could have been attempted. Recall, however, that the constant term in such a specification represents an estimate of the trend of the growth rate of the labor market variable. Since the post-1974 period amounts to only nine observations, we were concerned that the trend estimate might be spurious and partially reflect cyclical effects, thus biasing the output coefficient. Our interactive specification allows for a single overall trend term covering the entire sample period with separate output effects for the period before and after the implementation of the law.

28 Hamada and Kurosaka (1986) report that the adjustment speed of employment to changes in output declined after the 1973 oil crisis. They do not analyze hours or compensation adjustments, however.

29 An alternative explanation, suggested by Jacob Mincer, is that the Japanese economy became more cyclically volatile and, as a result, the firm-specific human capital impacts on labor market volatility became increasingly evident after 1975. This explanation implicitly views the Employment Insurance Law to be an endogenous factor.

30 An excellent summary of this literature is available from Hart (1984b).

# COMMENT

## JOHN P. MARTIN

This paper focuses on the differential patterns of labor market adjustment in Japan and the United States in response to short-run demand shocks. Hashimoto and Raisian argue that understanding these patterns will contribute to unraveling the mystery surrounding the better growth and unemployment performance of the Japanese economy in the postwar period.

Section 15.4 is the heart of the paper; it examines in great detail how employment, hours worked and wages vary with the cycle in the two countries. On the basis of their empirical analysis, the authors draw two key conclusions, namely that employment adjusts much more in the United States than it does in Japan in response to short-run changes in output growth, whereas wages (including bonuses) are much more variable in Japan over the cycle. These findings are not new; they were highlighted some years ago by Bob Gordon (1982), although Hashimoto and Raisian extend his analysis in a number of areas.

In so far as weekly hours worked are concerned, they find very similar cyclical elasticities in both countries. This latter result is somewhat surprising and not entirely in accordance with the literature. For example, a recent review by Tachibanaki (1987) concludes that most of the short-run adjustment in Japanese labor input comes through changes in hours worked. Tachibanaki also points out that changes in total hours worked in Japan over the past two decades have been strongly influenced by changes in overtime working, a factor that is not mentioned by Hashimoto and Raisian. This in turn presumably has something to do with the relative size of the overtime premium in both countries.

The finding that the cyclical elasticities of weekly hours worked are very similar in Japan and the United States may not hold for *annual* hours worked. When I investigated this, using annual data over the period 1960–85, I found that the estimated elasticity of average annual hours worked (total economy) was slightly larger (0.24) in Japan as compared with the United States (0.19).[1]

What factors might explain these differential patterns of labor market adjustment in Japan and the United States? The final section is entitled 'In Search of an Explanation for the Empirical Findings'. I can only applaud the authors for their frankness; they put forward some tentative hypotheses but admit that they are not well grounded in empirical evidence. Nevertheless, the reader is entitled to feel a bit disappointed at the thinness of this final section.

One possible explanation, which is often cited in the media, is different socio-cultural factors. Hashimoto and Raisian try to downplay this and prefer to emphasize economic explanations, appealing to differences in fixed costs of employment in the two countries. If the ratio of fixed to variable costs is typically higher in Japan than in the United

States, this suggests two predictions about employment adjustment: (i) employers would tend to substitute hours for employees; and (ii) a slower adjustment of employment in response to demand shocks. Hence, the fixed-costs hypothesis could account for some of the stylized facts about short-run employment adjustment in the two countries.

Unfortunately, data are not readily available on fixed and variable labor costs in Japan and the United States. In the 1986 OECD *Employment Outlook* we tried to assess the empirical significance of this issue by classifying the various elements of labor costs into fixed and variable costs. We were able to apply this classification to the EEC countries and to the United States but not to Japan. The results showed that fixed costs are not very significant in US manufacturing – ranging from 13 to 26 per cent of total labor costs depending upon whether a narrow or a broad definition of fixed costs is applied – nor does this ratio appear to have risen much over the 1970s (OECD, 1986).

Hashimoto and Raisian argue that the differential fixities of Japanese and US workers are mainly the result of differential investments in firm-specific human capital. I would feel more comfortable with this assertion if it were backed up with some direct evidence. As it is, statistics on the educational composition of the labor force, a proxy for human capital, do not show higher levels in Japan than in the United States or a much more rapid growth in education attainments over the 1970s (see Psacharopoulos and Arriagada, 1986).

Even if the assertion were true, it still begs the question why Japanese workers should be willing to invest relatively more in firm-specific human capital than their US counterparts. The authors respond that it reflects lower 'transactions costs' in Japan. However, they are not very explicit about the nature of these costs. When it comes to reasons why these costs are lower, the authors tend to appeal to differing socio-cultural factors. For example, they cite the family-type relationship between Japanese workers and their firms.

Some alternative explanations for these differential patterns of employment adjustment are ignored by Hashimoto and Raisian. The role of temporary layoffs in the United States has received much attention recently. They can be regarded as a mechanism for risk sharing between workers and employers in response to short-run shocks. In Japan, part of this role is played by the flexibility of working hours. The propensity of US employers to make use of temporary layoffs has been associated by some analysts with the lack of full experience-rating of employer unemployment insurance contributions. This may also be exacerbated by the strict operation of the seniority rule in unionized firms.

In sum, I applaud the authors' attempt to explain the differential patterns of hours and wage flexibility in the United States and Japan. The emphasis they put on investment in firm-specific skills is novel and interesting but the whole edifice is rather shaky at present. I hope they will continue this line of research and hunt down some convincing explanations.

# Notes

The views expressed here are my own and cannot be held to represent those of the OECD.

1 The basic regression equation fitted to time-series data on average weekly hours worked in the manufacturing sector and average annual hours worked in the total economy over the period 1960–85 was of the following form:

$$\ln HOURS_i = a_0 + a_1 \ln CYCLE + a_2 TT + \varepsilon$$

where $HOURS_i$ = average weekly or annual hours worked ($i$ stands for sector: either manufacturing or the total economy); $CYCLE$ = the ratio of actual to trend GDP (where trend GDP was calculated by the phase-average method); and $TT$ = a linear time-trend.

# CHAPTER 16

# *Sectoral Uncertainty and Unemployment*

## ROBERT TOPEL and LAURENCE WEISS

## 16.1 Introduction

Both the level and variability of measured unemployment in the United States have increased dramatically since 1975. The average unemployment rate has been 60 per cent higher than the average post-war rate up to 1975 (7.7 per cent vs. 4.7 per cent). Indeed, the recent cyclical low unemployment rate of 7.1 per cent (1984: IV) is only slightly below the maximum cyclical peak rate prior to 1975 (7.4 per cent in 1958: II). Similar, though more dramatic, increases occur in other OECD countries (OECD, 1986). Evidently, the level about which measured unemployment fluctuates is not higher than in comparable periods of the past.

In this paper we propose a new theory that may help to explain this phenomenon. The theory emphasizes the role of costly, irreversible, industry-specific human capital investments in determining an individual's lifetime labor supply decision. These costs require that agents consider future, as well as present, industry relative wages when choosing a job. In particular, we show that an increase in future relative wage uncertainty will tend to diminish the return to industry-specific human capital and increase the relative attractiveness of current period unemployment. We propose that much of the increase in recent unemployment can be attributed to greater sectoral uncertainty during this period. We present two distinct types of empirical evidence in support of this view. The first uses time-series evidence to show that several empirical proxies for agents' (unobservable) expectations of future relative wage uncertainty have increased in the period after 1975. The second kind of evidence uses cross-sectional data to show that the demographic incidence of unemployment and sectoral mobility are consistent with the theory.

There are few empirically convincing theories that attempt to explain the trend rise in unemployment. Factors thought to be important for determining the 'natural rate', such as unemployment insurance, minimum wage laws and union behavior, exhibit no sharp changes since the early 1970s (see Barro, 1984, Ch. 9). One common explanation stresses changing labor force composition. While it is true that there is greater participation among groups with traditionally higher measured unemployment (e.g. youths and women), this factor can account for only about one-third of the rise in aggregate unemployment (see Figure 16.1 and Table 16.1). A less easily dismissible explanation is that aggregate participation rates have risen over the recent past. Adherents of this view emphasize the relative constancy in aggregate employment to population ratios (see Table 16.2). However, we know of no completely articulated theory that explains a positive relationship between aggregate participation and unemployment. A third possibility is that the large influx of workers associated with the post-war 'baby boom' has lowered average labor productivity, which affects both earnings (Welch, 1979) and labor supply. By itself, however, this model has little to say about the concomitant rise in unemployment among older workers, nor does it address the sluggish behavior of aggregate output during this period.

Other papers in this volume do not seek to explain higher observed unemployment rates, though they do stress policies of labor demand management and work sharing that are designed to spread the costs of increased unemployment more widely by substituting hours for employment reductions. The theoretical foundations for these policies are open to serious questions in a world of long-term employment relations, since the explicit form of compensation in terms of straight-time and overtime pay is essentially irrelevant to employment decisions in this case. This (key) point aside, however, the efficacy of demand-side policies is not established when changes in observed unemployment are generated by optimizing behavior on the supply side of the labor market. We argue that the cause of higher unemployment is not a shortage of jobs or employment opportunities – whatever that may mean – but rather the supply response to structural uncertainty in the labor market. In our view this supply response is transitory, though policies to combat its symptoms are not. Our model has the additional advantage of being consistent with the facts.

The work that comes closest to ours it that of Lilien (1982, 1984), who has attempted to show that the rise in unemployment since the early 1970s is the result of the greater pace of reallocation of labor among different sectors over this period. Lilien's evidence for this is based partly on the observation that the fraction of employment in manufacturing has fallen sharply (from 30 per cent in 1964 to 26 per cent in 1974 and 20 per cent in 1984) and that periods of most rapid adjustment coincided with the aggregate contractions of 1971, 1975 and 1979–81. More formally, Lilien has documented a statistically significant positive relationship between measured unemployment and cross-sectional variation in industry employment growth rates, which he takes as a good proxy for relative sectoral changes.

Although Lilien's work is suggestive, two types of criticism have been raised. The first is that the model of unemployment underlying the sectoral shift hypothesis is not completely worked out. Thus it is not clear what features of the labor market give rise to an increase in

345

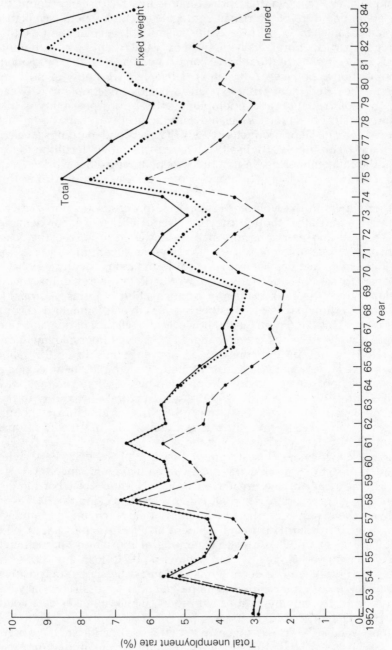

**Figure 16.1** Total, fixed demographic weight, and insured unemployment, 1952–84

**Table 16.1**

Total, Fixed Demographic Weight, and Insured Unemployment Rates, 1955–84

|  | 1955–9 | 1960–4 | 1965–9 | 1970–4 | 1975–9 | 1980–4 |
|---|---|---|---|---|---|---|
| Total unemployment | 5.01 | 5.72 | 3.06 | 5.36 | 7.00 | 8.30 |
| Fixed demographic weight | 5.08 | 5.68 | 3.60 | 4.78 | 6.12 | 7.26 |
| Insured unemployment | 4.22 | 4.58 | 2.42 | 3.44 | 4.14 | 3.74 |

*Source:* US Bureau of Labor Statistics, *Handbook of Labor Statistics* and *Handbook of Unemployment Insurance Financial Data.* The fixed-weight unemployment rate uses age × race × sex labor force shares for 1960.

**Table 16.2**

Labor Force Participation and Employment Rates, Persons Aged 16–64

|  | 1955–9 | 1960–4 | 1965–9 | 1970–4 | 1975–9 | 1980–4 |
|---|---|---|---|---|---|---|
| Labor force/population | 59.5 | 59.0 | 59.5 | 60.6 | 62.4 | 64.0 |
| Employment/population | 56.5 | 55.6 | 57.2 | 57.3 | 58.0 | 58.7 |

*Source:* US Bureau of Labor Statistics, *Handbook of Labor Statistics.*

unemployment as a response to a shock that requires labor to move between different sectors. The second criticism is that Lilien's formal evidence is consistent with a conventional view of business cycles (e.g. Mitchell, 1941) that incorporates non-neutralities across sectors (see Weiss, 1985). Indeed, measures of sectoral dispersion are concentrated around cyclical contractions in aggregate output. This leaves unexplained the higher, non-cyclical unemployment rates that have been observed throughout the past decade. This is not to deny that Lilien's tenet may be correct; it only points out that this work has little power to discriminate against the conventional view that attempts to explain aggregate output without reference to its sectoral composition, and that it fails to account for the secular increase in average unemployment rates.

Two other prime features of rising aggregate unemployment must be addressed by candidate theories. First, a demographic breakdown of unemployment rates (Table 16.3) shows that the increase in aggregate unemployment has fallen disproportionately on young workers. For example, unemployment rates among males aged 25–34 were only about 10 per cent higher than the post-35 group prior to 1970, but since that time their rate has been about 50 per cent higher. A possible objection is that these relative changes partly reflect the well-documented decline in labor force participation among older males, which may reduce measured unemployment in these groups. The more detailed breakdown by separate age intervals shows that unemployment of younger workers has risen relative even to prime age (35–44)

**Table 16.3**
Unemployment Rates of Males Aged 35 and over Relative to Unemployment of
Males Aged 25–34, 1955–84

| Age | 1955–9 | 1960–4 | 1965–9 | 1970–4 | 1975–9 | 1980–4 |
|---|---|---|---|---|---|---|
| ⩾35 | 0.90 | 0.88 | 0.92 | 0.71 | 0.66 | 0.62 |
| 35–44 | 0.82 | 0.80 | 0.83 | 0.68 | 0.67 | 0.69 |
| 45–54 | 0.90 | 0.86 | 0.84 | 0.67 | 0.64 | 0.59 |
| 55–64 | 1.01 | 1.00 | 1.06 | 0.76 | 0.64 | 0.58 |

*Source:* US Bureau of Labor Statistics, *Handbook of Labor Statistics.*

males, for whom changes in participation have been minor.[1] This evidence is difficult to reconcile with a pure sectoral shift hypothesis. Even if older workers remain longer in declining industries because of greater mobility costs or sector-specific human capital, should this not be offset by the greater opportunities for young workers in expanding sectors?

The second, related feature of aggregate unemployment comes from comparing the insured unemployment rate with the broader measure derived from the *Current Population Survey* (see Table 16.1). The insured rate is the fraction of covered workers currently receiving unemployment insurance benefits. It differs from the CPS measure by excluding (i) individuals who have exhausted their benefits and (ii) those who are ineligible for benefits. The latter are primarily individuals who have not worked long enough to be eligible. As shown in Table 16.1, the discrepancy between these measures has increased sharply. During the 1980s the insured rate was less than half of the total, compared to 80 per cent in the 1960s and 60 per cent in the 1970s. This, too, is difficult to reconcile with the view that the increase in aggregate unemployment is driven by a prolonged shift out of the traditional manufacturing sectors, whose experienced workers are mainly eligible to receive benefits. It is also inconsistent with an alternative view that the recent behavior of unemployment is due to a prolonged period of 'deficient' labor demand: insured unemployment is strongly cyclical (Figure 16.1), yet unlike total unemployment it displays no secular increase. Evidently, the increase in total unemployment is accounted for mainly by individuals with comparatively weak attachments to prior employment or the labor force (Murphy and Topel, 1987).

Our theory is formulated to be consistent with these facts. In contrast to Lilien, who implies that the *occurrence* of a sectoral shock that requires labor to be reallocated raises unemployment, we argue that *the prospect of future shocks* is a likely candidate for explaining the observed rise in unemployment during this period, especially among younger individuals. Of course, to the extent that the occurrence of sectoral shocks is correlated over time, a sectoral shock may increase expectations of future shocks, so it may be difficult to completely separate the two

348

theories empirically. In this sense, models of costly sectoral mobility and sectoral uncertainty are complementary theories of rising unemployment.

The paper is organized as follows. In Section 16.2 we present the basic model, emphasizing the role of training costs for determining agents' labor supply decisions. Section 16.3 is an empirical attempt to show that an appropriate measure of sectoral uncertainty has increased in the period after 1975. To do this we use evidence on sector-specific stock market returns and the observed sectoral composition of the labor force. Although the results are generally supportive, we were unsuccessful in formulating a testable time-series version of the model. Section 16.4 introduces new evidence on the differential incidence of unemployment by age and education and shows how the model may be extended to be consistent with observed patterns. Section 16.5 concludes.

## 16.2 The Model

Our model is designed to illustrate how the level of uncertainty about future relative wages may affect an individual's current employment decisions and, in particular, lead to voluntary abstentions from employment that are concentrated among young workers. In many ways this mechanism is similar to that of Bernanke (1983) who considers the effects of uncertainty on the decision to undertake costly irreversible physical investment. We emphasize the role of uncertainty on human capital acquisition.

Our model does not differentiate between non-employment and unemployment. As noted in Section 16.1, most of the variations in unemployment within the prime age male workforce are closely associated with variations in employment. Since our model is designed to explain variations within this group we simplify and identify non-employment as unemployment.

Consider a continuous time model in which all agents seek to maximize discounted utility of the form

$$U^i = \int e^{-\delta t}[c(t) - r^i l(t)] \, dt, \tag{16.1}$$

where $\delta > 0$ is a discount rate, $c(t)$ is consumption, $r^i$ is the individual-specific reservation wage and $l(t)$ is labor supply at $t$, taken to be either 0 (not working) or 1 (working). Note that the linear specification of individual preferences implies a labor supply income elasticity of zero. This rules out income effects as a possible source of cross-sectional heterogeneity and greatly simplifies the analysis.

There are two industries, or sectors, in which an individual may work. In order to work in either industry each individual must first pay an industry-specific 'training cost', $k^i$, which differs among individuals

349

(some individuals learn faster than others) but is common across industries. Incurring $k^i$ qualifies the individual to work in only one industry. Thus, the parameters that characterize an individual are his costs of learning and reservation wage $(k^i, r^i)$.

The pattern of industry relative wages arises from the following technology. At any point in time, one, and only one, of the two industries is 'productive'. If a trained worker is employed in a productive industry over any interval of time $dt$ he produces a 'lump' of perishable output of size $(2q/\mu)$ with probability $\mu\,dt$. If he is employed in a non-productive sector he produces nothing. With this technology the wage expressed as flow per unit time is $2q$ in the productive industry and 0 in the non-productive industry.

Aggregate uncertainty arises because sometimes it is common knowledge which of the two industries is productive. We call such intervals 'certain' periods. We assume that the duration of certain periods is random and generated by a Poisson probability distribution with parameter $\beta$. Thus the expected duration of a certain interval is $1/\beta$. When a certain period comes to an end, previous information on sectoral output becomes irrelevant. Everybody knows that each industry is productive with probability one-half, so that the expected wage in either sector is $(1/2) \times 2q + (1/2) \times 0 = q$. 'Uncertain periods' last until information is revealed via one of the two sectors producing output; this happens with probability $\mu\,dt$ over an interval $dt$, so that the expected duration of uncertain periods is $1/\mu$.

To simplify matters we make the following, somewhat artificial, assumption about the durability of industry-specific human capital. We assume that so long as an individual works in an industry his capital does not depreciate. An individual may also choose not to work during uncertain periods without jeopardizing his skills. However, should an individual decide not to work in an industry during a certain period, any skills previously acquired in that industry depreciate fully. Thus an individual will at any time be trained to work in at most one industry. These assumptions are designed to capture the idea that skills dissipate if not used. Since the duration of uncertain periods is taken to be relatively brief compared to certain periods (that is $\beta \ll \mu$), we take the depreciation during uncertain periods to be negligible and the depreciation during certain periods to be total.

Our model is designed to show how unemployment among young (inexperienced) workers will rise by a greater amount than unemployment among older workers during uncertain periods. The distinction between 'old' and 'young' in our model arises because experienced workers have already incurred the costs of training, while young workers must first pay the training cost in order to produce. We emphasize that all workers live forever or, alternatively, face a mortality probability independent of age, so the relevant distinction is between trained and untrained labor. It would be preferable to introduce finite working lives to explain the incidence of industry mobility by age (in Section 16.4 we document that older workers are less likely to change industries) but we neglect this additional complication to emphasize the role of training costs.

Each agent must decide when to enter the labor force, when to take temporary layoff and when to switch sectors. We first consider the problem of a young (untrained) worker who is born during 'certain' periods – that is, when the identity of the productive sector is known. It is clear that, should he enter the labor force, he will do so in the productive sector. His first non-trivial decision comes at the moment the uncertain period begins. His expected wage falls from $2q$ to $q$. Since he can 'rest' during this interval without forgoing the value of his human capital, his decision rule is simple – work if and only if $r^i < q$, that is, if his reservation wage is less than the expected wage. His next decision comes when the identity of the productive sector is announced at the beginning of a certain period. If he finds himself in the non-productive sector should he switch sectors? Since the value of either type of training is identical at the beginning of the next uncertain period, the decision to switch is governed by weighing the additional expected income generated by switching over the current certain period against the cost of training, $k^i$. Suppose the current certain period lasts exactly $T$ periods. The value of switching is the present discounted value of the difference in the wages between the two sectors: $\int_c^T - \delta s 2q \, ds$. Since the probability of the certain period lasting $T$ periods is $\beta e^{-\beta T}$, the expected value of switching is $\int \beta e^{-\beta T} \int^T e^{-\delta s} 2q \, ds \, dT = 2q/(\delta + \beta)$. Thus the agent will switch if and only if $k^i < 2q/(\delta + \beta)$, so switching is less likely when 'certain' periods are perceived as transitory. If the above inequality is not satisfied, the agent will remain in the non-productive sector even though the wage is zero in order to maintain his skills.

It remains only to determine if the agent will enter the labor force at all. This is governed by the requirement that the present discounted value of expected utility, under the optimum rest and switch decisions, be greater than zero. The results of this calculation are summarized in Figure 16.2.

Each individual's characteristics, his own reservation wage $r^i$ and cost of acquiring industry-specific training $k^i$, are represented by a point in the figure. If the individual lies above the regions marked A, B or C, he will never enter the labor force. People in A will work only during the certain periods and take leisure (unemployment) during the uncertain period, since they have a high reservation wage. They will always switch to the productive sector since their training costs are sufficiently low. More formally, individuals in area A satisfy

$$2q > r^i > q \text{ (employed during certain periods)}$$

$$k^i < \frac{2q - r^i}{\beta + \delta} + \frac{1}{2} \frac{k^i \mu}{\mu + \delta} \frac{\beta}{\beta + \delta} \text{ (choose to enter)}$$

$$k^i < \frac{2q}{\beta + \delta} \text{ (switch sectors)}$$

351

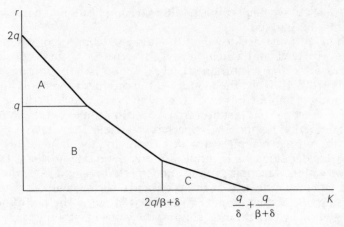

**Figure 16.2**

Similarly, agents in area B will always switch, but because of their lower reservation wage they will continue to work during the low-wage uncertain period. This continuous participation induces some workers with higher training costs than in A to enter the market. Specifically, area $\beta$ is defined by

$$r^i > q$$

$$k^i < \frac{2q - r^i}{\beta + \delta} + \frac{q - r^i}{\mu + \delta} \frac{\beta}{\beta + \delta} + \frac{1}{2} \frac{k^i \mu}{\mu + \delta} \frac{\beta}{\beta + \delta}$$

$$k^i < \frac{2q}{\beta + \delta}$$

Finally, agents in area C will never switch sectors because of their high costs of (re)training, and they will work in the sectors they originally entered, even if the sector is non-productive, in order to maintain their capital. Area C is defined by

$$r^i > q$$

$$k^i < \frac{q}{\beta + \delta} + \frac{q - r^i}{d}$$

$$k^i > \frac{2q}{\beta + \delta}.$$

Now consider the problem faced by a young (untrained) worker who comes of age during an uncertain period. Assume that $k^i < 2q/(\beta + \delta)$ so that the agent will always switch to the productive sector. (It is shown below that if this condition is not satisfied the agent should always wait

352

until a certain period to enter the labor force.) Should the agent join the labor force now, or should he wait until the certain period? If he decides to work now he pays $k^i$ and receives an expected wage of $q$ over the duration of the current uncertain period which has present value $(q - r^i)/(\mu + \delta)$. In addition, with probability one-half he will have selected the productive industry, so he will save the training costs at the onset of the certain period; this is worth $(1/2)k^i\mu/(\mu + \delta)$ in present value. Thus he should work today if $(q - r^i)/(\mu + \delta) + (1/2)k^i\mu/(\mu + \delta) - k^i > 0$. This region is shown as region D in Figure 16.3.

It is now clear why unemployment among untrained individuals will rise disproportionately in uncertain times. Only those agents with very low reservation and training costs will find it optimal to join the labor force during such periods. This occurs because there is a high probability that the individual's newly acquired industry-specific skills will soon become obsolete. The flow of untrained people into 'unemployment', defined here to be agents who will eventually work but choose not to do so immediately, consists of all people coming of age whose characteristics fall in regions A, B and C in Figure 16.3. The flow into employment consists only of those who fall into region D. Note that the size of this flow depends negatively on $\mu$, so participation is less likely (unemployment is more likely) if uncertain periods are expected to be short. It pays to wait until uncertainty is resolved before investing. By contrast, only those older workers who fall in region A above will choose temporary layoffs during uncertain periods. Other experienced individuals choose to work.

One might argue that our characterization of unemployment among young workers as a form of leisure is unrealistic, especially since most unemployment spells are comparatively short and do not constitute formal withdrawal from the labor force for an extended period. Our response is that the driving force of our model is postponement of sector-specific investments that generate attachments to continuous

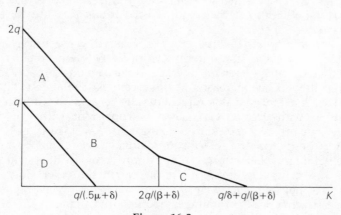

**Figure 16.3**

353

employment. The model could be extended to include intermittent spells of temporary employment during uncertain periods, which would formally incorporate the increased incidence of uninsured spells, but that model offers few additional insights.

Our specification of the human capital technology as point input–flow output is obviously unrealistic. It would be more natural, but more complicated, to introduce industry-specific 'learning by doing' as formulated by Arrow (1962) to capture the capital theoretic elements of labor supply. This would not alter our main conclusions that periods of sectoral uncertainty affect the employment of young workers relatively more, since a relatively higher proportion of their remuneration comes from acquiring skills to be used in future employment.

A more crucial and arguable assumption of our model is identifying human capital as sector or industry specific rather than occupational or task specific. Presumably elements of both are operative and both types of uncertainty may affect macroeconomic outcomes. A possible justification for our assumption is that 'learning by doing' affects primarily groups of people working together. This interpretation would point to individual firm or workplace uncertainty as affecting aggregate outcomes. To the extent that firms are correlated within an industry this is consistent with our emphasis on sectoral uncertainty. However, this focus is derived more from data availability than by any independent studies of the human capital process.

## 16.3 Time-Series Evidence

In this section we present evidence to support our contention that sectoral uncertainty increased in the period after 1975, which we interpret to mean that later experience was dominated by unusually long episodes of uncertain periods. We note at the outset that constructing a single convincing measure of sectoral 'uncertainty' is difficult. We focus on the ability to statistically predict various measures of relative sectoral performance.

The model emphasizes the role of relative wage uncertainty in individual's work decisions. Recent work by Bell and Freeman (1985) shows that the dispersion of average wages among broadly defined sectors in the US has increased in the recent past relative to historical norm. To the extent that this represents the realization from an *ex ante* distribution with greater variance it is consistent with our theory. However, we must be careful in utilizing *ex post* average wage data as a proxy for the distribution of *ex ante* relative wages faced by a typical worker. Changing labor force composition across sectors will greatly distort this view. Declining industries maintain older, high-skilled workers so their average wage might remain high even though their relative attractiveness to younger workers has fallen. In fact, this appears to have been the case in manufacturing: relative wages have risen in this sector in spite of its declining importance as a source of employment.

To circumvent this problem, we focus on employment data across two-digit industry classifications. Specifically, we show that there has been greater disparity in sectoral employment growth rates, which was unforeseen in the sense that it could not have been predicted from simple time-series models. We also show that this greater level of sectoral dispersion cannot be attributed to the greater level of aggregate fluctuations that have obviously occurred in the post-1970 period.

To implement these ideas, we use quarterly time-series data on employment in one-digit (SIC) industries in the United States. For each sector, $j$, let $E_{jt}$ denote the natural logarithm of employment in quarter $t$ ($t = 1948$: I–1983: IV). At each $t$, we estimate a rolling regression using the previous eight years' data of the form

$$E_{jt} = A^j(L)E_{jt-1} + B^j(L)Q_t + \varepsilon_{jt},$$

where $Q_t$ is the deviation of the natural logarithm of real GNP from quadratic trend, $A^j(L)$ and $B^j(L)$ are fourth-order polynomials in the lag operator $L$, and $\varepsilon_{jt}$ is a one step ahead prediction error. We then use this model to predict employment in sector $j$ at time $t + h$ conditional on the actual values of employment up to time $t$ and the actual values of aggregate income up to $t + h$. We condition the forecasts on *future* (period $t + h$) values of aggregate income in order to purge our measure of sectoral disturbances from 'pure' business cycle effects. We 'overcontrol' for these effects in the sense of using information that is not available to agents at time $t$. Note that the effects of aggregate fluctuations are allowed to be non-neutral across sectors. Denoting the forecasts by $\tilde{E}$, we then compute the share-weighted mean squared error of these predictions,

$$\eta_{t+h} = \sum_j (E_{jt}/E_t)(\tilde{E}_{jt+h} - E_{jt+h})^2.$$

We report two types of output from this procedure. The first simply reports the computed values of $\eta$ when $h$ is chosen alternatively as 4 or 8 quarters. The second set of estimates accumulates the value of $\eta$ from $h = 1$ to 4 or 8 quarters, alternatively. Means of the estimates over five-year intervals are reported in Table 16.4. Figure 16.4 illustrates the complete series for $h = 4$ quarters.

The results for employment provide support for the notion of increased sectoral uncertainty. Controlling for aggregate fluctuations, for $h = 4$ the average estimated mean squared errors in forecasting are more than twice as high in the post-1974 period as in earlier years. For the cumulative forecast errors, the difference is even larger. As Figure 16.4 shows, these differences are due mainly to a sharp increase in the volatility of $\eta_{t+h}$ in the 1970s and 1980s. Evidently, even controlling for the differential effect of the cycle across sectors, the sectoral composition

355

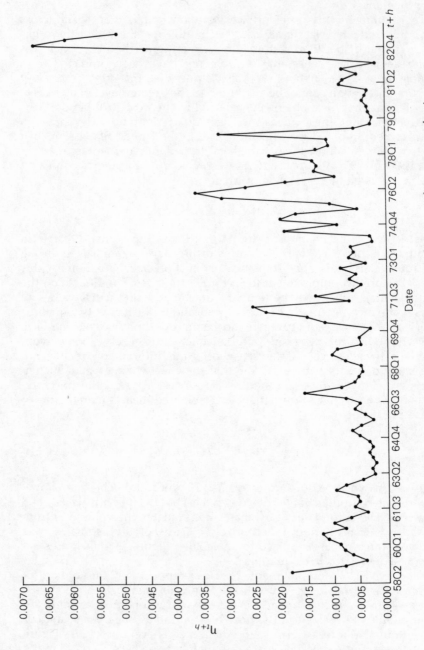

**Figure 16.4** Mean squared error of log employment forecasts: four-quarter horizons

**Table 16.4**

Weighted Mean Squared Errors in Forecasting Sectoral Employment, 1957–83

| | 1957–9 | 1960–4 | Period $t + h$ 1965–9 | 1970–4 | 1975–9 | 1980–4 |
|---|---|---|---|---|---|---|
| $h = 4$ *quarters* | | | | | | |
| $\eta_{t+h}$ | 0.88 | 0.57 | 0.60 | 0.90 | 1.54 | 1.84 |
| $\sum^{h} \eta_{t+i}$ | 2.14 | 1.23 | 1.29 | 1.65 | 3.51 | 4.84 |
| $h = 8$ *quarters* | | | | | | |
| $\eta_{t+h}$ | 2.89 | 2.77 | 2.38 | 5.24 | 4.06 | 4.25 |
| $\sum^{h} \eta_{t+i}$ | 11.72 | 8.74 | 7.35 | 14.19 | 14.75 | 12.43 |

*Note:* See text for description of variables. All estimates are multiplied by $10^3$.

of the demand for labor was much less predictable during this period than in the relatively docile decade of the 1960s.

An alternative source of information on changes in the sectoral composition of demand is the value of the capital stock in these sectors. For the same one-digit industry classifications, we constructed industry-wide stock portfolios for the period 1948I–1983IV. Denoting the rate of return on the sector $j$ portfolio by $\rho_{jt} = \log (P_t^j/P_{t-1}^j)$, where $P$ denotes average share price (value weighted), we purge these series of the effects of fluctuations in aggregate output by estimating

$$\rho_{jt} - \rho_t = \alpha^j + A^j(L)Q_t + V_{jt},$$

where $\rho_t$ is the market rate of return. We calculate the residuals from this model. Forecast errors for an $h$-period horizon are achieved by summing the unpredicted excess returns, $V_{jt+i}$. As above, this method 'overcontrols' for the cycle by using information on $Q_{t+i}$ that is not available to agents at $t$. We calculate mean squared errors for these series using sectoral employment shares as weights.

Weighted mean square errors for the stock market data are reported in Table 16.5 and displayed in Figure 16.5. The results are essentially similar to those for employment: controlling for sectoral non-neutralities in response to the cycle, the average ability to predict sectoral returns on these portfolios declined in the 1970s and 1980s. Over a four-period horizon, the average mean squared error in the post-1970 period is more than double the average in the period up to 1969, and for an eight period horizon the average is nearly three times higher. In conjunction with the similar findings for employment, we take this as evidence that the ability to predict relative sectoral performance declined sharply during a period of rising aggregate unemployment.

357

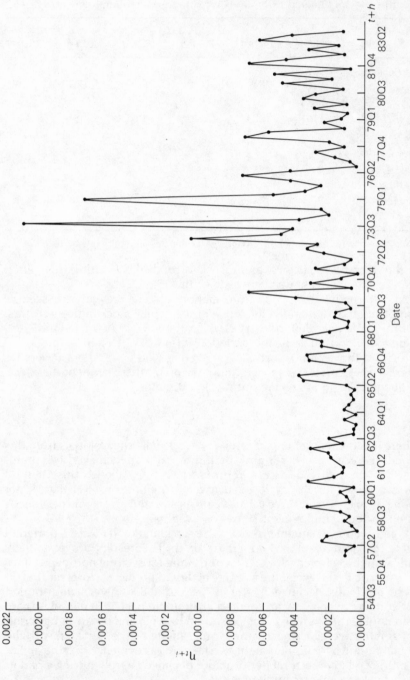

**Figure 16.5** Mean squared error of sectoral portfolio forecasts: four-quarter horizon

**Table 16.5**

Weighted Mean Squared Errors in Forecasting Sectoral Stock Portfolios, 1957–83

| | | | Period $t + h$ | | | |
|---|---|---|---|---|---|---|
| | 1957–9 | 1960–4 | 1965–9 | 1970–4 | 1975–9 | 1980–4 |
| $h = 4$ quarters | | | | | | |
| $\eta_{t+h}$ | 0.12 | 0.13 | 0.17 | 0.45 | 0.37 | 0.31 |
| $\sum^{h} \eta_{t+i}$ | 0.51 | 0.56 | 0.74 | 1.73 | 1.99 | 1.37 |
| $h = 8$ quarters | | | | | | |
| $\eta_{t+h}$ | 0.12 | 0.14 | 0.21 | 0.47 | 0.38 | 0.27 |
| $\sum^{h} \eta_{t+i}$ | 0.98 | 1.15 | 1.46 | 2.92 | 4.03 | 2.38 |

*Note:* See text for description of variables. All estimates are multiplied by $10^3$.

## 16.4 Further Demographic Evidence

Our model is designed to show how sectoral uncertainty may affect the demographic composition of unemployment. Further insight is gained by examining the incidence of unemployment by both age and education. Table 16.6 documents the well-known fact that more educated individuals are less likely to be unemployed. More surprisingly, the differential incidence of unemployment by education has increased

**Table 16.6**

Male Unemployment by Selected Age and Education Categories, 1968–83

| | 1968–9 | 1970–4 | 1975–9 | 1980–3 |
|---|---|---|---|---|
| Age 20–29 | 4.8 | 7.4 | 10.1 | 11.5 |
| Education: $<12$ | 8.1 | 13.4 | 19.5 | 23.4 |
| 12 | 4.5 | 7.2 | 10.9 | 13.0 |
| $\geqslant 16$ | 1.8 | 3.7 | 4.3 | 4.2 |
| Age 30–39 | 2.5 | 3.7 | 6.5 | 6.4 |
| Education: $<12$ | 4.0 | 5.5 | 8.2 | 11.6 |
| 12 | 2.0 | 3.2 | 5.0 | 6.9 |
| $\geqslant 16$ | 0.7 | 1.5 | 2.1 | 2.5 |
| Total: Age 20–65 | 3.0 | 4.3 | 6.5 | 7.7 |

359

since 1975, particularly for young people. Among workers aged 20–29, for example, the average difference in unemployment rates between high school and college graduate has been 7.6 percentage points since 1975, compared to about 3.2 per cent for 1968–74.

We sketch how the model presented above can be modified to account for these facts. In thinking about the return to education, economists have tried (generally unsuccessfully) to sort out two sets of issues. The first is how education changes the productivity of a given individual and the second is what innate characteristics of individuals may lead them to acquire more education. Our interpretation of the evidence suggests that both factors operate to explain the differential increase in the natural rate of unemployment by education.

Let the basic model be amended to include a new activity called education. In return for an individual-specific cost, $C^i$, the individual's productivity is augmented by fixed amount, $\partial x$ in any sector. Thus education provides general training in the sense of Becker (1964). Since the abilities to acquire general and sector-specific human capital will depend on an agent's innate ability, we would expect that $C^i$ is positively correlated with $k^i$, the cost of acquiring sector-specific training. Hence this model displays both a direct productivity effect as well as a self-selection effect, as those agents with relatively low cost of training will select education.

It is fairly easy to see that either one of these effects, separately, will lead to lower unemployment among educated workers during periods of uncertainty. Recall Figure 16.3. An $\partial x$ increase in productivity in any state is formally equivalent to an $\partial x$ reduction in $r$, the reservation wage (since only their difference enters individuals' utility). Thus even if education is allocated randomly throughout the population, we would expect that more educated people would fall into region D, which defines the region over which young (untrained) workers will elect

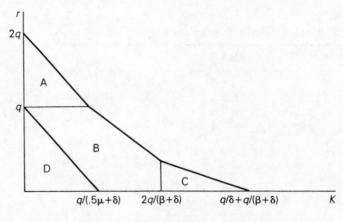

**Figure 16.3**

360

employment during uncertain times. Similarly, we would expect educated experienced workers to have lower unemployment as the productivity effect pushes those in the lower region of A (who choose temporary layoff during uncertain times) into region B.

The selectivity effect is more complicated. To the extent that the low $k$ young individuals are educated, they will have lower unemployment during uncertain times so long as $k$ and $r$ are not too negatively correlated, which seems plausible. However, owing to the assumed positive correlation between $C^i$ and $k^i$, older educated persons will include a disproportionate number of people with high reservation wages, so the selectivity effect works to increase their relative unemployment during uncertain times. Some selection working in the opposite direction occurs because individuals with high reservation wages, who participate only in certain times, are less likely to acquire an education for any level of $C^i$. Table 16.6 showed that the return to education in terms of differential unemployment has gone up for both groups. But the differential between college and high school educated young has gone up by more among inexperienced workers than among experienced ones, which is consistent with the differential selectivity effects between these two groups.

The model also predicts differences in education and the incidence of unemployment between individuals who choose to change sectors and those who do not. To the extent that the costs of general and specific training, $C^i$ and $k^i$, are positively correlated, more educated individuals will be more likely to move between sectors ($k^i < 2q/(\beta + \delta)$). Table 16.7 documents that, during the high-unemployment period 1976–83, college graduates were slightly more likely than those with a high school education or less to change the industry of their primary job between years $t$ and $t + 1$.[2] These figures probably understate the greater mobility of educated workers, since individuals who change place of residence are not counted in the table, and educated individuals are known to be more geographically mobile.[3] The result is surprising in light of the generally lower rates of job turnover found among more educated

**Table 16.7**
Year-to-Year Industry Mobility by Age and Education, 1976–83

| Education | Total | 20–29 | Age 30–45 | 46 |
|---|---|---|---|---|
| < 12 | −0.9 | 6.2 | −0.3 | −4.1 |
| 12 | −1.2 | 3.8 | −2.7 | −5.0 |
| 13–15 | 1.2 | 3.3 | 0.8 | −1.3 |
| 16 | 2.5 | 5.3 | 2.5 | −0.7 |
| > 16 | 2.6 | 4.9 | 3.0 | 0.4 |

Notes: Tabulated from matched CPS files 1977–84. Figures are proportion that change industry in one year expressed as deviation from the sample mean (= 20.2%) to adjust for measurement error. See note 2.

**Table 16.8**
Percentage of Reported Industry Changers from Years $t$ to $t+1$ Who Experience Intervening Unemployment Spells, by Age and Education, 1976–83

| Education | Total | 20–29 | Age 30–44 | 45+ |
|-----------|-------|-------|-----------|-----|
| <12 | 23.68 | 33.45 | 19.95 | 21.16 |
| 12 | 19.26 | 26.66 | 16.05 | 12.72 |
| 13–15 | 15.38 | 19.91 | 14.35 | 8.86 |
| 16 | 7.36 | 7.61 | 7.73 | 6.28 |
| >16 | 7.41 | 8.57 | 7.28 | 6.67 |

*Notes:* Tabulated from matched CPS files 1977–84. Reported figures are proportions of respondents reporting positive weeks unemployed during the previous calendar year.

workers. Evidently, job mobility among less educated workers occurs mainly within industry aggregates, indicating that the skills of educated workers are more portable across diverse sectors. An additional prediction is that unemployment will be more likely among individuals who choose to switch sectors (areas A and B). This is documented in Table 16.8, which also shows positive returns to education among industry movers.[4] To the extent that education shifts individuals into full-time participation (area B) and selects against persons who do not participate during uncertain times (area A), this pattern is consistent with the model.

## 16.5 Conclusion

Relative to historical norms, the trend rate of unemployment rose during the 1970s and early 1980s. We have documented that the incidence of this increase was widespread among various demographic groups, but fell disproportionately on individuals with less labor market experience and schooling, and on individuals whose previous labor force attachment did not qualify them for coverage under the unemployment insurance system. In light of these facts, we developed a prototypical model of costly, sector-specific human capital investment that generates a rising natural rate as a consquence of the optimizing behavior of individual agents. The key idea is that, in the face of sectoral uncertainty, individuals with less experience and those with greater costs of acquiring sector-specific human capital will rationally and optimally postpone employment and human capital investment until uncertainty has been resolved.

## Acknowledgements

An earlier version of this paper was presented at the July 1985 meeting of the NBER Research Program on Economic Fluctuations and to the Conference on

Employment, Unemployment and Hours of Work, Berlin, 1986. We are grateful to conference participants for their comments. This research was supported by the Alfred P. Sloan Foundation, the National Science Foundation and the US Department of Labor.

# Notes

1 Non-employment ratios show a similar pattern. For example, the non-employment rate of 25–34 year old males relative to that of 35–44 year olds averaged 0.86 in 1955–69 (0.82, 0.85, 0.92), but only 0.78 in 1970–84 (0.80, 0.79, 0.76). For older age groups, the decline in participation generated by social insurance programs (Parsons, 1980) dominates the data and makes comparisons of non-employment rates difficult. These calculations obscure a shift toward unemployment of prime aged workers that has occurred in the 1980s, especially relatively to very young (20–24) men. For details see Murphy and Topel (1987).

2 The data are based on tabulations of year-to-year matches of 34,245 males in the March *Current Population Surveys*, 1976–83. Industry changers are individuals whose reported three-digit industry in year $t$ was different than in year $t-1$. Because of measurement and coding errors, the reported proportion of the sample that changes industry will be overstated. (The sample mean rate is 20.2 per cent.) Thus we report the data as deviations from the sample mean on the reasonable assumption that errors in measurement are uncorrelated with age and education.

3 The CPS file is household, or 'rooftop', survey. Thus, the survey in year $t+1$ interviews persons who occupy the same dwelling unit as those interviewed in year $t$. Thus people who change dwellings leave the survey and are not counted in our tabulations.

4 Though not tabulated separately, we do find that reported movers are more likely than non-movers to report positive weeks unemployed in the previous year (17.5 per cent vs. 10.1 per cent). The difference in these proportions is understated because many individuals who do not actually change industry are misclassified as changers. For reference, the difference in unemployment between reported movers and non-movers is larger for young workers with less education: for high school graduates aged 20–29 the difference is 11.0 percentage points, but it is about 5.0 percentage points among older high school graduates and 4.3 points among college graduates.

# COMMENT

## WOLFGANG FRANZ

After 20 years of mostly negligible unemployment, European economies have suffered from long-lasting and high joblessness since the 1970s. As noted by the authors of this courageous and stimulating paper, these labor market problems cannot be explained fully and in a straightforward manner by conventional macroeconomic theories. Since the real wage gap has narrowed substantially in the 1980s this line of thought is less capable of providing an explanation of the rise in unemployment in these years. On the other hand, it is unlikely that demand deficiency is the sole candidate, since the non-accelerating inflationary rate of unemployment has been anything but stable in this time period. Moreover, structural factors may be at work, as is evidenced by the outward shift of the Beveridge curve.

This is the background against which Topel and Weiss offer their explanation of high and persistent unemployment. According to them, much of the increase in recent unemployment can be attributed to greater sectoral uncertainty during this period. More specifically, the increase in future relative wage uncertainty will tend to diminish the return to industry-specific human capital and increase the relative attractiveness of current period unemployment, especially for youths. So the basic question is: are millions of young people on the dole just because they do not know which sector to choose?

Since I am not competent enough to refer to the US labor market, I shall concentrate my discussion of the paper on two points:

(1) I shall comment on the theoretical model as it stands:
(2) I ask whether it is capable of explaining at least part of the increase in unemployment for my own country, the Federal Republic of Germany.

To begin with the theoretical basis of the model, there are various crucial assumptions that – in my view – are somewhat questionable:

1 There are training costs that must be paid by each individual. It is not clear to me what these training costs really mean. Presumably $k$ does not indicate a cash payment by the youth to the firm. One possible interpretation might be that $k$ represents opportunity costs. If so, these costs seem to be very small for an untrained youth – the case the authors frequently refer to.

2 A more crucial assumption is that incurring $k$ qualifies the individual to work in only one industry. There are certainly many jobs whose training costs are not lost when changing the industry. A youth may be well advised in a period of uncertainty to choose a job that provides as much general training as possible. Moreover, the failure

364

to differentiate between non-employment and unemployment pro-
hibits the authors from taking into account schooling as a reasonable
third choice.

3 More importantly, the assumption is made that, when a certain
period comes to an end, previous information on sectoral output
becomes irrelevant. This is hard to believe unless everything is
stochastic in the real world!

4 A somewhat unrealistic basic assumption of the model is that, if an
individual decides not to work during a certain period, *any* skills
previously acquired in an industry depreciate fully. This cannot be
justified by the notion that the duration of uncertain periods is
relatively brief compared to certain periods. If I have read the
empirical evidence presented by the authors correctly, the US
experienced a *long* period of uncertainty on the basis of the measure
employed. The major objection is, however, that I do not see any
theoretical justification for the important assumption that depreciation of human capital during uncertain periods is negligible but that
the *same* depreciation becomes *total* during certain periods.

5 As I understand the model, the reservation wage, which plays an
important role, is taken to be exogenous. Certainly it is not exogenous and its determinants should be spelled out within the framework
of the model. But, besides this, how important is a reservation wage
of an untrained youth who is probably not entitled to unemployment
compensation? Unless he or she has generous parents and/or the
welfare program in the US for these people is generous, my
suspicion is that the reservation wage is rather low. Since I have
mentioned already that I guess that training costs are also low, I
would conclude – in full agreement with the model and the implications spelled out – that most youths will choose to work even
during uncertain periods.

Given these objections, I am unconvinced that the model gives a
realistic picture of US youth unemployment. I think the major problem
is that the analogy to models that analyze investment into *non*-human
capital is stressed too much. I can, of course, imagine an investor who,
during uncertain periods, prefers not to invest his money but holds it
idle. I find it hard to believe that youths behave in the same manner.
Isn't it more likely that there are just no jobs available for them, rather
than that they do not know which job to take?

Let me very briefly touch on the empirical part. The time-series
evidence presented in the paper concentrates entirely on the issue of
whether or not uncertainty has increased since the 1970s. While this is
no test of the model, I fully understand the problems mentioned by the
authors. The major problem that I have with the various measures of
uncertainty is that they indicate different periods of uncertainty. For
example, employment uncertainty seems to me to be largest during
1974–9 and in 1982, whereas portfolio uncertainty is larger during
1972–6.

Let me turn to my last point. Both the US and West Germany have experienced a tremendous increase in (youth) unemployment. Therefore, both countries share the same problem. I have outlined why I think it doubtful that the model can explain this phenomenon for the US as is claimed by the authors. For Germany the verdict is even more doubtful. In Germany, the apprentice training system provides much non-specific human capital so that most of the investment made during the apprenticeship training can be used in different sectors. The problem for German youth is to find an apprenticeship training position and, later, a job.

# References

Åberg, Y. (1985), 'Produktionens och sysselsättningens bestämningsfaktorer i svensk ekonomi', DELFA, Arbetsmarknadsdepartementet, Stockholm (in Swedish)

Addison, J. T. and Castro, A. C. 'The importance of lifetime jobs: Differences between union and nonunion workers', *Industrial and Labor Relations Review*, 40(3), April, 393–405

Addison, J. T. and Portugal, P. (1987a), 'Job displacement, relative wage changes, and duration of unemployment', unpublished paper, University of South Carolina, August

Addison, J. T. and Portugal, P. (1987b), 'The effect of advance notification of plant closings on unemployment', *Industrial and Labor Relations Review*, 41(1), October, 3–16

Allen, R. (1980), 'The economic effects of a shorter working week', Government Economic Service Working Paper 33 (London: HM Treasury)

Altonji, J. and Shakotko, R. (1985), 'Do wages rise with job seniority?' *Review of Economic Studies*, 54(3), July, 437–61

Andrews, M. J., Bell, D. N. F., Fisher, P. G., Wallis, K. F. and Whitley, J. D. (1985), 'Models of the UK economy and the real wage–employment debate', *National Institute Economic Review*, 112, 41–56

Anxo, D. (1986), 'Beräkning av marginalelasticiteten med avseende på arbetstiden', Working Paper, Department of Economics, University of Gothenburg (in Swedish)

Appelbaum, E. (1986), 'Restructuring work: temporary, part-time and at-home employment', in H. I. Hartmann (ed.), *Computer Chips and Paper Clips: Technology and Women's Employment*, Vol. II, *Case Studies and Policy Perspectives* (Washington, DC: National Academy Press), pp. 268–310

Arrow, K. (1962), 'The economic implications of learning by doing', *Review of Economic Studies*, 29, June, 155–73

Arrufat, J. L. and Zabalza, A. (1986), 'Female labour supply with taxation, random preferences, and optimization errors', *Econometrica*, 54(1), 47–63

Azariadis, C. (1975), 'Implicit contracts and underemployment equilibria', *Journal of Political Economy*, 83, December, 1183–202

Azariadis, C. (1981), 'Implicit contracts and related topics', in Z. Hornstein *et al.* (eds), *The Economics of the Labour Market* (London: HMSO)

Backus, D. and Driffil, J. (1986), 'The consistency of optimal policy in stochastic rational expectations models', May (mimeo)

Baily, M. N. (1974), 'Wages and employment under uncertain demand', *Review of Economic Studies*, 41, January, 37–50

Baily, M. N. (1977), 'On the theory of layoffs and unemployment', *Econometrica*, 45, 1043–64

Bain, G. S. and Elsheikh, F. (1979), 'An interindustry analysis of unionization in Britain', *British Journal of Industrial Relations*, 18, July, 137–55

Ball, R. J., Burns, T. and Laury, J. S. E. (1977), 'The role of exchange rate changes in balance of payments adjustment – the United Kingdom case', *Economic Journal*, 87, 1–29

Ball, R. J. and St Cyr, E. B. A. (1966), 'Short term employment functions in British manufacturing industry', *Review of Economic Studies*, 33, 179–207

Ballard, B. (1984), 'Women part-time workers: Evidence from the 1980 Women and Employment survey', *Employment Gazette*, September, 409–16

Barro, R. (1984), *Macroeconomics* (New York: Wiley)

Barro, R. J. and Gordon, D. B. (1983), 'Rules, discretion and reputation in a model of monetary policy', *Journal of Monetary Economics*, 12, 101–21

Barron, J. M., Lowenstein, M. A. and Black, D. A. (1984), 'On recalls, layoffs, variable hours and labour adjustment costs', *Journal of Economic Dynamics and Control*, 8, 265–75

Bean, C. R. (1986), 'The estimation of "surprise" models and the "suprise" consumption function', *Review of Economic Studies*, 53(4), 497–516

Becker, G. S. (1962), 'Investment in human capital: A theoretical analysis', *Journal of Political Economy*, 70 (Supplement), 9–49

Becker, G. S. (1964), *Human Capital* (New York: Columbia University Press for National Bureau of Economic Research); 2nd edn 1975

Bell, D. (1982), 'Labor utilization and statutory non-wage costs', *Economica*, 49, 335–43

Bell, L. and Freeman, R. (1985), 'Does a flexible industry wage structure increase employment? The US experience', Working Paper No. 1604, National Bureau of Economic Research, April

Bernanke, B. S. (1983), 'Irreversibility, uncertainty, and cyclical investment', *Quarterly Journal of Economics*, 98, no. 390, February, 85–106

Bernanke, B. S. (1986), 'Employment, hours, and earnings in the Depression: An analysis of eight manufacturing industries', *American Economic Review*, 76, 82–109

Bielenski, H. and Hegner, F. (eds) (1985), *Flexible Arbeitszeiten: Erfahrungen aus der Praxis* (Frankfurt/New York: Campus)

Bienefeld, M. A. (1972), *Working Hours in British Industry: An Economic History* (London: Weidenfeld & Nicolson)

Blyton, P. (1985), *Changes in Working Time: An International Review* (London: Croom Helm/New York: St Martins Press)

Bodo, G. and Giannini, C. (1985), 'Average working time and the influence of contractual hours: An empirical investigation for Italian industry (1970–1981)', *Oxford Bulletin of Economics and Statistics*, 47(2), 131–51

Booth, A. and Schiantarelli, F. (1985), 'The employment effects of a shorter working week', Discussion Paper 263, Department of Economics, University of Essex

Booth, A. and Schiantarelli, F. (1987), 'The employment effects of a shorter working week', *Economica*, 54, May, 237–48

Booth, A. L. and Ulph, D. T. (1985), 'A bargaining model of wages, employment and trade union membership', The City University, London (mimeo)

Bosworth, D. L. (1981), 'Specification of factor demand models and shiftworking', *Scottish Journal of Political Economy*, 28, 256–65

Bosworth, D. L. and Westaway, J. A. (1986), 'Hours of work and employment in UK manufacturing industry: an empirical analysis', in R. A. Wilson (ed.), *Hours of Work* (University of Warwick, Institute for Employment Research), pp. 32–61

Brechling, F. (1965), 'The relationship between output and employment in British manufacturing industries', *Review of Economic Studies*, 32, 187–216

# REFERENCES

Bruno, M. and Sachs, J. D. (1985), *Economics of Worldwide Stagflation* (Cambridge, Mass.: Harvard University Press)

Brunstad, R. J. and Holm, T. (1984), 'Can shorter hours solve the problem of unemployment?' Paper presented at the European Meeting of the Econometric Society, Madrid

Bucher, A. (1984), 'Marché du travail et stabilité des fonctions d'emploi: le cas de la France et de la R.F.A.' in Daniel Vitry and Bernadette Marechal (eds), *Emploi-Chomage: Modelization et Analyses Quantitatives* (Dijon: Librairie de l'Université)

Büchtemann, C. F. (1988), 'Entwicklungstendenzen der Teilzeitbeschäftigung und Geringfügigkeitsgrenze', Discussion Paper, Wissenschaftszentrum Berlin für Sozialforschung (forthcoming)

Büchtemann, C. F. and Schupp, J. (1986), 'Zur Sozioökonomie der Teilzeitbeschäftigung in der Bundesrepublik Deutschland', Discussion Paper 86-15, Wissenschaftszentrum Berlin für Sozialforschung

Büchtemann, C. F. and Schupp, J. (1988), 'The socio-economics of part-time employment II: Further evidence for the Federal Republic of Germany', Discussion Paper, Wissenschaftszentrum Berlin für Sozialforschung (forthcoming)

Bull, C. and Tedeschi, P. (n.d.), 'Optimal probation for new hires' (mimeo)

Bulow, J. and Summers, L. (1986), 'A theory of dual labor markets with application to industrial policy, discrimination and Keynesian unemployment', *Journal of Labor Economics*, 4, July, 376–414

Burdett, K. and Wright, R. (1986), 'The effects of unemployment insurance on layoffs, hours per worker, and wages', Working Paper No. 363, Department of Economics, Cornell University, March


Calmfors, L. (1985), 'Job sharing, employment and wages', *European Economic Review*, 27, 293–309

Calmfors, L. and Hoel, M. (1985), 'Work sharing, overtime and shiftwork', Seminar Paper No. 336, Institute for International Economic Studies, University of Stockholm (mimeo)

Calmfors, L. and Hoel, M. (1988), 'Work sharing and overtime', *Scandinavian Journal of Economics*, 90(1), 45–62

Calvo, G. A. (1978), 'On the time consistency of optimal policy in a monetary economy', *Econometrica*, 46, 1411–28

Carey, M. L. and Hazelbaker, K. L. (1986), 'Employment growth in the temporary help industry', *Monthly Labor Review*, 109, April, 37–44

Carmichael, L. (1983), 'Firm-specific human capital and promotion ladders', *Bell Journal of Economics*, 14, 251–8

Carter, M. and Maddock, R. (1984), 'On the determination of working hours', Working Papers in Economics and Econometrics, No. 095, Faculty of Economics and Research School of Social Sciences, Australian National University

CBI (1979), *Reductions in Working Time* (London: Confederation of British Industry)

Chang, J. (1983), 'An econometric model of the short-run demand for workers and hours in the US auto industry', *Journal of Econometrics*, 22, 301–16

Chiarella, C. and Steinherr, A. (1982), 'Marginal employment subsidies: An effective policy to generate employment', *Economic Papers of the Commission of the European Communities*, No. 9

Chow, G. C. (1960), 'Tests of equality between sets of coefficients in two linear regressions', *Econometrica*, 28, 591–605

Cole, R. E. (1979), *Work, Mobility, and Participation* (Berkeley, Calif.: University of California Press)

Conradi, H. (1982), *Teilzeitarbeit – Theorie, Realität, Realisierbarkeit* (Munich: Minerva)

Craine, R. (1973), 'On the service flow from labour', *Review of Economic Studies*, 40, 39–46

Crawford, R. (1979), 'Expectations and labor market adjustments', *Journal of Econometrics*, 11, 207–32

Culliver, R. (1984), *The Reduction of Working Time* (Geneva: International Labour Office)

Dagsvik, J. K. (1988), 'The continuous generalized extreme value model with special reference to static models of labor supply', Discussion Paper, Central Bureau of Statistics, Oslo

Dagsvik, J. K. and Strøm, S. (1988), 'A labor supply model for married couples with non-convex budget sets and latent rationing', Discussion Paper, Central Bureau of Statistics, Oslo

Daniel, W. W. and Millward, N. (1984), *Workplace Industrial Relations in Britain* (London: Heinemann)

Davis, O. and Montgomery, E. (1986), 'Income security in the steel industry: A case study of US Steel Corporation', Washington, DC: School of Urban and Public Affairs, Carnegie-Mellon University; reprinted in *Daily Labor Report*, No. 95, Washington, DC, Bureau of National Affairs

Deardorff, A. V. and Stafford, F. P. (1976), 'Compensation of cooperating factors', *Econometrica*, 44, 671–84

De Neubourg, C. (1985), 'Part-time work: An international quantitative comparison', *International Labour Review*, 5, 559–76

Department of Health and Social Security (1983), *Abstract of Statistics for Index of Retail Prices, Average Earnings, Social Security Benefits and Contributions* (London: HMSO)

Deuterman, W. V., Jnr and Brown, S. C. (1978), 'Voluntary part-time workers: A growing part of the labor force', *Monthly Labor Review*, June, 3–10

Dickens, W. (1983), 'The effect of company campaigns on certification elections: Law and reality once again', *Industrial and Labor Relations Review*, 36, July, 560–75

Dickens, W. and Leonard, J. S. (1985), 'Accounting for the decline in union membership, 1950–1980', *Industrial and Labor Relations Review*, 38, April, 323–34

Dickens, W. T. and Lundberg, S. J. (1985), 'Hours restrictions and labor supply', Working Paper No. 1638, National Bureau of Economic Research

Disney, R. and Szyszczak, E. M. (1984), 'Protective labour legislation and part-time employment in Britain', *British Journal of Industrial Relations*, 22, March, 78–100

Durbin, J. (1970), 'Testing for serial correlation in least-squares regression when some of the regressors are lagged dependent variables', *Econometrica*, 38, 410–21

Ehrenberg, R. G. (1971a), *Fringe Benefits and Overtime Behavior* (Lexington, Mass.: D. C. Heath & Co.)

Ehrenberg, R. G. (1971b), 'Heterogeneous labor, the internal labor market, and the dynamics of the employment–hours decision', *Journal of Economic Theory*, 3, 85–104

# REFERENCES

Ehrenberg, R. G. (1971c), 'The impact of the overtime premium on employment and hours in US industry', *Western Economic Journal*, 9, 199–207

Ehrenberg, R. G. and Marcus, A. (1982), 'Minimum wages and teenagers' enrollment and employment outcomes: A multinomial logit model', *Journal of Human Resources*, 17, Winter, 39–59

Ehrenberg, R. G. and Schumann, P. L. (1982), *Longer Hours or More Jobs?* Cornell Studies in Industrial and Labor Relations No. 22 (Ithaca, NY: New York State School of Industrial and Labor Relations, Cornell University Press)

Ehrenberg, R. G. and Sherman, D. S. (1987), 'Employment while in college, academic achievement, and post-college outcomes: A summary of results', Journal of Human Resources, 22, Winter

*Employment Gazette*, various issues

Engle, R. F. (1982), 'Autoregressive conditional heteroscedasticity with estimates of the variance of United Kingdom inflation', *Econometrica*, 50, 987–1007

Epstein, R. A. (1984), 'In praise of the contract at will', *University of Chicago Law Review*, 51, 956–82

ETUI (1983), *The Reduction of Working Hours in Western Europe* (Brussels: European Trade Union Institute)

Evans, A. A. (1975), Hours of Work in Industrialised Countries (Geneva: International Labour Office)


Faini, R. and Schiantarelli, F. (1985), 'A unified framework for firms' decisions: Theoretical analysis and empirical application to Italy, 1970–1980', in Daniel Weiserbs (ed.), *Industrial Investment in Europe* (Amsterdam: Nijhoff)

Fair, R. C. (1969), *The Short-run Demand for Workers and Hours* (Amsterdam: North Holland)

Feldstein, M. S. (1967), 'Specification of the labour input in the aggregate production function', *Review of Economic Studies*, 34, October, 375–86

Feldstein, M. S. (1975), 'The importance of temporary layoffs: An empirical analysis', *Brookings Papers on Economic Activity*, 3, 725–45

Feldstein, M. S. (1976), 'Temporary layoffs in the theory of unemployment', *Journal of Political Economy*, 84, October, 937–57

Feldstein, M. S. (1977), 'Social security', in M. J. Boskin (ed.), *The Crisis on Social Security* (San Francisco: Institute for Contemporary Studies)

Fine, C. and Gibbons, R. (1986), 'Production smoothing and employee sorting: Factors in the demand for temporary employees', June (mimeo)

Fischel, D. (1984), 'Labor markets and labor law compared with capital markets and capital law', *University of Chicago Law Review*, 4, 1061–77

FitzRoy, F. (1981), 'On optimal unemployment', *Economics Letters*, 8, 275–80

FitzRoy, F. R. and Hart, R. A. (1985), 'Hours, layoffs and unemployment insurance funding: Theory and practice in an international perspective', *Economic Journal*, 95, 700–13

FitzRoy, F. R. and Hart, R. A. (1986), 'Part-time and full-time employment: The demand for workers and hours', International Institute of Management, Science Center, Berlin, April (mimeo)

Flaim, P. and Seghal, E. (1985), 'Displaced workers: How well have they fared?' *Monthly Labor Review*, 108(6), June, 3–16

Folbre, N., Leighton, J. and Roderick, M. (1984), 'Plant closings and their regulation in Maine, 1971–1982', *Industrial and Labor Relations Review*, 37, 185–96

Franz, W. (1984), 'Is less more? The current discussion about reduced working time in Western Germany: A survey of the debate', *Zeitschrift für die gesamte Staatswissenschaft*, 140, 626–54

Friedman, J. W. (1971), 'A non-cooperative equilibrium for supergames', *Review of Economic Studies*, 38, January, 861–74

Friedman, M. (1955), 'Comment', in *Business Concentration and Public Policy*, a Report of the National Bureau of Economic Research (Princeton, NJ: Princeton University Press)

Galler, H. and Wagner, G. (1983), 'Arbeitsangebotseffekte einer Arbeitszeit-verkürzung', *Sonderforschungsbereich 3: Mikroanalytische Grundlagen der Gesellschaftspolitik*, Discussion Paper No. 112, Frankfurt/M

Gennard, J. (1979), *Job Security and Industrial Relations* (Paris: OECD)

Gennard, J. (1985), 'Job security: Redundancy arrangements and practices in selected OECD countries', Paris, OECD

Gilbert, C. L. (1986), 'Professor Hendry's econometric methodology', *Oxford Bulletin of Economics and Statistics*, 48, 283–307

Ginneken, W. van (1984), 'Employment and the reduction of the work week: A comparison of seven European macro-economic models', *International Labour Review*, 123, 35–52

Gordon, R. J. (1982), 'Why US wage and employment behaviour differs from that in Britain and Japan', *Economic Journal*, 92(365), March, 13–44

Grossman, G. (1982), 'International competition and the unionized sector', Working Paper No. 899, National Bureau of Economic Research

Gustman, A. L. and Steinmeier, T. L. (1986), 'A structural retirement model', *Econometrica*, 54, 555–84

Hall, R. E. and Lazear, E. (1984), 'The excess sensitivity of layoffs and quits to demand', *Journal of Labor Economics*, 2, April, 233–57

Haltiwanger, J. (1984), 'The distinguishing characteristics of temporary and permanent layoffs', *Journal of Labor Economics*, 2(4), October, 523–38

Hamada, K. and Kurosaka, Y. (1984), 'The relationship between production and unemployment in Japan', *European Economic Review*, 25, 71–94.

Hamada, K. and Kurosaka, Y. (1986), 'Trends in unemployment, wages and productivity: The case of Japan', *Economica*, 53, Supplement, S275–96

Hamermesh, D. (1969), 'A disaggregative econometric model of gross changes in employment', *Yale Economic Essays*, 9, 107–46

Hamermesh, D. (1976), 'Econometric studies of labor demand and their application to policy analysis', *Journal of Human Resources*, 11, 507–25

Hamermesh, D. (1978), 'Unemployment insurance, short-time compensation and the workweek', in National Commission for Manpower Policy, *Work Time and Employment* (Washington, DC: NCMP)

Hamermesh, D. (1985), 'Job security and labor demand: Theory and evidence', July (mimeo)

Hamermesh, D. (1986), 'The demand for labor in the long run', in O. Ashenfelter and R. Layard, *Handbook of Labor Economics* (Amsterdam: North-Holland Press)

Hamermesh, D. (1987), 'The costs of worker displacement', *Quarterly Journal of Economics*, 102, 51–74

Hamermesh, D. and Rees, A. (1988), *The Economics of Work and Pay* (New York: Harper & Row)

Hanami, T. (1981), *Labor Relations in Japan Today* (Tokyo: Kodansha International)

## REFERENCES

Hanel, H. R. (1985), 'New data series on involuntary part-time work', *Monthly Labor Review*, March, 42–3

Hanemann, W. M. (1984), 'Discrete/continuous models of consumer demand', *Econometrica*, 52, 541–61

Harris, M. and Holmström, B. (1982), 'A theory of wage dynamics', *Review of Economic Studies*, 49, July, 315–33

Hart, R. A. (1984a), 'Worksharing and factor prices', *European Economic Review*, 24, 165–88

Hart, R. A. (1984b), *The Economics of Non-Wage Labour Costs* (London: Allen & Unwin)

Hart, R. A. (1987) *Working Time and Employment* (London: Allen & Unwin)

Hart, R. A. and Kawasaki, S. (1987), 'Payroll taxes and factor demand', *Research in Labor Economics*, 9 (Greenwich, Conn.: JAI Press)

Hart, R. A. and McGregor, P. G. (1988), 'The returns to labour services in West German manufacturing industry', *European Economic Review*, 32, 947–63

Hart, R. A. and Robb, L. A. (1980), 'Production and labor demand functions with endogenous fixed worker costs', Discussion Paper 1980-11, Wissenschaftszentrum Berlin

Hart, R. A. and Sharot, T. (1978), 'The short-run demand for workers and hours: A recursive model', *Review of Economic Studies*, 45, 299–309

Harvey, A. C. (1981), *The Econometric Analysis of Time Series* (Oxford: Philip Allen)

Hashimoto, M. (1975), 'Wage reduction, unemployment and specific human capital', *Economic Enquiry*, 13, 485–504

Hashimoto, M. (1979), 'Bonus payments, on-the-job training and lifetime employment in Japan', *Journal of Political Economy*, 87, 1086–104

Hashimoto, M. and Raisian, J. (1985a), 'Employment tenure and earnings profiles in Japan and the United States', *American Economic Review*, 75, 721–35

Hashimoto, M. and Raisian, J. (1985b), 'Productivity of Japanese and US workers in firms of varying size', presented at the Conference on Income and Wealth, National Bureau of Economic Research

Hashimoto, M. and Yu, B. T. (1980), 'Specific capital, employment contracts and wage rigidity', *Bell Journal of Economics*, 11, 536–49

Hausman, J. A. (1985), 'The econometrics of non linear budget set', *Econometrica*, 53(6), 1255–82

Hendry, D. F. (1983), 'Econometric modelling: The "consumption function" in retrospect', *Scottish Journal of Political Economy*, 30, 193–219

Hoel, M. (1984), 'Short and long-run effects of reduced working time in a unionised economy', Working Paper No. 10, Department of Economics, University of Oslo

Hoel, M. (1986), 'Employment and allocation effects of reducing the length of the workday', *Economica*, 53, February, 75–85

Hoel, M. and Vale, B. (1986), 'Effects of reduced working time in an economy where firms set wages', *European Economic Review*, 30, 1097–104

Hoff, A. (1983), *Betriebliche Arbeitszeitpolitik zwischen Arbeitszeitverkürzung und Arbeitszeitflexibilsierung* (Munich: Minerva)

Holt, C. *et al.* (1960), *Planning Production, Inventories and Work Force* (Englewood Cliffs, NJ: Prentice-Hall)

Homlund, B. (1981), 'Employment subsidies and the behaviour of the firm', in G. Eliasson and J. Sodersten (eds), *Business Taxation, Finance and Firm Behaviour* (Stockholm: Almquist & Wicksell), pp. 267–93

Houseman, S. N. (1985), 'Job security and industrial restructuring in the

European Community steel industry', PhD dissertation, Harvard University; forthcoming Harvard University Press

Houseman, S. N. (1986), 'Labor adjustment policies and practices: A study of US and European approaches in the steel industry', report prepared for the Bureau of International Labor Affairs, US Department of Labor

Hübler, O. (1987), 'Effort, overtime and standard working hours', Department of Economics, University of Hannover (mimeo)

Ichniowski, B. E. and Preston, (1986), 'New trends in part-time employment', *Proceedings of the Thirty-Eighth Annual Meeting of the Industrial Relations Research Association* (Madison, WI: IRRA)

IFO-Institute (1983), 'Gesamtwirtschaftliche Auswirkungen einer Verkürzung der Arbeitszeit', *IFO-Studien zur Arbeitszeitverkürzung*, 3/I, IFO-Institute, Munich

Ito, T. (1984), 'Why is the unemployment rate so much lower in Japan than in the US?' Working Paper No. 198, University of Minnesota

Johnston, J. (1960), *Statistical Cost Analysis* (New York: McGraw-Hill)

Jones, S. G. (1985), 'The worksharing debate in Western Europe', *National Westminster Bank Quarterly Review*, February, 18–29

Kamien, M. I. and Schwartz, N. L. (1971), 'Limit pricing and uncertain entry', *Econometrica*, 39, 441–54

Kane, P. (1982), 'The impact on employment of worksharing and shorter working week in twentieth century Britain', PhD thesis, University of London

Kennan, J. (1979), 'Bonding and the enforcement of labor contracts', *Economic Letters*, 3, 61–6

Kidd, D. P. and Oswald, A. J. (1987), 'A dynamic model of trade union behaviour', *Economica*, 54(215), 355–65

Killingsworth, M. R. (1983), *Labor Supply* (Cambridge: Cambridge University Press)

Kmenta, J. (1971), *Elements of Econometrics* (New York: Macmillan)

König, H. (1986), 'Arbeitslosigkeit: Fakten, Artifakte, Theorien', Discussion Paper No. 325-86, Institut für Volkswirtschaftslehre und Statistik, University of Mannheim

König, H. and Pohlmeier, W. (1986), 'Arbeitszeit und Beschäftigung: Eine Ökonometrische Studie', unpublished paper, University of Mannheim

König, H. and Pohlmeier, W. (1987), 'Worksharing and factor prices: A comparison of three flexible functional forms for nonlinear cost schemes', Discussion Paper No. 345-87, University of Mannheim

Labor Canada (1983), *Part-time Work in Canada: Report of the Commission of Enquiry into Part-time Work* (Ottawa)

Landenberger, M. (1983), 'Arbeitszeitwünsche, Vergleichende Analysen vorliegender Befragungsergebnisse', Discussion Paper 83-17, Wissenschaftszentrum Berlin für Sozialforschung

Latham, R. W. and Peel, D. A. (1979), 'A dynamic model of the demand for labour services', *Bulletin of Economic Research*, 31, 24–30

Lazear, E. (1981), 'Agency, earnings profiles, productivity and hours restrictions', *American Economic Review*, 71, 606–20

Leban, R. (1982), 'Employment and wage strategies of the firm over a business cycle', *Journal of Economic Dynamics and Control*, 4, 371–94

Leban, R. and Lesourne, J. (1980), 'The firm's investment and employment policy through a business cycle', *European Economic Review*, 13, 43–80

Leban, R. and Lesourne, J. (1983), 'Adaptive strategies of the firm through a business cycle', *Journal of Economic Dynamics and Control*, 5, 201–34

Leon, C. and Bednarzik, R. W. (1978), 'A profile of women in part-time schedules', *Monthly Labor Review*, October, 3–12

Leslie, D. (1978), 'A supply and demand analysis of the structure of hours of work for UK production industries', Discussion Paper No. 5, University of Manchester

Leslie, D. (1984), 'The productivity of hours in US manufacturing industries', *Review of Economics and Statistics*, 66(3), 486–90

Leslie, D. and Wise, J. (1980), 'The productivity of hours in UK manufacturing and production industries', *Economic Journal*, 90, 74–84

Levhari, D. and Liviatan, H. (1972), 'On stability in the saddlepoint sense', *Journal of Economic Theory*, 4, 88–93

Lewis, H. G. (1969), 'Employer interests in employee hours of work', unpublished paper

Lewis, H. G. (1971), 'Hours of work and hours of leisure', in J. F. Burton *et al.* (eds), *Readings in Labor Market Analysis* (New York: Holt Rinehart & Winston), Ch. 6

Lilien, D. (1980), 'The cyclical pattern of temporary layoffs in US manufacturing', *Review of Economics and Statistics*, 62(1), February, 24–31

Lilien, D. (1982), 'Sectoral shifts and cyclical unemployment', *Journal of Political Economy*, 90(4), August, 777–93

Lilien, D. (1984), 'A sectoral model of the business cycle', unpublished MS., University of Southern California, January

Linde, R. (1983), 'Beschäftigungseffekte von Arbeitszeitverkürzungen mit Lohnausgleich', *Jahrbücher für Nationalökonomie und Statistik*, 198, 425–36

Lucas, R. E., Jr (1970), 'Capacity, overtime and empirical production functions', *American Economic Review*, 60, May, 23–7

Lundberg, S. (1985), 'Tied wage–hours offers and the endogeneity of wages', *Review of Economics and Statistics*, 67, 405–10

McKersie, R. and Sengenberger, W. (1983), *Job Losses in Major Industries* (Paris: OECD)

Mairesse, J. and Dormont, B. (1985), 'Labor and investment demand at the firm level: A comparison of French, German and US manufacturing, 1970–79', Working Paper No. 1554, National Bureau of Economic Research, February

Mangum, G., Mayall, D. and Nelson, K. (1985), 'The temporary help industry: A response to the dual internal labor market', *Industrial and Labor Relations Review*, 40, July, 599–611

Matilla, J. P. (1981), 'The impact of minimum wages on teenage schooling and on the part-time/full-time employment of youths', in S. Rottenberg (ed.), *The Economics of Legal Minimum Wages* (Washington, DC: American Enterprise Institute)

Mayall, D. and Nelson, K. (1982), 'The temporary help supply service and the temporary labor market', report prepared for the Office of Research and Development, Employment and Training Administration, US Department of Labor, December

Medoff, J. L. (1979), 'Layoffs and alternatives under trade unions in United States manufacturing', *American Economic Review*, 69, June, 380–95

Medoff, J. L. and Abraham, K. G. (1980), 'Experience, performance, and earnings', *Quarterly Journal of Economics*, 95(4), December, 703–36

Meese, R. (1980), 'Dynamic factor demand schedules for labor and capital under rational expectations', *Journal of Econometrics*, 14, 141–58

Metcalf, D. (1984), 'On redundancies', Working Paper No. 640, Centre for Labour Economics, London School of Economics, May

Miller, M. and Salmon, M. (1985), 'Dynamic games and the time inconsistency of optimal policy in open economies', *Economic Journal*, 95, 124–37

Mincer, J. and Jovanovic, B. (1981), 'Labor mobility and wages', in S. Rosen (ed.), *Studies in Labor Markets* (Chicago: University of Chicago Press)

Mitchell, O. (1982), 'Fringe benefits and labor mobility', *Journal of Human Resources*, 17, 286–98

Mitchell, O. (1983), 'Fringe benefits and the costs of changing jobs', *Industrial and Labor Relations Review*, 37, October, 70–9

Mitchell, W. C. (1941), *Business Cycles and their Causes* (Berkeley, Calif.: University of California Press)

Morris, C. (ed.) (1983), *The Developing Labor Law*, 2nd edn (Washington, DC: Bureau of National Affairs)

Morrison, C. and Berndt, E. (1981), 'Short-run labor productivity in a dynamic model', *Journal of Econometrics*, 16, 339–65

Moy, J. and Sorrentino, C. (1981), 'Unemployment, labor force trends, and layoff practices in 10 countries', *Monthly Labor Review*, 104(12), December, 3–13

Mueller, D. C. (1986), *Profits in the Long Run* (Cambridge: Cambridge University Press)

Murphy, K. M. and Topel, R. H. (1987), 'The evolution of unemployment in the United States: 1968–1985', in S. Fisher (ed.), *The NBER Macroeconomics Annual*, vol. 2 (Cambridge, Mass.: MIT Press for the National Bureau of Economic Research)

Nadiri, M. I. and Rosen, S. (1969), 'Interrelated factor demand functions', *American Economic Review*, 59, 457–71

Nadiri, M. I. and Rosen, S. (1974), *A Disequilibrium Model of Demand for Factors of Production* (New York: National Bureau of Economic Research)

Nakakubo, H. (1985), 'Actual conditions and legal problems relating to part-time employment', *Japan Labor Bulletin*, 1 January, 5–8

Nardone, T. J. (1986), 'Part-time workers: Who are they?' *Monthly Labor Review*, February, 13–19

Nash, P. and Blake, G. P. (eds) (1979), *Appropriate Units for Collective Bargaining* (New York: Practising Law Institute)

Neale, A. J. and Wilson, R. A. (1985), 'Average weekly hours of work in the UK 1948–80: A disaggregated analysis', University of Warwick (mimeo)

Nerb, G. (1986), 'Employment problems: Views of businessmen and the workforce', *European Economy* (EEC), No. 27, 5–110

Neumann, M. (1984), *Arbeitszeitverkürzung gegen Arbeitslosigkeit* (Berlin: Duncker und Humblot)

Nickell, S. J. (1974), 'On the role of expectations in the pure theory of investment', *Review of Economic Studies*, 41, 1–19

Nickell, S. J. (1978), 'Fixed costs, employment and labor demand over the cycle', *Economica*, 45, 329–45

Nickell, S. J. (1979), 'Unemployment and the structure of labor costs', *Journal of Monetary Economics*, 11, 187–222

Nickell, S. J. (1982), 'The determinants of equilibrium unemployment in Britain', *Economic Journal*, 92, 556–75

Nickell, S. J. (1984a), 'Dynamic models of labour demand', Discussion Paper No. 197, London School of Economics

Nickell, S. J. (1984b), 'An investigation of the determinants of manufacturing employment in the United Kingdom', *Review of Economic Studies*, 51, 529–57

Nickell, S. J. (1987), 'Dynamic models of labour demand', in O. Ashenfelter and R. Layard (eds), *Handbook of Labour Economics* (Amsterdam: North-Holland)

Nissim, J. (1984), 'The price responsiveness of the demand for labor by skill: British mechanical engineering, 1963–1978', *Economic Journal*, 94, 812–25


OECD (1983), *Employment Outlook, 1983*, Paris

OECD (1984), *Employment Outlook, 1984*, Paris

OECD (1985), *Employment Outlook, 1985*, Paris

OECD (1986), *Employment Outlook, 1986*, Paris

OECD, Steel Committee (1985), 'Steel manpower policies', SC (85) 10, Paris

Oi, W. (1962), 'Labor as a quasi-fixed factor', *Journal of Political Economy*, 70, 538–55

Owen, J. (1979), *Working Hours* (Lexington, Mass.: Lexington Books)


Parsons, D. (1974), 'The cost of school time, forgone earnings and human capital formation', *Journal of Political Economy*, 82, March/April, 251–66

Parsons, D. (1980), 'The decline of male labor force participation', *Journal of Political Economy*, 88, February, 117–34

Pelsmacker, P. de (1984), 'Long-run and short-run demand for factors of production in the Belgian car industry', in D. Vitry and B. Marechal (eds), *Emploi–chomage: Modelization et analyses quantitatives* (Dijon: Librairie de l'Université)

Pindyck, R. (1984), 'Risk, inflation and the stock market', *American Economic Review*, 74, June, 335–51

Pindyck, R. S. and Rotemberg, J. J. (1983), 'Dynamic factor demands under rational expectations', *Scandinavian Journal of Economics*, 85, 223–38

Piore, M. (1980), 'Dualism as a response to flux and uncertainty', in S. Berger and M. J. Piore, *Dualism and Discontinuity in Industrial Societies* (Cambridge: Cambridge University Press)

Psacharopoulos, G. and Arriagada, A. M. (1986), 'The educational composition of the labour force: An international comparison', *International Labour Review*, 125, September/October, 561–74


Raisian, J. T. (1978), 'Cyclical variations in hours, weeks and wages', PhD dissertation, University Micro-films International, Ann Arbor, Michigan

Raisian, J. (1979), 'Cyclic patterns in weeks and wages', *Economic Inquiry*, 17, 475–95

Raisian, J. (1983), 'Contracts, job experience and cyclical labor adjustments', *Journal of Labor Economics*, 1, 152–70

Regt, E. R. de (1984), 'Shorter working time in a model of the firm, theory and estimation', Working Paper, Institute for Economic Research, Erasmus University, Rotterdam

Richardson, R. and Catlin, S. (1979), 'Trade union density and collective agreement patterns in Britain', *British Journal of Industrial Relations*, 15, November, 376–86

Robinson, O. and Wallace, J. (1984), 'Part-time employment and sex-discrimination legislation in Great Britain. A study of the demand for part-time labour and of sex-discrimination in selected organizations and establishments', Research Paper No. 43, Department of Employment, London

Rosen, H. S. (1976), 'Taxes in a labor supply model with joint wage–hours determination', *Econometrica*, 44, 485–507

Rosen, S. (1968), 'Short-run employment variation on class-I railroads in the US, 1947–1963', *Econometrica*, 36, 511–29

Rosen, S. (1978), 'The supply of work schedules and employment', in National Commission for Manpower Policy, *Work Time and Employment* (Washington, DC: NCMP)

Rosen, S. (1984), 'Commentary: In defense of the contract at will', *University of Chicago Law Review*, 51, 983–7

Rosen, S. (1985), 'Implicit contracts: A survey', *Journal of Economic Literature*, 23, 1144–75

Rossana, R. J. (1983), 'Some empirical estimates of the demand for hours in US manufacturing industries', *Review of Economics and Statistics*, 65, 560–9

Rossana, R. J. (1984), 'A model of the demand for investment in inventories of finished goods and employment', *International Economic Review*, 25, 731–41

Rossana, R. J. (1985), 'Buffer stocks and labor demand: Further evidence', *Review of Economics and Statistics*, 67, 16–26

Rothschild, M. (1971), 'On the cost of adjustment', *Quarterly Journal of Economics*, 85, 605–22


Santamäki, T. (1983), 'The overtime pay premium, hours of work, and employment', Working Paper F-75, Helsinki School of Economics

Santamäki, T. (1984), 'Employment and hours decisions, and the willingness to work overtime hours', Working Paper F-86, Helsinki School of Economics

Santamäki, T. (1986), *Cyclical Adjustment of Hours and Employment. An Optimal Control Approach to the Behaviour of the Firm* (Helsinki: Helsinki School of Economics), Publications A:46

Sargent, T. (1978a), 'Estimation of dynamic labor demand schedules under rational expectations', *Journal of Political Economy*, 86, 1009–44

Sargent, T. (1978b), *Macroeconomic Theory* (Orlando: Academic Press)

Schellhaass, H.-M. (1984), 'Chancen und Gefahren von Sozialplänen', *Wirtschaftsdienst*, 64, 287–90

Schoer, K. (1987), 'Part-time employment: Britain and West Germany', *Cambridge Journal of Economics*, 11, 83–94

Shapiro, C. and Stiglitz, J. (1984), 'Involuntary unemployment as a worker discipline device', *American Economic Review*, 74, June, 433–44

Shapiro, M. (1986), 'The dynamic demand for capital and labor', *Quarterly Journal of Economics*, 101, 513–42

Simon, M. and Cruz, J. B. (1973), 'Additional aspects of the Stackelberg strategy in nonzero-sum games', *Journal of Optimization Theory and Applications*, 11(6), 613–26

Sims, C. A. (1974), 'Output and labor input in manufacturing', *Brookings Papers on Economic Activity*, 3, 695–728

Sorrentino, C. (1976), 'Unemployment compensation in eight industrial nations', *Monthly Labor Review*, 99, 18–24

Sorrentino, C. (1984), 'Japan's low unemployment: An in-depth analysis', *Monthly Labor Review*, 107, 18–27

Strøm, S. (1983), 'Is a reduction in the length of the work day an answer to unemployment?', Memorandum No. 29, Institute of Economics, University of Oslo (mimeo)

## REFERENCES

Tachibanaki, T. (1987), 'Labour market flexibility in Japan in comparison with Europe and the US', *European Economic Review*, 31, 647–78

Taira, K. (1970), *Economic Development and the Labor Market in Japan* (New York: Columbia University Press)

Taira, K. (1983a), 'Labor productivity and industrial relations in the United States and Japan', in B. D. Dennis (ed.), *Proceedings of the Thirty-Fifth Annual Meeting* (Madison, WI: Industrial Relations Research Association)

Taira, K. (1983b), 'Japan's low unemployment: Economic miracle or statistical artifact?' *Monthly Labor Review*, 106, 3–10

Taira, K. and Levine, S. B. (1985), 'Japan's industrial relations: A social compact emerges', in H. Juris, M. Thompson and W. Daniels (eds), *Industrial Relations in a Decade of Economic Change* (Madison, WI: Industrial Relations Research Association Series), 247–300

Tatom, J. A. (1980), 'The problem of procyclical real wages and productivity', *Journal of Political Economy*, 88, 385–94

Telser, L. (1981), 'A theory of self-enforcing agreements', *Journal of Business*, 53, 27–44

Tobin, J. (1958), 'Estimation of relationships for limited dependent variables', *Econometrica*, 26, 24–36

Topel, R. H. (1982), 'Inventories, layoffs and the short-run demand for labor', *American Economic Review*, 72, September, 769–87

Topel, R. H. (1983), 'On layoffs and unemployment insurance', *American Economic Review*, 73, 541–59

TUC (1984), 'Working time objectives and guidelines for trade negotiators: 1984–85 pay round', pamphlet, London, Trades Union Congress

United States Bureau of the Census (1986), *County Business Patterns 1984, United States, CBP-84-1* (Washington, DC: USGPO)

Van der Ploeg, F. (1987), 'Trade unions, investment and employment: A non-cooperative approach', *European Economic Review*, 31(7), 1465–92

Wallis, K. F., Andrews, M. J., Bell, D. N. F., Fisher, P. G. and Whitley, J. D. (eds) (1985), *Models of the UK Economy: A Second Review by the ESRC Macro-economic Modelling Bureau* (Oxford: Oxford University Press)

Wallis, K. F., Andrews, M. J., Fisher, P. G., Longbottom, J. A. and Whitley, J. D. (eds) (1986), *Models of the UK Economy: A Third Review by the ESRC Macroeconomic Modelling Bureau* (Oxford: Oxford University Press)

Walters, A. A. (1963), 'Production and cost functions', *Econometrica*, 31, January–April, 1–66

Weiss, L. (1985), 'Asymmetric adjustment costs and sectoral shifts', *Essays in Honor of Kenneth Arrow*

Welch, F. (1979), 'The effect of cohort size on earnings: The baby boom babies' financial bust', *Journal of Political Economy*, 87, October, S65–97

White, M. (1982), 'Shorter working time through national agreements', Research Paper No. 38, Department of Employment, London: HMSO

White, M. (1983), 'Shorter hours through national agreements', *Employment Gazette*, 91, 432–6

White, M. and Ghobadian, A. (1984), *Shorter Working Hours in Practice* (London: Policy Studies Institute), No. 631

Whitley, J. D. and Wilson, R. A. (1986a), 'The impact on employment of a reduction in the length of the working week', *Cambridge Journal of Economics*, 10, 43–59

Whitley, J. D. and Wilson, R. A. (1986b), 'Hours reductions within large-scale macroeconomic models: Conflict between theory and empirical application', Discussion Paper No. 8, ESRC Macroeconomic Modelling Bureau, University of Warwick

Wickens, M. R. and Breusch, T. S. (1986), 'Dynamic specification, the long run and the estimation of transformed regression models', Discussion Papers in Economics and Econometrics 8618, University of Southampton

Williams, B. (1984), 'Shorter hours – increased employment? *The Three Banks Review*, 143, September

Wilson, N. (1985), 'Work organisation, employees' involvement and economic performance: A survey of the UK metal working industry', Management Centre, University of Bradford (mimeo)

Wilson R. A. (ed.) (1986), *Hours of Work* (Institute for Employment Research, University of Warwick)

Winston, G. C. and McCoy, T. O. (1974), 'Investment and the optimal idleness of capital', *Review of Economic Studies*, 41, 419–28

Yamamoto, T. (1982), 'An empirical analysis of employment adjustments in terms of the number of workers and manhours', *Mita Gakukai Zasshi*, 65–91; cited in K. Koshiro, 'Job security: Redundancy arrangements and practices in Japan', unpublished paper, OECD, 1985

# Index

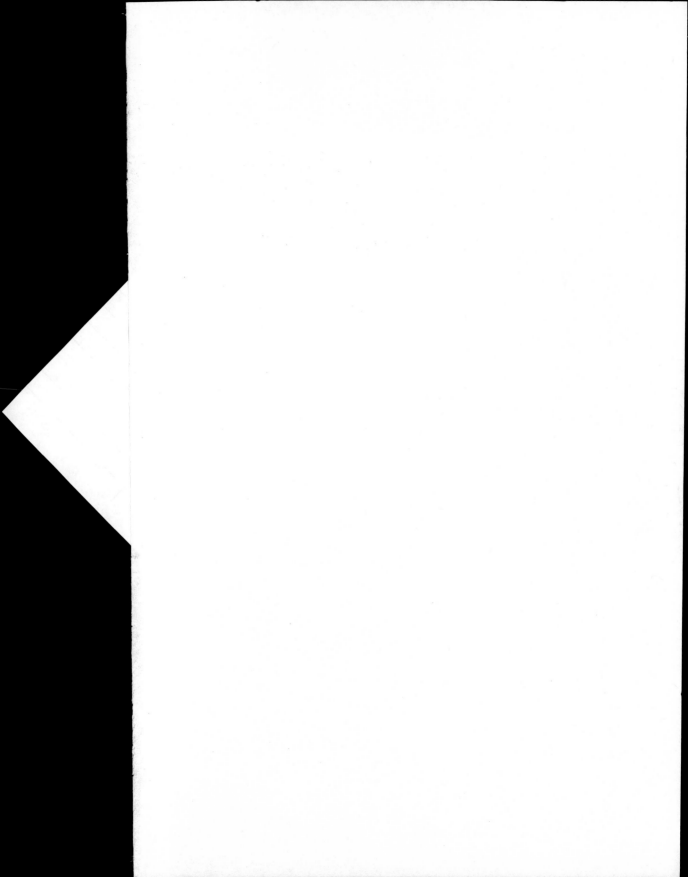